PostScript & Acrobat/PDF

Springer
Berlin
Heidelberg
New York
Barcelona
Budapest
Hong Kong
London
Milan
Paris
Santa Clara
Singapore
Tokyo

Thomas Merz

PostScript & Acrobat/PDF

Applications, Troubleshooting, and Cross-Platform Publishing

With 153 Figures and a CD-ROM

Springer

Thomas Merz
Tal 40
80331 München
Germany

Title of the Original German Edition:
Die PostScript- & Acrobat-Bibel
© Thomas Merz Verlag 1996

CIP-Data applied for

Die Deutsche Bibliothek – CIP-Einheitsaufnahme
PostScript & Acrobat, PDF: applications, troubleshooting, and cross platform
publishing / Thomas Merz. – Berlin ; Heidelberg ; New York ; Barcelona ;
Budapest ; Hong Kong ; London ; Milan ; Paris ; Santa Clara ; Singapore ;
Tokyo ; Springer.
Medienkombination
Orig.-Ausg. u.d.T.: Die PostScript- & Acrobat-Bibel
ISBN 3-540-60854-0
NE: Merz, Thomas; PostScript and Acrobat, PDF
Buch. – 1997
CD-ROM. – 1997

ISBN 3-540-60854-0 Springer-Verlag Berlin Heidelberg New York

Typesetting: Camera ready by author
Cover design and illustrations: Alessio Leonardi, agorà, Berlin
Translated from German by Richard Hunt, Tadcaster, UK, and the author
SPIN 10527305   Printed on acid-free paper   33/3142 – 5 4 3 2 1 0

Preface

I don't want to bore the reader with longish explanations about this book – the table of contents gives a much better overview.

What type of background do you need to take advantage of this book? Nothing specific. You should simply have some general experience in using computers and, of course, a certain degree of interest in the topic. Programming experience is definitely not required, each topic covered in the book is explained from the very beginning.

However, even developers and programmers can profit from the book since much of the information is either hardly accessible or hasn't been compiled in this way before.

I have tried to cover each and every subject related to PostScript and Acrobat. However, this doesn't include questions like "which problems will be encountered when using PostScript driver 5.28 and QuarkMaker 3.6?". Although the book considers current software features as they relate to PostScript and Acrobat, in most cases it doesn't take into account short-lived version numbers. Detailed descriptions of software bugs and current program updates are better suited for magazines. Here, I've just presented the basics of PostScript and Acrobat usage, explained their inner workings, and transferred know-how you can use in real-world situations.

A word of thanks

Many people were involved in preparing the German edition, modestly given the title "PostScript and Acrobat Bible". The network of proof-readers included software engineers, magazine editors, "ordinary" users, and typographers. I'd like to thank them all for helping improve the text and the presentation of the material. Without these people the book would be only half as good.

Richard Hunt from Tadcaster/UK not only translated the first four chapters accurately but also quickly replied to scores of e-mails I sent to him asking silly questions.

As with the German edition, the "Bavarian Lino-Tiger" Markus Wolfram was incredibly helpful in preparing films, late-night RIP-ping, and giving a helpful hand.

Last, but definitely not least, I'd like to thank Alessio Leonardi for his expertise and never-ending patience, and the whole Agorà crew for being so helpful and providing such a pleasant atmosphere whenever they hosted me in Berlin.

August 1996   Thomas Merz

Table of Contents

6 Gray Levels and Color *199*

Basics

1

PostScript gained wide distribution because of the rise of DTP and is accepted as the standard for control of printers and other output devices. To start with, we see what the success of PostScript is based on. The following description of the PostScript Interpreter is the basis for later chapters. An overview of the most important hardware and software applications in which PostScript is used makes it clear that PostScript is by no means restricted to laser printers.

1.1 Overview

1.1.1 What is PostScript?   PostScript is a programming language with powerful graphics functions. It is often called page description language because it can be used to specify the contents of a page that is to be printed. A "page" is always understood as a graphic that can contain various types of elements:

- ▸ Basic geometric components, such as lines, rectangles, circles, and curves. The lines can be drawn with any stroke weight or be dashed, surfaces can be filled with grays or colors.
- ▸ Text in various typefaces, of any size and orientation. Text characters are always treated as graphical objects. There are no restrictions as to size, color, or orientation.
- ▸ Bitmaps, that is pictures whose content is described not by objects but by individual pixels, in a rectangular grid. Individual pixels can have various grayscale or color values. Photos, for example, can be digitized using a scanner and stored as a bitmap.

All of these elements can be combined as desired and subjected to mathematical operations such as rotation, reduction, enlargement, or distortion.

PostScript is not only capable of describing graphics, but can also be used to depict them on various devices. The majority of output devices are raster-oriented, that is, they have to resolve each picture and piece of text to a series of individual pixels. According to the type of device, these pixels can take the values black or white (most laser printers), shades of gray between black and white (grayscale monitors) or random color values (thermal sublimation printers, color monitors). The fundamental problem of computer graphics is the transformation of an object-oriented graphic consisting of the above-

Fig. 1.1.
Rasterization of graphical elements

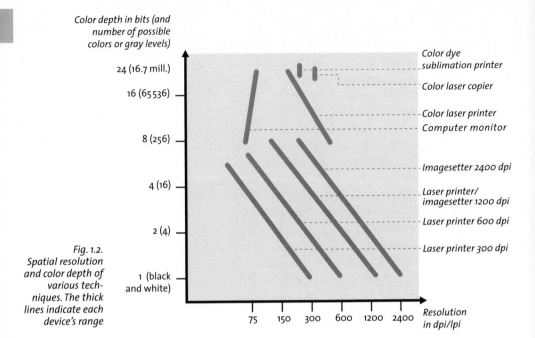

Color depth in bits (and number of possible colors or gray levels)

24 (16.7 mill.)

16 (65 536)

8 (256)

4 (16)

2 (4)

1 (black and white)

Color dye sublimation printer

Color laser copier

Color laser printer

Computer monitor

Imagesetter 2400 dpi

Laser printer/ imagesetter 1200 dpi

Laser printer 600 dpi

Laser printer 300 dpi

75   150   300   600   1200   2400

Resolution in dpi/lpi

Fig. 1.2. Spatial resolution and color depth of various techniques. The thick lines indicate each device's range

mentioned elements to raster oriented devices. This process is called *rendering*. Two main problems arise:

▸ Lines that do not run exactly horizontally or vertically are only approximated by pixels. This means that the representation is very coarse and sloping lines appear jaggy.

▸ If a device cannot output grayscales or colors, they must be simulated in a suitable manner. The simulation of grayscales by merging pixels together is known as *screening* or *halftoning* and is fully covered in Chapter 6.

Output quality is determined by the physical resolution, that is, the number of dots per unit of length, and the number of colors which can be represented (the color depth). Resolution is normally expressed as *dots per inch (dpi)*. Color depth is expressed in bits per pixel. The number of possible colors can be calculated as a power: for example 8-bit color depth makes it possible to use $2^8 = 256$ colors.

Figure 1.2 contains sample values for the resolution and color depth of some typical printing processes and monitors. This takes it for granted that a monitor only has a low resolution, but offers (with a suitable graphics card) a color depth of 24 bits. As the majority of printing processes can only generate a few colors, the number of available colors is increased by the raster processes which we will get to know in Chapter 6. These processes simulate grayscales or colors, but reduce the usable detail resolution. Example for interpreting the diagram: a laser printer with a 300 dpi engine can print a pure black and white picture at 300 dpi or simulate 25 gray levels at 60 dpi.

1.1.2 **The Evolution of PostScript.** The PostScript page description language – developed in the early 1980s by Adobe Systems – first became available in the Apple LaserWriter, the ancestor of all modern laser printers. From these humble beginnings, PostScript has since evolved to an industry standard which, because of the huge investment in hardware and software and its wide distribution, will be important for a long time. Because of the possibilities which it offers and the widespread availability of PostScript-compatible devices, many software vendors support this page description language in programs running under most operating systems.

Adobe licenses PostScript technology to printer manufacturers, in return for a license fee. As these fees were initially very high, and because PostScript printers require a higher level of hardware equipment, they were for a long time more expensive than devices without PostScript capabilities. As Adobe had published the specification of the language in the famous "Red Book" (see bibliography) some manufacturers developed their own PostScript implementations to avoid paying license fees for the printer control software. These clones were cheaper than printers using Adobe-licensed software, but could not initially keep up quality-wise. Adobe implemented a corporate policy of always being one step ahead of the competition in processing fonts (see Chapter 4). Today most of the clones are of high quality and have largely caught up in font processing. The PostScript Level 2 language extension has existed since the beginning of the 1990s and was intended to modernize PostScript whilst retaining compatibility with existing software. It was only accepted hesitantly by many software manufacturers and therefore suitable Level 2 drivers are still not available for some operating systems.

In the mid-1980s the idea had already occurred to make use of the advantages of PostScript for screen display as well as for printers. The first implementation of this idea, called Display PostScript, came in 1988 as a part of the NEXTSTEP operating system. Later, Adobe persuaded more and more Unix manufacturers to integrate Display PostScript into the X Window system and deliver it along with the operating system. Although PostScript files cannot in general be edited after creation, PostScript has been able to establish itself as an exchange format for graphics and multipage documents. The fact that the documents cannot be edited is often a big disadvantage, but in many situations documents do not need to be altered, merely distributed or archived digitally using a predetermined layout. For the

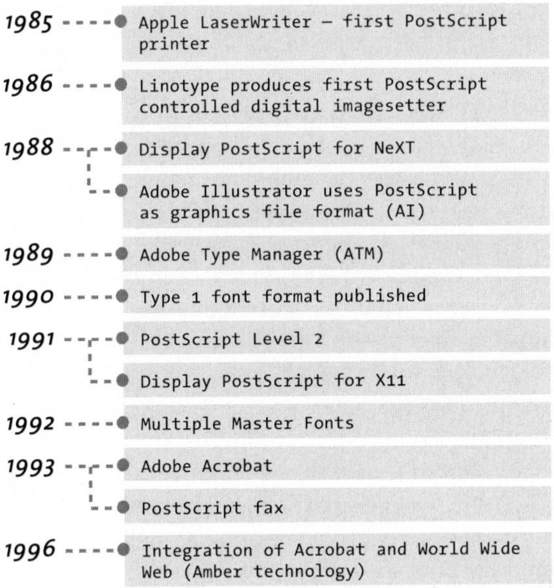

1985 ----●	Apple LaserWriter – first PostScript printer
1986 ----●	Linotype produces first PostScript controlled digital imagesetter
1988 --┌-●	Display PostScript for NeXT
└-●	Adobe Illustrator uses PostScript as graphics file format (AI)
1989 ----●	Adobe Type Manager (ATM)
1990 ----●	Type 1 font format published
1991 --┌-●	PostScript Level 2
└-●	Display PostScript for X11
1992 ----●	Multiple Master Fonts
1993 --┌-●	Adobe Acrobat
└-●	PostScript fax
1996 ----●	Integration of Acrobat and World Wide Web (Amber technology)

Fig. 1.3.
Milestones of PostScript
and Acrobat development

exchange of individual graphics, EPS files consisting of PostScript instructions with supplementary data are the standard.

Adobe used its experiences with PostScript when developing the Acrobat technology that should make the exchange of documents between operating systems and programs possible. Acrobat uses the PDF document format, which is based on PostScript but overcomes its difficulties with storing documents.

Adobe is constantly working to expand PostScript from a page description language with a limited range of uses to a universal communications standard. This corporate policy is pursued not just through cultivated co-operation with other companies but also through continuous development. PostScript fonts have become a standard format since the appearance of the *Adobe Type Manager* (ATM) software, which makes possible the display of these fonts on screen under Windows, Macintosh, OS/2, and (partly) Unix. The standardization of PostScript and the Type 1 font format as an ISO standard makes it clear that the PostScript page description language has established itself.

1.1.3 Advantages and Disadvantages of PostScript. The
biggest advantage of PostScript is device independence. Graphics are defined not according to the characteristics of a particular device (page size, color depth, resolution, etc.) but independently. During

output, the PostScript interpreter (introduced in the next section) takes over the conversion of user coordinates to device pixels, taking into account the device's technical limits. This makes it possible to output a PostScript file with more or less identical results on various machines – the only visible difference is the increasing reproduction quality as the resolution increases (and, if relevant, the representation of colors on color-capable devices). If there was no device-independent page description language it would not be possible to carry out test prints on a 300 dpi laser printer and to later feed the same files into a high resolution imagesetter.

The device independence also relates to the device's output method. With PostScript one can control not just monitor displays and dot matrix or laser printers, but also exotic devices, for example vinyl cutters with page lengths of up to 6 meters (e.g., to make signs for the sides of trucks) or a box of tricks to create film sub-titles.

The second important aspect is the independence from the operating system. PostScript files are simple text files which use the ASCII character set and which can be generated on every widely used operating system. The ASCII character set relates only to the PostScript instructions and not to the text to be output. These can use any character set, because flexible character encoding is a central component of font handling in PostScript. In conjunction with fonts, PostScript offers further advantages. For example, letters can be rotated, colored in, or scaled just like normal graphics elements. Special algorithms in the interpreter ensure quick and high-quality character redrawing. The typographic quality is so high that PostScript revolutionized the so-called pre-press stage, the preparation of printing plates (e.g., for offset printing). Where manufacturers once used competing and incompatible processes, PostScript and Type 1 fonts have established themselves as a standard that transcends manufacturers. In the meantime, an incredible variety of PostScript fonts is available: the total number of available fonts is already over 50 000!

As a PostScript user, however, one must also face up to the disadvantages of this page description language. The commonest point for criticism is the performance: on some pages an old laser printer sits calculating for an hour or longer while the user, frustrated, waits for the output. But with new printers with higher performance hardware – above all a faster processor – processing times are much shorter. Modern laser printers work, even with complex PostScript files, at close to the print engine speed of several pages per minute. The interpreter only poses a bottleneck with very complicated pages. But the software helps further: PostScript Level 2 and modern PostScript drivers also smooth the output process.

Especially when using multiple fonts and large graphics, the size of PostScript files can grow rapidly, and can easily reach several megabytes per page. Hardware and software development is taking away the strength of this argument more and more: apart from larger hard disks, more memory, and faster data transfer rates the data compression allowed by PostScript Level 2 also brings advantages.

We can also use this opportunity to get rid of a widespread misconception. Even if some software and hardware manufacturers claim that their products are "PostScript compatible", this does not mean that you can use a program to generate a PostScript file and then modify it with another program. In most cases PostScript is a one-way street for files, i.e., PostScript files cannot usually be further edited, but only be output whole. However, there are more and more exceptions to this rule, as we will see in the next section.

Finally, mention must be made of PostScript errors, which can make life very hard for the user. What's the point of all these great possibilities, if instead of the desired page, all that appears is an error message? A little know-how (which I shall try to pass on in Chapter 2), will help combat some problems, but in the case of massive integration problems the only cure is often to hope for an improved version of the program. One particular source of errors, namely the non-standard control of device-specific functions like paper bin selection and paper format setting, was a weakness in PostScript Level 1, but has largely been fixed in Level 2.

1.2 The PostScript Interpreter

The PostScript programming language instructions do not control the processor directly, but are evaluated by the so-called PostScript interpreter. In certain configurations, this is also referred to as the Raster Image Processor (RIP). The interpreter is a complex piece of software which is absolutely necessary for most of the areas in which PostScript is used (Type 1 fonts/ATM and the Adobe Illustrator file format are exceptions and are described at the end of the chapter). It works in several steps: firstly it analyzes the PostScript files, so that it can recognize the individual instructions. These instructions can either describe elements on the page or code for calculations, because PostScript is a fully blown programming language with many data and control structures. The interpreter builds up an internal representation of the page from the input instructions. Many interpreters generate a so-called display list. This is a data structure which contains all of the page elements in a compact form. Finally, with the help of the display list, the interpreter generates the various types of output:

- In a printer it controls the print engine, in an imagesetter it controls the laser beam. The end product is the printed page or the exposed film used for making printing plates. These are the largest uses for PostScript interpreters.
- Many RIPs convert PostScript files into instructions that can be understood by a normal printer (e.g., PCL for LaserJet models or QuickDraw for Apple printers) or display the pages on screen.
- Some RIPs rasterize the PostScript files and save them in a bitmap graphic format. The result is a pixel based TIFF, GIF, PCX, PICT, WMF, or other file.
- As well as rasterized versions of the page, a few interpreters can produce an object-oriented graphics format, e.g., PICT and WMF with objects (instead of with bitmaps as above), or CGM. Acrobat distiller for example creates the object oriented PDF format (see Section 1.3 and Chapter 8).

As well as these main functions the interpreter carries out various housekeeping tasks. Among these are the communication between computer and printer and the control of the print engine or the management of a hard disk connected to the printer. Many interpreters give the programmer the additional opportunity to enter PostScript instructions directly into the interpreter for test purposes (see Section 2.3.4). Therefore, the interpreter in certain respects represents the operating system of a printer.

The complexity of a PostScript interpreter can be made clear by looking at the size of the source code: the program sources in C, in which the majority of interpreters are written, vary between 100 000

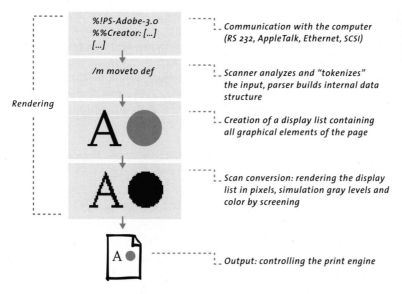

%!PS-Adobe-3.0
%%Creator: [...]
[...]

:_ Communication with the computer
(RS 232, AppleTalk, Ethernet, SCSI)

/m moveto def

:_ Scanner analyzes and "tokenizes" the input, parser builds internal data structure

:_ Creation of a display list containing all graphical elements of the page

:_ Scan conversion: rendering the display list in pixels, simulation gray levels and color by screening

Rendering

:_ Output: controlling the print engine

Fig. 1.4.
General structure of a PostScript interpreter

and 200 000 lines. This is the order of size of a full-featured word processor with several add-on modules. So that the interpreter is able to feed modern printer engines and imagesetters with data at the required speed, the interpreter needs to run on a fast processor and requires plenty of memory to work in. As the interpreter is sometimes supported by a hard disk, its hardware equipment does not lag behind the PC and may exceed it. The interpreter requires the RAM as working memory for its own processes, for the processing of the PostScript data, and for interim storage of the rasterized page.

The page pixels must, on most printers, be built up fully in memory before output. The memory requirement for this *frame buffer* depends on the resolution and color capability. For a black and white 300 dpi laser printer an A4 or US Letter size page (about 8 × 11.5 inches, 1 bit) it requires about one megabyte, whereas a 400 dpi 24-bit color page needs 42 megabytes[1]. As such a memory requirement pushes the price of the device upwards, some manufacturers use techniques such as compression and banding (processing the page in multiple narrow strips). Adobe refers to a combination of both techniques as a *memory booster*.

1.3 PostScript Configurations

PostScript is no longer confined to the control of printers, but is evident in several variants throughout the computer and publishing world. I would therefore like to introduce the most important configurations in which PostScript appears.

PostScript controller in a printer.   The classical and still the most common usage is a laser printer with an integrated PostScript controller. This is a special circuit board with memory and processor as well as the interpreter on one or more ROM chips. A variant is the PostScript cartridge, which allows the upgrading of a non-PostScript printer by inserting a supplementary cartridge. These cartridges are popular, above all, for upgrading HP LaserJets and compatible models.

Hardware RIP.   Imagesetters are distributed in much smaller numbers than laser printers, but they are the backbone of the prepress industry. They generate the films from which offset printing plates are etched or expose transparencies. Most of them are driven by an external RIP (*Raster Image Processor*). A RIP is a special computer which does not run any of the conventional operating systems, but only the

---

1.   *The memory requirement in bytes is derived from the page size in inches, the resolution in dpi and the color depth in bits: required memory = width × height × resolution^2 × (color depth)/8 .*

PostScript interpreter. The RIP receives the PostScript data from a connected Macintosh, PC or Unix server. A more recent development is digital printing machines with an integral PostScript RIP, which outputs the PostScript data without intermediate film exposure straight to the printing plates.

For several years, RIPs have also been available for color copiers. A modern color copier can be used not just as a copier, but also as a scanner for digitizing picture information or in conjunction with a PostScript RIP as a high quality color printer. Pre-eminent in this area were Canon color copiers and EFI's *fiery* RIPs, which made it possible to output PostScript files in A3 format at 400 dpi.Since then, other manufacturers have also begun to introduce digitally controlled copiers and various firms are producing RIPs for color copiers. Hardware RIPs have the advantage that they can be integrated into a computer network and used from all the connected workstations; this spreads the investment cost to all users.

Software RIP.   Unlike hardware RIPs, software RIPs run on an existing computer under whichever operating system is in use. Whilst a few years ago one still talked of "true" PostScript printers and "PostScript Emulators", software RIPs are no longer seen as PostScript on a shoe-string, but as sensible alternatives to hardware RIPs or integrated PostScript controllers. The environment of a PostScript interpreter is no longer a criterion to differentiate between original and clone: Adobe markets its own interpreter under the description *Configurable PostScript Interpreter* (CPSI) for workstations and Macintosh computers.

The concept of a software RIP using standard hardware and operating systems makes sense because a RIP requires RAM, a quick CPU, possibly a network connection and a hard disk. These components are present in every computer – more cheaply in comparison to specialized hardware. Unlike a controller built into a printer such a configuration works more flexibly as the PostScript interpreter profits from every computer hardware upgrade. If the desktop PC already has enough processing capacity anyway, no extra hardware investment costs are incurred for the RIP. But the argument does not hold in the other direction: an already slow computer should not be further burdened by a PostScript RIP, to avoid the investment needed for a PostScript printer.

The majority of software RIPs can control various output devices. To do this, they convert the rasterized version of the PostScript file into the target printer's language (e.g., PCL or QuickDraw). However, if you want to use a software RIP to revitalize an existing printer, take care to ensure that the interpreter supports the printer model. In

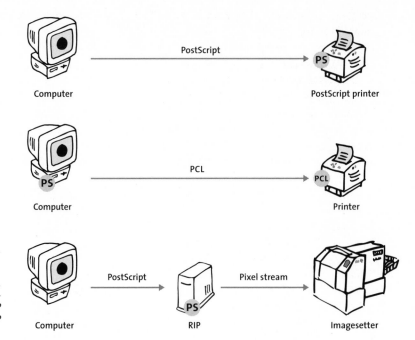

Fig. 1.5.
PostScript Con-
troller, Software RIP
and Hardware RIP

Computer   PostScript   PostScript printer

Computer   PCL   Printer

Computer   PostScript   RIP   Pixel stream   Imagesetter

addition, the level of integration into the whole system plays a role: some interpreters can only process finished PostScript files, others integrate themselves cleanly into the system – disguised as drivers – so that a user does not even have to think about emulation after installation.

Adobe offers ScreenReady as a software RIP, which specializes in preparing text and picture data for use in multimedia presentations. This Macintosh program converts PostScript files of any origin to PICT files (the standard graphic format on the Macintosh) for screen display. It is possible to specify a color depth, and the onscreen appearance is improved by anti-aliasing (the clever use of grayscales to smooth out jaggies) during rasterization. This method has the advantage that the same tools can be used to create online products and printed materials – except that the PostScript files do not go to a service bureau but are instead rasterized for the screen.

As well as various commercial products there has for years been a free interpreter called Ghostscript. It is quick and reliable. You can find versions of Ghostscript for several operating systems and the related C source on the accompanying CD-ROM. Apart from making possible the output of PostScript files to screen or printer, Ghostscript enables the carrying out of many other functions, and because of this we will often encounter it in this book. Appendix B contains detailed instructions on its installation and use, so here are just a few of the highlights:

- ► Interpreter for PostScript Level 2.
- ► Ghostscript can generate output for over 100 different printers, monitors and bitmap graphic formats.
- ► Display and print PDF files.
- ► Runs under MS-DOS, Windows (3.x, 95 and NT), OS/2, Macintosh, Unix/X11, Amiga, VAX/VMS, and other operating systems. C source code supplied.
- ► Offers many auxiliary programs to solve PostScript application problems. Appendix B offers an overview of possible uses for Ghostscript.
- ► The supplementary programs GSview (for Windows and OS/2) and Ghostview (for the X Window System) make it easy to use Ghostscript. If you wish to use Ghostscript's utility programs, view PostScript files on screen or give PostScript capability to an existing printer, then you should install Ghostscript on your system before following the remaining chapters. A detailed description of the necessary steps for each system can be found in Appendix B.

Acrobat Distiller. Distiller is a central component of the Acrobat software and consists of an interpreter for PostScript Level 2. However, it does not control any devices and does not generate bitmap graphics, but converts the PostScript data to *Portable Document Format* (PDF). Distiller can also be used for other purposes, e.g., to convert from Level 2 to Level 1 or to make PostScript files editable again. Comprehensive information on Acrobat can be found in Chapter 8.

Display PostScript (DPS). With the advantages of PostScript it is obvious to use the language not just for output to paper or film, but also for screen control, and to integrate this capability into the operating system. However, to do this Adobe had to implement some extensions to PostScript. Unlike output to paper, which uses a static page description that is discarded after printing, a dynamic window system with user input has totally different requirements: individual windows overlap each other on screen, are moved, and have to be constantly redrawn. The corresponding extensions, under the name Display PostScript, were first integrated in the NEXTSTEP operating system and also appeared some time later as DPS/X in the X Window System (X11). Today DPS/X is supported by several Unix manufacturers, but it has not found the same level of acceptance as with printers. For the PostScript control of X servers without integral DPS support there is the NX agent, which converts DPS calls to normal X11 protocol calls. This enables application software to use DPS functions on normal X terminals.

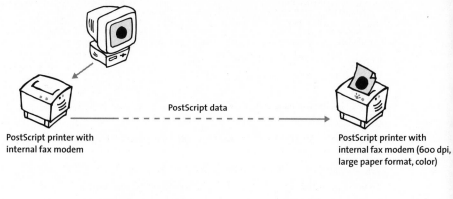

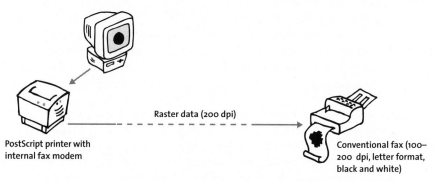

PostScript data

PostScript printer with
internal fax modem

PostScript printer with
internal fax modem (600 dpi,
large paper format, color)

Raster data (200 dpi)

PostScript printer with
internal fax modem

Conventional fax (100–
200 dpi, letter format,
black and white)

Fig. 1.6.
How PostScript
Fax works in
connection with a
normal fax
machine and a
PostScript Fax
printer

The advantages of using PostScript for screen control are obvious: a unitary model for describing screen and printer functions increases the quality of screen representation and makes programming easier. Data does not have to be converted for printing, but it is sufficient to redirect the PostScript instructions from screen to printer.

PostScript Fax. In the Unix world there are some fax software packages that accept PostScript files as input, using a PostScript interpreter (often Ghostscript) to convert them to the normal G3 fax standard and then relaying this data via a modem. Under Windows or on the Macintosh a special printer driver generates the fax data. Although this does mean that a fax can be sent from any program, this is really outmoded technology: first of all the documents are created digitally, then rasterized using PostScript, transmitted in analog mode, and when received possibly converted back to digital form by a fax modem – and finally maybe even converted back to individual letters using *optical character recognition* software!

In contrast to the process described above, Adobe has developed PostScript Fax, which expands the possibilities offered by conven-

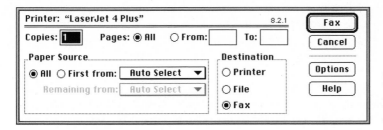

Fig. 1.7.
Controlling Post-
Script Fax with
the Macintosh
driver

tional faxing. PostScript Fax works with a fax modem, which is integrated into a PostScript printer and which extends the fax protocol so that as an alternative to bitmap data, PostScript data can be sent. If the receiving device is also a PostScript printer with fax facilities, the originating machine transmits PostScript data which is then rasterized by the receiving device. This means that the full quality of the receiving device's output can be used, e.g., a resolution of 600 dpi instead of the normal fax resolution of 200 dpi; even color output is possible and, according to the printer type, larger formats than A4 can be used.

The communications protocol used by PostScript Fax is designed so that the sender recognizes the recipient's machine type, and when linked to a conventional fax machine it rasterizes the data itself and uses a conventional process. In order to use PostScript Fax an extended printer driver is needed, e.g., the *Adobe Printer Driver* for the Macintosh. The user can choose as a target either the local printer, a PostScript file, or fax transmission from the print menu.

Apple, Compaq, DataProducts, NEC, Panasonic, and Xerox offer devices with extensions for PostScript Fax. Because of the relatively small choice of fax-capable printers and the difficulty of obtaining telecommunications regulatory authority in Europe, PostScript Fax has not yet become widespread.

Graphics Programs.   On the Macintosh and under Windows the format of the graphics program Adobe Illustrator (AI), a PostScript variant, has established itself as a quasi-standard for the exchange of graphics files. Although Illustrator does not contain a PostScript interpreter, it can read in PostScript files in AI format (but only those – not PostScript output from any old program!). In contrast to placing EPS files in a DTP program, where the graphics can only be scaled or moved, AI files remain fully editable. Details about this are given in Section 3.3.4. Picture editing programs like Adobe Photoshop are even capable of converting AI files into bitmap files. This rasterization also takes place without a PostScript interpreter and because of this only works with PostScript files which comply with the limitations of the AI formats.

Some graphics programs – e.g. CorelDraw and Adobe Illustrator 6.0 – go one step further and incorporate a complete PostScript interpreter. This makes it possible, in contrast to Illustrator compatible programs, to read in and process any PostScript file.

Adobe Type Manager (ATM). ATM software, available for Windows, Macintosh, OS/2, and some versions of Unix, as well as the Type 1 rasterizer built into the X Window system, process Type 1 fonts, the most important PostScript font format. It makes possible accurate text display on screen without Display PostScript. ATM only contains the part of the PostScript interpreter that rasterizes Type 1 fonts, and because of this it cannot be used to display normal PostScript files on screen. You can find more information on this topic in Chapter 4.

PostScript and Acrobat on the World Wide Web. With the huge growth of the Internet (mostly due to the World Wide Web), PostScript will become more and more important as an exchange format for files with a text and graphic content. However, as PostScript was conceived and optimized for printed output, it is not as suitable for use as an online format. It has relinquished this role to Acrobat and the Portable Document Format PDF, which was specially developed for document exchange across platforms, systems, and programs. Recently, Acrobat has become closely linked to the World Wide Web. We will examine this and other aspects of Acrobat in more detail in Chapter 8.

Between Monitor and Printer

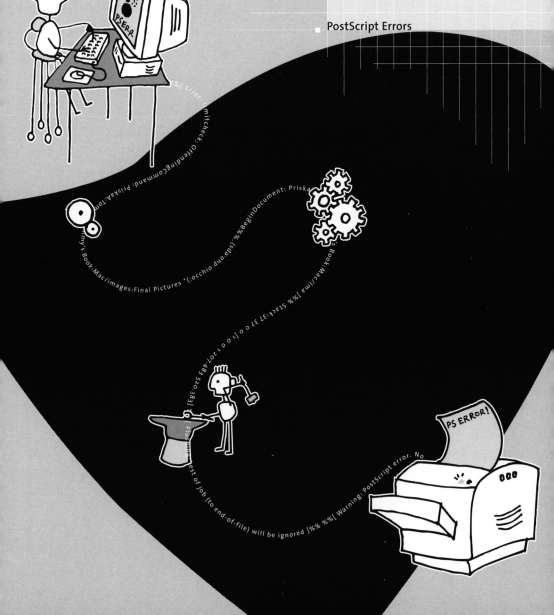

Many programs and components may play a part in the process of getting a document from the monitor to the printer or other output device: drivers, spoolers, converters, supplementary files. The properties of the interface being used also play an important role in the actual transfer of print data. In this chapter we look at these components more closely and focus on the ways in which they differ on different operating systems. A section on PostScript errors rounds off the chapter.

2.1 Creating PostScript Data

2.1.1 PostScript Drivers.
Both Windows and Macintosh use system-wide printer drivers: the component that converts data from the application program into a form the printer can understand is not part of the application, but is integrated into the operating system. Applications can call the functions of such system drivers using a standard programming interface. Windows refers to this as the GDI (*Graphics Device Interface*) and on the Macintosh it is called Quick-Draw. As these interfaces are responsible for monitor display as well as output to the printer, programmers can very easily make their software ready to print, as in principle they only have to divert the screen display instructions to the printer. The concept of a system-wide driver has several advantages:

- ▶ A new printer driver can be used by all programs. This means that not only will all applications benefit from an improved version of the driver, but also that they will be able to work with new printer models without being rewritten.
- ▶ Software developers are relieved of having to write their own printer drivers for each new model.
- ▶ The standardized printer interface can also be "abused" to utilize application data in other ways. Examples of this include fax drivers which are installed like printer drivers, or the PDF driver (see Chapter 8).

However, the first two points can also cause problems. In the case of a buggy driver, the user will first curse his or her text or graphics program as it appears not to be able to print correctly – only a second look will show that it might be a driver problem. In addition, some software manufacturers might be able to deliver better printer compatibility just as well. In this case the system driver actually prevents direct control of the printer.

2.1.2 Programs with Integrated PostScript Drivers.
In some environments there are no system-wide printer drivers available, and so each application program must have its own drivers for each supported device. This is mainly the case for operating systems without integrated graphics and output conventions, in particular MS-DOS and Unix. Under MS-DOS there is a long tradition of direct hardware control (e.g., writing to the video memory or reading from hardware registers). Under Unix the X Window System has established a wide-reaching standard for graphical output, but this standard does not extend to all flavors of Unix and does not offer any support for printing; it is only for screen output. This means that MS-DOS and Unix programs have to generate their own PostScript

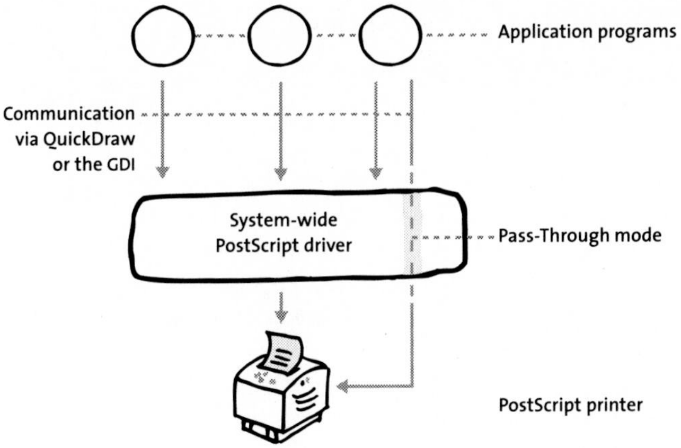

Fig. 2.1.
PostScript architecture
with a system driver,
used by all application
programs. Only in
Pass-Through-Mode
do programs generate
PostScript instruc-
tions themselves

output without calling on preinstalled drivers. The same goes for MS-DOS programs running in Windows' MS-DOS emulation. There are also some Windows or Macintosh programs which largely bypass the system-wide driver. They use the driver in Pass Through Mode, in which the driver relays the PostScript instructions generated by the program unaltered. Adobe has shown with its own products that this approach can make sense if:

► The program is already working internally with data in PostScript form and so further conversion to PostScript by the driver is superfluous. Adobe Illustrator for example uses PostScript to save its graphics files (see Section 3.3). These files are passed almost unchanged to a PostScript printer.

► The program has particular requirements in respect of PostScript output, which the system driver cannot fulfil. If, for example, the output process needs exact color reproduction or a particular spot function has to be used, one cannot risk the data being altered by the PostScript driver. This is why Adobe PhotoShop generates its own PostScript output.

► The program generates cleaner PostScript code than the driver. This is, for example, the case with Adobe Acrobat: above all in conjunction with PostScript Level 2, Acrobat can generate much better optimized PostScript output for PDF files than the system driver (see Section 5.5).

2.1.3 PostScript Converters.

PostScript converters, which convert a particular input format to PostScript for output, are also a possibility (filters in Unix jargon). It does not matter where the data were produced, or by which program, only that the data are received in a format which the filter understands. The difference between text and

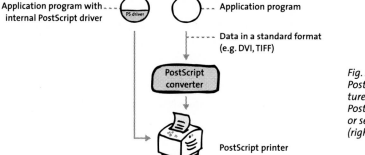

Application program with .... internal PostScript driver

Application program

Data in a standard format (e.g. DVI, TIFF)

PostScript converter

PostScript printer

Fig. 2.2.
PostScript architec-
tures with integrated
PostScript driver (left)
or separate converter
(right)

graphics filters should be noted. Text filters typically generate Post-
Script data for files of arbitrary length and also take care of, according
to the complexity of the filter, page breaks, or paragraph formatting.
Graphics filters convert graphics in one of the commonly used formats (TIFF, GIF, JPEG, PCX, etc.) to PostScript. In general they can only
process one graphic at a time, giving one page of output. The majority of graphics converters generate EPS files that not only can be
printed separately but also can be embedded in other documents,
using word processing or DTP software (see Chapter 3). In Sections 9.4
and 9.5 you will find details on the conversion of various formats to
and from PostScript.

2.1.4 PPD Files.   As already described, independence from a particular
output device is one of the greatest advantages of the PostScript page
description language. A PostScript printer driver will work for any
model of printer, won't it? As so often, the answer is yes, but...

It is possible to program a printer driver so that the PostScript instructions it generates work on all devices. However, this means that
the driver is unable to make use of the printer's special functions and
properties. The PostScript operators for graphics and text are the
same for each printer, but if the printer driver is to offer the user the
option of changing the paper tray (for example to give access to various types or sizes of paper) it must first know whether the printer in
use actually has multiple trays and the instructions to control them.
However, if one had to program a custom driver for every printer
type, then the advantage of a device-independent page description
language would be lost!

The solution is a splitting up of the PostScript driver into parts:
the main part of the driver works device-independently and generates the universal PostScript instructions for the output of graphics
and text. A smaller part of the driver generates the device-dependent

instructions. This part can be externally configured for a particular type of printer and lets the user control the printer's individual functions. The device-dependent part of the driver is configured using tables or description files which are usually supplied by the printer manufacturer. Because of this you do not need a customized driver (needing a lot of programming effort) for every printer, instead the same driver can be used with different tables for various models.

Adobe has defined PPD files (*PostScript Printer Description*) as a cross-platform standard. They contain all the relevant information regarding the configuration of an output device that the driver needs. PPD files are ASCII text files and can therefore be modified by the user. They are structured so that the driver program can evaluate their content automatically. The typical size of a PPD file is between 10 and 30 KB – a real waste if it "only" describes the paper trays. The information in a PPD file arises from several areas:

- ▸ Printer hardware: Is a hard disk connected to the printer? Which resolutions can be used?Can a fax expansion be installed? Is this a black and white or color printer?
- ▸ Description of the PostScript interpreter: Which language level does it support, how much RAM is built in, and which extensions (e.g., CMYK for Level 1 printers or rasterization of TrueType fonts for Level 2) are implemented?
- ▸ Connection and operation of the printer: Which transfer protocols are possible, can the printer emulate other printer languages?
- ▸ Fonts: Which fonts are available in the printer, and are they built in or do they need to be loaded from the hard disk? Which character sets do they support?
- ▸ Grayscales and color: Which color functions does the device support, which spot functions, screen frequencies and screen angles can realistically be used? Are other screening options like AccurateScreens available?
- ▸ Which further functions are available? Some printers can print on both sides of the paper. High performance machines can often punch, staple, fold or sort the printed paper in one pass.
- ▸ Print media: Which sizes of paper, film, transparency, etc., can be used? From which trays can the media be fed? Is there a manual paper feed?

PPD files do not just contain exact answers to these questions, they also contain the corresponding PostScript instructions. Many printer manufacturers ship their printers together with a suitable PPD file on floppy disk or at least make it available by request. Adobe's FTP site contains a comprehensive collection of PPD files for the printers of manufacturers who use the Adobe PostScript interpreter. The format of PPD files is so flexible that a well programmed printer driver is even able to support features that were unavailable when it was first written! The user interface (menus and options) for the printer driver configure themselves dynamically with the help of the information in the PPD file. The following extract is from the PPD file of a 600 dpi laser printer:

```
*PPD-Adobe: "4.1"
*FormatVersion: "4.1"
*FileVersion: "1.0"
*LanguageVersion: English
*LanguageEncoding: ISOLatin1
*PCFileName: "HPWINPS.ppd"
*Product: "(HP LaserJet 4 Plus)"
*PSVersion: "(2013.111)1"
*ModelName: "HP LaserJet 4 Plus"
*NickName: "HP LaserJet 4/4M Plus PS 600"
*LanguageLevel: "2"
*Protocols: PJL TBCP
*TTRasterizer: Type42
*ColorDevice: False
*DefaultColorSpace: Gray
*FileSystem: False
*Throughput: "12"
*FreeVM: "679680"
...
*DefaultPaperDimension: A4
*PaperDimension Letter/Letter: "612 792"
*PaperDimension Legal/Legal: "612 1008"
*PaperDimension A4/A4: "595 842"
...
*DefaultResolution: 600dpi
*DefaultFont: Courier
*Font AvantGarde-Book: Standard "(001.006)" Standard ROM
...
*Font ZapfDingbats: Special "(001.004)" Special ROM
```

As stated above, PPDs are text files and can be altered by hand. Typical candidates for such additions are entries to output a particular page size in landscape format to save film on an imagesetter or newly installed fonts (on the printer's hard disk).

Nevertheless, PPD files also have their drawbacks. Firstly, they are relatively large, especially if a driver only uses part of the information in the file. Secondly, plain text files cannot be read as quickly as optimized binary files. For this reason, other formats, as well as PPD files, are used to describe the printer properties, and we will look at them later during the description of PostScript processing on the most important operating systems.

2.1.5 DSC Comments.   What is (or isn't) good programming style can be disputed, but in the case of PostScript files, the answer is obvious: if the file produces the page correctly, it must be OK. Wrong! Problems can very quickly arise, even with "working" PostScript files, if they are not printed out immediately after being generated. The file may be transferred to another operating system or printed on another output device. But also during transmission and processing of PostScript files – examined in more detail in the next section – the wheat is separated from the chaff:

- ▸ Device dependence: does the file contain operators that are only available on a particular device? Is it conditional on a particular hardware property being present on the output device?
- ▸ Page independence: can the individual pages of the document be extracted and printed separately, or can the pages only be printed sequentially in the original order?
- ▸ Embedding as an EPS file: if the file is to be embedded in another document the correct BoundingBox parameters are crucial (see Section 3.2.1). If this is missing or contains incorrect values, the embedded graphic will be printed at the wrong size.
- ▸ Does the file contain only PostScript instructions or does it also contain elements of the transfer protocol being used? This problem mainly affects Windows and the serial or parallel interface (see Section 2.4.1).

These criteria affect not just the actual PostScript instructions for producing the page, but also the structure of the document as well as supplemental information which is not used by the PostScript interpreter.

Adobe has provided a tool to solve these problems: the Document Structuring Conventions (DSC) . These comments are an extension to the actual page description language. DSC comments have become an integral part of PostScript. Sticking to these conventions ought to guarantee "good" PostScript, i.e., portability of PostScript files between systems and devices, and making post-processing possible. As the page description instructions are not affected, this "Meta Post-Script" hides itself in comments which are ignored by the PostScript interpreter and therefore do not affect the eventual appearance of the page. Sticking to these DSC conventions is regarded as an important step towards creating "good" PostScript files. Many application problems would not arise if all PostScript files were DSC compatible. However, not all developers bother with DSC, either out of ignorance or because they only test their PostScript data in a limited environment ("It prints fine on my LaserJet, so it must be OK").

The first step towards DSC is the division of a PostScript file into prolog and script. The prolog contains the procedures and definitions required to print the document and which do not have to be repeated on every page. You can think of the prolog as a function library to which each individual page description has access. The prolog does not contain any instructions to output text or graphics but is loaded into the printer before outputting the first page. The script (or body) of the document contains the PostScript instructions to describe the pages.

If only a single page of the document is to be printed it is sufficient to send the prolog and the page to be printed to the printer. This only works if the pages are independent of one another. If the page to be printed uses a font that is defined in a previous page instead of the prolog, it can only be printed together with that page.

For DSC compatibility it is not enough to maintain the separation between the prolog and the script, but the individual parts must also be marked so that they can be identified without a PostScript interpreter. As this marking is done using comments, it has no effect on the PostScript instructions processed by the interpreter.

The most important DSC comments. DSC compatible PostScript files identify themselves with the entry

`%!PS-Adobe-3.0`

in the first line of the file. With the exception of this line, DSC comments always begin with two percent symbols (a percent symbol always begins a PostScript comment line which is ignored by the interpreter). The end of the prolog is marked by the comment

`%%EndProlog`

The page descriptions follow, each page beginning with

`%%Page: x y`

where x is the logical number of the page and can be any value (e.g., Roman or Arabic page numbers), and y describes the physical page number within the file; the first y-value is always 1. In many cases x and y are equal.

So that the comments contained in embedded files do not cause any confusion, the PostScript code of imported document parts is always bracketed with the *%%BeginDocument:* and *%%EndDocument* comments. Without this bracketing, the page numbering goes crazy, e.g., if the comments Begin/EndDocument are missing and a graphic containing the comment *Page: 1 1* is being imbedded on page 3 (it only consists of one page), the page numbers will be, confusingly, 3-1-4.

The setup section can be between the prolog and the script. It contains operations that affect the whole document (such as the choice

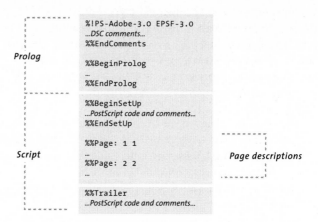

Fig. 2.3.
Structure of a
DSC compatible
PostScript file

Prolog

```
%!PS-Adobe-3.0 EPSF-3.0
...DSC comments...
%%EndComments

%%BeginProlog
...
%%EndProlog
```

```
%%BeginSetUp
...PostScript code and comments...
%%EndSetUp
```

Script

```
%%Page: 1 1
...
%%Page: 2 2
...
```

Page descriptions

```
%%Trailer
...PostScript code and comments...
```

of paper trays and sizes) and is bracketed by *%%BeginSetup* and *%%EndSetup*.

Finally, the DSC comments also contain information about the document: *%%LanguageLevel:* indicates whether the document can be printed with Level 1 or whether a Level 2 printer is required; *%%DocumentData:* indicates whether the file contains 7 or 8-bit data. The comment:

```
%%DocumentNeededResources: <List of resources>
```

is very important. It contains a list of all resources needed to output the document successfully, above all, font definitions and sometimes also procedures definitions in their own prologs (*ProcSets*). Device dependent operators which only function with certain printer types are bracketed with the comments *%%BeginFeature:* and *%%EndFeature*, so that they can be replaced or removed if the output device is changed. Without being signposted by comments the automatic replacement of PostScript fragments would not be possible. The *PostScript Language Reference Manual* (see bibliography) contains a complete description of DSC comments.

A good PostScript driver keeps to the format described and generates all the required DSC comments. In the next section we will see which programs utilize the DSC comments and where they can be useful (apart from in printing).

2.2 Transferring PostScript Data

2.2.1 The Tasks of a Spooler.
A spooler is a program which receives print data from application programs, if need be modifies it, and relays it to the chosen output device. Although this is really a job

for the operating system, none of the current generation of operating systems contain a really complete spooler for PostScript files. Some supplementary products attempt to fill this gap, which is very important in networked environments. The following idealized listing contains the most important tasks of a PostScript spooler and the relationship with DSC comments.

The spooler maintains a waiting queue for each connected device so that several users can share a device. The spooler compares the properties of the target printer (which it knows from the PPD files) with the requirements of the documents, and recognizes files that are being sent to an unsuitable printer (e.g., Level 2, color, or duplex printing). If desired, it will automatically divert such jobs to another printer.

In the case of incomplete PostScript files the spooler makes use of the resource comments to determine which fonts and prologs the document requires, and inserts them into the correct place in the PostScript file. In the same spirit, the importing program should also examine the comments in embedded EPS graphics. If, for example, an embedded graphic needs extra fonts then they must also be integrated – or the whole document's PostScript file must "inherit" the corresponding resource requirement comments from the EPS file. This inheritance is the same for all resources in embedded files. The spooler replaces device dependent PostScript code, characterized by corresponding DSC comments, if the document has to be diverted to another printer. It also fetches the necessary PostScript instructions from the corresponding PPD file.

Our idealized spooler receives error messages from the printer via a bidirectional connection and reacts to situations like paper jams or transfer problems by sending the page again or, in the case of pages which have "got lost" extracts their descriptions and sends them, together with the prolog, to the printer again.

Using the *%%Page:* comments the spooler is also able to rearrange the pages of a document. This means that the pages can be printed in reverse order or several actual pages can be printed at reduced size on one sheet of paper.

The *Open Prepress Interface* (OPI) and *Desktop Color Separation* (DCS), which we will discuss in more detail in Section 3.3, are extensions of the DSC principle which enable extra functions. An OPI compatible spooler or server for picture data replaces the low resolution proxy images contained in the file (e.g., 72 dpi pictures, used for layout on the screen) with high resolution versions (say, 2540 dpi for an imagesetter) before output, which makes the file processing and transfer much easier. Finally, DCS comments allow color separations to be handled.

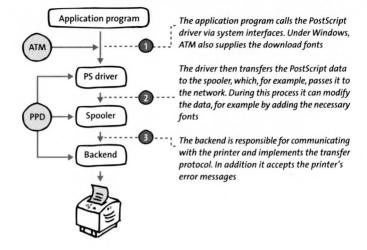

Fig. 2.4.
Many components are involved in the output of a Post-Script document, which may melt together into a single program

The application program calls the PostScript driver via system interfaces. Under Windows, ATM also supplies the download fonts

The driver then transfers the PostScript data to the spooler, which, for example, passes it to the network. During this process it can modify the data, for example by adding the necessary fonts

The backend is responsible for communicating with the printer and implements the transfer protocol. In addition it accepts the printer's error messages

2.2.2 Manipulation of PostScript Files.

Even without a Post-Script spooler, DSC compatible PostScript files have their advantages. If you want to look at a file on screen using a previewer, you can navigate to any page if the *%%Page:* comments are present. If these important comments are missing you will only be able to leaf through the pages sequentially from front to back. For example, amongst the previewers which make use of DSC comments is *GSview* for Windows, the Windows frontend for Ghostscript. You can use this to select any page of a document which is DSC compliant.

Using the PostScript Utilities (*PSutils*) for MS-DOS and Unix, which you will find on the accompanying CD-ROM, you can carry out the rearrangement of pages described above and many other operations as well, even without a spooler.

The program *psselect* from the PSutils package can be used in many different ways: To extract a particular page or several parts from a document, if the whole document is not to be printed. The rearrangement of all pages into reverse order saves you having to sort a stack of printed paper. In conjunction with extracting all the odd or even pages this *psselect* function also allows printing on both sides of the paper: first print the odd pages, then place the paper in the printer the other way up and print the even pages. Depending on the paper feed and store of your printer (does the printed page face down or up?), you might have to output the first or second half in reverse order.

The program *psnup* (from *n*-up printing) prints multiple pages on one sheet; you must enter the page format, orientation and margin.

An overview of all programs in the PostScript Utilities can be found in Appendix A.

2.2.3 Archiving PostScript Files.

PostScript is often used as a format for storing and archiving documents. The advantages and disadvantages of doing this will be explored more fully in conjunction with Adobe Acrobat and PDF, but here your attention is drawn to a couple of points you should note when making PostScript files for archival:

▸ DSC compatibility: the files should always include DSC comments to facilitate later processing.

▸ Completeness: all necessary fonts, prologs, and other resources must also be saved, so that the documents can be printed at a later date without problems.

▸ Optimization: if you are saving a considerable number of similar documents, you can save a lot of space by extracting common resources. Saving documents without the prolog gives a particularly big saving.

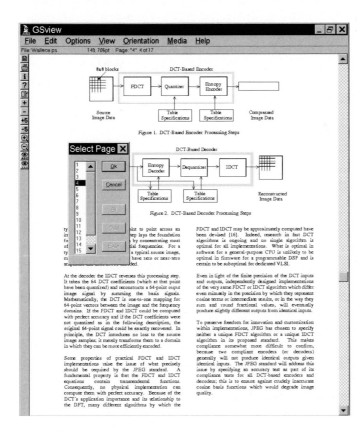

Fig. 2.5.
Choosing a page in a PostScript document with GSview

- Avoid using device dependent operators so that a particular device will not be needed to print the document later. Many drivers have a "generic" option which you can use to configure a PostScript file without device specific operators.
- The files should not contain any elements of the data transfer protocol as you may want to print them using a different operating system.

Even if you cannot use a spooler which takes advantage of all the procedures described above, the DSC comments play an important role in the long-term archival of PostScript files. At the current pace of software development it is very probable that in a few years DSC comments will be interpreted in the same way on all operating platforms. You should not fail to take advantage of this opportunity!

2.3 Sending PostScript Data to the Printer

2.3.1 Connection Types for PostScript Printers. The following criteria play a role in deciding how to connect printers:

- Speed: how fast should the print data be transferred from computer to printer?
- Standardization and distribution: which operating systems or architectures support the chosen interface?
- Bidirectionality: can the interface only transfer data from the computer to the printer, or can data be transferred in the other direction as well (to query the printer status, for example)?
- Transparency: Can the interface handle binary data or only 7-bit data?
- Simultaneous access: can only one computer at a time send data to the printer (point to point connection) or can several computers share an output device (networking)?

Serial interface. The serial interface, also known as the RS-232C interface, has been standardized for many years and is supported by almost all operating systems. This advantage must be weighed against the slow transfer rate and the difficulties of configuration: the user has to manually set the computer and the printer to use the same parameters (baud rate, parity, stop bits, etc.).

Although the serial interface does allow binary files to be transferred, most PostScript printers use a protocol that reserves some characters and is therefore only capable of transferring 7-bit files (see below). Using a serial connection, data can be transferred in both directions. But in many cases the return channel from printer to computer is not used.

Parallel interface. The parallel or Centronics interface is a standard item on all PCs using an Intel processor and can also be found on many Unix workstations. It offers a much faster data transfer rate than a serial interface. As with the serial interface, it is theoretically possible to transfer binary files; however, the protocols used normally rule this out. In its standard form, the parallel interface only transfers data from the computer to the printer and not vice versa. This is only made possible by using the bidirectional parallel interface, which requires specially screened cables and is incorporated into some new printer models (Hewlett Packard, for example). (For bidirectional data exchange over a parallel link, e.g., using MS-DOS 6.x's InterLink, a different protocol is used that has nothing to do with the Centronics standard.)

AppleTalk. All Macintosh computers are network ready. The protocol used, AppleTalk, changes name according to the available hardware; it may also be known as LocalTalk, EtherTalk, or TokenTalk. Whilst the speed depends on the type of network, all variants allow binary file transfers and bidirectional communication. AppleTalk interfaces are only found on Macintosh computers, but many printer manufacturers include them as standard on their printers.

SCSI. The *Small Computer System Interface* (SCSI) is a powerful interface for connecting a wide range of peripheral devices (hard disks, scanners, tape streamers, etc.) which allows high speed data throughput and bidirectional binary transfers. Unfortunately, the SCSI interface has not been able to establish itself as a standard for connecting printers. Some printers do have a SCSI interface, which is used not to connect the printer to the computer, but to attach a hard disk on which the PostScript interpreter stores fonts and other data.

Ethernet. It is possible to connect computers and printers – depending on the printers and operating system – using an Ethernet network and various network protocols. Apart from AppleTalk/ EtherTalk (Macintosh), Novell SPX/IPX (above all on MS-DOS/Windows) and TCP/IP (mainly Unix) are other important protocols. According to the operating system, extra communications software (possibly only available from the printer manufacturer) may be needed to connect a network printer. This allows bidirectional binary transfer. However, many printers connected via Ethernet simulate the serial interface protocol so that only 7-bit data can be transferred. An example of connecting a printer via Ethernet is included in Section 2.4.2.

2.3.2 Transfer Protocols.

Every time data is transferred between computers or between a computer and a printer control data – which ensures correct transfer – is transmitted as well as the user data (in our case PostScript files). The two important parts of this process are synchronization and identifying the beginning and end of a transfer. Synchronization prevents data going missing if the computer is transmitting data faster than the printer can process it.

The identification of the beginning or end of a transfer ensures that the PostScript interpreter returns to its "ready" state at the end of the print job (to free up the memory used). With printers the protocol often does a further job: apart from PostScript most printers also understand other printer languages or emulations. The protocol makes it easier to switch between the various modes.

In true networking of several devices these control functions are always a component of the relevant network protocol. On an Ethernet network, the TCP/IP or SPX/IPX protocols are used; AppleTalk uses the Printer Access Protocol (PAP). These network protocols signal the end of a transfer by sending a special packet type.

In the case of point to point connections (serial and parallel) the control functions are partly carried out at the hardware level (using specially reserved wires), and partly by the transfer software (for example, the serial XON/XOFF protocol), and sometimes as part of the transferred user data. This means that the PostScript instructions within a file are mixed with control functions via a particular channel. If such a file is printed on another system or via another channel, the "foreign" control characters cause problems. EPS files must not contain any control characters from one of these protocols!

Next, the common protocols for point to point connections will be described. In Section 2.4, you will find hints on the use of these protocols and the problems associated with them.

Standard protocol. The standard protocol is used with both serial and parallel interfaces. Some characters are reserved for use as control codes and therefore may not be contained in the PostScript data. For this reason, any old binary data cannot be transferred, but only characters in the ASCII range 32 to 127 – even if binary transfer was possible physically! The most important control character is Control-D (byte value 4), the "end-of-job" marker. This character marks the end of a print job or the start of a new one. If this character were to be included in the PostScript data (for example, as part of a bitmap picture), it would have disastrous consequences: the interpreter would think the print job is over! A list of all the control characters in the standard protocol can be found in the *details.pdf* file on the accompanying CD-ROM.

Binary data, which appear above all in bitmap pictures or with compressed data, cannot be transmitted using the standard protocol and need to be "wrapped" as an ASCII file. In PostScript Level 1 this can only be achieved using hexadecimal representation, which almost doubles the size of the data. In Level 2, ASCII85 encoding enlarges the file by a factor of 1.25 only. However, most drivers and converters use hexadecimal representation. On most printers the standard protocol is the only one for both serial and parallel interfaces and does not have to be set up specially. On printers that also support the Binary Control Protocol (see below) you can use the PostScript program *stdprot.ps* from the CD-ROM to switch back to the standard protocol from BCP.

Binary Control Protocol (BCP).   This relatively unknown protocol makes it possible to transfer any binary data via the serial or parallel interface and is supported by some Level 1 and many Level 2 printers. A precondition for BCP is an 8-bit capable relay channel, so, for example, a serial interface configured for 7-bit transmission cannot be used. The entry

```
*Protocols: BCP
```

in the printer's PPD file indicates that the device can use BCP. The protocol must solve the problem of being able to transfer 256 different characters plus the necessary control characters. These contradictory requirements are solved by the technique of *quoting*. Every control character contained in the user data is replaced by two characters which have no special meaning as control characters. When the data are received by the PostScript printer (but before being processed by the interpreter) this sequence is recognized and replaced by the original characters. The protocol uses further processes to ensure that data are not wrongly interpreted if such a sequence occurs by chance in the original data. Quoting allows any binary data to be transferred, without increasing the amount of data as much as the standard protocol: most characters are transmitted unchanged, and an extra byte is only added for a few control characters. You can find details on *Quoting* in the Acrobat file *details.pdf* on the CD-ROM.

AdobePS and the Windows 95 driver support BCP, so that you only have to activate the relevant driver function to enable binary file transfer. You can also make use of these functions in some circumstances to speed up printing if your printer driver is not BCP capable. The PostScript program *binprot.ps* on the CD-ROM activates the binary protocol and the program *quote* serves as a filter to ensure that the control characters are handled in accordance with BCP. You can find further details in Section 2.4.4.

Devices which support BCP

Manufacturer	Models
A. B. Dick	Digital Duplicator
Agfa	DuoProof, Elan 500 SF
Apple	LaserWriter 16/600, Select 310, Select 360f, Select 610, IIf, IIg, NTR, Pro 600, Pro 630, Pro 810, Color
Compaq	PAGEMARQ 15, PAGEMARQ 20
CalComp	EcoGrafix, TechJET
Digital	DEClaser 1152, DEClaser 1152, DECcolorwriter 1000
Canon	LASER SHOT A404PS, A406PS, LBP-860, LBP-1260, MDC PS, PS-IPU
ColorPoint	820, 830
CompuPrint	PageMaster 825/1025
DataProducts	LZR 1560, LZR 2080/F5, Typhoon 8, Typhoon 16, Typhoon 20
Digital	DEClaser 1152, 3500, 5100, DECcolorwriter 1000
Epson	EPL-7500, LP-8200PS2, LP-9000PS2
Fuji	Xerox Able Model-PR, Xerox Laser Press 4150, 4160, 4160 II
Hewlett-Packard	CopyJet M, DesignJet 650C, DeskJet 1200C/PS, Laserjet III, IIID , IIIP, 4, 4 Plus, 4ML, 4MP, 4Si/4SiMX, 4V/4MV, 5Si, PaintJet XL300,
Hitachi	Koki Typhoon 8, Koki Typhoon 16
IBM	4029
IDT	OracC Velociraptor
JVC	Trueprint SP5600J
Kodak	ColorEase PS, XLS 8400, 8600, Digital Science DCP 9000
Lexmark	Optra series
Mitsubishi	S3600-40, S6600-40
NEC	Silentwriter2 Model 90, Silentwriter 1097, 95, 97, S62P, 80PS2, PC-PR3000PS/4
Okidata	MICROLINE 800PSII, 801PSII, 802PSII, 810PSII, OL400, OL410, OL870, OL1200/PS
Panasonic	KX-P5400, KX-P5410
Ricoh	LP-M32, NRG3131/D431/2031, DS5330
Scantext	2013, Largo L2, Othello L2 , Rondo L2
Scitex	Dolev PSM, Dolev2Press, Dolev400, Station, IRIS INK Jet, Realist5015, 5030
Texas Instruments	microLaser PS17, PS35, Pro 600, XL, 6 Turbo, 9 Turbo, 16 Turbo, microWriter PS23, PS65
Tektronix	Phaser 140, 200, 220, 300, 340, 440, 480, 540, PXi, II PX, IISD, IISDJ, IISDX, III PXi
Xanté	Accel-a-Writer 8200, 8300, PlateMaker 8200, 8300
Xerox	4215, 4219, 4220, 4505

Tagged Binary Control Protocol (TBCP).   This protocol is much the same as BCP, but contains extra control sequences, which mark the beginning and end of a transfer. Unlike using Control-D, which marks the limits of an individual print job, a transfer sequence can consist of several PostScript print jobs. Once the sequence is over, print jobs can be sent in another emulation, for example, PCL. Devices which can use the Tagged Binary Control Protocol can be identified by the following entry in the relevant PPD file.

```
*Protocols: TBCP
```

Devices which support TBCP

Manufacturer	Models
Apple	LaserWriter Color
Compaq	PAGEMARQ 15, PAGEMARQ 20
CalComp	EcoGrafix, TechJet
Canon	LBP-860, LBP-1260, MDC PS
ColorPoint	820, 830
Digital	DEClaser 3500, 5100
Epson	LP-8200PS2
Fuji	Xerox Able Model-PR, Xerox Laser Press 4150, 4160, 4160II
Hewlett-Packard	CopyJet M, DesignJet 650C, DeskJet 1200C, LaserJet 4, 4 Plus, 4ML, 4MP, 4Si/4SiMX, 4V/4MV, 5Si, III, IIID, IIIP, PaintJet XL300
Kodak	Digital Science DCP 9000
Mitsubishi	S3600-40, S6600-40
Okidata	OL 1200
Xanté	Accel-a-Writer 8300, PlateMaker 8300
Scantext	Scantext 2013, Largo L2, Othello L2, Rondo L2
Xerox	4215/MRP, 4219/MRP, 4220 LPS, 4505, 4520

Printer Job Language (PJL).   This protocol, defined by Hewlett Packard for the LaserJet family, and also implemented in some other printers, controls supplementary printer functions.

PJL instructions work outside the individual print jobs and are therefore independent of the page description language (PostScript, PCL, etc.) in use. PJL instructions consist of ASCII text, as can be seen in the following examples:

```
@PJL JOB
@PJL SET RESOLUTION = 600
@PJL ENTER LANGUAGE = POSTSCRIPT
```

These instructions set the resolution to 600 dpi and specify Post-Script as the page description language. In practise, PJL is often combined with TBCP, which adds a few TBCP sequences to the instructions above. PJL compatible printers can be identified by the entry

```
*Protocols: PJL
```

in the relevant PPD file. PJL makes it easier to share a printer using various settings and page description languages, but must of course be supported by the printer that is in use.

Devices which support PJL

Manufacturer	Models
Canon	LBP-860, LBP-1260, MDC PS
Digital	DEClaser 5100
Hewlett-Packard	Color LaserJet, CopyJet M, DesignJet 650C, DeskJet 1200C, Laserjet 4 Plus , 4Si, 4V, 5M, 5MP, 5Si, IIISi, PaintJet XL300
Texas Instruments	microLaser Pro/8, PowerPro/12
Xerox	4215/MRP, 4219/MRP, 4220 LPS, 4220/MRP, 4230/MRP, 4505, 4517, 4520, 8808

Automatic emulation sensing.   As already stated, many printers can, apart from PostScript, accept one or more emulations or page description languages. Apart from various versions of the widely used Hewlett Packard Printer Control Language (PCL – used by LaserJet compatible printers), HPGL, Diablo, Epson and Proprinter emulations may be encountered. The majority of newer printers switch automatically between the possible emulations. This function is sometimes described, rather euphemistically, as "artificial intelligence". It is usually done by using the start of a print job to identify the language in use. So that PostScript files are recognized as such, they often have to be preceded by the characters %!, %!PS or %!PS-Adobe. If these characters are missing, then PostScript data can be wrongly interpreted as ASCII text causing the printer to churn out page after page of PostScript code!

Differentiation between various emulations can also be carried out by the transfer protocol (see above).

2.3.3 Resident Loading.   The various transfer protocols should make sure that the interpreter recognizes the beginning and end of print jobs and returns to ready mode after the end of each job. This is necessary to make sure that each print job can use all the printer memory and parts of the memory do not remain blocked by remnants of previous jobs. However, in some situations it can be useful if repeatedly-used data are available for every print job. The two most

important uses for this are the retention of fonts, and application specific PostScript prologs. The interpreter must have access to all of the fonts and prologs needed by a document in order to print it. If a lot of documents use the same fonts, transfer time can be reduced by downloading the fonts once to the printer and not erasing them after printing a document. This process is called *resident loading*, as the data stays resident in printer memory until the printer is turned off or reset (not to be confused with storing fonts on the printer's hard disk!).

Printer jobs, sensibly, are not normally resident loaded as this would unnecessarily block up the printer's memory. The PostScript instruction for resident loading is only effective for the current print job and ends at the start of the next job. The necessary instructions can be found in the PostScript file *resident.ps* on the CD-ROM. Resident loading of font definitions is usually carried out using a special downloading program. Details can be found in Section 4.4.

2.3.4 Interactive Access to the Interpreter.

Normally, the PostScript interpreter in a printer processes one PostScript job after the other, that is, it works in batch mode. When learning PostScript programming or for error trapping it is however useful to be able to communicate interactively with the interpreter. Doing this not only allows PostScript instructions to be tried out, but also allows the interpreter's internal state to be checked or – with PostScript programming knowledge – to track down errors more precisely. Some software RIPs, including Ghostscript, can be used interactively.

If you have established a connection to the printer in one of the ways described below, you will have to type

```
executive
```

blind and press the return key. If you have made (or think you have made) a typing error, hit Control-D to end the current session and try again. This instruction starts interactive mode and the interpreter makes itself known with a message similar to this:

```
PostScript(r) Version 2013.111
(c) Copyright 1984-1993 Adobe Systems Incorporated.
Typefaces (c) Copyright 1981 Linotype-Hell AG and/or its subsi-
diaries.
All Rights Reserved.
PS>
```

The *PS>* prompt shows that the interpreter is waiting for input. You can now type PostScript instructions, which are executed after pressing return:

```
PS>vmstatus pstack
655104
13104
2
PS>
```

This example returns the size of the available and utilized memory. If you make an error or give an unknown command, the interpreter will complain:

```
PS>help
%%[ Error: undefined; OffendingCommand: help ]%%
PS>
```

You can use the command *quit* to leave interactive mode again. According to the connection method in use, you can send files in interactive mode, for example, to analyze faulty PostScript files. Note, however, that it is not possible to process fonts or bitmap graphics in interactive mode. If you want to see the interpreter's messages, but not the files being sent, you can turn off the echo function using the command *false echo*.

To work with a printer in interactive mode, you need both a suitable connection and software. Therefore, we will cover this separately for each operating system. With most variants the printer has to be connected with the computer via a *null modem cable*. This is a serial cable with wires 2 and 3 (Transmit Data and Receive Data) crossed. You can buy a null modem cable at your local computer dealer or simulate it with a switch box and a straight cable. If your printer has automatic emulation recognition, you should turn permanent Post-Script mode on. Otherwise, your interactive instructions may be printed as ASCII text.

ASCII terminal. If you have an ASCII terminal (for example, VT 100) then you do not even have to connect the printer to a computer: simply connect printer and terminal using the serial interface and a null modem cable. If you set the communications parameters on both sides correctly, then you can communicate directly with the printer's interpreter from the terminal.

MS-DOS and Windows. You only require a terminal emulator. This software is often used in comms and emulates the functioning of a terminal. There is a wide range of shareware and public domain programs for this purpose. Interactive mode works perfectly well using Windows 3.1's built in Terminal accessory.

Here as well, you must connect the computer and printer with a serial null modem cable. After starting the terminal emulation, set

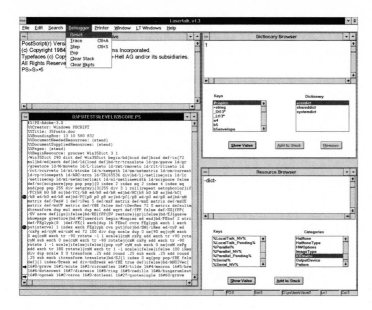

Fig. 2.6.
LaserTalk supports
PostScript de-
bugging with a
wealth of features

the data transfer speed and other serial interface parameters as for
the printer and then type *executive.*

If the transfer goes correctly, it is a good idea to map the command to a function key so that you do not always have to type the
command blind. Via the menu entry Transfer, Send Text File Post-
Script files can be sent to the printer and all the messages which
occur can be viewed.

For PostScript developers the program LaserTalk provides an easier method of accessing the PostScript interpreter. This program has
long been available for the Macintosh and is now being offered by
Adobe in a Windows version. Apart from interactive access with some
printer models, LaserTalk offers onscreen viewing of PostScript files
(with some printers only) as well as help tracing errors. Unfortunately, LaserTalk supports neither the bidirectional parallel interface or
networked printers.

Macintosh. The Macintosh also makes it possible to "converse" with
the printer using terminal emulation. As this connection does not
use AppleTalk, but uses the serial interface, you must set up the
printer accordingly. For example, on Apple's LaserWriter printer series there is a small switch at the back of the machine for setting the
various types of communication. Set it (as per the handbook) to serial
communication and PostScript mode (not *AutoSense*). Connect the
device using a null modem cable, not to the printer port but to the
modem port of your Mac. You must also set the communications

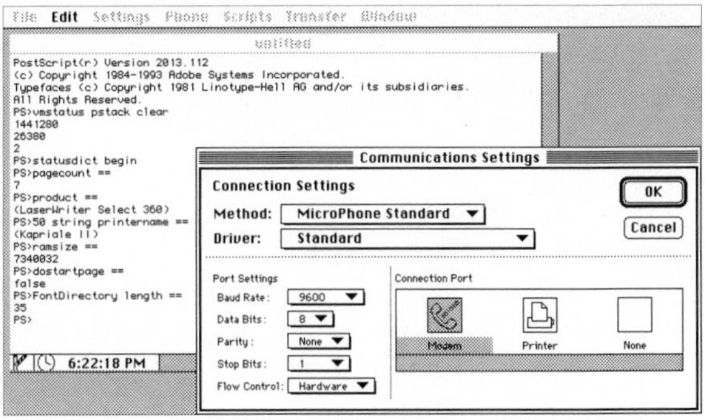

Fig. 2.7.
Interactive connection with the PostScript interpreter using terminal emulation software on the Mac

parameters of your terminal software to match those used by the printer.

Alternatively, you can use *LaserTalk* to communicate with a printer that is connected using AppleTalk. Like the Windows version of this software, LaserTalk for Macintosh allows, with some printer models, screen display of PostScript files and offers help to the developer in fixing PostScript errors.

Unix.   Under Unix you must also connect the printer to the computer's serial port using a null modem cable. If the *tip* command is available on your system, enter a line into the file */etc/remote* which reads

```
ttya:dv=/dev/ttya:br#9600:el=^D:
```

but be careful to enter the correct designator for the interface and the correct data transfer rate. If the parameters match the printer settings, use the command

```
tip ttya
```

to open dialog with the interpreter. A further possibility is the program *cu*, which allows you to select all the required parameters as command line options.

If you have networked the printer using TCP/IP it is possible to establish an interactive connection using telnet (port 23).

2.4 PostScript Drivers for Different Operating Systems

2.4.1 PostScript Under Windows 3.x.   Windows 3.1 and 3.11 come
with a standard PostScript printer driver which can be configured for many printers. There were very often problems (mostly related to the use of imagesetters) with the first versions of this driver. The current

version has fixed most of these problems and there is also now an alternative in the form of the Adobe PostScript drivers. Before describing these drivers, we draw your attention to a general Windows problem.

The Control-D problem.   Under Windows the driver sends data either directly to the interface or to the Print Manager, which puts print files unaltered into the printer queue. As there is no software component to communicate with the printer and to carry out the relevant protocol, the printer driver must carry out this function as well. However, it does not know which protocol will later be used to send the PostScript data to the printer. As the parallel and serial interface and therefore the standard protocol are dominant under Windows, the driver takes the precaution of adding a Control-D character to the start and end of the data, so that the interpreter recognizes the boundary between various print jobs. This works as long as the PostScript data are actually sent via a serial or parallel link. However, if the data are sent to a file for output on another system, the Control-D characters become superfluous and cause huge problems. If PostScript files are to be passed to another system, the Control-D characters at the beginning and end of the file must be removed or better still not be created at all.

There is a lot of argument about this feature, which at best is regarded as an error in the printer driver. In reality, it is a structural weakness in Windows that is to blame, namely the absence of a backend (printer communications software). This leads to user data (the PostScript code) being mixed with parts of the protocol (the Control-D). Hints on avoiding this problem are given below. In an editor which allows control characters to be entered, a missing Control-D can be entered with the keyboard sequence Alt-004.

The Microsoft driver.   The PostScript driver, which comes as standard with Windows, was jointly developed by Microsoft and Aldus and serves as a basis for many printer manufacturers' driver adaptations, as the C source code is included in the *Windows Device Driver Kit* (DDK).

This driver can be configured for various printer models by using WPD (*Windows Printer Description*) files. WPD files are shortened versions of PPD files, which for reasons of space and speed are translated to a binary format. Above all they contain details about possible paper formats, the available printer memory and font availability. The program, which converts PPD files to WPD files, is also part of the Windows DDK, but is not usually available to the user. Because of this, a suitable WPD file is delivered with some (but not all) printers. The driver can control various printers using different WPD files.

Unfortunately, it is not possible to configure the driver using the standardized PPD files.

Font handling with the Microsoft driver is somewhat laborious (see Section 4.4.4). It is not just the tiresome font entries in *win.ini*, but also the fact that the font installation depends on the interface to which the printer is connected. So it can happen that if a print-out (for which all the correct fonts are available in a test print) is to be re-directed to create a print file with the printer connected to FILE:, the required fonts are no longer loaded! The Microsoft driver converts TrueType fonts, which a PostScript printer cannot process into Type 3 bitmap fonts at small sizes and to Type 1 outline fonts at larger point sizes. However, the quality of the converted fonts is not very high, for example, they are unhinted.

Users who create PostScript files under Windows often have nothing good to say about the Microsoft driver. Apart from the disastrous Control-D problem, the driver also has difficulties generating DSC comments. This makes output on other systems or the further processing of the PostScript files much more difficult. The BoundingBox in EPS files generated with this driver is usually incorrect, which does not add to its popularity. The "Options". "Advanced... " menu in the driver setup dialog does make it possible to generate DSC compliant files. This setting only cures some idiosyncrasies of the driver (for example, pages that are dependent on other pages) but does not generate complete DSC compatible files. To prevent a Control-D being output at the beginning of the file, you have to locate the printer section of *win.ini* – for example [PostScript,LPT1] – and insert the line:

```
CtrlD=0
```

This inconvenient method means that after making a print-out (with Control-D) you will always have to edit the file to create a proper print file (without Control-D). The Control-D at the end of the output file is unfortunately not always suppressed by this line. Using the program

Fig. 2.8.
Setup Options for
the Microsoft driver

PSCtrld from the accompanying CD-ROM you can specify, for each installed printer, whether or not Control-D characters should be generated.

The final shortcoming to note is that this driver does not support PostScript Level 2 at all and therefore throws away functionality and speed advantages (see Chapter 5).

The AdobePS driver. PostScript's inventor, Adobe, was naturally not very happy with the Windows driver situation, as the bad reputation of the driver – so it was feared – would quickly rub off on PostScript itself. For this reason Adobe soon developed its own Windows Post-Script drivers. The first version of Adobe's Windows driver was a modified version of the Microsoft driver. In 1993 a complete re-write, version 2.1, was introduced which differed radically from Microsoft's driver. Version 3.01 has a reworked interface and groups the possible settings together in tabs. The new driver architecture is supposed to have speed advantages over the old driver. This is brought about not just by optimizing the Level 1 code, but also by integrating the functions of PostScript Level 2. This driver makes it possible to utilize the advantages of a Level 2 device under Windows for the first time.

Some manufacturers deliver the Adobe driver with new printers or make it available on-line (for example, Hewlett Packard's FTP-Server ftp-boi.external.hp.com). Although Adobe sells the driver to end users in the USA at a nominal price, it is difficult to obtain in Europe unless you buy other Adobe software.

On the "Paper" tab AdobePS allows to select, as well as the normal range of paper sizes and orientations, several "effects". These include printing a watermark all over the page or printing several reduced size thumbnails on one page ("*n*-up printing").

As to be expected, the driver is configured using Adobe's PPD files. The driver does not just evaluate the usual information about paper sizes, but uses all the entries in the PPD file, even those whose func-

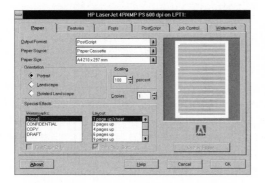

Fig. 2.9.
Settings for the Adobe driver. Unlike other drivers, the Adobe driver offers three page orientations – portrait, landscape and rotated landscape

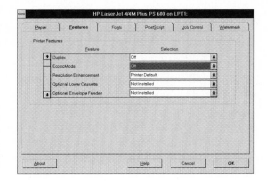

Fig. 2.10.
The Adobe driver
gathers special
printer functions
together dynami-
cally in a list (the
"Features" tab)

tion was not known at the time of the driver's development! This includes for example new functions for resolution enhancement or
hardware expansions like a duplex unit. The driver is able to put together an interface from entries in the PPD file which can be used to
control these functions. As the printer description file also includes
the necessary PostScript code, the driver does not need to understand
which functions it concerns. This list, unique to each printer, appears
in the "Features" tab.

As there was no possibility until Version 2.11 of the AdobePS driver
to add new PPD files, it was necessary to laboriously alter the *oemset-
up.inf* installation file to configure an already-installed driver for a
new printer model. Version 3.01 of the AdobePS driver contains a
small extra program called from Control Panel which serves to integrate new PPD files. The user does not see the cryptic file names, but a
full description of the printer.

The integrated font downloader is started from the "Fonts" tab.
This downloader makes font handling much easier and can transfer
PostScript print files as well as fonts to the printer. The user can use
the downloader to send individual fonts to the printer. The driver
worries about all fonts not already loaded when a file is printed. In
the "Job Control" tab, font download can be turned off completely,
such as when generating a print file for a system on which the fonts
already exist. For TrueType fonts, apart from the usual possibilities
(replacement by equivalent PostScript fonts, conversion to Type 1 or
Type 3) there is also the possibility, on newer printers, of wrapping
them as a Type 42 font.

The division of features between the "PostScript" and "Job Control" tabs does seem a little odd, as both influence the eventual Post-
Script output. The parameters which can be altered include Level 1/
Level 2 (normally, the driver reads this from the PPD file), ASCII and
binary transfer as well as the integration of prologs, error handling,
and font definitions.

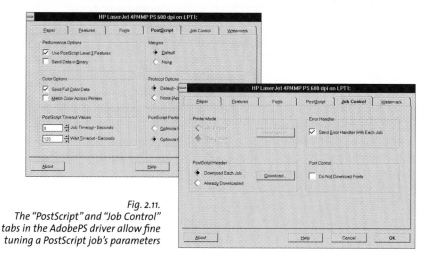

Fig. 2.11.
The "PostScript" and "Job Control"
tabs in the AdobePS driver allow fine
tuning a PostScript job's parameters

Control-D generation hides under "Protocol Options". For immediate output you should usually select the Standard protocol (using Control-D). Output without extra characters is hidden under the confusing description "None (AppleTalk)". This the preferred option when producing PostScript print files. This also gets rid of the need (as with the Microsoft driver) to make changes to win.ini.

The Adobe driver does have its own problems: because of the fundamentally different architecture with respect to the Microsoft driver, there are compatibility problems with some application programs. Adobe insists that these are problems in the application software which simply did not manifest themselves with the old driver, but such problems can render the driver useless. At least the problems should reduce if the driver is more widely distributed and software developers have more incentive to adapt their products to AdobePS. The Adobe driver cannot adequately resolve the Bounding-Box error problem as this would require modifications to the program being printed from.

Downloader. Microsoft overlooked a not insignificant detail when it was developing Windows: no method is included to dump existing PostScript files to the printer! Copying the file to LPT1 with the File Manager does work, but gives a pointless error message and ties up the whole system for the duration of the copying process. This also happens when the file is copied to the printer port with the copy command in a DOS box. Some printers therefore have download software included. For example, Apple includes Macintosh and Windows versions of the LaserWriter utility program with its LaserWriter models which (like the Adobe Downloader) is suitable for downloading fonts and PostScript files. Alternatively you can use the *bprint* (*binary printing*) program on the accompanying CD-ROM. You can drag&drop files to it for sending to the printer.

2.4.2 PostScript Under Windows 95.
Microsoft took heed of the problems with the drivers in earlier Windows versions: The Windows 95 PostScript driver has been jointly developed by Microsoft and Adobe. Many similarities can be seen between these drivers and the AdobePS driver for Windows 3.x both in functionality and appearance. The new driver has many of the characteristics which one expects from a modern PostScript driver:

► Support for PostScript Level 2
► Configuration using PPD files and support for device specific functions
► Support for binary transfer protocols
► DSC compatible PostScript output
► Various output options: device specific functions or "generic PostScript" for easy archiving.

To set up a PostScript printer driver the corresponding printer description file and a *.inf* file are required. The installation is carried out in the normal manner for Windows 95. As the driver does not evaluate all the entries in PPD files, Windows 95 uses abbreviated versions of the PPD files, which have the suffix SPD. Like PPD files, these contain a description of the printer properties in text format, but are a little smaller than the original PPDs. Inserting an individual PPD file without a corresponding .inf file is unfortunately – unlike the Windows 3.1 AdobePS driver – not possible (but note the tip further down). The PostScript driver configuration menu is reached from "Desktop", "Printers", choose printer, "File", "Properties" or (limited options) from application programs' "Printer Setup" menu entry. It is divided

Fig. 2.12.
The "Paper" and
"Graphics" tabs of the
Windows 95 printer
driver

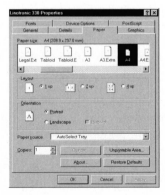

into several tabs (see Figure 2.12). The "Paper" tab shows paper format and orientation, and paper tray options. Under "Graphics" resolution, halftoning, scaling, and reverse options can be set. The "PostScript" tab is particularly interesting. A drop-down menu allows various options to be chosen: the standard setting of "PostScript (Optimize for Portability – ADSC)" gives DSC compatible PostScript output and should therefore be used generally.

There are also options for generating EPS files as well as "archive format". The latter excludes all printer-dependent functions (paper trays, etc.) and is suitable for making PostScript files which will be distributed to various recipients or archived. The PJL archive format contains additional control sequences for HP printers (to change printer languages). However, such files are unsuitable for other printers. The other options in the "PostScript" tab relate to loading prologs, error handling routines and timeouts. The extended options allow switching between Level 1 and Level 2, which should not usually be changed, however, as the driver reads the printer's language level from the PPD file. Bitmap compression is handled in Level 2 by the relevant filter operators. In Level 1 the driver reduces the size of bitmap graphics using RLE compression. Under the description "Data Formats" you can find the settings for various transfer protocols: "ASCII Data" generates 7-bit output, suitable for all printers and interfaces; "Tagged Binary Communications Protocol" must be supported by the printer. As binary transfer can halve the volume of picture data, you should use this setting if the printer supports it. "Pure Binary Data" on the other hand is seldom used. Independent of ASCII or binary transfer it allows you to specify separately whether a Control-D should be generated at the start and end of the file. This removes the need to laboriously edit the ini file as was necessary in Windows 3.x.

The TrueType font options on the "Fonts" tab are almost the same as the options which were available under Windows 3.x. The driver

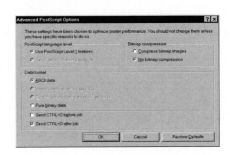

Fig. 2.13.
The "PostScript" Tab and the
advanced PostScript options

Fig. 2.14.
TrueType fonts in Windows 95
are treated almost the same
as in Windows 3.x

can convert TrueType fonts into PostScript Type 1 fonts (outline fonts), Type 3 fonts (bitmaps), or Type 42 (TrueType fonts wrapped as PostScript). In addition, you can specify the font height in pixels at which the driver changes from converting TrueType fonts to Type 3 to changing them to Type 1.

Installing a new PPD file.   As already stated, Windows 95 needs not only the PPD file when installing a new printer, but also an .inf file, which has details of all the files required by the printer. However, you may need to install a new PPD file, for example, for an imagesetter, without having a manufacturer's installation disk to hand.

Luckily, Windows 95 is easily fooled! Follow these steps to install a new PPD file:

- ▶ Install any PostScript printer, so that Windows copies the basic files.
- ▶ Make a temporary directory and copy the PPD file to it. Change its extension to .spd.
- ▶ Create a file called speedy.inf in that directory with the following contents, altering the sample entries for the manufacturer ("Speedy"), model ("Printwonder") and the name of the SPD file ("speedy.spd") as required (in case of doubt you will find the model name in the PPD file):

```
[Version]
Class=Printer
[Manufacturer]
"Speedy"
[Speedy]
"Speedy Printwonder"=SPEEDY.SPD
[SPEEDY.SPD]
CopyFiles=@SPEEDY.SPD
DataSection=PSCRIPT_DATA
[PSCRIPT_DATA]
```

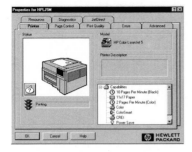

Fig. 2.15.
JetAdmin and the extended setup
dialog for a networked printer

```
DriverFile=PSCRIPT.DRV
[DestinationDirs]
DefaultDestDir=11
```

▶ Now you can "install" a new printer, using the above directory as a substitute for the installation disk. The name of the printer can now be selected from the installation menu.

Connecting a printer to a network.　Windows 95 makes it easier to connect a printer to a network than earlier versions. Built-in support is provided for DEC Printserver, HP JetAdmin, and RPC printing. As an example we shall describe the connection of an HP LaserJet 4M Plus via an Ethernet network, as this printer comes with a network connection built in, but the connection of printers to a network is not covered adequately in the Windows 95 handbooks.

After physically connecting the printer to the Ethernet several layers of software have to be configured using the Control Panel's Network item: this begins with a driver for the network card, then a driver for the IPX/SPX network protocol, and finally, under the heading "Services" the HP Jet-Admin software. If everything went successfully a new item for the JetAdmin management software should appear in the Control Panel. After starting, JetAdmin searches for all the printers which are accessible via the network or parallel port. If the networking is successful, the device address of the printer, which can be used to define a new interface with "Printer", "New" (see Figure 2.15), appears. As soon as you connect a printer driver to the new interface, three new tabs – Diagnosis, Status, and Functions – are added to the setup dialog. They make it possible to call up various printer settings and network parameters as well as the control of printer functions.

If your printer has a network interface, it should definitely be used – particularly if the low cost of PC network cards is taken into account. Using a network does not just offer advantages for workgroups who want to share a printer, but often also give a speed boost to standalone workstations. A more detailed analysis of performance can be found in Section 9.1.

Downloading under Windows 95.   Unfortunately there is no direct way to download PostScript files or fonts to a printer queue, and yet again it is necessary to use third party programs. Unfortunately, the PostScript driver (unlike the Windows 3.1 AdobePS driver) does not contain a font downloader.

AdobePS 4.1.   In Spring 1996, Adobe came up with its own Windows 95 PostScript driver called AdobePS 4.1. It offers several enhancements over the Windows 95 standard driver. These include some minor features as well as major improvements:

- a greater choice of thumbnail variations (e.g., print 16 pages on one sheet);
- the ability to install new PPD files without a corresponding INF file;
- extended help feature;
- support for Image Color Matching (ICM), device-independent color specifications, and device profiles. This brings color matching among different devices to specially enabled Windows 95 applications.

Adobe seems to bundle this driver with new application software releases. At the time of writing, it is not clear whether AdobePS will be available free of charge to all users or marketed as a separate product.

2.4.3 PostScript on the Macintosh.   The Macintosh operating system contains a PostScript driver which is named after the Laser-Writer range of printers. The LaserWriter 8.0 drivers, introduced in 1993, began a new generation of drivers developed jointly by Apple and Adobe. This driver replaced the old versions of Apple's Laser-Writer and was therefore included with every copy of the Mac operating system. In addition, it is included with many printer models and is also distributed separately by Adobe under the name PSPrinter.

Adobe made use of all the knowledge about PostScript programming then available when developing PSPrinter: it supports Post-Script Level 2, can be configured using PPD files, enables EPS files with preview generation and generates DSC compatible output. The Level 2 capability delivers speed advantages and also makes device independent color definition possible.

The driver does not just take paper format, paper tray, and available font information from the PPD file, but also makes use of information about device specific functions. It then allows the user to

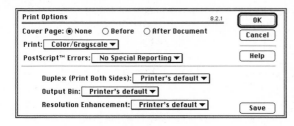

Fig. 2.16.
LaserWriter/
PSPrinter print
options. Extra
printer functions,
described in the
PPD file, appear
in the lower
section

select them. Configuring a new printer can be carried out without re-
installing the driver: if the driver can communicate with the printer
using AppleTalk, it can find out the correct type classification and select the appropriate PPD file automatically. In order for this to work,
the PPD file's name must exactly match the name of the printer
which it describes. In exceptional cases (or if the printer is not directly connected) the user can select a suitable PPD file. This makes sense
if the printer has extra features added (such as a hard disk with extra
fonts) or if several examples of the same series are to be operated using different feature levels and the corresponding PPD files are adjusted by hand. When generating EPS files (see Chapter 3) using the
printer driver, PSPrinter offers several options for the preview section: no preview, black and white bitmap or object QuickDraw image
(PICT) in color (extended preview).

If a document is to be output to a PostScript file rather than printed straight away, PSPrinter offers several possible settings: ASCII or binary, Level 1 or Level 2, type of preview picture and number of fonts to
be embedded. The DSC compatibility of the PostScript files makes it
easier to process the files on other systems. The driver also makes use
of DSC compatible output for other functions, e.g., printing "thumbnails" on a page.

PSPrinter processes a file in two passes: firstly it creates a Quick-
Draw version of the document on the hard disk. It then analyzes this
in order to make decisions about the fonts required and optimization
strategy. In the second pass the QuickDraw version is converted to
PostScript and sent to the printer or spooler. PSPrinter, unlike earlier
versions of LaserWriter, does not download the required PostScript
prolog (in Apple-speak, LaserPrep) to be resident in the printer, but
downloads it for every job. This ensures that users with different
driver versions can share a network printer and also that problems do
not arise because of a missing prolog when sending a PostScript file
on floppy disk.

Downloader.   Apple includes the LaserWriter utility program with
its LaserWriter printers. Apart from various management functions it
makes it possible to send fonts and PostScript files to the printer.

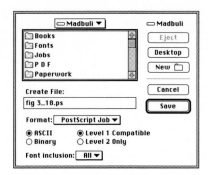

Fig. 2.17.
Macintosh driver
options for
creating a Post-
Script file

When loading PostScript files you must be aware that the LaserWriter utility only accepts files of type TEXT. If need be, change the file type with ResEdit or a similar program.

2.4.4 PostScript Under Unix.   As there are no standardized printer drivers used by all programs under Unix, we will confine ourselves to the transfer of PostScript data. The PostScript data is created by the printer driver for the program in use or by a converter, but can also originate from other systems (for example, Macintosh) on the same network.

Spoolers and OPI servers.   As the classic multiuser system, Unix has to manage the access of several users to the available printers. The spooler manages queues of individual print jobs, sent by the users of a computer or several computers attached to the network. Apart from these basic functions, there are many extra functions available in conjunction with PostScript which are implemented to varying degrees on different systems:

- Inserting the required font descriptions or prologs.
- Extracting individual pages or printing in reverse order.
- Differentiation between text and PostScript files. Text files are automatically converted to PostScript.
- Printer error messages are sent to the user by e-mail.
- OPI functions: replacement of low resolution proxy images with high resolution image data.

Many of these functions are already performed by the system software or other freely available programs (see below). However, to implement OPI extensions extra software is needed. One example is Helios EtherShare, which combines the functions of spooler and OPI server and allows a Unix server to be integrated into a Macintosh network.

Backend. The spooler does receive the PostScript data from the user, but another program, the backend, is responsible for actually communicating with the printer and processing the protocol. Depending on the Unix derivative, this may be implemented as an independent program which is activated as required from the spooler, or it may simply be a made up of a few shell scripts. The basic job of the backend is to keep to the protocol, and if a parallel or serial connection is in use, to generate the Control-D which separates the print jobs.

The package *lprps* on the accompanying CD-ROM contains a backend for the standard protocol, a program to differentiate between text and PostScript data as well as two filters to convert text data to PostScript and to reverse the page order in a print document. Printer error messages are processed via the syslog facility, other printer output is sent by e-mail to the user by *lprps*.

If you need to print large amounts of picture data and have a BCP compatible printer, then you may be able to increase the data throughput by using binary communications. To do this you also need a printer driver or a converter which is capable of generating binary PostScript data. If using a Level 2 device you may also use the JPEG and TIFF converters described in detail in Section 5.5.1. When using parallel or serial communications, the binary data must, in accordance with BCP, employ "quoting", that is convert the control characters which it may contain. You can either do this before sending the PostScript file to the spooler by using the quote program from the accompanying CD-ROM, for example:

```
cat image.ps | quote | lpr
```

With a good knowledge of the system, you can perform the BCP conversion in the backend or integrate it into a filter called by the backend.

Download. Under Unix a separate downloader is not required, as the spooler and backend carry out the communication with the printer. One exception is the resident loading of fonts to the printer. In Section 4.4.6 it is explained how this works, even without a special downloader, using the spooler and a small PostScript program.

2.5 PostScript Errors

2.5.1 Various Types of Error.
There are two classic situations for turning a PostScript user's hair gray: the feed light blinks and blinks and blinks and then stops blinking without spitting a page out. Or: the PostScript file prints beautifully on the laser printer, all the fonts are there, the instructions are correct – but the imagesetter continu-

ally throws out the message *Error: limitcheck, Offending Command: clip.* Like it or not, PostScript errors are part of everyday life, just like program crashes on the PC.

PostScript files are programs in the PostScript language, and programs may contain errors. This observation can be used to place responsibility for PostScript errors at the door of the creator of the PostScript files – usually the developer of the driver or converter. However, many PostScript errors are not caused exclusively by errors in the print file but have other causes which can be fixed even by a user without knowledge of PostScript:

- ► Data transfer. Errors can arise when the file is sent to the printer; for example, not sticking to the protocol, using an inadequately screened printer cable which loses data, or if binary data are sent on a 7-bit link.
- ► Configuration problems. Some applications assume that the corresponding PostScript prolog is resident in the printer even if this is not the case. This problem can be fixed easily by loading the correct prolog (if it is available).
- ► Device specific operators. A PostScript file which contains device specific operators should not be output on a device that does not support those operators. This happens when a file is prepared for a specific device but is output on another. However, good PostScript drivers generate code which recognizes this situation and reconfigures itself accordingly.
- ► Execution problems. The device does not have enough memory to process the PostScript file. This problem can usually only be solved by altering and simplifying the original file (or increasing the amount of RAM in the printer).
- ► Programming errors. This category is unavoidable if you start to write your own PostScript programs. In commercial software, genuine programming errors in the PostScript code are happily very rare. If they do occur, then they require detailed PostScript programming knowledge to solve, or, better, a new driver.

It is important for the user to immediately recognize PostScript errors as such (if the printer stops blinking, the power might simply have failed...). Only then can you decide whether the error can be fixed from outside and take the appropriate measures.

The printer does not give an error message in some cases, but nevertheless doesn't do the right thing. For this reason, some irritating problems have to be dealt with before going on to real PostScript errors. In Section 3.4.2 you can find further information on the errors that can occur in conjunction with EPS.

PostScript data does not reach the printer.   Most printers show that they are processing a printer file by, for example, displaying a *Processing* message in the printer display or by a blinking light. But your PostScript file does not cause any reaction. Usually a backend or spooler (especially under Unix) is responsible for this. These programs often try to check whether the printer file actually consists of PostScript data. To do this, they interrogate the file header. PostScript files must (depending on the spooler) start with *%!, %!PS* or *%!PS-Adobe- 3.0*. Files which do not comply are rejected and not sent to the printer at all. The user often receives a message in the form of *File ... is not a PostScript file*. Apart from home-made PostScript programs without DSC comments, (Windows) print files which have the Control-D character at the start and end, and therefore do not fulfil the check conditions can be to blame.

The printer prints pages of PostScript code.   Many printers have an automatic emulation detector which investigates the data sent to the printer and decides whether it consists of PostScript instructions, PCL code, or ASCII text and activates the appropriate emulation software in the printer. If PostScript data are not identified as such, it can happen that all the instructions are printed as plain text. The best solution is to create PostScript files which pass the test. Alternatively, the automatic emulation software on many printers can be turned off and the PostScript interpreter left active permanently.

Sometimes this autorecognition function is also built into the spooler or backend. Instead of totally rejecting the file, the system software then creates PostScript instructions which print the whole file as ASCII text. The advice here is also to either find out and stick to the test criteria for PostScript data or to permanently activate PostScript mode.

2.5.2 Error Handling Routines.

PostScript error messages from a printer or imagesetter can appear on screen or be printed out. Output to the screen is particularly desirable on machines which use expensive consumables (e.g., thermal transfer printers) but is not possible on all platforms.

Error messages on screen.   The interpreter always tries to send the error description and the name of the offending PostScript instruction to the computer. This means that the user can see which error has occurred. A bidirectional communications link is needed so that the computer can receive messages from the computer. On the Macintosh using AppleTalk this is always the case. Under Unix you require a suitable print spooler or backend as well as a serial or network connection to the printer. The form of parallel interface control usual under MS-DOS and Windows does not allow the computer to receive error messages, and special software is required to receive error messages when using a bidirectional parallel cable. The return channel of the serial interface is not normally used.

Printed error messages.   As a substitute (or a supplement) for an error message on screen, the printer can also print any error messages. Before the error message, it may print out the part of the page for which instructions were sent before the error occurred. An *error handler* (a piece of PostScript code) is needed for this function. Some newer devices have an integral error handler, which you can activate via the printer control menu or the RIP's management software. Even if this is not the case, then you can still activate such an error handling routine very easily.

Often, no special action is necessary because the software or driver has already loaded an error handling routine as part of the prolog or has at least offered to load it as an option.

If you are using the Microsoft driver for Windows 3.x, you can activate the error handler by choosing "Options", "Advanced..." and enabling "Print PostScript Error Information" in the printer setup dialog. You can find the corresponding option in the Adobe driver setup submenu "Job Control" and "Send Error Control with each job".

In Windows 95, you can enable the error handler in the driver's "PostScript" tab by clicking "Print PostScript error information".

On the Macintosh in the print dialog of LaserWriter 8.0 (or higher versions) and PSPrinter you can choose between "No Special Reporting", "Summarize on Screen" or "Print Detailed Report" from the "Options" submenu. If "Print Detailed Report" is selected, LaserWriter (unlike the Windows drivers) does not print out the page which caused the error.

Fig. 2.18.
The LaserWriter/
PSPrinter print
dialog with error
handling options

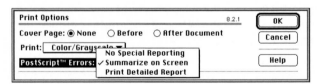

If you are working under MS-DOS or Unix, and your software has not made an error handling routine available, use the file *errorh.ps* on the accompanying CD-ROM. Send this file as a separate job to the printer before the problem file. This makes the routine resident and it then keeps an eye on all subsequent print jobs until the printer is turned off or reset.

All error handling routines report the name of the error, and then the name of the instruction which triggered the error and possibly the operand stack. A PostScript programmer can use the data to gather more detailed information about how the error occurred or the point in the PostScript file which caused the error. errorh.ps prints further information which looks unintelligible to most users, but makes it easier for a specialist to analyse the errors.[1] In the next section you will find a list of the commonest errors as well as notes on possible causes and how to fix the errors.

With some errors, the PostScript code recognizes the cause itself and prints an understandable error message for the user. For example, the Microsoft driver uses this procedure if it concludes that the relevant prolog is not loaded. It prints a message describing the problem in plain text (PostScript prolog not loaded) and the remedy (Load prolog manually). The Adobe driver for Windows recognizes more errors and reports them with suitable messages in plain text. This affects incorrect protocol settings (driver creates binary data, but printer cannot handle them), the wrong language level (some jobs require Level 2), or insufficient memory. A further example is the embedding of EPS graphics: it is increasingly the case that the embedding software catches forbidden operators from the EPS file and prints an error message instead of the graphic (see Section 3.4.2). Such plain text messages are easier to understand than the usual PostScript error messages, but are not possible for all errors.

2.5.3 Remedying PostScript Errors. PostScript error messages always take the form

```
%%[Error: <error name>; OffendingCommand: <operator> ]%%
```

To determine the cause of the error you must take note of the error name as well as the PostScript operator that triggered it. The following listing contains all thirty possible PostScript errors. However, many of them only occur very occasionally and cannot be remedied by the user. In the descriptions you will also find hints on the operators which often trigger the errors. You can find detailed descriptions of the operators in the *PostScript Language Reference Manual*. If an operator is not described there, this fact is in itself important: such operators are not part of standard PostScript, but belong to the group of device specific operators and point to an incorrect driver configuration or output on the wrong device. If an error message contains no

---

1. *Namely execution stack and dictionary stack as well as the errorinfo dictionary with detailed information about the occurrence of certain errors.*

operator name but just random characters, this points to problems sending the PostScript data.

Cause of the Error.   In complex print environments it is not sufficient to identify the actual cause of the error, but it is important to find out which part of the document triggered the error. To do this you must check not just all the elements in the document, but everything which plays a part in the output process. If the culprit is not evident from the partly printed page or the error message, find it out by altering the document or the path to the printer. Take note of the following points:

- ▸ Embedded EPS files can cause errors, especially if they do not adhere to the EPS standards.
- ▸ When configuring a printer with PPD files: are you using the correct PPD file for your printer?
- ▸ Printer driver: does the error also occur with a different driver?
- ▸ Embedded fonts: Does the document use too many fonts or are some font files damaged?
- ▸ High resolution data embedded by an OPI server: does the application software generate DSC compatible output and the correct OPI comments? If in doubt, remove embedded graphics, which are replaced by the OPI server.
- ▸ Communications protocol: Who is ensuring compliance? Are binary data generated, but sent via a 7 bit connection?
- ▸ Printer type: Can you work around the error by printing on another device (with more memory or a different PostScript interpreter)?

When searching for errors it is often very useful to use a screen previewer (such as Ghostscript). It is quicker, saves resources, and you can see how the page builds up, as far as the point which causes the error. However, some errors that depend on memory resources or the PostScript implementation will no longer occur. If the file absolutely cannot be printed out, but will display on screen, you can try using Ghostscript to rasterize the file in another format (e.g., PCL) and print out that file, providing of course that your printer can use different emulations. A further possibility is to convert the file to a simple PostScript bitmap with Ghostscript's psmono device (providing that the error does not occur in Ghostscript). After these general hints, we will look at the possible errors individually.

undefined.   This is the one of the commonest PostScript error messages. Its cause can be seen from the offending command which triggered it. Often an application specific prolog, needed to print the file, is missing. Most prologs define their own dictionary, a PostScript data structure, which contains the required procedures and variables. Its name often points to the offending software. A few examples: *Win35Dict* (Microsoft driver for Windows), *msdict* (Microsoft Word), *Adobe_Win_Driver* (Adobe driver for Windows), *md* (LaserWriter or PSPrinter), *FMdict* (FrameMaker for Unix). Some PostScript files also print a message if the PostScript prolog is missing. If you see an error message in the form:

```
Error: undefined, OffendingCommand: md
```

then the PostScript file does not contain the required prolog and you must make sure that it is loaded before the actual page description. If you have access to the software or driver which generated the file, you can usually set an option to determine whether or not to download the prolog to be resident in the printer. If you cannot generate the PostScript file (perhaps you have received it from another system), then you must obtain the correct prolog and download it to the printer before output.

The error *undefined* can also occur with PostScript files which carelessly use device specific operators. In this case the error may be triggered by one of the operators like *setduplexmode, setpapertray, manualtray*, etc., which are not implemented on all PostScript devices. To get around this you should recreate the file using the driver for the actual target printer if possible. Otherwise, you can render these commands ineffective using dummy definitions at the start of the PostScript file, e.g.:

```
/setduplexmode {pop} def
```

Unfortunately, there is no simple solution for users without PostScript programming knowledge.

If you see the error message *undefined in EPSF* (or four odd characters instead of EPSF), then you have tried to print an EPS file with a TIFF preview (see Section 3.3) directly. The PostScript interpreter cannot cope with the binary data at the start of such a file and produces an error message. To get round the problem, embed the file in a word processor or DTP document or extract the PostScript part of the EPS file and print that. You can find further tips in Section 3.4.2.

An error message in the form

```
Error: undefined; OffendingCommand:
```

without a more precise description of what caused the error points to hidden control characters which the printer cannot understand in the PostScript file. This can happen for example if you are printing a PostScript file from a Macintosh, but the PostScript file was created under Windows and contains Control-Ds or if a binary PostScript file is transmitted via a 7-bit link.

A peculiarity of the Adobe downloader in conjunction with Multiple Master fonts can cause the error message

```
Error: undefined; OffendingCommand: makeblendedfont
```

A more precise explanation and tips on fixing this error can be found in Section 4.4.4.

The following error appears if the driver for a PostScript printer is configured with Hewlett-Packard PJL but the printer does not understand PJL instructions.

```
%%[ Error: undefined; OffendingCommand: @PJL ]%%
```

This error message often appears when using Acrobat Distiller with an HP printer driver. In this case the driver has to be configured so that it does not produce HP specific commands any more. If you often switch between output on an HP printer and Acrobat and do not want to have to alter the printer driver configuration every time, you can put this definition in the Distiller startup file to render the HP commands harmless:

```
/@PJL { currentfile //=string readline { pop } if } bind def
```

limitcheck and VMerror.   Both of these error messages (VM stands for *virtual memory*) occur if the interpreter is exhausted, i.e., if the page description makes too high a demand on the device's memory. When using Level 2 PostScript these errors occur very rarely, thanks to optimized memory management. The usual candidate for limitcheck is the drawing path: complex graphics and above all silhouetting contain very large numbers of line elements (points, line segments, etc.), more than the interpreter can handle. With many Level 1 interpreters the limit lies at 1500 elements, but in Level 2 there is no fixed limit. Some particularly nasty memory problems cause the printer to return to standby mode without issuing an error message.

To solve *limitcheck* errors you must simplify the path using your graphics software. If you are converting bitmap graphics to vector graphics with autotracing software like Adobe Streamline then you can alter the tolerances. In graphics you have created yourself, you can remove unnecessary line segments to minimize the memory requirements. Finally, there is the *flatness* parameter: this specifies how accurately the interpreter should approximate curves with short line segments. The more precise the conversion, the more line segments are created. The flatness can be changed by hand in most graphics programs (flatness in Illustrator, coarseness in FreeHand). The flatness is measured in device pixels. A larger value (e.g., 3 instead of 0) slightly reduces the precision of the representation and therefore also the demands on memory.

Memory problems (VMerror) can often be fixed by reducing the number of fonts required. If you do not want to do without the fonts, then you should try to make sure that only those character outlines that are actually required are loaded. Modern graphics programs also allow text to be converted to graphics. This needs less memory and the graphic might then be capable of being printed. As hinting is lost if you use this technique, it should only be used for large-sized text.

LaserWriter 8.0 for the Macintosh offers the option "Unlimited Downloadable fonts in a document". If you activate this field the printer uses a different type of memory management which is slower, but uses the available memory more efficiently, with the memory. Sometimes a VMerror can be cured without amending the document by using this setting.

Too many nested EPS files can also trigger a limitcheck error: An EPS graphic containing an EPS graphic, which also contains an EPS graphic. With most interpreters the limit for the number of nested items, governed by memory management, is 15. However, you cannot actually use this number as some levels are already used by the embedded document.

On the Macintosh unusual folder names can trigger a limitcheck error! When generating EPS graphics some programs using Illustrator format include the full path name as a PostScript string in the EPS file, without treating special characters (if present) correctly. In such cases avoid using commas and backslashes in the names of folders containing EPS graphics. If you use an error handling routine that prints out a corresponding message, you will usually be able to spot the problem from the folder names in the error message.

If you often encounter the limitcheck error you ought to consider fitting more RAM to your printer. On many printers it is easy to add more RAM (often in the form of industry standard SIMMs). The investment may be justified depending on the applications you are running

If another device with more memory is available, try printing on that device. Another possibility is to rasterize the PostScript file with a software interpreter (e.g., Ghostscript) and output as a PostScript bitmap or using the printer's Laserjet mode. These are viable alternatives particularly if your computer has a lot more memory than your printer.

syntaxerror. A syntax error occurs when the PostScript data exceed the programming rules. One possible cause is the cutting of data by various conversion processes, e.g. 7-bit transmission of binary files or incorrect conversion of linefeed characters.

syntaxerror in ≪ occurs when a PostScript program generated for a Level 2 interpreter is output on a Level 1 machine without checking the language level of the interpreter. The only solution here is to do the output on a Level 2 device.

timeout. This error message signifies that a timeout limit has been exceeded. It occurs most often with serial or parallel transfer to a PostScript printer. The individual print jobs must be separated by the Control-D character. If the character is missing then the interpreter will wait for more data for a specified amount of time after finishing a job. If it is not "nudged", the timeout error is triggered. This is especially annoying and inexplicable if all the print jobs have been correctly worked through and an error handler is loaded. As if by magic a few minutes after the last page of the job, a page with an error message appears. To get rid of this problem you must configure your printing environment so that print jobs are separated by Control-D (using driver settings, or under Unix a suitable backend; as a last resort add a Control-D at the end of the PostScript file). Further notes on the Control-D problem can be found in Section 2.4.1).

ioerror. (*input/output error*) This message is caused by faulty data transfer to the interpreter. Possible causes include parity errors (with serial transfer) or faulty termination in a network. It is in the nature of things that these errors cannot be solved by attacking the PostScript file, but need a secure transfer of data. For confirmation, you can check whether or not the problems occur with different types of PostScript file, for example, long and short files.

ioerror can also occur when the XON/XOFF protocol in the printer has been turned off and the entry buffer overflows.

interrupt. In practise this error is not so important. It signals interruptions to the flow of data. In interactive mode you can enter Control-C to cause an interrupt to stop a program or process prematurely.

invalidfont. This message is caused by incorrect font data. In a few rare cases a font file on the hard disk is corrupted and the error shows up later when the font is used. Attempt to identify the font, then remove it from the (printer's or computer's) hard disk and reinstall it.

configurationerror. This error only happens on Level 2 devices and says that the device cannot fulfil a particular demand. This is usually a particular page format, paper tray or other hardware requirement. The errorinfo message tells you what the requirement is.

Programming errors.   The following error messages are almost always caused by programming errors and can only occasionally be solved by user intervention. Attempt to work round the error by installing a different or updated PostScript driver. Under some circumstances the PostScript file may have been damaged (for example, whilst in transit via diskette, e-mail or on the network).

dictfull, dictstackoverflow, dictstackunderflow, execstackoverflow, handleerror, invalidaccess, invalidcontext, invalidexit, invalidfileaccess, invalidid, invalidrestore, nocurrentpoint, rangecheck, stackoverflow, stackunderflow, typecheck, undefinedfilename, undefinedresource, undefinedresult, unmatchedmark, unregistered.

2.5.4 Other Messages from the Interpreter.   When handling PostScript files you may encounter a whole series of messages from the interpreter which are not PostScript errors. Whether and how you receive such messages depends on the type of connection to the printer: with a Macintosh you see the messages during the print process; spoolers or backends under Unix trap some of the messages and deliver them to the user by e-mail (for example, the backend *lprps* on the accompanying CD-ROM). Windows users, because of the lack of bi-directional communication, do not usually see these messages.

```
%%[ exitserver: permanent state may be changed ]%%
```

This message precedes a resident loading process (see Section 2.3.3). The "permanent state" contains the data which should be made available for future print jobs, such as fonts and prologs.

```
%%[ Flushing: rest of job (to end-of-file) will be ignored ]%%
```

This message usually follows an error message and signifies that the interpreter will not process further data until the end of the current print job.

```
%%[ status: waiting; source: Serial ]%%
```

This is a normal status message which the interpreter sends to the computer. It can contain these conditions: *waiting/idle/busy/warming up,* depending on what the interpreter is doing. Possible sources are: *serial9, serial25, AppleTalk, LocalTalk, EtherTalk, TokenRing, Centronics* or *Fax.*

```
FontName not found, using Courier
```

This message appears if a PostScript file requests a font which is not available to the interpreter. The Courier font, which is almost always available, is used instead.

```
%%[ PrinterError: cover open ]%%
```

Messages like this inform of a specific printer problem, in this case an open printer cover. The possible messages are dependent on the type of printer, and are usually self-explanatory or are expanded on in the printer documentation.

Encapsulated PostScript (EPS)

3

Encapsulated PostScript (EPS) has for many years been the standard format for graphics exchange between various system platforms. It is suitable not just for exchanging data between programs, but also for transferring data across operating systems. In this chapter we will take a look at the principle of EPS and then examine variants of EPS under Macintosh, Windows, and Unix as well as some newer extensions to the EPS format. After the theory, we will concentrate on practical aspects, including tips on what to do if things go wrong, how to give inadequate software a helping hand, and how to generate or tweak EPS files.

3.1 How Does EPS Work?

3.1.1 Exchanging Graphics Data.   Data exchange plays a decisive role with modern software. A few years ago, software manufacturers hoped to gain advantages in the market by using proprietary file formats which were kept secret and did not offer any way to exchange data with other manufacturers' programs.

Luckily, these times are (mostly) over: the importance of data exchange is shown not just by the number of filters and converters supplied with most programs, but also by the efforts made by the major operating system manufacturers. Microsoft's OLE and OpenDoc from Apple and other firms do not define a document as a single file any more, but as a "container" for a series of different objects, each created, edited, and managed by a different specialized program. For example, such a document might contain a table created with a spreadsheet, and a diagram created with a graphics program.

EPS is meant to solve the data exchange problem, at least in the graphics area, across operating systems. As EPS was defined in the mid-1980s and is meant to work as far as possible on all operating systems, it cannot make use of the modern dynamic techniques named above, but uses its own file format. This has the following main aims:

- EPS uses PostScript's advantages, above all device independence.
- The preconditions for the exchange of data must not be too high: EPS does not require a PostScript interpreter.
- Graphics can be exchanged between various programs.
- Graphics can be transferred across various operating systems.
- EPS uses the functions available on each operating system and sticks to the usual conventions for programs and files.

The last two points of course contradict one another. To use all of an operating system's functions as fully as possible (for example, Display PostScript), the files will not then be transferrable to another system. A truly portable format has to use only the lowest common denominator of the available functions. We will shortly see how EPS solves this dilemma by using several variants to create a platform-independent format.

In this context, two definitions are useful: the creator of an EPS file, for example, a graphics program, *exports* the graphic in EPS format. A word processor or DTP program which can arrange multiple elements on a page, *imports* the EPS file. These are typical examples for exchanging EPS files:

- A graphics designer creates illustrations for a book using a Macintosh and sends them to the publisher in EPS format. They are then integrated into the layout using specialist typesetting software running under Unix.

- ► A consultant designs a new corporate image for a company. So that the graphical elements of the image, such as the company logo, are available for in-house document production, they are delivered in EPS format. Within the company, any computer system may be in use.
- ► A printed original, for example, a photo, is to be scanned. The scanner software produces a pixelized version of the picture in EPS format for further processing.
- ► A translator, who is doing the book layout at the same time, receives the illustrations from the original version in EPS format. The illustrations are to be the same in the translated version, except for the text.

These examples make it clear that when an EPS file is imported, it is often not necessary to edit the graphic, that is to alter or manipulate its content: that is the graphic artist's (and therefore the exporting program's) job – at the end of the day not every employee should be able to alter the company logo! However, it should be possible to adjust the graphic's size and positioning for different uses. The example with the scanner is somewhat different. If the scanned data are to be processed further (e.g., for color correction) they have to be read into image processing software. As these are bitmap data, not object oriented graphic data, one of the universal bitmap graphics formats should be used, such as TIFF.

The example of the translator describes a typical problem which arises in conjunction with EPS: if it is not known which program was originally used to create the graphics, or if that program is not available, it is necessary to edit the EPS files directly to change the text contained in the graphics. In general, this is not possible with EPS files. In Section 9.3 some ways to get around this problem will be introduced.

3.1.2 Screen Representation of PostScript Data. To make it easier to integrate a graphic into a document, the user should see, as nearly as possible, on screen what will later be printed. Manufacturers usually herald this as WYSIWYG (*What you see is what you get*), but usually what appears on screen is only an approximate representation of what will be printed later.

The main problem when working with PostScript data is that a PostScript interpreter is needed, and the majority of graphics packages do not have one – ideally this should be in the form of Display PostScript, which is for example part of NEXTSTEP or the X Window System with DPS extension (see Chapter 7). This means that the lay-

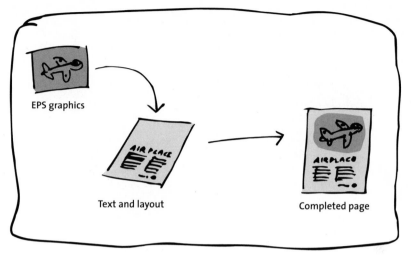

EPS graphics

Text and layout

Completed page

Fig. 3.1.
Embedding
an EPS file

out program can simply send the PostScript commands from the EPS to the screen. DPS interprets the commands and ensures the best possible on-screen representation for the monitor's resolution and color depth. However, as only a few users have the luxury of Display PostScript, on most platforms the exporting program has to make use of tricks to make screen display possible even without a PostScript interpreter. To do this, the PostScript commands are supplemented by a second description of the graphic, which can be used by the normal graphic functions or graphics format under the relevant operating system. The majority of EPS files contain a bitmap (made up of individual pixels) at a specified resolution rather than object oriented instructions (lines, curves, colored areas, etc.) in this preview section. The individual pixels can be black, white, gray, or colored. Although these pictures are often known as bitmaps, strictly speaking this term should only be used for black and white pictures. The importing program can read the bitmap version of the graphic without much effort and use it for screen display before printing. This is known as a bitmap preview. The bitmap preview is ignored during output to a PostScript device as the PostScript commands in the EPS file are used. However, the preview is used as a least-bad solution if the document is printed on a non-PostScript printer. If this is the case, the bitmap and not the PostScript commands are sent to the printer.

In comparison to object oriented graphics, bitmap files can be very large and also they cannot be enlarged without losing quality: during enlargement the steps that result from the square pixels are

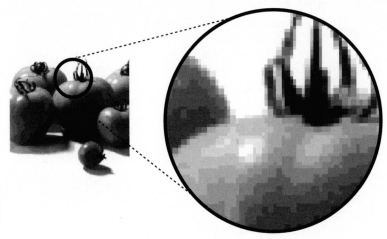

also enlarged, making for an unpleasing display. We can also get rid of a common misunderstanding at this point: PostScript files can contain not only vector graphics, but also bitmaps (e.g., from a scanner or a paint program). Such bitmaps have nothing to do with the preview bitmap, but they do cause the same problems when printed, that is they appear to become ragged when enlarged.

The systemwide graphic format on the Macintosh is PICT, used to record QuickDraw functions. QuickDraw is the name of the graphics model which is used by all applications on the Macintosh to draw screen displays and is therefore widely used. PICT files can contain both bitmap and object oriented graphics.

Windows offers the Windows Metafile (WMF) as an exchange format for PCs; in this case it saves the GDI calls used to generate the graphic. The GDI (Graphics Device Interface) is the Windows counterpart to QuickDraw. PICT and WMF are suitable to use as platform specific graphic descriptions for the preview portions of EPS files on the Macintosh or Windows PC. In addition, under Windows a bitmap representation in the well-known TIFF format can be created. This is a higly capable bitmap graphics format which, amongst other things, can make use of several data compression routines.

As there is no standardized picture format integrated into Unix systems, the *Encapsulated PostScript Interchange* (EPSI) format is used. This adds a bitmap version of the graphic, in the form of comment lines, imbedded directly in the PostScript commands. EPSI also serves as a universal format for exchanging EPS files between operating systems. Further details on the different types of EPS files can be found in Section 3.3.

3.1.3 Embedding EPS Graphics.

We have already seen that in many cases it is not necessary to change the contents of an EPS graphic. In most cases, all you want to do is fit the size and position of the graphic to the page layout and perhaps select a suitable part of the image. How can this work, if we assume that the importing software does not have a PostScript interpreter? The answer lies in the vocabulary of PostScript: there are instructions which enlarge, reduce, move, or clip the graphic as a whole. The importer (or the printer driver) has to generate the desired measurements and the appropriate instructions, and send them to the printer together with the unaltered Post-Script data from the EPS file. To enlarge the graphic on screen, the importer has to "inflate" the bitmap, either by duplicating individual pixels (the simplest method) or by calculating interpolated values (more complicated, but gives a better result).

What happens if the EPS file contains no preview because it was created by a program which does not generate previews, or if the file comes from another platform? In this case, it is still possible to import the file, but the importing program will have to use a place-holder instead of the graphic. Normally this is a simple gray box which shows information about the EPS file (file name, creation date, creator) or a simple crossed-out box.

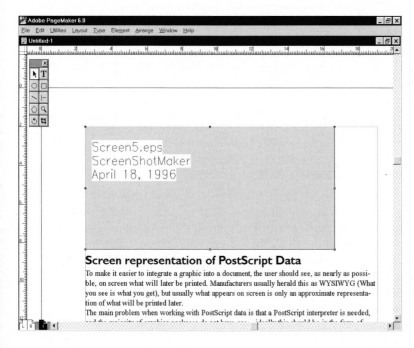

Fig. 3.3.
Importing an EPS file without a preview into PageMaker: graphics files like this go against the WYSIWYG principle and PageMaker has to make do with general information about the picture

3.1.4 Creating EPS Graphics.
There are many possible sources of EPS files. The usual way is to create a graphic using a drawing or paint program, and then to export it in EPS format. This method should always be the first choice as the creating program has all the information which is needed about the graphic. It can integrate the structure comments described below into the EPS file, and create an appropriate preview.

Bitmap graphic files are also an important source for EPS files. They can come either from a scanner which creates EPS directly, or by conversion from another bitmap graphics format. You can find further notes on this topic in Section 9.4.

It's also very common to create EPS using the system's printer driver. Many of the EPS files created like this are not worthy of the name as they usually ignore the EPS specification in some way. Difficulties when using these files, such as embedding in another document, are (pun intended) preprogrammed. The causes of these problems are explained in the next section, and hints on trouble shooting can be found in in the rest of this chapter.

Finally, it is possible, and sometimes can make sense, to write PostScript files "by hand". If you stick to the rules contained in the next section (and master the PostScript programming language), a legal EPS file, which can be embedded as usual, can easily be created. Such a manually created EPS file naturally contains no preview, i.e., when it is embedded in a document you will only see a placeholder on screen. In Section 3.4.3 you will find hints on converting any PostScript file to an EPS file. This conversion is always necessary if you cannot create a "real" EPS file (for example if the program used to create the graphic is not available).

3.1.5 Portability of EPS Graphics.
The PostScript part of an EPS file must meet certain requirements in order to ensure that the file can be printed successfully in a different environment (operating system, printer, communications protocol).

To achieve this, you must make sure that the EPS file does not rely on external resources and contains all needed elements, if possible. This includes all sorts of PostScript resources, that is fonts, procedures, character encodings, etc. If this is not the case it must contain corresponding DSC comments which describe the required resources. In theory the importing application is therefore theoretically responsible for seeing that missing fonts, etc., are available at print time. However, in practice this is hardly ever possible and the user must be aware of this, and ready, for example, to download the fonts manually.

Another point that plays an important role in the exchange of EPS files is the type of data encoding (not to be confused with character encoding). PostScript files can contain 7-bit data (ASCII) or 8-bit data (binary). As already explained in Section 2.3, binary data cannot always be printed out. On the Macintosh, EPS files in binary format are usually created as these take up less space than the ASCII versions and can finally be printed without problems via AppleTalk. If you create an EPS file on the Macintosh which is to be used under Windows, you must choose 7-bit encoding when creating the file, as only few Windows configurations can print binary PostScript files. The current generation of Macintosh graphics programs allow you to choose between ASCII and binary when exporting EPS files.

If the EPS file uses functions that are exclusive to PostScript Level 2, then the file will not print on all printers. Corresponding DSC comments must be included in the EPS file. Whilst the Level 2 operators simply increase print speed for some graphics and can be emulated on a Level 1 device, there are also cases where output on a Level 1 device is not possible (e.g., JPEG-EPS files, see Section 5.4).

3.1.6 Summary. When creating an EPS file, the creator must stick to certain rules so that the importer can read in the file without executing the actual PostScript commands. In addition it should integrate a preview version of the graphic so that the importer can display a simple preview on screen. Most EPS files contain a PostScript version of the graphic, used for printing, and a preview version of the same graphic, which is displayed on screen or output on non-PostScript printers. If a graphic is embedded in a document, the importing program has to evaluate certain information from the EPS file and incorporate the unaltered PostScript data with scaling instructions into the print-out.

For the user, the following points are important:

- ▸ The fonts used in the EPS file must be available at print time. They must be either included in the EPS file or sent separately. It is often a good idea to convert text elements to outlines to make the font problem less severe.
- ▸ If you intend to work on the file on different operating systems, then the data should be encoded as ASCII, not binary.
- ▸ EPS files should always be created using the export function of the program in use, or with a suitable converter. Creating them with the printer driver often causes problems and should only be used as a last resort!
- ▸ So that you can work reasonably with an EPS graphic on another system, you should always include a screen preview in the relevant format. If it is not known on which platform the file will be

worked on, it is safest to produce EPS files without a preview or in EPSI format (generic EPS file).

3.2 Differences Between PostScript and EPS

The question "What is the difference between PostScript and EPS?" has already caused heated discussions and caused programmers sleepless nights (to say nothing of user frustration). The answers "EPS is the diversion of PostScript print output to a file", "EPS is a Post-Script file with only one page" or "only the name" are all not completely wrong, but not completely right either. Therefore, we want to explore the differences and similarities between PostScript and EPS files in order.

EPS files contain three types of data:

- ► PostScript commands, used during printing or (with Display Post-Script) for output to the screen.
- ► An optional bitmap version of the picture *(preview)*, usually used for screen display and also printed if the graphic is output on a non-PostScript device.
- ► Information *about* the image (above all its size), which the DTP software needs for embedding.

3.2.1 EPS Requirements.
A PostScript file which is to work as EPS has to comply with a few requirements. It is immediately obvious that an EPS file may only describe one page (or part of a page) if the embedding process described above is to be of any use. In addition, the file must be DSC compatible, that is, it has to comply with the conventions described in Section 2.1.5. These comments always begin (except for the first line) with the characters %%. They are ignored by the PostScript interpreter, but contain extra information about the file which can be used by other programs.

Most of these DSC comments are optional, but the following lines must be placed at the beginning of the PostScript part of an EPS file:

```
%!PS-Adobe-3.0 EPSF-3.0
%%BoundingBox: llx lly urx ury
```

The first line ensures that the importing program can recognize an EPS file as such (and in particular distinguish it from a "normal" Post-Script file). The numbers do not, as often maintained, relate to the version of PostScript used (there is not yet any version 3 of Post-Script), but to the version of the DSC specification used when generating the file and to the underlying version of the EPS specification. Version 3, the current one, of the EPS specification makes no major changes to the previous one, but clears up some points and allows some extra comments.

The second line is needed when embedding a graphic in a document and is needed for the size calculations. As we have already seen, a PostScript interpreter is not usually available during embedding. The importing program must know how much space the graphic takes up so that it can enlarge, reduce, or move it accordingly. To do this, it makes use of the BoundingBox comments. The BoundingBox is the the smallest rectangle which totally encloses the drawing.

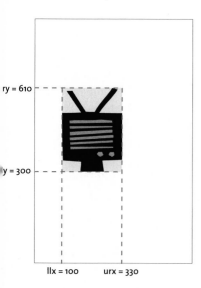
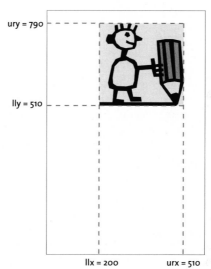

Fig. 3.4.
Two EPS graphics with their corresponding BoundingBox

ury = 790
lly = 510
ry = 610
y = 300
llx = 100   urx = 330
llx = 200   urx = 510

When working out the size during embedding, it is sufficient to know the coordinates of the rectangle, more precisely the *x* and *y* coordinates of the *lower left* and *upper right* corners. These are the values in the BoundingBox comment. The EPS specification lays down four integer values for this comment. Despite this, some programs generate floating point values, which other programs in turn reject during import. Newer programs (for example, Adobe Photoshop) give the BoundingBox more precisely, without breaking the specification; as well as the normal comment, they use the extra entry *%%HiResBoundingBox*, which describes the BoundingBox using four floating point values.

The PostScript coordinate system is used for describing the BoundingBox: the origin is at the lower left corner of the page (not always exactly in the corner for some printers); the x coordinates increase to the right and the y coordinates increase upwards. The DTP point *(pt)*, defined as $^1/_{72}$ inch, is used as the unit of measurement. One inch is 2.54 cm, which gives:

1 point = $^1/_{72}$ inch = 2.54 cm / 72 ≈ 0.35 mm

A U.S. letter format page measures 612 × 792 pt (215.9 × 279.4 mm). On the CD-ROM accompanying this book you will find the PostScript program *grid.ps*, which prints out a page showing the PostScript coordinate grid (to do this you must remove the % before the *showpage* operator at the end of the file).

Here is a sample calculation: Assuming that the comment in an EPS file reads:

```
%%BoundingBox: 100 300 330 610
```

This means that the lower left corner of the graphic's BoundingBox is 100 pt = 100 × 2.54 cm/72 = 3.52 cm from the left margin and 300 pt = 300 × 2.54 cm/72 = 10.6 cm from the bottom margin. The upper right corner is 330 pt = 11.6 cm from the left margin and 610 pt = 21.5 cm from the bottom margin.

Depending on the contents of the EPS file, extra DSC comments may be required. For example, if the EPS file uses operators that are only defined in PostScript Level 2 then attention must be drawn to them with the following comment:

```
%%LanguageLevel: 2
```

The information about the EPS graphic which are shown if a gray box is displayed instead of the picture are taken from these DSC comments:

```
%%Creator: Adobe Illustrator(TM) for Windows
%%For: (Thomas Merz)
%%Title: (sample.ai)
%%CreationDate: (12/14/95) (1:36 PM)
```

These comments should be present in every EPS file, and show which software was used to create the graphic, when it was created, and its file name.

Arguments are often sparked by the question of whether EPS files must contain the PostScript operator *showpage* or not. This operator instructs the print engine to eject the page when the individual graphic elements have been described and the image (which the interpreter has until now only built up in memory) is to be transferred to paper.

Calling *showpage* from an EPS graphic in the middle of a document page has catastrophic consequences: the part of the page that has already been built up is printed, but the rest lands on the next page! On the other hand an EPS graphic cannot be printed independently (that is without being embedded in another document) if it does not contain *showpage*. In this case, the interpreter does process the data but then "forgets" to dump the memory contents to paper.

The EPS format treats the *showpage* problem rather pragmatically: it allows the operator in EPS files and it is the importing software which has to render it harmless. This is done with the following instruction:

```
/showpage { } def
```

This defines a dummy operator called *showpage* which consists of just an empty procedure. This instruction is sent to the printer before the EPS file and cancelled afterwards. Many modern graphics programs integrate *showpage* into the EPS files which they generate, but some do not.

3.2.2 EPS Limitations.

The example of the *showpage* problem has already shown that there are some PostScript operators that can cause problems in an EPS file. Whilst *showpage* is allowed in EPS files because of its importance and is handled by a special routine, other operators are taboo for EPS files as they disrupt the embedding process. This category contains all operators which do not describe elements of the graphic, but which change the state of the interpreter (for example, select a different paper tray, or change the page size) or which destroy the environment of the embedding PostScript program. This is a fundamental difference between EPS and "normal" PostScript files! Whilst a print file is naturally allowed to change the paper tray settings before output using the relevant PostScript commands, an EPS file, which is probably executed in the middle of a page description, should never be allowed to do this as it will flush the whole page from memory. This problem has often caused attempts at embedding supposed EPS files to fail!

The "Red Book" lists these forbidden operators. If an EPS file contains one of them (for example, *initmatrix, initclip, initgraphics, setpagedevice, clear, quit, a4, letter, legal, copypage, erasepage*), difficulties during embedding in a document will be almost unavoidable.

The following table shows the most important differences between EPS and "regular" PostScript files.

	EPS file	"Regular" PostScript file
Number of pages	1	arbitrary
Output to PostScript printer possible?	yes, possibly the preview section will have to be removed and the showpage operator be inserted	yes
Output to non-PostScript printer possible?	yes, if there is a preview section present in the file	no
Output to screen without PS interpreter possible?	yes, if there is a preview image present	no
File is DSC compatible?	yes	recommended
File contains Bounding Box comments?	yes	recommended
Critical operators allowed?	no	yes
File contains showpage?	not always	yes
Exchange between various operating systems possible?	EPSI or EPS without preview: yes, Mac or Windows EPS with preview: only restricted exchange.	print only
File may be created using the printer driver?	restricted	always

3.3 EPS Flavors

3.3.1 Macintosh. EPS files on the Macintosh (EPS-PICT) usually have file type EPSF, sometimes also TEXT. If you want to edit the contents of an EPS file as text, and your word processor cannot read the file, then you can use ResEdit to change the file type from EPSF to TEXT. The data fork of an EPS file contains the PostScript commands, the resource fork contains a QuickDraw representation of the graphic. This PICT resource always has the number 256.

When creating EPS files on the Mac you can often choose between 7 -bit and 8-bit encoding (see Section 3.1.5). If you want to use the file further on a Mac, you should choose 8-bit (binary), but otherwise play safe and choose 7-bit (ASCII) unless you are certain that 8-bit files can be used in the target environment. In addition, you can specify the type of preview picture: no preview, black and white, or color; a black and white preview needs less space than a color one. Most Mac graphics programs can also create EPS files for Windows.

The LaserWriter 8 and PSPrinter drivers are capable of generating EPS files with standard 72 dpi black and white bitmapped preview ("Mac Standard Preview"), an object oriented QuickDraw preview ("Mac Extended Preview"), or EPS without preview. The latter is suitable for interchange with other systems. Extended preview usually

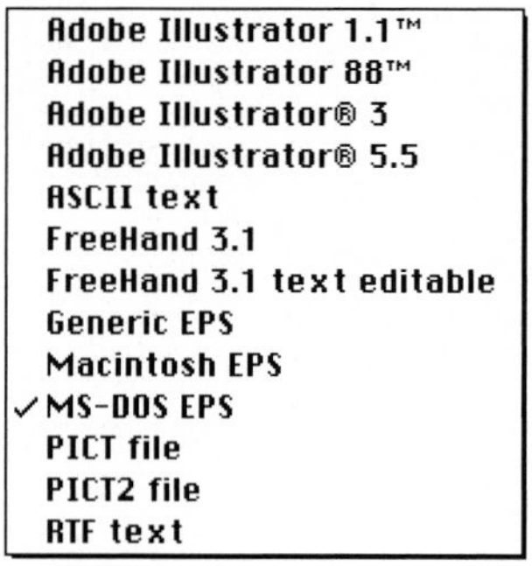

```
Adobe Illustrator 1.1™
Adobe Illustrator 88™
Adobe Illustrator® 3
Adobe Illustrator® 5.5
ASCII text
FreeHand 3.1
FreeHand 3.1 text editable
Generic EPS
Macintosh EPS
✓ MS-DOS EPS
PICT file
PICT2 file
RTF text
```

Fig. 3.5.
Freehand's export
dialog: on the
Mac, you can also
create EPS files for
other systems

has the advantage of smaller size and higher quality, especially for text.

Note that most applications generate bitmapped PICT preview images when exporting in EPS format. A notable exception is FreeHand which in some cases creates object oriented QuickDraw previews for EPS files.

3.3.2 Windows.

While the naming conventions are not uniform, EPS files under MS-DOS/Windows (and OS/2) are often designated as EPSF, which actually simply means *Encapsulated PostScript Format*. As the MS-DOS/Windows file system, unlike the Macintosh system, does not have a forked method of structuring files, both the PostScript and preview part of an EPS file have to be saved together in a "flat" file. To do this, the file contains a binary table at the beginning, which specifies the starting positions and lengths of the individual sections of the EPS file. This table and the binary preview data are responsible for the fact that such an EPS file can no longer be printed directly, that is sent to the printer without preparation, or be edited with a text editor. The importing application must therefore, when printing to a PostScript printer, make use of the table to extract the PostScript section. In Section 3.5.3 you will see how to remove the preview manually, for example, to print an EPS file without embedding it in a document.

As already mentioned, the preview part of an EPS file under Windows can contain a TIFF bitmap or GDI instructions in *Windows Metafile* (WMF) format. The TIFF variant is far more useful. In practise, EPS files with WMF previews are hardly ever used. An EPS file can contain either a TIFF or a WMF preview, but not both.

The table at the start of an EPS file contains 30 bytes. Details of its construction and the meaning of the individual entries can be found in the file *details.pdf* on the accompanying CD-ROM.

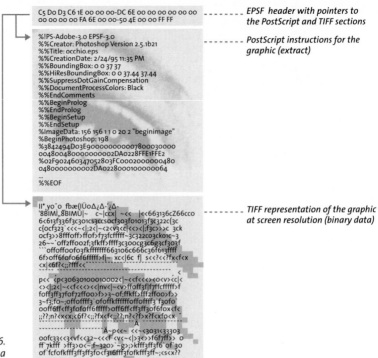

C5 D0 D3 C6 1E 00 00 00-DC 6E 00 00 00 00 00 00
00 00 00 00 FA 6E 00 00-50 4E 00 00 FF FF

— — — — EPSF header with pointers to
the PostScript and TIFF sections

%!PS-Adobe-3.0 EPSF-3.0
%%Creator: Photoshop Version 2.5.1b21
%%Title: occhio.eps
%%CreationDate: 2/24/95 11:35 PM
%%BoundingBox: 0 0 37 37
%%HiResBoundingBox: 0 0 37.44 37.44
%%SuppressDotGainCompensation
%%DocumentProcessColors: Black
%%EndComments
%%BeginProlog
%%EndProlog
%%BeginSetup
%%EndSetup
%ImageData: 156 156 1 1 0 20 2 "beginimage"
%BeginPhotoshop: 198
%3842494D03E90000000000007800030000
004800480000000002DA0228FFE1FFE2
%02F902460347052803FC000200000000480
0480000000002DA0228000100000064

...

%%EOF

— — — — PostScript instructions for the
graphic (extract)

II° yo˘o fbæ(lÛoΔ¿Δ-'¿Δ-
'8BIMI,,8BIMU|~   c-|ccx| ~<< |<<663136cZ66cco
6<613f336f3c301cs3ccs0cf303f01013f3c322c(3c
c{ocf323 <<<~<|;2<|~<2<v3<c|<<><|;f3c>>< 3ck
ocf3>>8fffoff>ffof>f73fcfffff~3c322c03ck01c~3
26~~˘off2ffoo2f;3fkff>ffff3c300cg3c6g3cf303f
```offoffoofo3fkffffff663106c666c36f613ffff
6f>off6fofo6f6fffff>f|~. xc<|6c_f| s<<?<<?fx<f<x
<x|<6f?<;;?fff<<

— — — — TIFF representation of the graphic
at screen resolution (binary data)

p<<˘<p<30630100010002<|~<<f<<<><0<v><c|<
<><|;2<|~<<f<<<><<|nv<|~<v>ffoff3f|f7ffcfffff>f
foff3ff37fof72ffoo>f>>3~of;ffkff>fff2ffoo>f>>
3~f3;fo~;offoffff3˘ofoffkfffffffoffoffff3˘f3ofo˘
ooff6ff<ff3fofoff6fffff>off6ff<ff3f3of6fox<f<
;;??;n?<x<x;<6f?<;;?fx<f<;;??;n?<?f>x?f<xfo<x

— — — — — — — — — — — — — — — Ā
— — — — — — — — — — —Ā~p<<~  <<~<3031<33303
oofc33<<3<vf<<32~<<<f˘<v~<<|>3<>>f6f7ff>>  o
ff˘7kfff  >ff3>o<~;f~320>˘~g>;>kfff3ff3f6˘of˘30
of˘fcfofkfff3ff3ff3fo<f316fff3fofkfff3ff~;<s<x??

...

*Fig. 3.6.*
*An EPS file with a*
*Windows preview*

The four bytes C5 D0 D3 C6 at the start of the file (the *magic number*)
differentiate an EPS file with a preview from a file that contains exclu-
sively PostScript data without a preview. In the second case, accord-
ing to DSC conventions the sequence %! must be present at the start
of the file.

### 3.3.3 Device Independent Preview (EPSI). The *Encapsulated PostScript Interchange* format (EPSI) is the most generic EPS variant.
Its only requirement of the operating system is that it is capable of
working with ASCII files. EPSI is suitable for use as an exchange for-
mat, but does not play any role for Macintosh and Windows, as the
corresponding EPS variants with PICT, TIFF, or WMF previews are domi-
ant. Even Unix applications are more likely to support the Windows
variant than EPSI. One notable exception is FrameMaker, which can
import and display EPSI files on screen on all platforms.

EPSI encodes graphic previews not in a platform-dependent for-
mat but as an uncompressed bitmap, whose content is stored in
ASCII hexadecimal representation as a comment in the EPS file. EPSI
files only contain ASCII characters and no binary data: this means
```

they can be edited with any text editor. EPSI previews cannnot contain colors, only gray scales or black and white. It should come after the introductory comments and is bracketed by two special comment lines. (The four parameters after *%%BeginPreview* are integers and describe the width and height of the bitmap in pixels, the number of bits per pixel (usually 1, 2, 4, or 8) and the number of comment lines in the preview):

```
%!PS-Adobe-3.0 EPSF-3.0
%%BoundingBox: 100 100 200 125
%%Title: (triangle.ps)
%%Creator: Ydraw
%%For: York
%%CreationDate: Thu Oct 26 22:16:53 1995
%%Pages: 1
%%EndComments
%%BeginPreview: 73 19 1 19
% 0000000008000000000
% 000000003E000000000
% 00000000FF8000000000
% 00000003FFE000000000
% 0000000FFFF800000000
% 0000003FFFFE00000000
% 000000FFFFFF80000000
% 000003FFFFFFE0000000
% 00000FFFFFFFF8000000
% 00003FFFFFFFFE000000
% 0000FFFFFFFFFF800000
% 0003FFFFFFFFFFE00000
% 000FFFFFFFFFFFF80000
% 003FFFFFFFFFFFFE0000
% 00FFFFFFFFFFFFFF8000
% 03FFFFFFFFFFFFFFE000
% 0FFFFFFFFFFFFFFFF800
% 3FFFFFFFFFFFFFFFFE00
% FFFFFFFFFFFFFFFFFF80
%%EndPreview
%EndProlog
%%Page: 1
100 100 moveto
150 125 lineto
200 100 lineto
closepath
fill
showpage
%%Trailer
%%EOF
```

Even if the preview has low resolution, EPSI files can become very large. This is caused partly by the fact that the bitmap (unlike the TIFF variant) cannot be stored in compressed format. Each data byte is stored in hexadecimal ASCII and therefore requires two bytes for storage. The total amount of data is (width and height are expressed in pixels):

```
(color depth × width × height × 2) / 8.
```

A letter size graphic which contains a 72 dpi bitmap with 256 levels of gray (8 bits per pixel) needs 1 MB of storage, only for the preview! As the bitmap section in the comments will be ignored by the PostScript interpreter anyway, the importing program should remove the preview data before printing, to speed up the print process, although none of the well known programs actually does this.

3.3.4 Adobe Illustrator File Format (AI).

Adobe Illustrator is a powerful graphics program, available for Macintosh, Windows, and Unix platforms (e.g., Sun and SGI). The developers of this program not only implemented multifaceted functions for creating complex graphics, but also went down a new path for storing any graphics created: whilst most programs save new documents in their own, often undocumented, formats and allow the document to be converted to PostScript commands by the printer driver during printing, Illustrator saves its graphics directly as PostScript files – and can naturally also read and manipulate them. This technique does have some advantages but has also contributed to confusion amongst users: whilst EPS files in general cannot be further edited, this is not a problem with Illustrator files. This goes for Illustrator as well as for many other programs that support this file format. As well as commercial programs which at least import AI files and convert them to their own format, you can use the Windows graphics program PageDraw, on the accompanying CD-ROM, to create and edit AI compatible files. However, as PageDraw only understands a subset of AI instructions, it cannot read all kinds of AI files.

In practice, as the difference between AI and other EPS files is often not clear, misunderstandings arise easily: EPS files from non-AI compatible programs cannot be read and altered using Illustrator but can only be placed and scaled in a document. The FreeHand file format causes further problems as it is not fully compatible with the AI format (though very similar).

As already mentioned, a PostScript interpreter is needed to process a PostScript file. So, does the fully featured Illustrator software giant also include an interpreter? If yes, why can't it read all EPS files? Firstly, AI files are regular EPS files, which stick to the conventions of the platform in use and may contain a preview. However, it is a little more complicated than that: Illustrator cannot read just any Post-Script and does not contain an interpreter. Files in AI format are valid PostScript programs, which the printer can output directly, but they may contain only a subset of PostScript operators, and only use these when structured in a particular way. Illustrator does not understand the programming meaning of the AI commands when it reads them; it only uses their textual values. If you alter an Illustrator file so that the graphic operators have a different appearance (such as consistently renaming procedures), the interpreter in the printer will, as before, give the same result, but Illustrator (with its limited understanding of PostScript) will have to pass. These admittedly somewhat unclear circumstances make for difficulties for both users and software developers!

AI files contain the usual DSC comments at the beginning of the PostScript section. There then follows some supplementary information which is required for processing the file, but not for printing: these include, for example, details about the rulers or a background mask if one is used. Illustrator stores this supplementary information in comment lines of the form *%AI3_...*. After these, in the Post-Script *header*, follow definitions which define the PostScript operators for the Illustrator language's instructions. This prolog is only required for printing and so is left out of the standard file format, reducing the file size by about 20 KB. Illustrator obviously knows the meaning of its own instructions and can therefore also read files without a prolog. This is in contrast to the PostScript interpreter in the printer, which will have to pass on such files! In addition to the actual instructions, AI files can also contain the relevant platform specific preview and are therefore "normal" EPS files – only editable.

To keep the graphic files as small as possible, the instructions in AI files have "names" with only one or two letters (most PostScript driv-

```
f
*u
165.6601 393.8568 m
169.8347 402.0089 L
184.8983 406.3575 L
178.6251 408.3965 L
165.6601 393.8568 L
f
*U
*u
1 0.72 0 0.38 (color A) 0.6 x
161.8512 395.0768 m
156.1606 406.3856 L
161.6907 413.7849 L
161.8512 395.0768 L
f
*U
Q
%%PageTrailer
gsave annotatepage grestore showpage
%%Trailer
```

Fig. 3.7.
An Illustrator graphic and an extract from the corresponding AI instructions

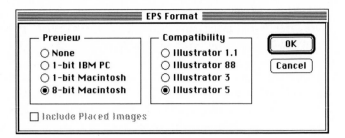

Fig. 3.8.
Illustrator files can
be saved in several
variants

ers do the same). PostScript procedures with the same names are defined in the prolog for these instructions. It should now be clear why Illustrator chokes on "foreign" EPS files: it only looks in the PostScript data for instructions from its own limited PostScript dialect, and cannot do anything with other instructions, in particular PostScript operators and procedures.

It is perhaps easier to understand this odd behavior by comparing the PostScript interpreter to a univeral translator which can understand any PostScript dialect with the help of a suitable dictionary (the prolog). Illustrator, on the other hand, is fluent only in its own dialect which it can understand without a dictionary. Although AI files contain valid PostScript commands they cannot be understood by an interpreter without a dictionary(prolog). The situation has changed with Adobe Illustrator 6.0 which does contain a PostScript interpreter, which can process any PostScript files and not just those in AI format.

The AI format is much too complicated to describe it in full detail here. The file *details.pdf* on the accompanying CD-ROM contains some important AI format operators. The functionality of the AI format has been extended several times for new versions of Illustrator. On compatibility grounds, Illustrator and other graphics programs offer the option to save files in all versions of the format. Some graphic properties can be lost when saving in older versions of the format.

The AI format is based on PostScript, but does not offer the same possibilities. Illustrator, as an object oriented drawing program, does not offer any possibility (apart from embedding) to handle bitmap graphics; because of this the AI format cannot transport bitmaps. AI also has to pass on fonts: font descriptions always come from the operating system in use. AI cannot keep up with some of the newer developments, such as the filters from PostScript Level 2. It may be assumed that the AI format served as a test bed for the definition of a document format based on the graphical model provided by PostScript: it's definitely no coincidence that many of the PDF operators (see Chapter 8) have the same names as the corresponding Illustrator format operators.

In addition, the socalled *riders* file allows you to include custom Post-Script commands into an Illustrator document. (The details vary among versions and operating systems – Illustrator 5.5 has a riders Plug-In, older versions expect a file called *Adobe Illustrator EPSF Riders* (Mac) or *riders.ai* (Windows) in the Illustrator folder/directory. Check your documentation for details.) You can use this feature to embed elements such as a logo or copyright notice which has to be printed with every graphic, or to activate special screening options (see Section 6.2.5). Illustrator does not make use of these instructions on screen, but passes them unchanged to the printer.

In Section 9.3 you can find solutions for the problem of converting PostScript files into AI files in order to make them editable again.

3.3.5 Open Prepress Interface (OPI). OPI is an extension to EPS which was defined by Aldus (before the Adobe merger) to facilitate the workflow in the professional prepress stage, that is the generation of films as originals for producing printing plates.

The typical production environment looks similar to this: the layout is done on workstations (usually Macs), which are networked with each other and and with a file server that runs in the background and looks after enough storage capacity for all the users (this is often a Unix machine). A high resolution scanner to digitize photographs and an imagesetter are also integrated into the network. To make a printed item, the DTPers combine text and images on a workstation to produce a layout. Whilst the text files mostly come from the customer, the scanner usually passes the bitmap data over the internal

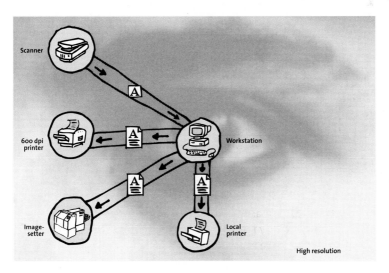

Fig. 3.9.
Conventional
work flow
without OPI

network to the file server and then to the work stations. This creates large amounts of data: A letter size page at 600 dpi in four colors (8 bits each color) uncompressed requires about 130 MB of storage! It is clear that this amount of data reduces speed greatly: for each image incorporated into the layout the bitmap files are sent from the file server to the workstation. For screen display, their resolutions are usually reduced to 72–100 dpi. For each proof on a laser printer the picture data are sent over the network again. Finally, the finished layout is output on an imagesetter, which is often connected to the fileserver or addressed via the network. The PostScript data for the whole document, which can contain any number of bitmap images, are sent again from the workstation to the fileserver and from there to the imagesetter. These multiple transfers of scanned data not only puts a heavy load on the network (and frustrates the user by causing long delays), but is also largely unnecessary as positioning on screen and proofing on the laser printer do not use anything like the full resolution of the scanner. Lower resolution versions of the images suffice. The high resolution data are really only needed for output at 1000 dpi or more on the imagesetter.

The basic idea of OPI is to transfer only high resolution image data from the scanner to the fileserver. The server then generates a lower resolution version, which is sufficient for positioning on screen and for laser or color printer proofs. The server usually sends this low-res data to the workstations as TIFF files, and high-res data are parked on the server. This relieves the network and thanks to the slim TIFF files the layout data can be processed more quickly. When the layout is finished, the workstation user creates a PostScript output file which

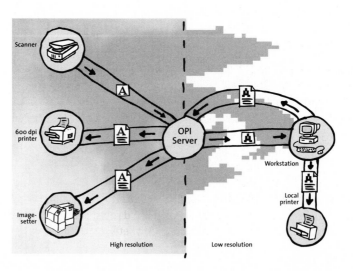

Fig. 3.10.
Workflow
with OPI

is sent to the fileserver which further transfers it to the imagesetter. The file server filters the PostScript data and replaces the low-res data with the high-res data which is still on the server. Only then is the PostScript data fully prepared for the imagesetter, and it is then output at high resolution.

So that the fileserver, which now may proudly trade under the name OPI server, knows which data to replace, the PostScript files must contain additional information. As usual in such cases, comment lines which are ignored by the PostScript interpreter are used. OPI files must fulfil the normal requirements for DSC. As OPI is an extension, special comments starting with %ALD... (Aldus was the inventor) are used. These OPI comments must at least identify the high-res data stored on the server (usually with complete path name to the corresponding file) and the positioning coordinates. In addition there are further comments which describe further image manipulations. When transferring picture data to the layout, it is not just scaling and cropping that are important, but also other picture editing functions like adjustment of lightness and contrast. These manipulations are not actually carried out on the image data on the workstation, but are described by corresponding OPI comments. When the server inserts the high-res data, it carries out these extra instructions and adjusts the data accordingly. To further reduce the network load and save storage space, CMYK versions of the image data (color separations) are not stored at all; if they are needed the server calculates them from the stored RGB data.

An EPS file which complies with OPI Version 1.3 must contain the following comments:

```
%ALDImageFileName:Filename
%ALDImageDimensions: Width Height
%ALDImageCropRect:left upper right lower
%ALDImagePosition:llx lly ulx uly urx ury lrx lry
```

Filename is the name of the low resolution TIFF file, from which the name of the high-res file on the server can usually be derived. The next comment shows the dimensions of the placed TIFF file in pixels as well as the dimensions of the crop rectangle which specifies a section of the placed image (again in pixels). The image position comment describes the positions of the four corners (using the standard PostScript coordinate system) of the desired image section after all the effects (such as reflection, rotation, and shearing), have been applied. The PostScript transformations which have to be applied to the image can be calculated from these values and the coordinates of the crop rectangle. The actual image data is bracketed by the following comments:

```
%%BeginObject: image
%%EndObject
```

If an EPS file contains low-res image data, it will be between these two comments. The OPI server removes all data between the comments and inserts the high-res data in its place. The low-res data may be missing altogether, in which case just the two comments will remain as a placeholder in the EPS file.

In addition, there are optional OPI comments to describe the resolution of the high-res data, various color properties and the color depth as well as a comment for the transfer curve. This alters the picture's brightness (see Section 6.2.4).

Obviously, the PageMaker DTP program, made by the inventors of OPI, Aldus (now part of Adobe), can generate OPI comments, but so can the competing Quark XPress. Examples of OPI capable server software are Archetype's InterSep for Novell networks, Adobe Color Central for Macintosh networks, Adobe TrapWise, and Helios Ether-Share-OPI for Unix file servers in heterogeneous networks.

Open Prepress Interface Version 2.0.   With the merger of Aldus and Adobe, Adobe took over responsibility for further development of the OPI specification. In summer 1995 a draft for OPI 2.0 was published, and although it is not yet finalized, it is not likely to change significantly.

OPI 2.0 defines an OPI producer as a program which generates OPI comments, typically a layout program like PageMaker or Quark XPress. An OPI consumer is any software that makes use of OPI comments in PostScript files, e.g., an OPI server. However, it is important that the OPI consumer does not have to be the final link in the workflow from the user via spooler and server to the imagesetter. Before being rasterized in the imagesetter's RIP the PostScript data can be modified by other software. For this reason, the majority of OPI consumers ara at the same time OPI producers, as they re-embed OPI comments into their output.

Thee most important design change between OPI 1.3 and 2.0 consists of different work assignments: in the old version the consumer was responsible for the correct positioning and scaling of embedded images, but in OPI 2.0 this task falls to the producer. As it can require a lot of effort to process the PostScript data from another program (neither the consumer nor the producer contains a PostScript interpreter), this makes implementing an OPI consumer much easier. The consumer no longer has to generate the PostScript commands for the correct scaling of the picture, but only has to replace low-res data with high-res data and possibly perform a color separation.

In OPI 2.0 all information concerning image embedding are bracketed by these comments:

```
%%BeginOPI: 2.0
%%EndOPI
```

The comments listed above that describe the picture's size and crop rectangle are preserved, but lose the "ALD" from their name (e.g., %%ImageDimensions). As the consumer is no longer concerned with the embedding parameters, the comment "%%ALDImagePosition" vanishes entirely. In addition a whole series of new commands, describing further aspects of the embedded image, are added.

A producer can generate comments simultaneously for OPI 1.3 and 2.0, so that data can be processed by both old and new consumers. However, Adobe has indicated that support for OPI 1.3 will be discontinued once the most important consumers and producers have switched to OPI 2.0.

3.3.6 Desktop Color Separation (DCS).
DCS is another extension to the EPS format which, like OPI, is meant to simplify the stages of the prepress workflow. DCS was defined by the software manufacturer Quark and relates to the handling of color separations (see also Section 6.4). Unlike OPI, no special server software is needed to use DCS, but the programs on the workstation used to generate the graphics and import them into documents must be DCS compatible. Like OPI, DCS also uses special PostScript comments and allows you to connect multiple files. DCS is supported by many important publishing applications including Quark XPress, FrameMaker, PageMaker, and Photoshop.

The problem when working with color separations is that a single main file holds the complete (composite) color information and several dependent separation files hold the color information for the individual print colors, typically *cyan, magenta, yellow,* and *black* and possibly extra *spot colors.* DCS makes it possible to mark the individual color extracts and set up a link between the main file and the separation files.

The main file is a regular EPS file which can (but does not have to) contain a full color version of the image. This full color version is used if the document is output on a color printer (without separations). If the full color PostScript version of the image is missing, then the preview section is used for proofs.

The separation data only contain the color information for the corresponding color (for example, the *cyan* file for the *cyan* plate). As the separation files are not needed for proofs or screen display, they contain neither previews nor complete color information. DCS 2.0

Eye.CMYK

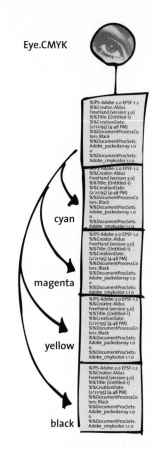

Fig. 3.11.
DCS file with integrated
separation data

cyan

magenta

yellow

black

offers two ways to establish a link between the main and separation files, which both use the special comment *%%PlateFile*.

In the first variant the available data are divided amongst several files. At the start of the PostScript data for the full color version is a comment similar to:

```
%%PlateFile: (color name) filetype location Filename
```

Color name is the name of the corresponding process or spot color (for example, *magenta* or PANTONE184 CV). *Filetype* describes the separation type and primarily attains the value EPS. Location can have the value *Local*. In this case the separation file is sought on the local file system. If a different storage location is specified, the file type can be different from EPS. However, in this case supplementary software is responsible for creating the separation data. *Filename* shows the name of the separation file.

The second variant packs all the data into one file. In this case the comment is similar to:

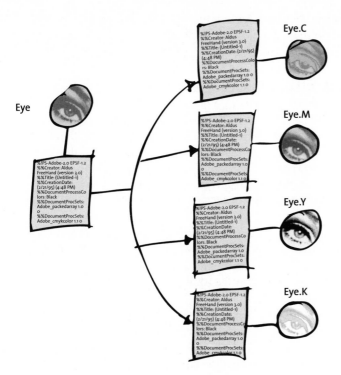

Fig. 3.12.
DCS file with
pointers to four
individual separation
files

```
%%PlateFile: (color name) filetype #offset size
```

Color name and *filetype* have the same meaning as above. *Offset* and *size* indicate the starting position and length of the corresponding separation data within the composite file. The separation data to which this comment refers are normal EPS data without a preview section.

3.4 Troubleshooting EPS Files

Embedding and printing an EPS graphic can fail for the most differing reasons. Theoretically, embedding should always work. Within homogenous environments or when working with highly integrated programs – especially on the Mac – it does definitely work. It becomes more interesting when working on different platforms, or if the programs in use do not generate "correct" EPS files. Most problems can be traced back to the EPS generating program not sticking to the rules explained in Sections 3.2 and 3.3. As this hint is not of much use in the real world, let us review the most common problems that occur when embedding and printing EPS graphics, and look at some possible solutions.

For clarity, this section only contains brief descriptions of the necessary steps. For more detailed information on carrying out these procedures on various operating systems, refer to Section 3.5.

3.4.1 Problems with Embedding EPS Graphics.
The most common cause of errors when embedding an EPS graphic into a document seems to be an incorrect or missing BoundingBox comment. If a normal PostScript print file is doing duty as an EPS file this comment is often missing altogether and the file can't be embedded. If the EPS file was generated using the PostScript printer driver and not the original program's export function, then the BoundingBox often describes not the size of the graphic, but the dimensions of the whole page.

If a file with a wrong BoundingBox is not rejected in the first place when you try to import it, when it is printed it will not give satisfactory results, due to incorrect size calculations. In the commonest case – the BoundingBox describes the whole page – the imported graphic will appear much too small.

In the case of EPS files that do not contain binary data, it is usually quite easy to modify the incorrect lines with a text editor. EPS files with binary data are usually only created by specialist graphics programs which luckily usually get the BoundingBox right. If the EPS file contains a TIFF preview, you will have to remove it before editing the comments.

The BoundingBox is not just a problem with rather dubious software, but also with standard programs of the better sort: this can be shown by a simple experiment with Adobe Illustrator: If the graphic contains a single letter at a font size of 800 points, then Illustrator generates a completely false BoundingBox. Only if the letter is converted to curves are the BoundingBox values at the start of the AI file correct. One cause of problems when calculating the BoundingBox are the Bézier curves, used by all graphics programs to draw arbitrary curves and also used to define character shapes in a font: the control points of these curves can lie off the curve and therefore increase the size of the BoundingBox if they are included in its calculation.

There is an easy fix for problems with a BoundingBox that is too small. This fix is available directly within the graphics program: simply draw an invisible (e.g., white) line of minimal width or a rectangle of the desired dimensions. This rectangle assists the program to calculate the correct BoundingBox, without affecting output.

Another problem when embedding an EPS graphic makes it a lot harder to work with the compound document: if the graphic does not contain a preview, only a gray rectangle or similar placeholder appears on screen. The following methods for adding a preview should

Fig. 3.13.
Even good graphics
programs some-
times work out the
BoundingBox
wrongly

be regarded as a last resort. The first choice should always be the program with which the EPS file was generated. Only if this is not available or did not generate a preview should you attempt to integrate a preview manually.

Symptom	Cause	Remedy
File is rejected by importing program	Required comments are either not present or contain errors	Insert comments
Only a placeholder appears on screen	EPS file contains no preview	Generate preview
Only a substitute placeholder on screen, although the EPS file contains an ASCII preview	The importing program can only use TIFF or PICT previews	Generate the required preview and possibly remove the ASCII preview
The file displays correctly on screen but the print output is too small	The BoundingBox in the EPS file is too large	Work out and insert the correct BoundingBox values

3.4.2 Problems with Printing EPS Graphics.

When EPS files are printed separately (without embedding in a document) various problems can arise. Only problems specific to EPS are discussed here; general problems affecting the PostScript output are discussed in Section 2.5.

First of all, EPS files must not contain a binary preview if they are to be printed separately. Because of this you should find out whether the file contains a preview and if need be remove it. After this change you can send an EPS file to the printer and in most cases get a printout. However, some EPS files do not contain the *showpage* operator to eject the finished page. You can easily insert this command with a text editor: simply add the word *showpage* at the end of the file on a line of its own. You can also use the program *epsffit* and the command line option -s from the PostScript Utilities *(psutils)* on the accompanying CD-ROM to do this (see also below).

If the printer outputs a blank page after this change, your graphic has probably been positioned outside the printable area. In this case you will have to move or scale the graphic using the program *epsffit* from the PostScript Utilities. To do this, indicate the target rectangle on the command line:

```
epsffit 100 100 300 300 file.eps new_file.eps
```

The coordinates represent the corners of the desired new Bounding-Box (as usual in PostScript units).

If odd errors occur after embedding an EPS graphic in a document (for example, pages are only printed half way), the primary suspects are illegal PostScript operators contained in the EPS file. Under Windows you can check this with GSview by choosing "Options", activating "EPS Warn" and checking the Ghostscript text window for messages while the file is being processed. Some programs (e.g., FrameMaker) use special PostScript commands to trap illegal operators in EPS graphics and instead of the graphic print an error message (*"EPS must not use initgraphics"*). In this case you do not have a valid EPS file! However, you can try to remove the offending operators from the file by hand.

If text elements of the graphic are not printed in the correct font but Courier instead, then you will have to download the required fonts to the printer manually. The comments *%%DocumentFonts:* or *%%DocumentNeededResources:* should contain the names of the required fonts. If this is not the case, display the file using Ghostscript or GSview and note which error messages Ghostscript displays in its text window. There you will see the names of all the required fonts.

EPS files generated under Windows (which are not really worthy of the name) often contain the control character Ctrl-D as the first and last character. Such files can be printed under Windows, but are not suitable for embedding and cause problems on other systems. In this case you must prevent the Windows driver from inserting these control characters into the file. Details of how to do this and a detailed description of the Ctrl-D problem can be found in Section 2.3. Another common cause of errors is a missing PostScript header in the EPS file. Without this header, the file can not be printed, and because of this the program that generates the file should include the PostScript header! As a last resort, you can download the header to the printer before the file (like a font). The table below lists key points on the commonest sources of errors when printing EPS files:

Symptom	Cause	Remedy
Odd error messages including binary code (cryptic characters)	EPS file contains preview section	Remove the preview
No error message, but no output either	showpage operator is missing	Insert showpage
File generates an empty page	Graphic is positioned outside the page	Move the graphic on the page
Pages of a document including an EPS graphic are only printed half way	EPS file contains illegal PostScript operators	Under Windows: check with GSview; remove these operators
Sending an EPSI file to the printer takes too long	File contains a large ASCII preview	Remove preview before printing
File displays correctly using Ghostscript or GSview but does not print	EPS file contains Ctrl-D characters	Regenerate file without Ctrl-D characters
The composite document is printed including the EPS file, but the rest of the page is missing and an error message appears	There is no linefeed character at the end of the EPS file (sometimes the case with Mac files)	Read the EPS file (without preview section) into a text editor and save it again; add a linefeed at the end manually

3.4.3 Converting EPS Graphics. This section contains notes on the various conversions which may be necessary in conjunction with EPS files: conversion of a "normal" PostScript file to an EPS file, as well as exchanging EPS files across operating systems. In Section 9.3 you can find methods to make EPS files editable again if the original file or the software used to create them is not available. Conversion between EPS and other graphics formats is covered in Section 9.4. In Section 4.7.2 you can learn how to create your own logo font from EPS files and the advantages of doing so.

Converting a PostScript print file to an EPS file. As already mentioned, many users face the problem of having to use a PostScript print file as an EPS file, as the available software does not have a suitable export option. This check list repeats the topics that you should be aware of:

▸ Make illegal PostScript operators harmless. Unfortunately, you cannot do this without detailed knowledge of PostScript, as the operators can have very different forms. In simple cases it may be enough to remove the operators from the file, in other cases it may be necessary to insert a dummy definition for the operator to prevent the "actual" PostScript operators from being called. However, it is possible for the EPS file to bypass these dummy operators...

- ► Correct or insert BoundingBox comments.
- ► Ctrl-D control characters must not be present at the start and end of the file.
- ► The file should end with a line feed character. If necessary, insert it manually. The type of line feed is not relevant (CR, LF or CR/LF).
- ► Insert a preview section. This is not strictly necessary, but does make it easier to embed the EPS file in a document.

Converting EPS files for Windows.   EPS files from a Macintosh often have to be used under Windows. If you're lucky, your Mac graphics software can generate a Windows EPS file with a preview so that no further conversion is required. When converting an EPS file for use on a different platform, it may also be necessary to convert any fonts used. This process is detailed in Section 4.6.

Main topics for Windows conversion:

- ► EPSI files from the Unix environment: if possible remove the preview comments on the Unix computer to speed up printing.
- ► If you have to edit existing EPS files, you may have to change the line-end characters with the *lineend* utility (under MS-DOS).
- ► Insert a TIFF or WMF preview.

Converting EPS files for Unix.   As Unix programs differ greatly in their range of functions and supported formats, the necessary steps depend on the program in use:

- ► EPS files from the Macintosh: change line end characters with *lineend*.
- ► If your application makes use of TIFF previews: generate a TIFF preview for Mac files.
- ► If your application only uses ASCII previews: remove the TIFF preview and generate an ASCII preview.
- ► EPS files from Windows: remove the Ctrl-D control characters.

Converting EPS files for the Macintosh.   Because of the Mac's peculiarities, this route is more complicated. The best solution is to convert to AI format, import into a suitable graphics program, and save as EPS with preview. Another option is to use the ShareWare *EPScon-verter* or one of several software PostScript RIPs that can generate AI format (e.g., Transverter Pro, Tailor). But not every user will have the necessary software, so here are some hints on manual conversion:

- ► EPS files from Windows: remove the TIFF preview.
- ► EPSI files from Unix: remove the ASCII preview.
- ► If possible: convert to AI format, import to an AI compatible graphics program and save as EPS with PICT preview (for details see Section 9.3.1).

▶ If it is not possible to convert to AI format, you can use the Mac version of Ghostscript and ResEdit to insert a PICT preview into the EPS file.

3.5 Procedures for EPS Troubleshooting

The following sections each describe several options for the operations that may be necessary to fix broken EPS file. The program *epstool* is very versatile when doing this: it can generate or remove preview bitmaps in various formats and runs under MS-DOS, Windows, OS/2, and Unix. Under MS-DOS or Windows a supplementary program is needed; check out the details in Appendix A.

Figure 3.14 shows an overview of the steps in the conversion process, the programs used to convert between platforms and how to deal with previews. AI conversion, covered in detail in Section 9.3.1 is also included. Commercial solutions are not included, only those which can be implemented with the programs on the accompanying CD-ROM.

3.5.1 Determining the Correct BoundingBox.
There are several methods of determining the correct BoundingBox. The easiest method is to print the graphic and measure it with a ruler. The problem arises that the origin of the PostScript coordinate system is theoretically located in the lower left corner of the paper, but may in

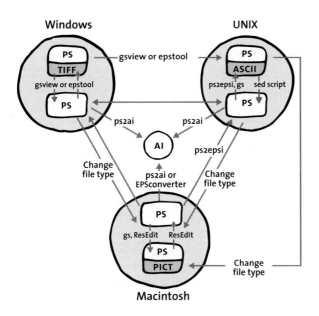

*Fig. 3.14.
Converting EPS files between Mac, Unix and Windows, and conversion to AI format*

practice be a few points "off" because the paper was not pulled through the printer exactly straight. Alternatively, the origin may be on the page but outside the printable area. In this case, the PostScript program *grid.ps*, on the accompanying CD-ROM, is useful. It prints PostScript coordinate system grid lines on the paper which you can use to read off the BoundingBox. Proceed as follows:

Method 1: grid.ps (all systems).
- Print the file *grid.ps* and your EPS file together as a single print job. Under MS-DOS use the command
  ```
  copy /B grid.ps+file.eps lpt1:
  ```
  The corresponding Unix instruction is
  ```
  cat grid.ps file.eps | lp
  ```
- If the printer does not eject any paper at all, then the file probably does not contain the *showpage* operator. In this case, add the operator as detailed above. If a page is ejected, but the graphic is only partly visible or not visible at all, it is positioned outside the printable area. If this is the case, it is best to use the second method as detailed below.
- Draw a rectangle whose sides are parallel to the edges of the page and which fully encloses the graphic.
- Read the following four values from the scale:
  llx = horizontal coordinate of the lower left corner
  lly = vertical coordinate of the upper left corner
  urx = horizontal coordinate of the lower right corner
  ury = vertical coordinate of the upper right corner
- The comment required at the start of the EPS file reads:
  ```
  %%BoundingBox: llx lly urx ury
  ```
  Enter this comment, inserting the four values above as integers. If need be, round *llx* and *lly* down, *urx* and *ury* up.

Because it is not possible to combine the two files on the Macintosh, in this case it is best to print the two files separately and lay the two pages on top of one another to determine the BoundingBox (or run the page with the printed grid through the printer a second time). So that the file can be printed at all, first use a text editor to remove the % character before the *showpage* operator in the last line of the file.

Method 2: epsfinfo.ps (all systems except Macintosh).   The second possibility is easier, as all the coordinates are calculated automatically. However, it does require bidirectional communication with a PostScript interpreter (see Section 2.3.1) and can occasionally give wrong results. Unfortunately, you cannot use Ghostscript as an interpreter (for reasons unknown to me) as it delivers incorrect results. To work out the BoundingBox automatically use the PostScript program *epsfinfo.ps* from the accompanying CD-ROM. Proceed as follows:

- Send the contents of *epsfinfo.ps* together with the EPS file to the PostScript printer *as a single print job* (as with method 1 and *grid.ps*).
- The PostScript interpreter outputs the required coordinates via the standard output channel. It is a good idea to check these coordinates by making a test print.
- Enter the values into the EPS file as described above.

If you notice when entering the comment that it is already present and also contains correct values, make sure that the four coordinates are not given as floating point numbers, but as integers. Watch for the exact syntax: in the case of one particular Unix software I had difficulties with embedding because a colon was missing after %%BoundingBox!

Method 3: GSview (Windows or OS/2).   Under Windows and OS/2 using the combination of Ghostscript/GSview is another way to determine the BoundingBox. It is interactive and easy to use, but does require precise use of the mouse.

- Open the EPS file in GSview.
- Choose "File", "PS to EPS".
- Click with the mouse on the left, right, upper and lower edges of the bounding rectangle as indicated in the four info panels that appear. Use the screen display of the graphic as a guide. If needed, you can scroll the GSview window.
- Save the file under a new name. GSview will create a BoundingBox comment using the coordinates you clicked on.

Method 4: epstool (MS-DOS, Windows, OS/2, Unix).   Epstool starts Ghostscript and makes it rasterize the PostScript file. Afterwards epstool analyzes the bitmap that has been generated and uses it to calculate the correct BoundingBox. For example, the following command inserts a TIFF preview and calculates the correct BoundingBox:

```
epstool -b -t4 -ofile.eps file.ps
```

3.5.2 Adding a Preview Image.   The type of preview depends not just on the target system but also the software.

Method 1: GSview (Windows and OS/2).   This method is again based on GSview and is therefore only suitable for Windows and OS/2. It can be used to create TIFF, WMF or ASCII (EPSI) previews. The most important steps are described below. A more detailed description can be found in the GSview help file:

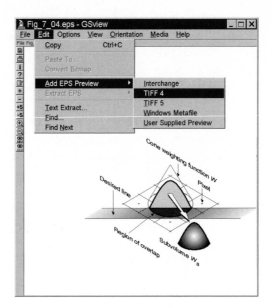

Fig. 3.15.
Adding an EPS
preview using
GSview

- ► Make sure that the file contains a correct BoundingBox comment (see above). In addition the file should contain the *showpage oper-ator.*
- ► Open the file in GSview.
- ► Choose "Edit", "Copy", to copy a bitmap version of the graphic to the clipboard. The resolution of the bitmap also determines the size of the preview. If the image is too large for the clipboard (or if you are happy with a lower resolution), reduce the resolution using "Media", "Resolution".
- ► The image copied to the clipboard contains the whole page and so is usually too large. To correct this, you can clip off the white margins around the graphic in a paint program and then copy the image back to the clipboard.
- ► Choose "Edit", "Add EPS Preview" and the type of preview to use (for use under Windows choose TIFF4, under Unix choose Inter-change).
- ► Save the file under a new name.

Method 2: Ghostscript (all systems). This method only requires Ghostscript and can therefore be used on any platform for which Ghostscript is available. On the Macintosh, ResEdit and image editing software are also needed. For MS-DOS use the batch file *ps2epsi.bat* or for Unix the shell script *ps2epsi* and obey the instructions in the file *ps2epsi.doc.* All these files are part of the Ghostscript package. On the Macintosh, proceed as follows:

- Start Ghostscript and open the PostScript file you wish to use. For Windows EPS you must first remove the preview section.
- If the graphic is displayed fully on screen, copy it (in PICT format) to the clipboard.
- Start an image editing program, open a new file and paste the contents of the clipboard into it. Crop the bitmap, to remove the surplus white area around the graphic. After doing this, select the remaining part containing the graphic and copy it to the clipboard.
- Now open the EPS file with ResEdit and paste in the contents of the clipboard. ResEdit generates a PICT resource. Double-click on the new PICT resource and choose "resource info". Change the resource ID in this dialog to 256 and save the file.

Method 3: epstool (MS-DOS, Windows, OS/2, Unix). Epstool can create all types of preview. It makes GhostScript generate the required bitmaps. However, it is also possible to embed an existing file into an EPS file as preview section. This makes sense if a program can export as EPS and WMF or TIFF but not as EPS with preview. Here is an example of the epstool command for generating a TIFF preview:

```
epstool -ttiffg3 -ofile.eps file.ps
```

Method 4: Converting to AI format. If the graphic is already in AI format or if you can convert it to this format, read it into Illustrator or another AI compatible program and save it again *with* preview. Various methods of converting files to this quasi-standard format can be found in Section 9.3).

3.5.3 Deleting a Preview Image.

Method 1: epstool (MS-DOS, Windows, OS/2, Unix). Epstool's *Extract PostScript* option allows you to extract the PostScript section from an EPS file with a preview. The command line is as follows:

```
epstool -p -ofile.ps file.eps
```

Method 2: GSview (Windows and OS/2). Open the file with GSview using "File", "Select File..." (not "Open"!) and choose the menu command "File", "Extract...". Save the extracted PostScript section under a different name.

Method 3: The sed stream editor (Unix). If you can live without the screen preview, you can remove the preview comments from EPSI files to make the file smaller and speed up printing. The easiest way to do this is with the following *sed* stream editor command which removes all characters between %%BeginPreview and %%EndPreview:

```
sed -e/%%BeginPreview/,/%%EndPreview/d <file.epsi >file.eps
```

Removing the preview comments also makes sense if you are porting an EPS file from Unix to Windows and are embedding a TIFF preview (as the ASCII preview is no longer needed in this case).

PostScript Fonts

4

Type is one of our most important communication media. The accurate representation of type characters has been decisive in the universal propagation of PostScript. The many areas and operating systems in which PostScript fonts are used has brought with it a variety of file and font formats, which at first glance make the topic somewhat unclear. However, with the necessary background knowledge and some well-chosen utility programs, you can make your way through the font format jungle.

4.1 Digital Typography

4.1.1 **Some History.** In ancient prehistory – that is 20 or 30 years ago – most computer users didn't have to distinguish a monitor from a printer. They worked at a "terminal" which consisted of a keyboard and a printing mechanism and which resembled an electric typewriter. The terminal printed all of the computer's output, and the user's input, on to continuous paper. As the teletype-like terminals were replaced by screens and printers, matrix technology developed on both classes of devices: on printers, needles made impressions on paper in a grid to form individual characters. On screen, rectangular cells of the sizes 8 × 8 or 8 × 16 dots served to represent letters. The bitmaps which represented the letters were built in to both classes of device, either in the printer's memory or in the graphic card's ROM.

Bitmap fonts. This bitmap technology was retained, even after hardware developed further: the printer needles and screen pixels became smaller, so that more dots were available for each letter, leading to a more detailed representation. Now the disadvantages of bitmap fonts became more and more apparent: if the fonts were enlarged (scaled) the unavoidable stepping increased too, so that characters became increasingly ugly as their size was increased. This could be avoided by using extra bitmap data for all the desired font sizes, but this drove up memory requirements correspondingly. Rotating font characters – except in multiples of 90° – made the problem more evident: the character was no longer in line with the grid and only approximated the original form.

Stroke fonts. Plotters use a different technique: they "know" the shape of a character and guide the pen around the shape. This concept does allow better scaling (possibly using different pen thicknesses) and only uses one set of data for each character, independent of size. However as the pen width is constant the character elements always have the same weight. However, aesthetically pleasing letters require, for example, strokes of differing widths.

Outline fonts. These requirements could only be implemented using a font technology which describes the outline of a character geometrically using lines and curved elements and then fills the shape created with black. Errors still arise when the curves are mapped to a grid for output but with increasing resolution (that is, grid points per unit) these decrease. When the first 300 dpi laser printers were delivering the technical capability of using outline fonts, PostScript was providing the necessary software for their efficient use and their translation to pixels.

Fig. 4.1.
Digital font technologies:
bitmap and outline fonts

The success of PostScript fonts is based on the fact that a character in a font is handled like a normal graphic object bounded by lines and curves, which can be filled or hollow or, as earlier, represented by a bitmap. A PostScript interpreter contains complex algorithms which convert these geometric descriptions into a pixel pattern for whichever output device is in use. This might sound like a "routine" programming job; in fact it is anything but trivial: there are various standard procedures for determining which pixels are inside or outside an outline curve. However, it is the pixels that are on or close to the line which are critical: because of rounding errors, they can give rise to inaccuracies, holes, or unwanted thickening. The real challenge in implementing a font technology is in the satisfactory treatment of these irregularities.

That such effects can be seen with the naked eye can be shown by a simple calculation: at the normal font size of 10 points, upper case letters are about 7 points high. At a resolution of 300 dpi about 30 rows of pixels are available to represent an upper case letter. Only one or two pixels are left to depict fine serifs, but the jump from one to two means a doubling of thickness!

The advantages of outline fonts (lower memory requirements and scalability) are balanced by disadvantages. The outlines can be rasterized at any size, but this process is time consuming – bitmaps on the other hand are simply copied from a font file or from memory without any extra processing overhead. In addition, at small sizes, automatically rasterized fonts do not match the quality of hand crafted bitmap fonts which have been optimized pixel by pixel for readability by an experienced type designer.

To be truly WYSIWYG *(What you see is what you get)* the fonts used on screen should be exactly the same as those in the printer. The increasing dominance of PostScript caused an increase in the need to display PostScript fonts on screen. The next step should therefore have been the integration of the PostScript interpreter into the oper-

Times
Times
Times

Fig. 4.2.
Rasterization of 10
point text (enlarged):
at 75, 300, and 600 dpi
respectively 7, 30, or 60
pixels are available for
the height of an upper
case letter

ating system – but the peculiar nature of the software market complicated things.

Font wars. Adobe – inventor and distributor of PostScript – achieved a strong position during the 1980s, not just because of the (expensive) licenses for PostScript printers, but also because of the rapidly growing font software business. To maintain this advantage, Adobe had kept one card up its sleeve: unlike the rest of the Post-Script specification, it had never published the Type 1 font format. This hindered the development of 100 percent compatible printers, as their manufacturers could not make use of the growing number of Type 1 fonts. Adobe charged heavily for the software to create such fonts. This monopoly situation naturally upset the competition: Adobe's former partner, Apple, allied itself with Microsoft and announced the development of its own font format under the description *TrueType*, to be integrated into both manufacturers' future operating systems and be used for both screen display and printing, and in addition it would be PostScript compatible.

Adobe reacted very cleverly to this threat: they lifted the fog of secrecy surrounding Type 1 fonts – at the beginning of 1990 they published the complete Type 1 specification. This information made it possible for other manufacturers to make their PostScript clones Type 1 compatible or to implement suitable font editors. The second counterattack was the introduction of the *Adobe Type Manager* (ATM) software, first on the Apple Macintosh, and a little later for Windows as well. ATM is basically the part of the PostScript interpreter which processes Type 1 fonts, and it installs itself as a driver between the operating system and application programs. If a program (such as a word processor) requests a PostScript font that the operating system cannot offer, then ATM falls back on its stock of PostScript fonts and rasterizes it at whatever size is required on screen. In addition to this, ATM supplies all graphics capable printers, including non-PostScript devices, with rasterized PostScript fonts and makes it possible to use Type 1 fonts even without a PS printer.

These two steps caused an enormous strengthening of the Type 1 format's position; it has even been "honored" as an ISO standard. TrueType has come to market and does dominate mainly the low cost sector, but it plays no role in the high quality sector (after the image-setting studios had mastered PostScript fonts they certainly did not want to start grappling with new compatibility problems). In spite of this, TrueType has proved itself worthwhile: the emergence of a competing standard did at least open up the Type 1 format, and the "font war" caused prices for digital fonts to crash in their wake.

Whither Unix? In the Unix (workstation) market, the X Window System (X11) has for some years been the manufacturer-independent standard for graphical user interfaces. Until Release 4 (X11R4), screen display was based, like Mac and Windows, on bitmap fonts only. Only with Release 5 of X11 (1991/92) were scalable screen fonts and the font server for network wide font supply introduced. Some contributions from the industry to the free X Window System made a marked improvement, from R5 on, to font processing: Bitstream contributed a rasterizer for fonts in its own Speedo format as well as some Speedo fonts. In conjunction with PostScript one contribution from IBM is important, namely the Type 1 rasterizer which makes it possible to use Type 1 fonts under X. So that it also had something to rasterize, IBM contributed its own version of the standard Courier font (this is not the "normal" Courier, but a font with interesting extra characteristics, see Section 4.5). Adobe enlarged this package with the freely distributable Type 1 font Utopia. On many X systems these two fonts still form the standard range of PostScript fonts. How to install extra fonts and configure the X11 font server for PostScript is explained in Section 4.3.6.

Copyright and fonts. The theme of fonts also touches on legal aspects. Fonts are software, which the purchaser cannot do with as he likes, but for which he obtains the right (according to the manufacturer) to use the fonts on one or more output device. This means that fonts, just like application programs, may not be legally copied and distributed at random. Conversion of a font to a different format or for different operating systems, also discussed in this book, falls into a gray area between "only just allowed" and "not really allowed, but tolerated". If in doubt, consult the manufacturer's license conditions. In any case, you are responsible for observing the conditions of use!

A further important point is the level of protection for the underlying typeface design. There are different rules in different countries. In the USA, it is not possible to protect the form or shape of a character, but only its conversion to a particular digital format (font). In Europe on the other hand the designer can also protect the shape, but it is difficult to have copyright upheld even if only minor changes have been made to the letterforms. The American interpretation has led to the practice of re-digitizing a large printout of a font, making minor changes and thus creating a "new" font which is then marketed as an original product. As there is no creative effort in making products of that kind, they are offered at dumping prices and deprive many type designers of the fruits of their labor. On the other hand, the widespread distribution of digital fonts and the democratization of fonts has lead to the appearance of many genuinely new fonts.

Finally, a designer can also protect a font's name. This does not afford any protection from clones of the font (that is, digitization of an existing design). It does mean that the clones have to have other names and cannot simply be passed off as high value original works. For the user, this usually means that there are two almost identical fonts with different names.

4.1.2 Typographer's Jargon.   In the world of digital type (as in every specialist area) there is a wealth of jargon which makes it easier to understand the subject but frightens off the uninitiated.

Metrics.   When using fonts on a computer, the width of individual characters plays an important role: if a word processor, for example, is to justify a block of text, then it must know the width of each character in the current font and size. These width values are added together to work out how much text will fit on a line and how the empty space between the words should be distributed. For advanced DTP functions the width information on its own is not enough. It is supplemented by general information about the font; for example, ascender and descender lengths, stroke weights, optimal line spacing, and so on. As the PostScript interpreter can output text not just character by character but also in large blocks at once, it has to be able to work out the width of a character. For this reason, PostScript fonts always contain width information for all characters.

Kerning.   The font metrics only give one width value for each character. This value is fine usually, but can lead to an unpleasant appearance with some combinations of letters: two "V"s next to each other can look like a W, and the distance between T and e must be reduced, or too much ugly white space appears. This compensation is referred

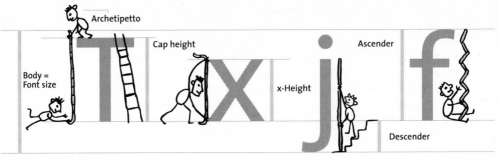

Fig. 4.3.
Character metrics

to as kerning; in the days of metal type, the characters of the letter pairs were actually filed down to reduce their width.

A good font always contains a comprehensive kerning table, which should contain the kerning values for several hundred letter pairs. The kerning information is only used by application programs and does not play any role in the PostScript interpreter, as all calculations about correct character positioning have already been carried out by the application software. They are therefore not contained in the actual PostScript font file and are stored, according to the operating system, in various supplementary files and formats.

Fig. 4.4.
Unmodified
character spacing
compared to
kerning

Tele Vaso
No kerning

Tele Vaso
Kerning applied

Te   Va
Character movement caused by kerning

Apart from pair kerning there is also track kerning (or tracking). Behind this is the fact that the letter spacing depends on the font size as well: in general, the larger the font becomes, the closer the characters can be set. The track kerning tables use a mathematical function to describe how font size affects letter spacing. The track kerning files are also stored in supplementary files rather than the font files themselves.

Ligatures. Ligatures are special characters for particular letter pairs, for example, *f* and *i*. In much work produced using DTP, they are simply ignored, but for high quality publications they are a must. The most commonly used ligatures are those for fi and fl.

The practical use of ligatures varies according to the operating system and application software in use: the Mac character set (see Appendix C) contains the ligatures for fi and fl in all character sets; the so-called expert sets, in a well-constructed font family, contain extra ligatures. But these can only be accessed by changing font. The

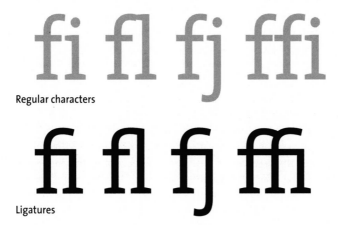

Regular characters

Ligatures

Fig. 4.5.
The most commonly
used ligatures

QuickDraw GX system extension makes it easier to use ligatures by automatic substitution of the individual characters. As the Windows character set contains no ligatures, under Windows ligatures must always be inserted from a supplementary expert font, if available.

Small Capitals. This term describes reduced size upper case letters, which are often used to draw attention to an author's name. Small caps are also used for abbreviations and acronyms, which – if set in full size upper case – would cause ugly gaps in the text flow. They should emphasize an expression, without disturbing the visual effect of the text. Small caps are not simply smaller letters, but are fonts in their own right: when normal capital letters are reduced, so are the stroke widths of the letters so that reduced-size "normal" upper case letters look too "thin" in the text. HIGH QUALITY SMALL CAPITALS ALSO HAVE WIDER LETTERS. COMPARE THIS SENTENCE, COMPOSED WITH REDUCED SIZE UPPER CASE LETTERS, WITH THE "REAL" SMALL CAPS IN THE PREVIOUS SENTENCE! Well constructed font families usually offer both proper small caps and an expert set with further typographic "goodies".

4.2 PostScript Font Basics

There are various font types in PostScript, some of which only have historical importance, but thanks to their differing properties have their own areas of use.

4.2.1 Type 1 Fonts and ATM.

The Type 1 format (T1) is without doubt the most important PostScript font type. The name is derived from the internal classification property *FontType* which has the value 1 for this font type. Type 1 fonts and *Adobe Type Manager* (ATM) are so closely associated with each other that the terms are often used interchangeably ("ATM fonts"). However, we will see later that this is not quite correct.

Output quality and hinting. Type 1 fonts give excellent quality output, are processed quickly, and do not need much storage space. The quality of the font is related to hints, which are special data within the font that improve the font's appearance mainly on low resolution output devices (such as monitors or printers up to 600 dpi).

Figure 4.6 shows a Type 1 font in its standard version and for comparison without hints (unhinted)[1]. This clearly shows that hints ensure equal-sized stems and help to avoid asymmetry. As the human eye is very sensitive to irregularities and asymmetries, the font description contains additional hints which the interpreter uses when it rasterizes the font. They relate partly to the whole font (in that they ensure the same stroke weight for all characters) or various points within a letter ("the two vertical strokes in the H should be the same width"). As these hints only describe the desired appearance of the character, they are also known as declarative hints.

The interpreter is responsible for converting the hints. This has the advantage that an improved algorithm in a new version of the interpreter will also have a beneficial effect on older fonts. In TrueType fonts the corresponding supplementary information is referred to as an instruction. They do not just contain mere descriptions, but also hold the instructions for carrying out the desired regularization. This is why TrueType files are usually larger than Type 1 font files. However, a TrueType font developer can implement his own procedures and is not limited to the capabilities of existing interpreters. You will find further details on hints at the end of this chapter.

1. *The strange test word "Hamburgefons" is often used as it contains characters with all the important characteristics (ascenders and descenders, straight and rounded characters, etc.).*

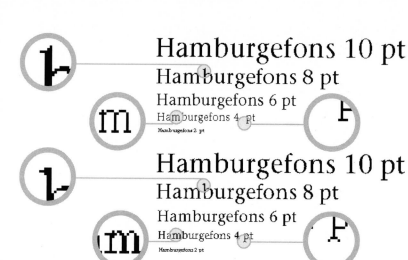

Fig. 4.6.
Various font sizes
rasterized at
300 dpi; above:
with hints; below:
without hints

Encryption. If you have ever looked at the content of a font file or the font data in a PostScript file, you will have already have recognized one of the most important things: namely, you cannot see anything! The font file starts with some readable entries, for example, the complete font name and the character set, but the actual outline descriptions appear to be an illegible jumble of numbers. The normal end user will not be particularly surprised, as this is how normal software looks to him. However, unlike executable programs, Type 1 fonts are also unreadable for programmers – or, more accurately, they were until 1990. Adobe protected its font files using a sophisticated multi-level encryption procedure.

When the interpreter or ATM processes a font, it must first remove the *eexec* encryption. This step decrypts the *CharStrings* dictionary with the individual character descriptions. Next, it has to decipher the CharStrings encryption, as the data are protected by a second layer of encryption. Only then are the actual instructions describing the letter forms available. They offer similar possibilities to the normal drawing instructions in PostScript, but do not encompass all the graphical possibilities of the "mother language". The mini-PostScript used by Type 1 fonts does not consist of plain text instructions; the operators are encoded in one or two bytes. This means that Type 1 fonts are very compact and require less storage space than other font formats. In addition, the encryption achieves a random byte distribution which means that compression programs cannot greatly reduce the font file size.

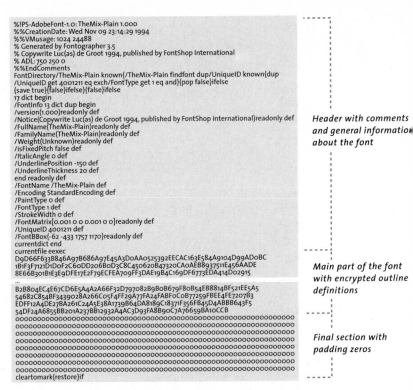

```
%!PS-AdobeFont-1.0: TheMix-Plain 1.000
%%CreationDate: Wed Nov 09 23:14:29 1994
%%VMusage: 1024 24488
% Generated by Fontographer 3.5
% Copywrite Luc(as) de Groot 1994, published by FontShop International
% ADL: 750 250 0
%%EndComments
FontDirectory/TheMix-Plain known{/TheMix-Plain findfont dup/UniqueID known{dup
/UniqueID get 4001211 eq exch/FontType get 1 eq and}{pop false}ifelse
{save true}{false}ifelse}{false}ifelse
17 dict begin
/FontInfo 13 dict dup begin
/version(1.000)readonly def
/Notice(Copywrite Luc(as) de Groot 1994, published by FontShop International)readonly def
/FullName(TheMix-Plain)readonly def
/FamilyName(TheMix-Plain)readonly def
/Weight(Unknown)readonly def
/isFixedPitch false def
/ItalicAngle 0 def
/UnderlinePosition -150 def
/UnderlineThickness 20 def
end readonly def
/FontName /TheMix-Plain def
/Encoding StandardEncoding def
/PaintType 0 def
/FontType 1 def
/StrokeWidth 0 def
/FontMatrix[0.001 0 0 0.001 0 0]readonly def
/UniqueID 4001211 def
/FontBBox{-62 -433 1757 1170}readonly def
currentdict end
currentfile eexec
D9D66F633B846A97B686A97E45A3D0AA0525392EECAC163E584A9104D99ADoBC
1B1F3F7121D1D0F2C60DD206B0D3C8C450620B47320CA0AEB8937511E456AADE
8E66B301B1E3E9DFE17E2F79ECFEA709FF3DAE19B4C169DF6773EDA414D02915
...
B2B804EC4E67CD6E5A4A2A66F32D797082B9B0B679F80B54EB8814BF521EE5A5
54682C854BF3439028A266C05F4FF29A77FA24FABF0C0B77259FBEE4FE7207B3
EDFF12A4DE27BA261C24A5E38A1739B64DA8189C18371F356FB45D4ABBB643F5
54DF24A6855BB201A237BB12932A4AC3D93FA8B90C7A76659BA10CCB
0000000000000000000000000000000000000000000000000000000000000000
0000000000000000000000000000000000000000000000000000000000000000
0000000000000000000000000000000000000000000000000000000000000000
0000000000000000000000000000000000000000000000000000000000000000
0000000000000000000000000000000000000000000000000000000000000000
0000000000000000000000000000000000000000000000000000000000000000
0000000000000000000000000000000000000000000000000000000000000000
0000000000000000000000000000000000000000000000000000000000000000
cleartomark{restore}if
```

Header with comments and general information about the font

Main part of the font with encrypted outline definitions

Final section with padding zeros

Fig. 4.7. Components of a Type 1 font

Limitations.   The Type 1 language's instructions have the same capabilities as the main PostScript language to describe curves and lines. Missing are some parts of the PostScript graphic feature set which are unimportant for fonts and would unnecessarily complicate the Type 1 format. The characters in a Type 1 font must always be defined by outlines as bitmap characters are not possible.

Type 1 also does not support color: a font can be printed in color, but the color information comes from the application software; it is not part of the font description. A Type 1 font cannot specify that it is always to be printed in a particular color or appear in two colors.

Adobe Type Manager.   ATM contains the part of the PostScript interpreter which processes Type 1 fonts. It sits between the operating system and the applications software and traps its calls relating to text output. If it concerns a PostScript font, it completes the call by rasterizing the required characters of a Type 1 font, in other cases it passes on the call to the operating system.

ATM is available for Windows, Mac, OS/2, and some Unix systems as well as part of Display PostScript. Unlike the interpreter, ATM cannot process all PostScript instructions (for example, to display EPS graphics on screen). There are some additional conditions for making a Type 1 font ATM compatible, for example, the order in which components are arranged. These formal conditions only affect the external format of the instructions, but do not result in any functional limitations. The majority of Type 1 fonts created with modern font editors are ATM compatible. In practice you can assume that Type 1 fonts almost always work with ATM. From time to time a complete PostScript interpreter demonstrates its superiority over ATM: a font might be printed, but cannot be displayed on screen.

We will look at the installation of fonts for ATM and the files required to do this separately for each operating system. In Section 4.5 we will take a closer look at some of the peculiarities of ATM.

Speaking of ATM, its *Application Programming Interface* (API) is of interest. This is a programming interface which allows application programs to make use of ATM's capabilities. Applications can use this interface to call on font variants which are not offered by the operating system, for example, certain geometric transformations or further processing of the character outlines. Some programs make use of this interface for special effects; such ATM effects only work with Type 1 fonts.

4.2.2 Type 3 Fonts.   For a long time, Type 3 fonts were the only way for PostScript developers to define their own fonts. Type 3 fonts make use of all PostScript's graphic functions to define a new font. As we saw above, the character instructions on their own are not enough. In Type 3 quality cannot be improved by hints, but there is also no irritating encryption. The PostScript interpreter uses different rasterization algorithms for Type 1 and Type 3. For Type 1 fonts, it blackens all pixels whose center lies within the desired outline. Type 3 fonts on the other hand do not use the normal PostScript procedure: a pixel is blackened if any part of the letter form overlaps any part of this pixel.

This process does prevent very thin lines from disappearing during rasterization, but does mean that lines and curves generally look rather heavier than in Type 1.

As Type 3 fonts can use any PostScript instruction and do not have to comply with Type 1 restrictions, you cannot display them on screen with ATM. However, they can be used for purposes which Type 1 can't be: they can contain bitmaps or color instructions. Contrary to popular opinion, Type 3 fonts are not always bitmap fonts, but can contain bitmaps *or* outlines (or even both kinds of characters). In addition to this, Type 3 fonts can use and modify fonts of any other type. You can use this for example to create a version of a Type 1 font with an embedded shadow or to construct a font containing characters from other fonts (such as extra symbols in a text font).

Type 3 fonts are not often encountered today, as they have been almost totally driven out by Type 1. They are sometimes still used for logos and symbols. For complex logos, Type 3 fonts are sometimes the only possibility due to the tighter limits set by Type 1 in respect of the total number of permitted path elements which restrict a character's complexity.

On the accompanying CD-ROM you will find as examples of Type 3 fonts a simple barcode font and a bitmap font which was created manually for taking MS-DOS screenshots. The font simulates a VGA graphic card's standard font and was created by reading the internal font from the graphic card's ROM and converting it to Type 3 format. Special fonts like this naturally have a very limited area of use as they cannot be used with ATM.

Mac users occasionally come across Type 3 fonts: if a required PostScript font is missing when a document is printed, the printer driver converts one of the existing bitmapped screen fonts to a Type 3 font which it sends to the printer instead.

As Type 3 fonts encompass a greater range of functions than Type 1 fonts, a Type 3 font cannot usually be converted to Type 1. In some special cases the conversion does succeed, if the font has a fixed structure, for example, Type 3 fonts created with Fontographer (see Section 4.7). Interested PostScript fanatics can find a converter in my *TerminalBuch PostScript*[1] which, with a little help, can convert (almost) any Type 3 font to Type 1. The converter itself is programmed in PostScript.

4.2.3 TrueType Fonts and PostScript.

As already mentioned, TrueType fonts (TT) brought a new dynamic to the font market, but from the PostScript user's point of view, they complicated procedures

---

1. *Unfortunately, it is available in German only – but the PostScript code on the accompanying disk is international! You can find the exact reference in the bibliography.*

on the PC. The main problem is that the operating system (Mac or Windows) rasterizes TrueType fonts for the screen or printer (that is, it delivers bitmaps), whilst a PostScript printer demands PostScript fonts, if possible described by outlines. The printer driver can achieve this in two ways: either by converting the installed TrueType fonts to PostScript fonts, during which discrepancies may creep in, or to substitute available PostScript fonts for the TrueType fonts. Professional users often bypass substitution related problems by turning off TrueType fonts and working exclusively with ATM fonts.

If you want to work with TrueType fonts, then you will have to get used to the different names for the standard fonts: Helvetica for example is replaced by Arial. The Microsoft and Adobe Windows printer drivers offer various options for converting TrueType fonts for PostScript printers. For some fonts, like Arial, for which an equivalent font is available on the PostScript side, it is enough to change the name correspondingly. The printer drivers do this with substitution tables in which the PostScript equivalent for each TrueType font can be specified.

TrueType fonts without a PostScript equivalent have to be converted to PostScript by the driver and embedded in the output so that they are available to the interpreter during printing. An option in the Windows driver setup allows you to choose between Type 1 fonts or bitmap fonts in Type 3 format. With the printer driver, a free True-Type to Type 1 converter is available, although the quality of the PostScript fonts created is not very high, as for example the driver does not generate hints for Type 1 fonts.

On some newer printers with Level 2 interpreters (version numbers above 2013), Type 42 fonts offer another method of converting from TrueType to PostScript. Type 42 fonts contain the data of a TrueType font, with the addition of PostScript instructions. Unlike the methods above for conversion to Type 1 or Type 3, the content of the font data is not changed, but suitably "wrapped". The TrueType rasterizer, which converts the fonts, is a part of these newer versions of the PostScript interpreter. Using the PostScript program *info.ps* on the accompanying CD-ROM, you can check whether your printer can cope with Type 42 fonts. Another possibility is to check the content of the printer's PPD file. The entry

```
*TTRasterizer:Type42
```

shows that the printer can use TrueType fonts as Type 42. In this case the font is rasterized using the printer's internal algorithms without the user having to worry about the printer's conversion capabilities.

Warning: print files with Type 42 fonts are not really suitable for printers other than the one specified in the driver, as Type 42 is not

yet included in the standard PostScript vocabulary. If you want to
play safe and have to transfer a print file to another printer or an
imagesetter, you should convert the TrueType fonts to Type 1. The
Adobe printer driver for Windows lets you convert TrueType fonts
to Type 1, Type 3, or Type 42.

4.2.4 Multiple Master Fonts.

Multiple Master fonts (MM) are not
simply a further technical variation of PostScript fonts, but offer
typographers and users wholly new possibilities. They contain, in
one font, a large number of variants, which are carefully matched to
each other. This matching is particularly important if you want to
avoid a typographic mess and instead pay attention to quality. Font
manufacturers and typographers who take their job seriously usually
offer their fonts in families which contain various weights *(light/reg-
ular/bold)*, styles *(plain, italic, caps,* etc.), or widths *(condensed/nor-
mal/expanded)*. Each typeface lives in its own font and is carefully
matched to the other members of the font family. MM fonts take this
principle a step further by making possible smooth transitions between the predefined faces. This way, not just the usual two to four
weights are available (for some well-made fonts like Univers or Thesis
there may be more), but many more weights in between. These faces
do not exist as separate font files, but are created by interpolation
(calculation of interim values) from two or more master designs contained in the font. The range of values is specified by the typographer
when the font is designed.

An MM font can contain up to four such parameters which can be
described as design axes. As the axes parameters are independent of
one another, each MM font has a design space with up to four dimensions. This all sounds very mathematical, here is an example: let's
take a look at the Multiple Master version of ThesisMonospaced. It
has a single design axis weight (stroke weight); this parameter can be

Fig. 4.9.
The Multiple Master
font ThesisMonoMM
with the Weight
design axis

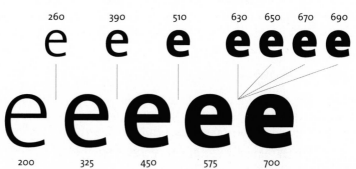

between 200 and 700 and any whole number interim value. The higher the value, the bolder the font.

The Adobe font MyriadMM contains the two design axes weight (215 to 830) and width (300 to 700). These allow for almost 250 000 variations! Figure 4.10 shows some of the available faces, arranged in the two-dimensional design space (which can, because of this, be represented well on paper). Apart from the two design axes weight and width, there are also fonts in which the style changes (from a sans serif to a serif design).

One very interesting design axis is called *optical size*. It is based on a property which was for hundreds of years a component of printing technology but was lost with the advent of digital processes: The term "scalable font" means, with most modern typesetting methods, that a single outline shape is used to describe a letter at all sizes. This may seem to be obvious, but does degrade quality: at small sizes (below 12 points), for example, the serifs have to be more pronounced so that they do not "break off" when printed; the distance between letters and the insides of the letters have to be larger to ensure optimal legibility at small sizes. At large sizes on the other hand the difference between serifs and main stems becomes more pronounced.

With traditional metal type, the type designer had to cut an individual matrix for each size; this allowed such subtle differences at various sizes to be built in. With normal PostScript fonts, you cannot do this: all the sizes have to make do with a single outline description. A Multiple Master font with the optical size design axis on the other hand can be adjusted according to the font size in use and achieve the same range of variations as was possible before.

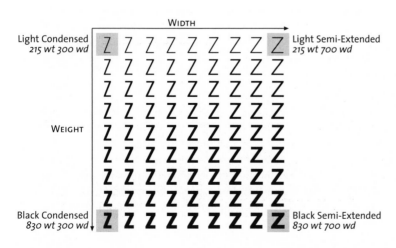

Fig. 4.10.
The MyriadMM design matrix with the Weight and Width design axes

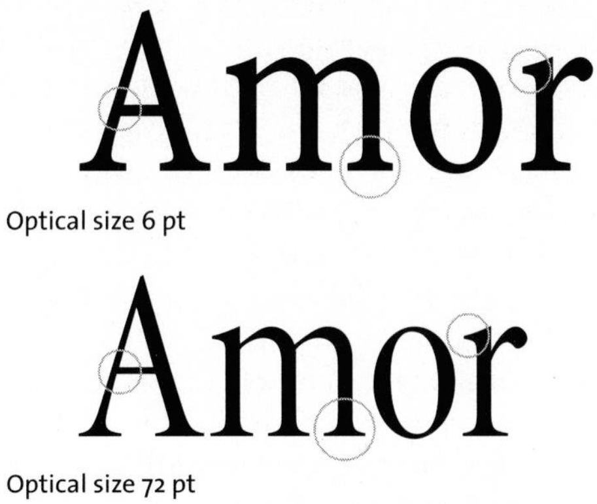

Amor

Fig. 4.11.
*Letterform differences
with MinionMM using
the optical size design
axis. The examples
shown are for 6 points
and 72 points, but
they are printed at the
same size for
comparison*

Optical size 6 pt

Amor

Optical size 72 pt

Where to use Multiple Master fonts.   Multiple Master fonts open up a whole new area of possible uses, which today's applications software can only partly exploit:

▸ The problem of *copyfitting* is to fit a predefined amount of text into a fixed space, such as fitting a headline exactly across the width of a column. Until now, you have either had to change the type size of the text (not always what you want) or modify the letterforms manually using a graphics program (which does not always give satisfactory results). MM fonts make this task easier by choosing a suitable parameter for width (and possibly also for the weight).

▸ Some typographic effects, like the transition from light to bold in a piece of text, are very difficult to achieve with conventional fonts.

*Fig. 4.12.
Dynamic transition
from light to bold*

Metamorfosi

▸ The correct optical scaling property described above is very easy to integrate into application programs: the software automatically chooses the correct typeface variation for the size in use.

▸ Documents published with several languages next to one another often suffer as the amount of text can change with the language and cause layout problems (for example, more space is needed for the German version than the English). You can use an MM font to change the text width so that all the language versions fit in the same layout.

- Font substitution: Many users receive digital documents to work on, only to find that their system does not have all the necessary fonts. When opening such a document the fonts are often replaced randomly with others, changing the line breaks – the document loses its original character. MM fonts remedy this situation by simulating missing fonts. Adobe, with SuperATM (only for the Mac), offers software to automatically replace missing fonts with similar ones which at least have the same metrics. Font substitution using MM fonts is a core component of Adobe's Acrobat technology (see Chapter 8).
- Animations and morphing using MM fonts have opened up a new field whose boundaries are not yet clear. A pioneer in this area is Luc(as) de Groot with his "porno font" MoveMeMM. In this Multiple Master font, the design axis disguised as optical size is actually an axis in which the letters morph to erotic illustrations!

Fig. 4.13.
Metamorphosis of a letter in the "Porno Font" MoveMeMM

Multiple Masters in practice.   Adobe has implemented MM technology as an extension to the Type 1 format so that MM fonts can also be used on older printers. It's widely held that you need a Level 2 capable printer to use MM fonts, but this is not true. However, there are some facts which can get in the way of using MM fonts successfully. To display the fonts on screen, you need a Multiple Master compatible version of ATM (Version 3.0 or higher on both Mac and Windows). For printing, you need a fully compatible PostScript interpreter; some clones have difficulties (for example, users of Sun NeWSprint report problems). A genuine Adobe interpreter is no guarantee of success: both the Apple LaserWriter NT and the HP Level 1 PostScript Cartridge for LaserJet printers contain an error in the interpreter which affects MM fonts. This problem can manifest itself with the error message *invalidfont*, an incorrect font display or a sudden crash. MM fonts need a lot of memory; your printer might need a RAM upgrade before it can use them.

An MM font can, depending on the number of design axes, generate millions of variations; they cannot be named conventionally, but the parameters used form part of the font name. This gives rise to awkward names like *MyriaMM 492 wt 447 wd*. To enable the user to take his first steps into the tide of font variations, the type designer can use *primary instances* to integrate equivalents to the usual faces (for example, regular, semibold, bold). It must be hoped that applica-

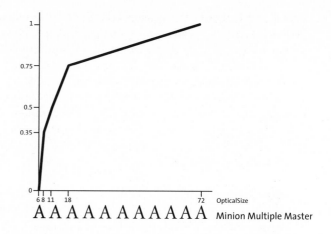

Fig. 4.14.
Multiple Master
Analyzer shows the
parameter range
and limits, in this
case optical size for
MinionMM. The
design differences
are hard to see at
small sizes

tion software will take more and more MM functionality from the user, and make higher level functions available. It's possible that we might see, for example, automatic choice of optical size or a special copyfitting function.

Using ATM you can generate and view as many faces of an MM font as you like, but there is no way of comparing them or getting an overview of what the parameters do. I have written the PostScript program *Multiple Master Analyzer*, which prints out all the design axes of an MM font with examples. Using it, you can for example see that MinionMM's optical size design axis is not linear but is made up of multiple straight segment.

You can find further platform-specific hints on MM fonts in Section 4.3. Although PostScript documents with MM fonts can be printed on all systems, it is at the moment only possible to display and create new variations under Windows or on the Mac.

Multiple Master fonts with a weight axis can have an MMM file entry which describes the difference of the weight parameter between a normal and a bold weight. With such fonts you can click on "Bold" in the ATM control panel's "Create..." menu to create a font with the attribute BOLD, but which really just has an increased weight parameter. For example, by using the bold attribute you can, from ThesisMonoMM_550, create the bold font ThesisMonoMM_750, 200 units heavier. At the upper end of the weight axis there is no difference between normal and bold, as the maximum weight parameter cannot be exceeded. Using this attribute, it is possible to create two identical, but differently named fonts, for example ThesisMonoMM_550 BOLD is identical to ThesisMonoMM_750. The second check box for italic does not generate an italic version using an algorithm, but can only be enabled if a real italic version of the font is available.

4.2.5 The Font Cache. As the characters in most PostScript fonts are described by their outlines, to output a document the PostScript interpreter would have to rasterize the same letter countless thousands of times – an enormous waste of time! Because of this, the PostScript interpreter uses a cache, which in many situations can speed up hardware and software. A cache is a part of the available memory which stores the pixelized versions of characters that have already been rasterized and which makes them available when called again, without having to recalculate them.

As the various sizes are recalculated every time from the outline description, the interpreter saves all used sizes of a letter separately in the font cache. In addition to this, rotated characters have to be treated differently, as bitmaps cannot be be rotated without losing quality (unless the rotation is 90° or a multiple thereof). For each saved character, the font cache has to remember its size, rotation angle, and font name, so that it can correctly identify characters which have already been rasterized. Mix-ups can cause a correct PostScript program to suddenly deliver output with the wrong fonts!

As it would be far too laborious to save the font name along with each character, fonts can be given a unique identification number *(UniqueID)*, which can be used to clearly identify it. However, in the early years of DTP Adobe did not properly coordinate the distribution of these ID numbers, so it can sometimes happen that two fonts have the same number. To solve this problem, the UniqueID was expanded in Level 2 and can in theory be any length, so the total of available numbers is no longer limited. However, few fonts have been numbered with the new scheme in order to maintain Level 1 compatibility.

As long as there are no ID conflicts between various fonts, the font cache speeds up PostScript text output unnoticed. There is one situation in which the cache makes its presence known in an unwelcome manner: when designing and testing a new font. As the contents of the cache are preserved between print jobs, it can happen that a downloadable font is not actually downloaded, but the previous version from the cache is used instead (which usually is exactly what is wanted). If the two fonts concerned are different versions of the same font which you want to test (for example, with altered letter forms), the cache must not be allowed to cut in at all. In this case you will usually only be able to flush the cache by switching the printer off. Tip: some font editors allow you to create fonts without a UniqueID. They only stay in the cache until the end of the current print job, so problems with subsequent print jobs can be avoided. Some printers and RIPs fitted with a hard disk save the font cache's contents on the disk. You cannot flush this cache by switching off, but only by using an appropriate downloader or utility program.

Adobe Type Manager, with which speed (because of its interactive nature) plays a greater role than with printing, also uses a font cache whose size you can change in the ATM Control Panel. Depending on the amount of memory in your computer and the number of fonts in use, you may be able to increase screen display speed dramatically by allocating more memory to the cache. As a rule of thumb, you should reserve 50 KB in the font cache for each frequently used font.

4.3 Installing PostScript Fonts

The actual PostScript data is the same on each operating system, but the packaging of the PS data and extra information (above all the metrics) largely differs between systems. To ensure the cross plat-form exchange of supplementary PostScript font information, Adobe defined a simple format which is valid on all operating systems. Although some information in this section also goes for Type 3 fonts (for example, about font and file names) it mostly relates to Type 1 fonts, as only they can be displayed on screen using ATM.

4.3.1 AFM Files. AFM (*Adobe Font Metrics*) files are an important source of information when working with fonts. They contain, in ASCII plain text (or whatever the software industry thinks is "plain" text) general information about a PostScript font as well as metrics data. Most font manufacturers deliver AFM files with their fonts or at least make them available on request. Here, I want to introduce the most important entries or blocks. The complete specification isn't contained in any of Adobe's PostScript books, but is only available from the *Adobe Developers Association*.

Located at the start of an AFM file is general information about the font. This includes Copyright, font name, weight (normal or bold), italics and various font metrics information:

```
StartFontMetrics 2.0
Comment Copyright (c) 1985, 1987, 1990, 1992 Adobe Systems In-
corporated.  All Rights Reserved.
Comment Creation Date: Fri Jul 24 13:40:47 1992
Comment UniqueID 39729
Comment VMusage 40013 50905
FontName Garamond-Bold
FullName ITC Garamond Bold
FamilyName ITC Garamond
Weight Bold
ItalicAngle 0
IsFixedPitch false
```

...

EncodingScheme AdobeStandardEncoding

The name entries in this part of the AFM file are particularly important, especially with regard to installation under various operating systems. *FamilyName* indicates to which family the font belongs. This is just the basic name. If you add extra information about the style (for example, Italic), weight (for example, SemiBold) and character set (for example, Expert), you get the *FullName* entry. This is the most expressive description and it can contain spaces. The separation of family name and style information is important, so that the application software can treat font names and emphasis separately, without losing the link between them. For example, if you italicized one word in a paragraph and altered the base font for that paragraph, the italicization should be carried forward to the new font. This is not possible if the software does not recognize a link between the normal and italic members of a font family. The same goes for bold fonts, but here the situation is a little more complex as well designed font families contain not just normal and bold, but also a larger variety of weights (such as Light, ExtraLight, Bold, SemiBold, Black, etc.). Some type designers reject automatic choice of a bold face for this reason and require you to choose the font variant directly.

Finally, *FontName* is the name which identifies the font to the PostScript interpreter and because of this is the only one permitted in page descriptions. As shown in the following sections, a PostScript font's name differs between operating systems. *FontName* is the only way of describing the name of a PostScript font in a platform independent manner. For this reason, many DTP programs use this name when exchanging documents between platforms. For compatibility reasons, *FontName* should be limited to 29 characters. The convention is to separate the style (such as *Italic*) from the family name by a hypen character.

After this general part follows detailed metrics information on all characters in the font, both coded and unencoded characters (see Section 4.5):

```
C 32 ; WX 280 ; N space ; B 0 0 0 0 ;
C 33 ; WX 280 ; N exclam ; B 52 -15 229 639 ;
C 65 ; WX 660 ; N A ; B -22 -4 680 639 ;
C 102 ; WX 360 ; N f ; B 10 -2 451 688 ; L i fi ; L l fl ;
C -1 ; WX 760 ; N copyright ; B 63 -15 706 639 ;
C -1 ; WX 560 ; N brokenbar ; B 243 -175 324 675 ;
```

On a separate line for each character follow (the examples relates to the fourth line of the above section):

- ▸ The encoding number of the character (if it is contained in the font's default encoding vector, otherwise -1): C 102

- its width: `WX 360`
- the character name: `N f`
- four values describing the character's BoundingBox: `B 10 -2 451 688`. These values relate to a 1000-unit coordinate system, that is, the total character height including ascenders and descenders is 1000 units.
- After this the character's ligature combinations may follow: `L i fi ; L l fl ;`

The block with the character metrics is followed by the kerning data. In the *KernPairs* block each line contains the name of the two characters to be kerned, together with the amount by which the characters are to be moved together or apart. In most cases, this value is negative, that is the characters are to be moved closer. The kerning block can also hold tracking information, but in practice this is not widely used.

```
KPX A y -23
KPX A w -24
KPX r d 16
KPX r comma -68
```

Finally, the AFM file can contain details about composite characters. This gives application programs information about the positioning of accents relative to the base character (example: A plus ´ gives Á). However, programs rarely use this information:

```
CC Aacute 2 ; PCC A 0 0 ; PCC acute 130 146 ;
CC Acircumflex 2 ; PCC A 0 0 ; PCC circumflex 60 146 ;
CC ydieresis 2 ; PCC y 0 0 ; PCC dieresis 110 0 ;
```

Multiple Master fonts use AMFM files (*Adobe Multiple Master Font Metrics*), an extension to the AFM format which contains information on the parameter axis and master (primary) instances of the font.

4.3.2 Installing Fonts in MS-DOS. As MS-DOS has neither a system-level method of displaying fonts on screen nor a system-wide printer driver, software developers had to keep reinventing the wheel and come up with their own mechanisms to handle fonts and write their own printer drivers; this means that the font installation procedure depends on the software in use.

The font names are always processed by the application program in use, and because of this it is not possible to make a general statement. There is a small extra file with a INF suffix, which contains information for the use of the fonts in some PC applications. It repeats some of the information from the AFM file, such as the font names for Microsoft Word and Ventura Publisher:

```
FontName (Garamond-BoldItalic)
```

```
FullName (ITC Garamond Bold Italic)
FamilyName (ITC Garamond)
...
Serif true
Pi false
MSMenuName (Garamond)
VPMenuName (ITC Garamond)
WORDMenuName (Garamond)
VPTypefaceID 22
VPStyle (T)
```

There is a convention for font names, which can, because of the DOS
file naming limitations, produce rather cryptic file names; it is also
not followed by all manufacturers. The eight characters before the
dot are used like this:

```
1,2:  Font name (ga)
3,4,5:Style (bi_)
6,7:  Point size for bitmap fonts
8:    Device code (various graphics cards)
```

The corresponding parts of the file name *gabi____* are shown in
brackets; they relate to the font *Garamond-BoldItalic*. Irrelevant parts
are replaced with an underscore character _. As only two characters
are reserved for the font name, and MS-DOS is not case sensitive, it's
obvious that this convention cannot be adhered to because of the
limited number of combinations. It is especially annoying that the
last three characters are only meaningful for bitmap fonts and are of
no use for PostScript fonts. MS-DOS and Windows users will have to
put up with unintelligible font names as long as the 8 plus 3 file
names are around!

    The basic file name is extended by three letter suffixes: AFM, INF,
or PFB. The latter stands for *Printer Font Binary*, and it is this file which
contains the actual PostScript instructions.

4.3.3 Installing Fonts in Windows 3.x and Windows 95.

To use PostScript fonts (or more precisely Type 1 fonts) under Windows, you need to have Adobe Type Manager (or one of the competing products which were not successful in the market) to display
them on screen. Since version 3.01, ATM also works under Windows
95, making the installation of PostScript fonts the same under all
ersions of Windows. For several years, ATM lacked support for Windows NT. However, ATM Deluxe 4.0 will support Windows NT 4.0. You
can read more about this version at the end of Section 4.3.5.

    ATM is responsible not just for displaying the fonts on screen, but
also manages the installed fonts with functions for adding or removing them and sends font data to the printer. When using a PostScript

printer, ATM sends it the PostScript data for the font; on non-PostScript printers ATM generates the bitmaps at the desired size itself and sends them to the printer.

The mere PostScript data are not enough to install a new font. ATM requires additional information, above all the width information and kerning tables, but also some additional general information about the font. There are two ways of supplying this additional information: most fonts are delivered with a corresponding PFM (*Printer Font Metrics*) file. This file contains metrics and other font information in a non-readable binary format.

The PFM file is made available by the font manufacturer. If an INF file is available, ATM can extract the data from the AFM file and does not need the PFM file, as the details about the font's Windows name and other categories are contained in the INF file. Both the AFM and INF files are ASCII files which can be modified with a text editor. Do not worry if you cannot install a font under Windows because of a missing PFM file: you can find out what to do by reading Section 4.6.1.

If you want to look at the contents of a PFM file, you can use the shareware program *FontMonster* (unfortunately, this could not be included on the CD-ROM). FontMonster opens the PFM file and shows the entries in easy to view menus. You can also change many of the entries using FontMonster.

The font's PostScript instructions, that is outline descriptions of the individual characters, which ATM and the PostScript interpreter make use of, have to be capable of being sent over 7-bit links and are

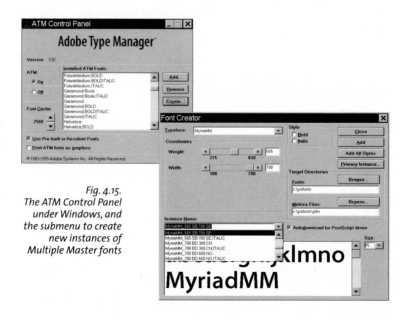

Fig. 4.15.
The ATM Control Panel under Windows, and the submenu to create new instances of Multiple Master fonts

therefore in ASCII format. As this is wasteful with disk space, there is a more compact binary format. This PFB (*Printer Font Binary*) format contains most of the font data in 8-bit form, and only needs about half as much storage space as the ASCII version.

The PFB format is needed to install the font, but cannot be sent directly to the printer. ATM or the printer driver perform the necessary conversions. Font files in ASCII format are referred to as PFA *(Printer Font ASCII)* files. You can convert PFA and PFB files to and from each other using the utilities *t1binary* (PFA to PFB) and *t1ascii* (PFB to PFA) from the *T1 utilities* package, which you can find on the accompanying CD-ROM.

Font and file names.   File names are not really open for discussion under Windows: you have to use DOS filenames for PostScript fonts (see above). The Windows font names – the names under which fonts appear in applications' font menus – are more interesting; they are usually different from the fonts' PostScript names.

Windows 3.0 forced each font family to be grouped into *normal, bold, italic,* and *bold italic.* This scheme might at first glance sound sensible, but is too limiting for larger font families. In this case the font manufacturer has to make the fonts fit the scheme somehow and then draw the user's attention to it. For example, the StoneSans family contains the weights normal, semibold, and bold, each in normal and italic versions. After installation in ATM, these six faces appear in the font menus as two families, *StoneSans* and *StoneSansBold.* The first family contains four faces: when choosing bold you get the normal face of the semibold version, and the same goes for italic and bold italic. The second (Windows) family *StoneSansBold* only contains the *StoneSans-Bold* and *StoneSans-BoldItalic* faces (PostScript font names) and cannot automatically be made bolder. ATM uses the font classification given in the *MSMenuName* entry of the INF file.

A font's PostScript and menu names as well as the bold and italic attributes are contained in the PFM file. As already pointed out, ATM can read the extra information from the PFM file or if need be generate it from the AFM and INF files.

Menu names for fonts under Windows can be up to 31 characters, although Adobe recommends that, for compatibility reasons, a maximum of 30 characters are used.

Copying fonts.   If you try to copy fonts from the hard disk to a diskette, you will find that the obscure file names make it very difficult to select the correct font file. You can check the font file names in *win.ini* or *atm.ini* but the following method makes it easier: start the ATM control panel and click on "Add...". Swap the source and target directories: in the upper part with the list of available fonts choose the directory in which you have installed your fonts (for example, *C:\ps-fonts*), and specify the disk drive as the target directory. If you click on "Add...", ATM will copy the selected fonts PFB and PFM files to the diskette, without you having to worry about the font names. Important: after specifying the diskette you must carry out the process again in the opposite direction, or ATM will look for the fonts on the diskette. Install the copied fonts to the hard disk again. They are already there, but this will make sure that ATM looks for them in the right directory on the hard disk, instead of the diskette.

Font management.   Various manufacturers offer programs to simplify font management under Windows, for example, *Ares FontMinder* or *Font Consultant*. They let you build project-oriented font groups which can be easily installed and uninstalled without using the ATM control panel. Their ease of use and the substitution of actual font names for the awkward file names are very useful, and these programs also get round the download problem when using the Microsoft driver (which is discussed more fully later on). If you often change your font installation, you ought to consider buying a font management program.

ATM Deluxe 4.0, discussed at the end of Section 4.3.5, will incorporate its own font management features for PostScript and TrueType fonts.

Multiple Master fonts.   Since version 3.0 you can also install Multiple Master fonts in ATM. As an MM font always contains multiple instances (individual fonts) which each have their own width and may require different kerning tables, Adobe had to define a new standard for the extra information in an MM font. The MMM (*Multiple Master Metrics*) file also holds information about the MM font design axes which are in use. ATM creates a PFM file for each instance of the font, using the data from the MMM file, to ensure compatibility with printer drivers and application programs.

Installing MM fonts is not, to start with, any different from installing normal fonts: simply choose the required font variation using the ATM control panel. You have to differentiate between the *base font*, for example, *TektoMM*, and the *primary instances*, for example, *Tekto_240 RG 564 NO*. Although both the base font and the primary instance appear in ATM as normal fonts, there is one big difference: only the base font's PFB file (containing the character descriptions) is installed. According to the number of design axes, it can vary in size between 80 and 160 KB. The primary instances reference PSS files which are about 200 bytes in size. These *PostScript stubs* do not contain any character descriptions, but only a reference to the corresponding base font and the MM parameters. For this reason, stubs are of no use on their own: primary instances can only be installed with the corresponding base font. If you remove the base font, you must also remove all the primary instances.

By using "Create..." in the ATM control panel (see Figure 4.15) you can create a new instance of a multiple master font at any time. However, some application programs only build their font menu when the program is started and do not notice when new fonts (or instances) are added. In this case you will have to exit and restart the program. The names of newly created MM fonts with three axes can unfortunately become so long that in some programs they are cut off in the font menu (for example, *MinioMM 367 wt 585 wd 12 op*).

The documentation states that if a document using uninstalled versions of MM fonts is opened, then ATM will generate them, but in practice this is not so. Adobe Illustrator 4.0 for example issues a missing font warning and replaces it on screen with Helvetica, but the "missing" MM font appears fine when printed.

4.3.4 Installing Fonts in OS/2.   OS/2 has contained ATM as part of
the operating system since version 1.3. You can therefore install a new font from the fonts palette in the system configuration folder and do not need a special ATM control panel. The installation of new fonts is hidden behind the rather confusing menu entry "Edit font type", "Add". As usual you have to specify the directory or drive containing the new fonts. OS/2 understands Windows PFB files but expects the metrics information in the form of AFM files, which are converted during installation into a special binary format called OFM *(OS/2 font metrics)*. As Windows fonts are usually supplied with PFB, AFM, and INF files, they can be installed without problems under OS/2. If you only have the PFM file but no AFM file, you can convert it using the procedure described in Section 4.6.3.

When using Windows under OS/2 you must remember that the fonts are installed separately for both environments, that is, to use a font under Win-OS/2 which is already installed in OS/2, you must install it again.

4.3.5 Installing Fonts on the Mac.   ATM also takes care of stScript
font screen display on the Mac. The installation of new fonts is very easy, since System 7: simply drag the PostScript font file and the screen font to the system folder – that's it! The operating system copies the font to the "System extensions" folder (on System 7.0) or to the "Fonts" folder (since System 7.1). PostScript fonts have the type LWFN (LaserWriter font).

You will perhaps wonder why you have to install a bitmap font, if ATM is taking care of screen display: because the font metrics are contained in the bitmap file, you have to install at least one size of the bitmap version. You only need to use the ATM control panel to, for example, change the size of the font cache, and to create Multiple Master instances.

The FOND resource.   The bitmap font file contains, in the FOND resource, general information about the font, metrics tables, pointers to the corresponding bitmaps (in NFNT resources), as well as the PostScript names of all the fonts in each font family in the *Style Mapping Table*. As the FOND resource can also contain the metrics tables for all "family members", to install a whole font family it suffices to install one file for each PostScript typeface and one bitmap file for each family.

The POST resource.   The PostScript font file contains the actual PostScript instructions for the font, not in plain text, but in several POST resources. ATM or the printer driver extract these resources if they need to display this font on screen or send it to the printer. A more precise description of the POST format can be found in the file *details.pdf* on the accompanying CD-ROM. You can extract the POST resource using the Mac program *unadobe* which you will also find on the accompanying CD-ROM. In Section 4.6.1 you can also find out out how to convert the resource format to a Windows font.

Font management.   Using System 7.1 you can have up to 128 font suitcases in the Fonts folder. As one suitcase can contain pointers to all the PostScript fonts in a family, consolidating fonts to families increases the number of fonts which can be installed. You should bear in mind that installed fonts not only use main memory, but can also slow down the loading of the system and applications. Word processors and DTP programs build their font menus when started by querying available fonts from the system. Therefore you should only install those fonts which you actually need for a project. Programs like *Suitcase* and *MasterJuggler* can help here. You can use them to consolidate fonts to groups, and then simply install and uninstall the groups.

At the end of this section you'll find some remarks on ATM Deluxe 4.0 which sports font management features, too.

Font and file names.   The names in the font menus are derived from the corresponding FOND resources. These names can be up to 31 characters long, but for compatibility reasons Adobe recommends using a maximum of 30 characters. In System 7 the font names must also not overlap in the first 28 letters. As the font menus on earlier Mac programs were often so narrow that the style at the end of the font name (*bold, italic,* etc.) were often not visible, old fonts have a style abbrevi-

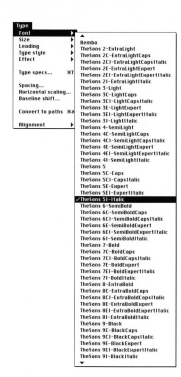

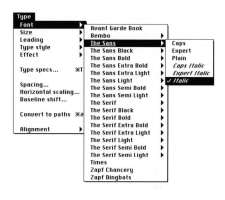

Fig. 4.16.
Adobe Type Reunion
(right) ensures clear
font menu entries for
all Mac programs

ation (*B, I*, etc.) at the beginning. This solution has, among others, the disadvantage that the fonts are no longer sorted alphabetically, as the style abbreviation confuses the sort procedure.

This style convention is no longer used as the utility program *Adobe Type Reunion* has made the font menus much easier to use. The program interprets the PostScript font names in the FOND resource and replaces the normal font menu with a more compact one in which all the fonts are sorted by family, and the individual weights in each family appear in a submenu. This only works if each member of the font family has its own FOND resource. Type Reunion uses the hyphen in PostScript font names to differentiate between family name and style attribute. The attribute *Condensed* is an exception, as it is counted as part of the family name, even if placed after the hyphen.

Finally, PostScript font files are named according to the 5:3:3 rule. To apply this rule, the PostScript name of the font (from the FOND resource *Style Mapping Table*) is split into several words, which always begin with the next capital letter. Hyphens, if present, are ignored. *Helvetica-BoldOblique*, for example, gives the words *Helvetica*, *Bold*, and *Oblique*. You take the first five letters of the first word and the first three letters of the following words to get the file name: *HelveBolObl*. This rule can result in different fonts having the same file names; in this case you cannot install them at the same time.

Multiple Master fonts. The Mac was the first system to use Multiple Master technology. The MM capable versions of ATM (3.0 and higher) are supported by the program *Font Creator* which makes it possible to create new variations of installed MM fonts. MM fonts store the design axis information in the BLND resource.

Due to the earlier appearance of MM technology on the Mac compared to Windows, there are already some Mac programs with direct support for Multiple Master fonts. For example, Adobe Illustrator calls FontCreator from the font menu to create new faces *on the fly*. When it opens a graphic which needs an uninstalled MM font, Illustrator has the font generated automatically, as long as the corresponding basic MM font is installed.

QuickDraw GX. The Mac graphic model has been extended by GX (*Graphical Extension*) , which makes it easier to use enhanced typographical functions. QuickDraw GX contains rasterizers for TrueType and Type 1 fonts; the Type 1 rasterizer can also cope with Multiple Master fonts. The *Line Layout Manager* (LLM), which takes care of text output under GX, also looks after, amongst other things, context-sensitive character substitution, such as the automatic insertion of ligatures, fractions and small caps. Of course, the font in use also has to contain these special characters. QuickDraw GX allows the user more precise control over letter spacing than previously by using intelligent kerning and tracking. Finally, Multiple Master style font

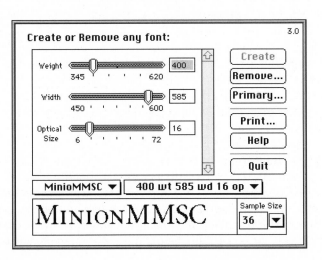

Fig. 4.17.
Creating a new
MM variant on the
Mac using Font
Creator

variations are also possible with TrueType fonts; under QuickDraw GX they are called *Style Variations*.

To implement all these functions, an extension to the Mac Type 1 font format was necessary. The new GX fonts contain (in the sfnt resource) various tables to control character substitution and orientation. So that LLM can access the individual character descriptions directly, Type 1 fonts can no longer be encrypted. When changing to QuickDraw GX the *Type 1 GX Enabler* utility takes care of converting existing Type 1 fonts to the new format.

ATM Deluxe 4.0. At the time of writing ATM 4.0 was not available. Judging from Adobe's announcements, this version will be loaded with new features. ATM Deluxe 4.0 will supposedly be released in summer 1996 and support the Macintosh, Windows 95, and Windows NT 4.0 platforms.

ATM's font rendering algorithm was enhanced to allow anti-aliasing (Adobe calls it "font smoothing") which has advantages for online documents and presentations (anti-aliasing is also implemented in Acrobat 3.0).

Adobe also integrated font management in ATM. It is not restricted to Type 1 fonts but also supports TrueType. You can group fonts in font sets which can be installed and activated together. These font sets are compatible across platforms.

Font substitution, formerly only implemented in SuperATM for the Mac, uses a font database to substitute missing fonts with Multiple Master fonts (similar to font substitution in Acrobat). This mechanism preserves line and page breaks when opening a document for which the necessary fonts are not available. Font substitution now also works in the Windows version of ATM.

4.3.6 Installing Fonts in the X Window System. The X Window System allows the use of PostScript fonts in various configurations:

- ► A workstation whose display is served by an X server with an integrated Type 1 rasterizer.
- ► A font server, running on any machine on the network and supplying workstations or X terminals with font data (for example, HP-UX 9.0, NCD).
- ► Display PostScript or X server with the DPS extension (for example, Solaris, OSF/1, AIX, SGI-Irix).
- ► Integrated version of ATM (for example, Onsite SVR4.2)

As already mentioned, since Release 5 a Type 1 rasterizer has been available for the X Window system, but it is not supplied by all manufacturers. If the X server you are using does not support the Type 1 format, the font server *fs* can help. It greatly simplifies font configu-

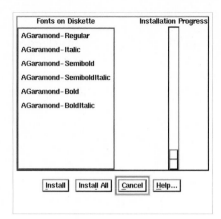

Fig. 4.18.
Easy PostScript font
installation under
Unix System V,
Release 4.2

ration on a Unix network. It makes rasterized font data available across the network, even to servers which cannot directly use Type 1 format. In addition, it makes possible the integration of new font formats without having to install a new X server. This is useful for X terminals on which new server software cannot be loaded or isn't available.

On some Unix derivatives, such as SVR4.2, it is just as easy to install new PostScript fonts as on the Mac or Windows PC: after inserting a new DOS format font diskette (with PFB and AFM files) the font manager recognizes the fonts which it contains and offers their PostScript names for installation. The font manager takes care of all the steps necessary to install the fonts in the X Window system.

Installing fonts manually. Unfortunately, the automatic installation of PostScript fonts is an exception. As with most Unix topics, there are minor differences between systems, for example, the path names used. We assume that the font files are available in ASCII (PFA) format. Such fonts can be found on many Internet FTP servers. In Section 4.6.3 you can read how to prepare fonts from other platforms for use under Unix. You do not need the corresponding AFM file to install a font under X, but it makes it easier to construct the X file name (see below); if the fonts are to be used in a DTP or graphics program, the software will need information about the character metrics. The integration of fonts into applications varies from package to package, but usually requires the AFM files.

The relationship of font file names to the corresponding X11 font names is determined by the file *fonts.dir,* which must be present in each font directory. This ASCII file contains the number of fonts which it describes in its first line and after that each line contains the

Example	Meaning	Comments, corresponding AFM entries
FontShop	Manufacturer	Copyright or Notice
TheSans	Font name	FamilyName without manufacturer's name
Bold	Weight	Weight
r	Angle: r=regular, i=italic	Usually can be determined from FullName, for italic fonts the ItalicAngle is negative.
- -	Style: sans/serif	often left empty
0	Font size in pixels	0 for scaleable fonts, sometimes (for compatibility with old programs) 12
0	Font size in 1/10 point	0 for scaleable fonts, sometimes (for compatibility with old programs) 120
0	horizontal resolution in dpi	0 for scalable fonts
0	vertical resolution in dpi	0 for scalable fonts
p	p=proportional, m=monospaced	IsFixedPitch=true means monospaced
0	average character width	usually 0 (is ignored)
iso8859-1	Character set/ encoding	If EncodingScheme has the value AdobeStandardEncoding, the font can be encoded according to iso8859-1; if it is FontSpecific use "adobe-fontspecific" instead

name of a font file and the corresponding X11 font name. The latter is built according to the XLFD (*X Logical Font Description*) convention, which can give rather long and clumsy font names. Because of this it would be easiest if you could create this file automatically (as for bitmap fonts) using the program *mkfontdir*. However, on most systems this utility cannot process Type 1 files, so you have to construct the X font names yourself. One notable exception is HP-UX: the *stmkdirs* tool recognizes PFA files and creates the required entries in *fonts.dir*.

The table explains the meaning of the individual entries in an XLFD font name using Thesis as an example. The table also contains some comments on constructing the values using the AFM file. The XLFD font name in the example is:

```
FontShop-TheSans-Bold-r-normal--0-0-0-0-p-0-iso8859-1.
```

As the individual entries are a little bit ambiguous, some human intervention is usually required (that is, XLFD construction cannot be fully automated). If there is no AFM file available, you can also find some information at the start of the font file (before the encrypted *eexec* section).

The last two fields of the XLFD name, which describe the font's character set, are the most interesting. The entries *iso8859-1* for West European language text fonts or *adobe-fontspecific* for symbol fonts cover most cases, but on some systems (with suitable fonts) "exotic" character sets can also be installed, You can find details in Section 4.5.2. For our sample Thesis installation, *fonts.dir* looks like this:

```
144
FontShop-TheSans-Bold-r-normal--0-0-0-0-p-0-iso8859-1
FontShop-TheSerif-Bold-r-normal--0-0-0-0-p-0-iso8859-1
...similar entries for the remaining 142 faces...
```

The entries in *fonts.dir* are the most difficult part of the font installation. Next, you must register the new fonts on the server. Experienced X users will know the command by heart:

```
xset +fp /the/font/file/directory
xset fp rehash
```

This command makes the server read *fonts.dir* and make the newly installed fonts available to programs.

If you want to use the font server *fs*, you will have to enter the new font directory into the configuration file (usually */usr/lib/X11/fonts/fs/config*) and restart *fs* or "kill" it with the HANGUP signal, so that it reads the configuration file again. Every X server on the network

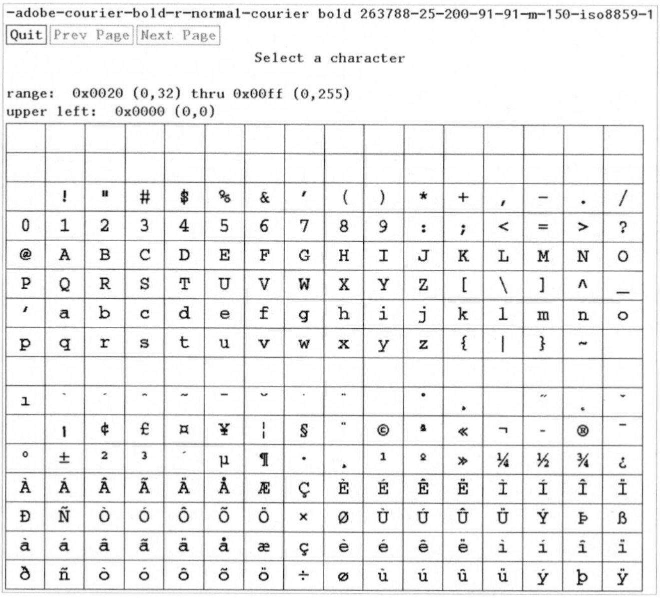

Fig. 4.19.
xfd display a newly installed font

138 | Chapter 4: PostScript Fonts

(workstation or X terminal), which is to use the new fonts, is made aware of the existence of the fontserver with these commands:

```
xset +fp tcp/Harkie:7000
xset fp rehash
```

Harkie is the name of the computer on which the font server is running, and 7000 is the port address. (Most font servers use this standard port number.) If X servers or the font server return an error message after the first *xset* call, it could mean that Type 1 functionality is not implemented. This makes the outlook bad for your PostScript fonts.

You can check the successful installation immediately using the programs *xfontsel*, *xfd* or *xlsfonts* which should offer the new font names or display the new fonts. The font server also makes it possible to easily convert Type 1 fonts to the BDF format for systems which can only use bitmap fonts: the command *fstobdf* fetches a rasterized version of the font from the font server and generates the corresponding BDF file.

Font and file names. You have already seen above how to construct the name of a font in the X Window system from a font's AFM properties. But this long XLFD name is not necessarily the name which you, as the user, see in applications. As fonts are not installed globally under Unix, but only appear, via the X Window system, on screen, it depends on the application how the useable fonts are configured and presented to the user. Simple applications can make do with the XLFD names, but programs with higher typographic requirements split the font names into their components (family, weight, angle, width, etc.) and allow these components to be chosen separately.

As almost all Unix systems allow long file names, font files often use the PostScript font name as the file name. Some applications can only find fonts if this convention is adhered to. However, fonts installed from MS-DOS disks often use the original cryptic file name. If you want to rename a font file (for a better overview, or because an application requires it), you can find the corresponding PostScript names in the AFM or INF file under the key word *FontName*. If neither of these files are available, you can also work out the name from the font's PFA or PFB file:

```
grep FontName Fontfile.pfa
```

The PostScript name appears after the *FontName* key, following the "/" character which is not part of the name.

The table in Section 7.2.2 shows the names of the directories for various systems (with and without Display PostScript) where fonts are installed by default.

4.3.7 Installing Fonts in Display PostScript. In DPS/X the fonts as well as AFM files, character sets, and prologs are treated as resources. There are unified installation and search procedures for such resource; they are described in detail in Section 7.2.2.

4.4 Downloading PostScript Fonts

4.4.1 Manual Versus Automatic Download. When printing a document, the interpreter must have access to all PostScript fonts used in the document. Printing is not stopped if a font definition is missing, but the interpreter replaces the missing font with Courier, which very likely results in a useless printout. There are several ways of making fonts available to the printer's interpreter:

- ▶ The document only uses fonts which are permanently available to the printer. These can be built into the printer ROM or stored on a hard disk which is directly connected to the printer (*permanently loaded fonts*). A list of built-in fonts can be printed out with some downloaders (see the next section), referred to in the printer handbook or worked out from the printer's PPD file.

- ▶ Fonts which are present in printer RAM and available until it is next switched off (*resident* fonts).

- ▶ Fonts whose definition is sent to the printer as part of the print job (*inline* fonts).

- ▶ The PostScript file contains no fonts, but only pointers with the names of the required fonts (DSC comments). The print spooler interprets these pointers before sending the data to the printer, compares them with the fonts available in the printer, and then loads any additional fonts required.

In the first case there is from the user's point of view nothing further to do, as all the required fonts are already in the printer. Otherwise, you mostly have the choice of two methods: either you send the required fonts manually to the device before printing (download them) and make them *resident,* or let the software load all the fonts automatically together with the actual page description. Both methods have advantages and disadvantages. You should bear in mind that font files are between 30 and 60 KB large, and sending them to the printer takes time – which can slow down printing.

In the case of *manual download* you only have to send the fonts to the printer once. They are installed as memory resident using special PostScript instructions and remain available until the printer is turned off. All the documents which are printed up to then and which require these fonts are therefore freed from the "ballast" of font definitions and are printed more quickly.

This method has the disadvantage that responsibility for making the fonts available passes from the software to the user, which makes printing more complicated and more prone to errors. The fonts' memory requirement also plays a role: if several users share a printer and all use different fonts, the printer memory is often not sufficient to hold all the required fonts at the same time. This is also the case if, as a single user, you wish to print several documents with different fonts. In this case, manual downloading is not suitable.

With *automatic download* the software which generates the Post-Script commands (application software or printer driver) ensures that the page description – that is, the PostScript file – contains all the required fonts. It may happen that fonts are loaded unnecessarily, as they are already present in the printer, but on the other hand the user no longer has to worry about font handling.

The best solution is a spooler, which sits between the PostScript driver and the printer: it recognizes the font requests from the print files, checks which fonts are already present and loads any which are additionally required. With a little extra intelligence it even recognizes the most-used fonts and and loads them as resident, to speed up data transfer. This all sounds very interesting, but is in the realms of fantasy for most users: there is extra software which goes in this direction, but an intelligent spooler as part of the operating system will remain on the wish list for some time. You can find further details in Chapter 2.

Concerning download of Multiple Master fonts, you shouldn't forget that an MM font always requires the corresponding *base font*. Instances derived from it do not contain the letter shapes, but only a pointer to the base font and the design axes parameters. Special Post-Script instructions in these mini font files generate new instances from the base font as required. For printing, it suffices if the base font is available to the printer. This does not work in the opposite direction: if a PostScript file contains an instance but not the base font, a PostScript error occurs. For this reason if you see the following error message when working with MM fonts:

```
Error: undefined, Offending Command: makeblendedfont
```

then the printer cannot access the base font and you will have to download it to the printer manually (even if it is not used in the document). To avoid problems like this, Adobe recommends that manual download is not used at all with MM fonts, but to integrate all the required fonts directly into the PostScript output using the printer driver.

To store fonts on the printer's hard disk, use a special hard disk down-loader or the PostScript program *diskload.ps* from the accompanying CD-ROM.

4.4.2 Memory Requirements for Fonts.

Each downloaded font requires space in the printer's (limited) RAM. This means that you cannot download as many fonts as you want, but only a limited number according to the amount of printer RAM: six to eight (on a personal 300 dpi laser) or up to several dozen on a well-equipped departmental printer. The exact number of fonts which can be load-ed depends on many factors and unfortunately cannot be predicted accurately; if you get the error message *VMerror* during font down-loading, you have exceeded the limit!

The memory required by each font depends on the number and complexity of the characters which it contains and is not the same as the font file size. Most font files have a comment like this at the be-ginning:

```
%%VMusage:  41576  52468
```

These two values indicate how much memory the font needs in the interpreter. Due to the internal workings of the PostScript interpreter (object names are reused in memory) the memory requirement the first time a font is loaded is higher than when the same font is loaded a second time. The two values describe this situation. The second number shows the amount of memory needed the *first* time the font is loaded. For most fonts this is between 30 and 60 KB. Multiple Mas-ter fonts are the most memory hungry. According to the number of design axes they may require between 100 and 160 KB!

When talking about the available printer memory, you should not be misled by the amount of installed RAM (usually several MB), but only take into account the amount of memory left free by the inter-preter (the rest serves as, for example, frame buffer to store the page description). The useable fraction is about ten percent of the total memory, at most a few hundred KB. You can find this value after the key word *FreeVM* in the printer's PPD file. In addition, the size of the virtual memory can be worked out using the PostScript program *info.ps* from the accompanying CD-ROM or using various utility programs (such as the Apple LaserWriter utility program).

Here is an example which should be treated with caution because of all the possibilities involved: a 600 dpi printer with 6 MB of RAM has, according to the PPD file, 600 KB of memory free. If we deduct 100 KB for the actual page description and assume an average memo-ry requirement per font of 70 KB, we come to a total of seven fonts which can be loaded into the printer at the same time.

```
ADOBE FONT DOWNLOADER: Selecting Fonts For Downloading

Fonts available for downloading      Fonts available in printer

  BaskervilleBE-Italic                 AGaramond-Bold
  BaskervilleBE-Medium                 AGaramond-BoldItalic
  BaskervilleBE-MediumItalic           AGaramond-Italic
  BaskervilleBE-Regular                AGaramond-Regular
  Boton-Italic                         AGaramond-Semibold
  Boton-Medium                         AGaramond-SemiboldItalic
  Boton-MediumItalic                   AvantGarde-Book
  Boton-Regular                        AvantGarde-BookOblique
  Boulevard                            AvantGarde-Demi
  Brush                                AvantGarde-DemiOblique
                                       Bookman-Demi
                                       Bookman-DemiItalic
  Printer memory available: 341 KB     Bookman-Light

  ⬆ ⬇ PgUp PgDown will scroll through lists of fonts
  ENTER key will either select or deselect a font
  Select: D<o, R<eturn to main menu, or Q<uit program
```

Fig. 4.20.
The downloader
psdown for the
serial interface

The Adobe driver and some other PostScript drivers are capable of loading an unlimited number of fonts. The driver uses a trick to do this: it always takes into account the memory required by fonts which are already loaded. As soon as it approaches the memory limit, it deletes fonts which are already loaded to make way for new ones. This technique does slow down printing, but avoids the fatal *VMerror* message.

4.4.3 Downloading Fonts in MS-DOS.

Automatic font download under MS-DOS must be carried out by whichever software is in use, so there are not many opportunities for more control – MS-DOS users can only dream of an intelligent print spooler. This means that the only interesting option is manual download. Adobe includes two font downloaders with many font packages. Which one you can use depends on which printer interface you are using: *pcsend* for the parallel interface, or *psdown* for the serial interface. Both can download fonts as resident to printer RAM or to the printer's hard disk.

Fonts can be loaded as resident using *pcsend* or sent to the printer with a PostScript file so that they are only available for one job and are then removed from memory. *pcsend* is controlled by command line options, which makes it easy to automate downloading. Assuming that you use a limited number of fonts for all your print jobs, you can load them into the printer when you boot your PC by adding a suitable line to the *autoexec.bat* file. They will be available until the printer is switched off. *pcsend* has the disadvantage that you have to specify the font file names (and not the more intelligible font names).

The program *psdown* for the serial interface, on the other hand, works interactively: you can choose various functions from a menu and can see the full PostScript font names (no wrestling with the cryptic file names). Apart from the interactive method, there is another important difference between the two downloaders: *psdown* creates a bidirectional link via the serial interface and receives information from the printer. Because of this, you can display a list of all the fonts available in the printer and keep an eye on available memory. *psdown* also offers facilities for restarting the printer, printing a list of available fonts, and naturally also to transfer a PostScript file.

Download without a downloader.   You do not absolutely need a downloader to make fonts resident in the printer or to transfer a PostScript file. In principle all you have to do is copy the data to the relevant port with the *copy* command. Care must be taken, as Type 1 files are stored under MS-DOS in the compact PFB format which the printer cannot use directly. The program *t1ascii* from the T1-Utilities on the accompanying CD-ROM converts this binary format to 7-bit ASCII, which can be sent to the printer without problems.

Example: you want to use the font StoneSerif, stored in the file sr_____.pfb. Firstly, create the corresponding ASCII file:

```
t1ascii sr_____.pfb > sr_____.pfa
```

To make this font resident in the printer, send the PFA file, bracketed by the files *resident.ps* and *eof.ps*, which you will also find on the CD-ROM, to the appropriate port:

```
copy /b resident.ps+sr_____.pfa+eof.ps lpt1:
```

The /b option stops the copy command from adding an end-of-file marker (Ctrl-Z) to the file. A small batch file *down.bat* with the following contents saves typing and storage space for the PFA files:

```
copy /b resident.ps %2
t1ascii %1 > %2
copy /b eof.ps %2
```

The command is then simply:

```
down sr_____.pfb lpt1
```

You might have to configure a printer connected to a serial port using the *mode* command; the syntax for transfer via the second serial port at 9600 Baud, no parity, eight data bits and one stop bit is:

```
mode com2: 96,N,8,1
```

The Ctrl-D character in *eof.ps* is important: if it is missing you will not only provoke a *timeout error*, but also risk making your print files resident, which will quickly clog the printer memory.

If you are not making a font resident, but only want to send it with a print job, simply copy the font and the print file to the port:

```
copy /b sr_____.pfa+chap_1.ps lpt1:
```

There is even a way to download fonts to the printer's hard disk without a downloader: use the program *writedisk.ps* from the CD-ROM to

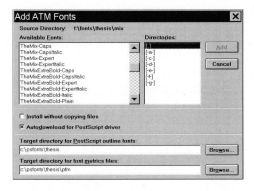

Source Directory: f:\fonts\thesis\mix

Available Fonts:
TheMix-Caps
TheMix-CapsItalic
TheMix-Expert
TheMix-ExpertItalic
TheMixExtraBold-Caps
TheMixExtraBold-CapsItalic
TheMixExtraBold-Expert
TheMixExtraBold-ExpertItalic
TheMixExtraBold-Italic
TheMixExtraBold-Plain

Directories:
[...]
[-a-]
[-c-]
[-d-]
[-e-]
[-f-]
[-g-]

Add
Cancel

□ Install without copying files
☒ Autodownload for PostScript driver

Target directory for PostScript outline fonts:
c:\psfonts\thesis   Browse...

Target directory for font metrics files:
c:\psfonts\thesis\pfm   Browse...

Fig. 4.21.
Installing new
fonts in ATM

save fonts on the hard disk. Enter the PostScript name of the font in
the correct place in this file, then send both writedisk.ps and the ASCII
font file together to the printer.

4.4.4 Downloading Fonts in Windows 3.x and Windows 95.
Downloading fonts in Windows 3.x and Windows 95 is a joint effort
by application software, printer driver, ATM and the user. This mix-
ture allows some degree of control, but is also a potential source of
errors.

Automatic download.   When installing new fonts, ATM offers a
checkbox to allow automatic downloaded. Automatic download is
the default; that is, the font descriptions are part of the print file. As
already noted, the print job then proceeds smoothly, but the fonts
hugely increase the size of the print job; under some circumstances
the PC sends fonts to the printer even if they are not needed.

Manual download.   To manually download fonts under Windows
you can use the same methods as for MS-DOS, described above. This
might sound masochistic, but does make sense; for example, if you
want to automate the download procedure and load all required
fonts at boot time using *autoexec.bat*.
    If you often change your font configuration, a proper Windows
downloader is naturally easier to use. Adobe supplies the downloader
windown with some fonts and application software and along with
the AdobePS printer driver. Some other manufacturers also supply
downloaders with their printers. The Apple LaserWriter comes with
the LaserWriter utility program in versions for both Mac and Windows. If you do not have a download program, you will find the program *winpsx* for Windows on the accompanying CD-ROM.
    With *windown* you load fonts, which are installed under Windows,
via a serial or parallel interface (unfortunately, the program cannot
use network interfaces) to the printer and also carry out other tasks

like transferring PostScript files. You cannot use the Adobe down-loader to send uninstalled fonts in PFB format to the printer. In this case you should switch to *winpsx* or one of the DOS methods de-scribed above.

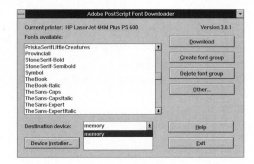

Fig. 4.22.
The Adobe
downloader for
Windows

Windown shows the PostScript names of all installed fonts in its main window – somewhat confusing for extensive font families, as the PostScript font names do not necessarily agree with the names in the Windows font menu (see Section 4.3.1).

Windown keeps track of downloaded fonts: the program saves the names of the loaded fonts and makes sure that the printer driver does not send them again. Every time it is called, it reminds the user that Windows is expecting particular fonts to already be in the print-er. The user has to either confirm this or choose to send the fonts to the printer again. This rather clumsy process is needed because the downloader does not communicate directly with the printer to check the available fonts. It only notices the loaded fonts, but cannot tell if the printer has been turned off in the meantime. This "memory func-tion" is very useful, but only works if you remember to launch the downloader!

The pairing of downloader and printer driver has the advantage that fonts which you have already downloaded manually are not au-tomatically sent to the printer again. This means that you can easily decide at any time, without editing *ini* files or other configuration settings, which fonts to send manually to the printer.

Fig. 4.23.
Windown's
"memory"
feature

As the downloader does not have a bidirectional connection to the printer, it cannot check the stored fonts. In addition, this defect shows up in memory management: the downloader cannot work out the free printer memory to find out whether or not more fonts can be loaded or whether the memory is already full. Because of this, *windown* uses a simple strategy: after downloading five fonts a warning appears (independent of the make and memory configuration of the printer) that the printer memory might be full. The user has to confirm this message for each subsequent font. It would be more elegant if the downloader took into account the printer in use, or at least its memory configuration (see also the hints in Section 4.4.2).

Download using the Microsoft driver for Windows 3.x.   With the Microsoft driver the loading of fonts cannot be controlled with menu entries, but it is necessary to edit *win.ini* instead. This file contains a section for every installed printer (and possibly port) such as [PostScript, LPT1]. These sections contain information about the installed PostScript fonts, inserted by ATM:

```
softfonts=77
softfont1=c:\psfonts\pfm\gabi____.pfm,
softfont2=c:\psfonts\pfm\pr_____.pfm,c:\psfonts\pr_____.pfb
...
```

The first entry shows the total number of installed soft fonts and then follows a line for each font. Each line contains a pointer to the relevant PFM file with a complete pathname and optionally a pointer to the PFB file, that is the actual downloaded font. The Microsoft driver will only send fonts to the printer if the line in win.ini contains both the PFM file and the PFB file. If you want to send fonts to the printer manually, you will have to remove the part of the line after the comma using a text editor. There are some utilities which take care of the tiresome editing of *win.ini* and which provide a convenient front end for font management.

An evil trap opens if the interface is changed. If you, for example, use the Control Panel to connect a printer to FILE instead of LPT1, a different entry in win.ini is responsible for the fonts: this may contain different font settings or the same PFM files without download entries. The danger arises that a file which your own PostScript printer prints fine may suddenly not contain the required fonts!

The Microsoft driver attempts to reduce the amount of memory required by the printer by using fonts which it has already downloaded for one page of a document on another page without downloading them again – a clear breach of DSC rules. If the document is printed in a different order, font descriptions may be missing. In this case, activate the driver's DSC option (you will find it under "Advanced..." in the driver setup. In addition, you can enter the amount of available memory if, for example, you have installed more RAM in your printer.

Download under Windows 95. Unfortunately the Windows 95 PostScript driver does not have an integrated downloader, and the Adobe downloader for Windows 3.x refuses to work under Windows 95, returning the lame "Font database error". Therefore you have to hope that the printer driver downloads the required font itself, or install a separate downloader. Another possibility is to edit the font entries in win.ini – a process which is decidedly not user friendly.

4.4.5 Downloading Fonts on the Mac. The printer driver uses the bidirectional AppleTalk connection with the printer to check which fonts are already present in the printer and which fonts are missing and have to be downloaded. This avoids the problem of fonts which are already present being downloaded again (unlike the Windows driver). Although this automatic download works in all situations, manual font download does have speed advantages. Suitable utilities for doing this include the *LaserWriter Utility program*. It is supplied by Apple with all LaserWriter printers and allows not just the loading of fonts and normal PostScript files but also offers various ways to access special printer control functions. Using the LaserWriter utility you can send any PostScript fonts to the printer including ones which are not installed in the system.

4.4.6 Downloading Fonts in Unix. Whether or not you have installed PostScript fonts under X11, you need to be able to send PostScript fonts from your computer's hard disk to the printer. Whilst there are easy-to-use downloaders for Mac and Windows, under Unix you have to do everything yourself. Downloading is however very straightforward; providing that the printer port is correctly configured and served by a backend or spooler, you only need to send the font data to *lp* or *lpr*. Decide first whether to make the fonts resident in the printer (available until it is switched off) or whether they are only required for one print job. In the first case send the font files to the printer using the program *resident.ps*, which you will find on the accompanying CD-ROM:

```
cat resident.ps TheSans.pfa TheSerif.pfa | lp
```

Note that if the fonts are to stay resident, you must send the files together as *one* job. If the fonts are only needed to print one document, making the font resident is not necessary. Simply send the font file to the printer before the PostScript file (again, bundled together as one job):

```
cat TheSans.pfa TheSerif.pfa chapter_1.ps | lp
```

If you want to use fonts in the Windows format, use the *t1ascii* utility to convert them to PFA format (see Section 4.6.3) before you send them to the printer:

```
(cat resident.ps; t1ascii TheSans.pfb) | lp
```

4.5 Character Sets and Encoding

4.5.1 Character Sets.   PostScript fonts can be used on many different platforms; they cannot therefore be limited to the character set used by any particular operating system or application program. Individual characters in a font are therefore referred to by descriptive names rather than numbers; they are usually derived from the meaning of the character (see examples). For fonts which are made up of symbols or pictograms it's not so easy to allocate names. While, for example, the *Carta* font has names for each of its map symbols, the symbols in ZapfDingbats simply have numbers as "names".

To use the fonts successfully on different platforms, two conditions must be met: on the one hand it is necessary to have some mechanism that arranges the characters in the order in which they are used on the target system. In addition, a font must contain all the characters which are available to the user on that operating system.

PostScript uses the *encoding vector* to arrange the character set in a font. When it outputs a character, the interpreter receives a single byte between 0 and 255. This number refers to an entry in the font's encoding vector. This is a data structure which contains 256 named entries; these names describe the character set of the font. Using the

A	WKing	fi	hiking	seven
Courier	*Cheq*	*TheSans-Italic*	*Carta*	*Palatino*

alpha	m	copyright	Schiwete	a12
Symbol	*Letterine*	*Scala*	*TimesCyrillic*	*ZapfDingbats*

Fig. 4.24.
Some examples of character names in various fonts. The character's name and font are shown under each glyph

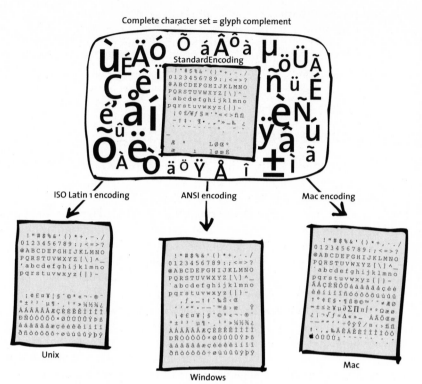

Fig. 4.25.
Re-encoding a font
by applying a new
encoding vector
to the font's
character set

names from the encoding vector, the interpreter then accesses the character definition containing the glyph's outline description. If the font contains no character with the requested name, the interpreter outputs the substitute character *.notdef* which is usually an empty space. The CharStrings Dictionary contains all the characters which belong to the font. The group of all characters available in a font is called character set or glyph complement. The CharStrings Dictionary is a requirement for Type 1 fonts; for Type 3 fonts the data structures and their names are not fixed. In PostScript Level 2 characters from the character set can be addressed directly, bypassing the encoding vector (see Section 5.5.6).

It is vitally important for the flexibility of the character arrangement that a PostScript file should be able to modify the encoding vector of a font. This process is called re-encoding – a mandatory exercise for all PostScript driver developers. So that a font can also be used without re-encoding, all PostScript fonts in their unmodified form must contain a default encoding vector. Application software or the PostScript driver re-encodes the font if necessary, so that it uses the respective operating system's character set. Text fonts usually use *StandardEncoding* as default encoding. This encoding is very thinly populated and does not match the character set used by any of the current operating systems. In practice it is only useful for plain English text, as it doesn't contain many special characters. A text font therefore usually has to be re-encoded by the printer driver.

The distinction between character set and encoding has big advantages:

▸ PostScript documents can be printed in any character set. This is true not only for the most widely used operating systems (Mac, MS-DOS/Windows, Unix, and OS/2), but also mainframes using the EBCDIC character set.

▸ Application software may position extra characters (for example, ligatures).

▸ A font may contain more than 256 characters. However, it is necessary to use multiple encoding vectors to access more than 256 characters.

▸ Special characters can be integrated without problems into 7-bit output (for example, an ASCII variant with umlauts).

▸ Foreign language software versions re-encode fonts for their requirements (for example, the Russian version of Windows).

The character set or glyph complement. The font designer must ensure that a (latin) text font contains all the characters for the most important languages. A character set has emerged which is suitable for most western languages. This standard character set includes 228 characters (plus the *.notdef* substitute character for undefined characters). The fonts in some very old PostScript printers contain 23 characters less, which either (according to the driver in use) go missing during printing or are replaced by the printer (usually by a small square). The majority of text fonts contain this standard glyph complement, which includes those characters needed by the Mac, Windows and Unix character sets. However, the Mac character set includes some Greek and math characters, which are not included in normal latin fonts. The driver takes them instead from the *Symbol* font.

As each operating system only presents a PostScript font encoded with that platform's encoding, the question arises of how to determine the range of available characters in a font. There are several ways of achieving this:

▸ A font's AFM file contains information on all the characters in the font, including the unencoded ones. It lists all characters along with their names and encoding vector positions (if the character is not included in the font's default encoding, the code is listed as -1).

- ▸ If you do not have the AFM file, but can establish a bidirectional link with a PostScript interpreter, you can use the PostScript instructions in the file *charname.ps* on the accompanying CD-ROM to create a list of the range of characters in a font.

- ▸ A Level 2 printer can use the program *allglyph.ps* to print out a list of all available characters (see Section 5.5.6).

- ▸ The *prfont.ps* utility from the Ghostscript package first of all lists all encoded characters in a font, then all the unencoded ones.

- ▸ Under Windows the program *pfbview* (on the accompanying CD-ROM) shows on screen all the characters which a font contains in its PFB file. Unlike many other font viewers, pfbview reads the PFB file directly and does not leave it to Windows or ATM.

- ▸ Using suitable font manipulation software (see Section 4.7) you can open the font file and examine the font's glyph complement. You can, for example, use the demo versions on the accompanying CD-ROM for this purpose.

Screen font encoding.   Re-encoding fonts is a PostScript technique which only works for printing. To display a font on screen, PostScript instructions cannot be used to modify it. In a similar way to the printer driver, which re-encodes the font using PostScript instructions, ATM sorts the characters in a text font so that they resemble the character set of the relevant platform (Mac or Windows). This happens transparently: if you install the same font on different platforms, you will get different encodings on each platform, assuming that the font uses StandardEncoding by default and contains the complete standard glyph complement. This assumption is usually correct, but not always.

The X Window system Type 1 rasterizer, on the other hand, exhibits (at least in the standard version) a rather limited view of font encodings: it tries to force all fonts to use the *ISOLatin1Encoding* character set, and will not allow this re-encoding to be turned off for new symbol fonts. It does however recognize the *Symbol* and *ZapfDingbats* character names and processes them using their original character sets. Some manufacturers offer an additional interface for specifying user-defined encodings (see examples below).

Text and symbol fonts.   Re-encoding a font using a suitable encoding vector only works if the font contains "real" letters which are identified with the correct names. However, there are fonts which do not contain (latin) characters, but symbols, pictograms, or non-latin characters. These symbol or pi fonts may not be re-encoded by a printer driver. If it does rebuild a symbol font with another encoding vector, it is possible that nothing will be printed as the font does not contain the characters with the requested names and the .*notdef* character appears instead.

A couple of real world examples show the importance of differentiating between text and symbol fonts:

- ▶ Some programs, such as Microsoft Word, support input of special characters via a window in which the user picks out the character from a table instead of using an unwieldy key combination. Only fonts classified as symbol fonts appear in this window.
- ▶ Cross-plattform applications like FrameMaker adapt the encoding of text fonts used in a document when the document is moved to another platform, but symbol fonts remain unchanged. If a symbol font is not designated as such (or not designated on all systems), characters get mixed up.
- ▶ Adobe Acrobat simulates text fonts using Multiple Master technology, but this does not work for symbol fonts. Because of this, Distiller and the PDFWriter always embed the symbol fonts used in the PDF file, but in order to do this symbol fonts must be designated as such!
- ▶ If, on the other hand, a normal text font does not use Standard-Encoding, ATM's re-encoding for Mac or Windows will not work and the user can't access the available characters.

This means that a criterion is needed to distinguish reliably between text and symbol fonts. This information is contained in the AFM file. Text fonts with the usual glyph complementand StandardEncoding as the default encoding have the following entry in their AFM file:

```
EncodingScheme AdobeStandardEncoding
```

Symbol fonts can be recognized by a "font specific" encoding vector:

```
EncodingScheme FontSpecific
```

These entries have corresponding entries in the Mac and Windows supplementary files need to install a font. Mac fonts contain, in the FOND resource, the *Style Mapping Table*. This table contains information on the style allocations of font family members and also says whether or not the font may be re-encoded using the normal Mac encoding vector.

Under Windows the entries *dfCharSet* and *dfPitchAndFamily* in the PFM file describe the font's encoding. The Microsoft PostScript driver uses these values to decide whether or not the font can be re-encoded. On the other hand, ATM does not use the PFM file for this distinction, but the font file itself, which (unlike the printer driver) it does not just pass on but analyzes it carefully. If the font files*Encoding* entry contains the value *StandardEncoding*, ATM takes the liberty of changing the encoding to Windows' ANSI encoding, that is, it re-encodes the font.

With the X Window system, the last two entries in the XLFD font name stand for the character set family and encoding. Text fonts usually have the entry *iso8859-1*, symbol fonts are designated as *adobe-fontspecific*.

4.5.2 Using Hidden Characters and Special Character Sets.

PostScript allows to combine unencoded characters from a font in an encoding, or (in Level 2) to address them directly. It would be nice if this was also possible when using fonts on screen, but unfortunately neither the Mac nor Windows PCs separate font and encoding in such a way that you can use a configurable interface to overlay different encodings into an existing font. You can alter the font file itself, but this is a relatively laborious task (see next section). It is possible to make PostScript fonts use a different character set without too much effort on some implementations of the X Window system.

For example, let's take a look at changing a font to use the ISO 8859-2 (Latin 2) encoding which contains the special characters needed for East European languages, such as Czech, Polish, and Hungarian. It is of course necessary to use a font whose glyph complement includes all those needed. In this example we will use the IBM version of Courier. While this font is not quite an aesthetic beauty, it has two advantages: It has a huge glyph complement containing 480 characters which include all the letters and special characters needed for Latin 1, Latin 2, and various MS-DOS codepages including linedraw characters. It can also be freely copied (like the Type 1 rasterizer it was a contribution from IBM to the X Window system). You will find the four IBM Courier typefaces on the accompanying CD-ROM.

Character sets in HP-UX and Solaris. The HP-UX 9.0 Unix derivative integrates PostScript fonts into the X Window system somewhat

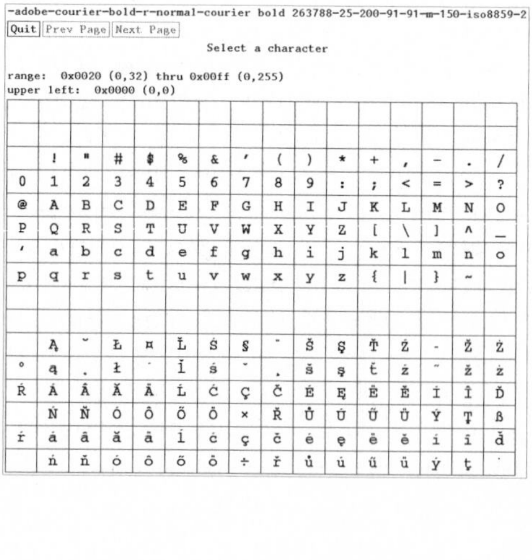

Fig. 4.26.
Flexible character set allocation under HP-UX: Courier, using the ISO Latin 2 character set

better than the standard X11 distribution. This is for example shown by the fact that the program *stmkdirs* reads the entries in PostScript fonts and automatically generates XLFD entries for the *fonts.dir* font list. For this, the last two parts of the name, which describe the character set, are not called *iso8859-1*, but *std-encoding*. This tells the font server that it can allocate different character sets to the font. As by default only the Latin 1 character set can be used, this feature is normally not accessible. To make use of it, you have to dig deep into the system to find the encoding files which are hidden in */usr/lib/X11/fonts/stadmin/type1/charsets/cp.**. These *cp* files (*cp* obviously means *codepage*) contain, in ASCII format, the allocation of code positions to character names, corresponding to PostScript's encoding vector. It is easy to create such a file in an ASCII editor:

```
# Codepage for ISO 8859-2
256
32 |space|
...
253 |yacute|
254 |tcedilla|
255 |dotaccent|
```

After creating such a *codepage* file, incorporate your changes into the font mechanism using the *kill* or *xset* commands (see Section 4.3.6). Now the font should appear in *xfontsel* in an additional flavor, which offers a 2 in the last field of the XLFD name. Using these names, you can for example view the complete font and the new character set using the program *xfd*.

Under Solaris 2.3 and higher, which uses Display PostScript, this trick also works. The encoding files (also in ASCII format) are stored in */usr/openwin/lib/X11/fonts/encodings/*.enc.* They look similar to those under HP-UX, except that there are no pipe characters before and after the character names.

Changing the encoding vector for X11 manually. On some X11 systems, if you only need a font for screen display and the metrics data are not important (or the integration with an application program has already been taken care of), the encoding vector of a Type 1 font contained in the PFA file may be changed manually using a text editor. (Note that some older X servers or font servers cannot re-encode fonts but always use the ISO Latin 1 character set.) To do this, replace the following line at the start of the font file (before the encrypted eexec section):

```
/Encoding StandardEncoding def
```

with the new encoding vector in the form

```
/Encoding 256 array
0 1 255 {1 index exch /.notdef put} for
dup 1 /SS000000 put
dup 2 /SS010000 put
...
dup 254 /filledbox put
dup 255 /space put
readonly def
```

This encoding vector must contain all the required characters (the names after the slashes). You do not have to include unused characters, as all characters are initialized with *.notdef* by default. On the accompanying CD-ROM you will find predefined encoding vectors for the most important operating systems and character sets.

A nice example for the use of this technique is modem communication with a BBS under Unix. Such BBSs usually use the extended MS-DOS character set, which is not normally available under Unix. Because only a monospaced font can be used, the freely available version of Courier which you can find on the accompanying CD-ROM is ideal. If you load the MS-DOS character set (encoding vector PC 437) into this font, you can also access the linedraw characters under Unix. To do this you need the 8 bit capable *ansi_xterm*, as the normal version of *xterm* ignores some characters in the upper half of the character set. When launching *ansi_xterm*, use the *-fn* option to specify the name of the MS-DOS emulation font. Do not forget to enter *adobe-fontspecific* in the last two fields of the XLFD font name. If you want to continue using Courier with the standard character set, you should install the MS-DOS character set version under a new name.

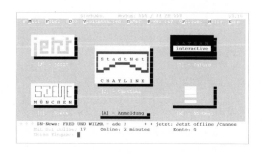

Fig. 4.27.
Xterm with an MS-DOS encoded font serves as terminal emulation for modem communications

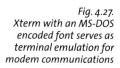

Composite characters and the seac problem under Windows. The Type 1 instructions include an operator which can create a new character by combining two existing ones. This operator is called *seac* (*standard encoding accented character*) and is used to construct accented characters. As an example, we will use the umlauted *ä* with the PostScript name *adieresis* (*dieresis* refers to the umlaut points).

To save space in the font file, such composite characters are not usually defined by their outlines but by pointers to the base and accent characters (that is, *a* and *dieresis*). As the position of the accents is not the same on all letters (such as upper and lower case letters), this pointer is completed with an offset vector for the accent. You can find this information in the AFM file:

```
CC adieresis 2 ; PCC a 0 0 ; PCC dieresis 63 0 ;
```

This line says: the character *adieresis* (ä) has two parts, namely *a* and *dieresis*; the base character a should be placed at (0, 0) in the 1000 unit font coordinate system and the umlaut at (63, 0) relative to its standalone positioning.

Using the seac instruction saves space in the font file. However, there are some restrictions which are imposed by the *standard encoding* in the operator's name. These restrictions in combination with some software bugs have caused a lot of confusion.

Firstly, the standard encoding vector must contain both parts of a seac character, that is the basic character and the accent. In addition, earlier versions of the Adobe PostScript interpreter required both parts of the character to be present in the encoding vector of the font. This condition was relaxed with in the course of further development, and disappeared altogether with Level 2.

The various versions of ATM for Windows cause further problems. With ATM versions before 2.6 there were some problems in combination with seac characters and the character set of the font:

▸ The character in position zero is not useable.
▸ If a character appears more than once in the encoding vector it is only recognized in the lower position, the higher position remains empty.
▸ If a font contains seac characters and is not using Standard-Encoding (which is changed by ATM to the ANSI character set), the composite characters have to be at particular positions in the font's encoding vector.

These restrictions may cause a font which is printed perfectly to be displayed wrong on screen or even to crash ATM! The first two issues affect some TeX fonts, the third is a problem when constructing a font with the classical MS-DOS character set (codepage 437, see Appendix C): such a font contains composite characters and therefore usually (according to its construction) seac characters, but does not use either StandardEncoding or the ANSI character set.

Figure 4.28 shows an example of such a font: ATM uses the wrong characters as "accents" and confuses graphic characters with normal letters! To check whether or not a font contains seac characters, you can either open it with a font editor (see Section 4.7) or convert it to

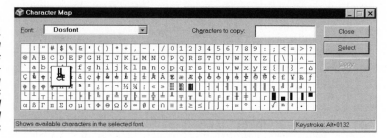

Fig. 4.28.
The seac problem
under Windows:
composite charac-
ters appear with
incorrect graphics
symbols instead
of the required
accent characters

plain text using the Type 1 utilities (*t1ascii* and *t1disasm*) from the accompanying CD-ROM and searching for the word *seac*. You can only solve such a problem with suitable software. Another hint for font designers: elements of letters can be combined to make new characters without problems by using *subroutines*. The capability of adding such subroutines to a font is not yet a standard feature of font editors.

4.5.3 CID Fonts. In PostScript Level 2 Adobe introduced Composite Fonts for processing scripts that require large character collections such as Chinese, Japanese, and Korean (CJK). This extended font format, discussed in Section 5.2.4, is very flexible and supports large character sets. However, to make handling of large fonts still more efficient, Adobe invented CID fonts. The name is derived from character identifiers which play an important role in this new font format.

CID fonts are based on concepts which should already be familiar to you: character outlines are described using Type 1 instructions, and the actual glyph definitions are separated from the character set information – much like an arbitrary encoding vector may be imposed on a Type 1 font's glyph complement. But since CJK fonts have huge character sets, things are more complicated. To economize on memory, the encoding vector, which is called CMap (character map) in the CID concept, is not stored along with each font but only once on each system. This way multiple fonts can share the same CMap file. The Cmap file maps character input codes to a character selector which is used to access the actual character shape definition in the CID font file. Unlike Type 1 fonts, characters are accessed by numbers instead of by names in order to improve performance. CMap files describe diverse character set standards which may be used for Asian fonts. This includes national standards and also provides for different mappings for horizontal versus vertical writing mode. CMap tables for most common standards are supplied by Adobe. This way a font manufacturer can use predefined CMaps and still has the flexibility to define his own map if need be. CMap files refer to character collections that contain all characters needed for a specific language.

CID fonts are meant to provide multi-byte Type 1 font support for a variety of environments, including embedded PostScript interpreters, ATM, Configurable PostScript Interpreter (CPSI), and Display PostScript systems. CID fonts require an interpreter capable of processing composite fonts. This holds true for all Level 2 devices. Starting with version 2015 of the interpreter, Adobe implemented direct CID support in the interpreter. Older interpreter versions require the so-called CID Support Library (CSL). This is a collection of auxiliary PostScript procedures which is also supplied by Adobe.

Fonts with ISO 10646 encoding (mostly identical with Unicode) can be implemented provided a suitable CMap file is available. CID also includes Type 42 font support for double-byte TrueType fonts. Adobe announced they would provide CID fonts in Japanese versions of ATM for Mac, Windows, and Unix.

4.6 Converting Fonts

Many users face the problem of having to convert fonts between operating systems or to different formats to use them with the available hardware and software. This section is concerned with conversion routines which you can carry out without commercial software, using just the programs on the accompanying CD-ROM or with generally available system software.

When carrying out conversions you should of course pay attention to the legalities and conditions of use: with many commercial fonts, you only acquire the right to use the font on one output device. As the conditions imposed by font manufacturers are different, and the legal situation varies from country to country, if in doubt you should check with the manufacturer! However, there is a gray area: for example, what should you do if you require a particular font for a platform which the manufacturer doesn't support?

Apart from the legal restrictions, there are a lot of technical considerations when converting fonts, not just for the typographer. These are partly related to the quality of the conversion software, but sometimes general problems arise from the basic procedure:

- ▸ Some conversions lose hints or other information, and output quality degrades.
- ▸ Often, the character set is affected: special characters vanish or become inaccesible because of an incorrect encoding vector.
- ▸ Extra information, for example, kerning data, gets lost.
- ▸ Some conversions which are basically correct fail because of problems in the rasterizer (PostScript interpreter or ATM).

The actual PostScript data, the outline descriptions of Type 1 fonts, are independent of a particular operating system, but are packaged differently on different platforms (PFA, PFB, resource format). Whilst these forms can be converted without loss of data in all directions, this is not true for the metrics data, which is also needed. Here you sometimes have to accept losses in conversion.

Taking into account these reservations, we are concerned with the conversion of PostScript fonts for use on different operating systems as well as conversion between PostScript and TrueType. Figure 4.29 shows the most often used file formats for PostScript fonts. Luckily, free convertors are available for most of the conversions and you can find them on the accompanying CD-ROM. As you can see from the diagram, you may have to carry out two conversions to achieve your aim.

4.6.1 Converting Fonts for Windows.
As explained in Section 4.3, to install a PostScript font under Windows you need the PFB file and either the PFM file or the AFM and the INF files.

Creating the font file. If you have a font file in the standard Unix PFA format, you can convert it to binary format with the program *t1binary* from the T1 utilities:

```
t1binary ti_____.pfa > ti_____.pfb
```

Mac font files are more difficult to manipulate: as Mac files are not "flat" but consist of two separate forks for resources and data, you first have to convert the Mac file to Windows PC format. To do this you need to have direct access to the data resource fork. In practice, exchanging data using MS-DOS formatted disks has proved reliable. However, you must not use the Apple File Exchange program to write the disk on the Mac, as it ignores the resource fork. It is better to use the *AccessPC* or *PC Exchange* utility, which write two files on to the disk, one each for the resource and data forks.

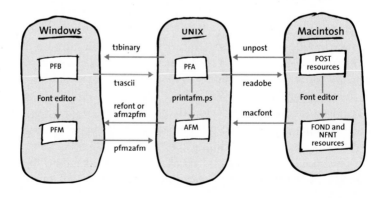

Fig. 4.29. Suitable converters allow the Post-Script and metrics information to be converted between platforms

The case of a heterogenous network is similar, for example, if various operating systems share disk space on a Unix server. In this case, Mac files are also usually split into two separate files on the server's hard disk. If you are using Helios EtherShare to network Mac and Unix computers, note that the resource fork of Mac files contains an extra 512 bytes at the beginning. Finally, there is the Binhex standard for transferring Mac files by modem. From binhexed files the Mac file's resource fork can also be retrieved using a suitable decoder on the PC.

If you have created the font resource with one of these methods (diskette, network, Binhex), you can extract the actual font data using the program *unpost* from the T1 utilities and convert the resulting font file to PFB format using the technique described above:

```
unpost thesans.res > thesis.pfa
t1binary thesis.pfa > thesis.pfb
```

With Mac files stored on a Unix server using Helios EtherShare, you have to use *unpost* with the *-r 512* command line option to skip the extra data at the beginning.

You can also leave the resource fork complications to the Mac printer driver if you are not frightened off by a rather clumsy procedure: use the printer driver to generate a print file in ASCII format which contains the desired font. Load a small document which uses that font into a word processor, and generate a PostScript print file. Open this file with an editor, if need be changing the file type to TEXT using ResEdit. Next, locate and cut out the font data in the file and save it in its own file. Use the example in Figure 4.7 to help recognize the start and end of the font data. Save this file extracted from the font file as a PFA file and process it using *t1binary*.

Creating the metrics file.   There are two distinct ways of doing this: if you have an AFM file for the font, make an INF file for the font, using an existing one as a model, and install the font (using both the AFM and INF files) into ATM. It will create the missing PFM file itself. Alternatively, the PFM file can be created using the programs *refont* or *afm2pfm*. If there is no AFM file available, you will have to extract the missing metrics information directly from the PostScript data. You can carry out this step with a font editor (see next section). There are not any public domain or shareware font editors, but if you need or want to manipulate fonts on a regular basis, they are worth the expense. Font editors let you open the font file, add some necessary extra information (such as the Windows name of the font) and then write a PFM file to the hard disk.

When a PFM file is generated from the PostScript data, then the kerning data will be missing. Depending on the type of font and its intended use, you can overlook this or (if you need high quality) you will have to pass on using the font.

4.6.2 Converting Fonts for the Mac.   Because of the complex structure of Mac font files, it is only possible to convert fonts from other platforms for use on the Mac using commercial software. Sometimes these programs also support data transfer between the Mac and other systems (see Section 4.7.1). I prefer a different method: starting with a PFA file (which, in the case of Windows fonts, you can generate from the PFB file, see below), you can use the Mac program *readobe*, from the accompanying CD-ROM, to create a file in the normal Mac resource format. The program opens an ASCII version of the font and creates a download font, which you still cannot install but which can be opened by FontMonger or Fontographer which can then create the required bitmap and metrics data. If present, kerning data will be lost, if you do not import it afterwards from the AFM file into the font editor. This method does have the advantage that the PostScript data are transferred unchanged. During conversion with a font editor hints are often lost or the character set does not survive the conversion.

4.6.3 Converting Fonts for Unix or OS/2.   Making an ASCII font file from a PFB file is performed with the program *t1ascii* from the T1 utilities:

```
t1ascii ti_____.pfb > ti_____.pfa
```

To convert a Mac font, proceed as described above for Windows, but omit the last step (PFA to PFB conversion). This font file is sufficient for installation under X11.

To install the font in an applications program, you normally need the AFM file as well. If an AFM is not at hand, create it according to what is available from a Windows PFM file, a Mac screen font, or direct from the font data.

Conversion from PFM to AFM is handled by the program *pfm2afm*. However, the PFM file only contains the metrics data for the Windows character set and not for the full range of characters in the font. If you are only going to use the default Unix character set (ISO Latin 1) this is not important, but with other character sets some characters may (because of the lack of metrics data) be unusable. The PFM file still contains the kerning data.

When converting a font which was installed on the Mac, it is best to use the metrics information from the corresponding screen font to create the AFM file. The program *macfont* opens such a file in resource or binhex format and generates the metrics information.

There are more likely to be problems with special characters than with Windows fonts as the Mac uses its own character set.

If neither Windows nor Mac files with metrics information are available or do not contain all the information required because of character set problems, the PostScript program *printafm.ps* from the Ghostscript package can deliver the AFM file for a font (see Appendix B). Ghostscript can access all the characters in a font and work out their metrics, but again it has no kerning data. You have to weigh up which is more important for your purposes.

4.6.4 Converting TrueType Fonts. The conversion of TrueType fonts to PostScript format is easiest when left to the Windows printer driver: First of all connect the (Adobe or Microsoft) PostScript driver to FILE in order to create a PostScript file. Set up the printer driver to convert TrueType fonts to Type 1. Using the Microsoft driver you do this with the sequence "Printer Settings", "Options", "Advanced...". In this dialog you will find an option for sending TrueType fonts to the printer as Adobe Type 1. Select this option and during printing the driver will convert all the required TrueType fonts (those not built in to the printer) to Type 1 and incorporates this font description into the PostScript output. Next, use a word processor to create a file which contains a test word in the desired font at a size of at least 72 points (the Microsoft driver always generates a Type 3 bitmap at small sizes) and create a PostScript print file. Extract the font data from this file: open the PostScript file in a text editor and locate the beginning and end of the font, following the example in Figure 4.7. Copy the font data to the clipboard and save it in a new file. Treat this font data as described in the Windows section above.

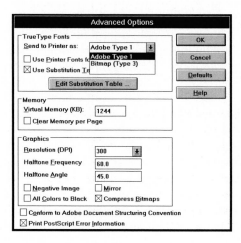

Fig. 4.30.
Settings for the
Microsoft driver
to convert True-
Type fonts to
Type 1 fonts

Using the Adobe driver, the corresponding setting is reached with the sequence "Printer Settings", "TrueType Fonts". This menu also has a setting governing how TT fonts are sent to a PostScript printer.

With both drivers, you must be careful that the actual font and not a substitute from the substitution table is used. You can use the same method to create Type 3 bitmap fonts, simply by choosing this format instead of Type 1.

4.7 Font Editors

4.7.1 Manipulating Fonts.
With the explosion in digital fonts since the end of the 1980s, it is not surprising that the market for software to manipulate fonts is booming. A typographer can use a font editor to design new fonts, and users can make changes to a font, either to correct technical faults or to add new characters for special applications. When modifying PostScript fonts not every action is as easy as changing the outlines; the various font editors do not support all features equally well. A font editor is really more than a graphics program which creates fonts instead of EPS files.

On the accompanying CD-ROM you will find demo versions of the Windows programs Type-Designer (from DTP Software Manfred Albracht, Germany) and FontLab (from SoftUnion). With the exception of the disabled save command, these are full working programs which allow you to try out all the functions addressed. In addition, the following sections contain some remarks about Fontographer and Ares FontMonger (both available for Windows and Mac).

Creating a new font. When designing a new font, the drawing functions, with which the designer draws curve segments, moves control points, and carries out geometric operations like scaling and translation, play an important role. As most designers, even in the digital age, start with sketches on paper, the import functions or the way in which the font editor interfaces with other programs are just as important: if the font editor's own drawing functions are inadequate or the font is to be built using existing graphics data, it is important that the font editor can accept information from other graphics programs. For example, the ability to import EPS files in Illustrator format is part of the de facto standard: you design a character in a trusted dull-function graphics program and integrate it into the font later. When importing scanned sketches, the capabilities of the auto tracing function are as important as the bitmap import.

Integrating and altering characters. Many users do not want to build a new font, but just to insert new characters in an existing font.

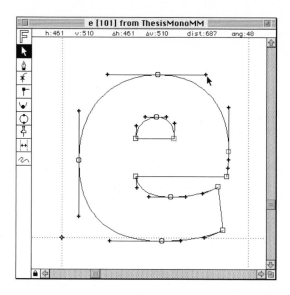

Fig. 4.31.
Fontographer's
drawing functions

Common applications are East European languages, fractions, small caps, and ligatures because the necessary characters are not normally contained in the font. Functions to automate this procedure are useful, above all if you are editing several fonts (such as a whole font family). To do this, FontMonger offers, in addition to predefined operations for individual characters (superscript and subscript, italicize, reduce), the opportunity of defining new operations using scaling, positioning, slanting, and rotating, which can be applied quickly to any character. FontLab also has a range of somewhat anarchic-looking effects, such as frayed or randomized edges.

Some of these automatic functions, in particular the automatic generation of bold and italic versions of a font, tend to give professional typographers a heart attack. The typographic quality of such autogenerated fonts often leaves a lot to be desired and cannot compare to a true italic or bold font. Autogenerated fractions or small caps are similar: if the letters or numbers are simply reduced in size, the stem widths become too narrow in comparison with the other characters in the font (in this case it sometimes helps to start with a bold or semibold variant).

Converting fonts.   Most font editors can also be used as font converters. The distinction must be drawn between converting between different operating systems (such as from Mac to Windows) and conversion between font formats (for example, from PostScript to TrueType). Whilst the first task can often be carried out with freely avail-

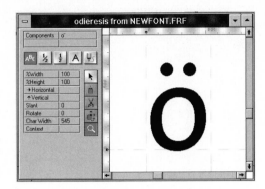

Fig. 4.32.
FontMonger's
editing functions

able software (see previous section) conversion between formats always requires commercial software (exceptions like the conversion of TrueType fonts to PostScript bear this out). Apart from the most important formats (PostScript Type 1, less often Type 3) and True-Type), less common formats like Agfa Intellifont and Bitstream Speedo amongst others must be considered. Creating a bitmap version of a font should not be regarded as a conversion any more, but rather as creating supplementary data (see below).

The converters usually convert the outline descriptions in such a way that they can be used on another system. Unfortunately it is often the case that during conversion additional information is left behind and the quality of the font suffers. Hints are often affected by such losses, causing the converted font to not be rasterized as well as the original. Sometimes there are also problems with the kerning data or the character set.

Some programs not only write file formats for other platforms, but also support file transfer. Problems arise, because of the different file structures, when transferring files between Mac and Windows. The manufacturer of FontMonger has devised something special for this problem: the program is available in both Mac and Windows versions, and contains a special converter module to enable (Mac) Font-Monger files to be transferred to DOS diskettes with the help of the *Apple File Exchange* without losing data.

Creating supplementary files. Supplementary font files include platform-specific metrics files with width and kerning information as well as bitmap versions of a font, that is, everything needed to use the font over and above the actual PostScript data. After opening or creating a font, a font editor should generate the corresponding metrics data correctly. It cannot be taken for granted that the users can access these files with the font editor. Especially under Windows

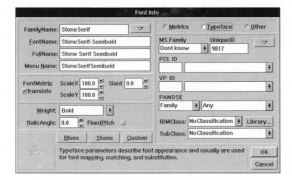

Fig. 4.33.
FontLab lets you access
the PFM file's details

there are very important entries in the PFM file which can affect the use of a font and should be accessible in the font editor.

When specifying individual character widths, you should always have several characters displayed in context so you can judge the effect of a letter in conjunction with others. With kerning it is helpful to make a list of test words which contains as many critical letter pairs as possible.

Bitmap versions of a font, thanks to ATM, do not play a large role any more. If they are required, the font editor ought to create them automatically and offer methods of editing them by hand. At small sizes such hand-tuned bitmaps are more readable on screen than automatically generated ones.

Accessing character set and encoding.   Although this point often plays an important role when crossing platforms, it was not addressed properly for a long time. Ideally, a font editor (like a PostScript font) should handle the character set and glyph complement separately. This separation is also obvious in the user interface:

► The names of the characters are not fixed, but can be freely defined.

► The encoding vector can be changed as you want.

In Section 4.5.1 the differences between text and symbol fonts were explained. Unfortunately many of the fonts which are available do not stick to these classifications or inhibit other problems with the encoding (for example letters, with the names of control characters like ACK, etc.).

Type-Designer permits an almost model treatment of encoding and character names: you can rename not just individual characters but also read in a complete encoding from a file; FontLab is similarily easy to use. This lets you change the encoding of several fonts in one go. FontMonger allows you to choose characters by name or from a list with previews of all encoded and unencoded characters.

Technical functions. Among the functions concerned with the internal workings of the Type 1 format, hints, which contain extra information used in rasterizing characters, must come first. A good font editor creates hints for a new font automatically, shows them to the user and allows them to be edited manually (only for experts!). In addition, it makes sense to have an interface to global hints, to allow quality-conscious typographers the most control possible.

The Type 1 command *seac* allows composite characters to be defined economically with regard to space – even with limitations, especially under Windows. A font editor should not just support compound characters, but also take precautions to prevent problems when using the font. Among these are the conversion of critical *seac* characters to individual outlines or their replacement with subroutines. Type-Designer gets round the *seac* problem by, for example, taking composite characters apart and replacing them with a proper outline description (which does not refer to other characters). This does make the font file larger, but there are no problems with composite characters

Subroutines are a generalization of *seac*: they allow parts of letters, such as horizontal and vertical serifs, to be defined as subroutines and reused for other characters. This method not only saves space in the font file, but also guarantees that all character parts which should be the same appear the same throughout the font. FontLab is, at the time of writing, the only font editor allowing direct access to the subroutines.

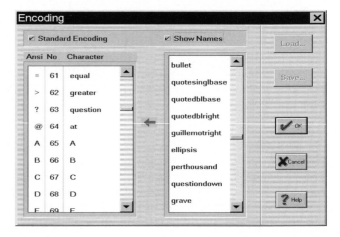

Fig. 4.34. Type-Designer allows to re-encode fonts easily

Finally, among the expert functions is the creation of Multiple Master fonts. The effort needed to create a Multiple Master font far exceeds the requirements for creating a normal font: the individual masters have to be drawn separately and still show common characteristics, but must also fulfil MM requirements. At the time of writing, Fontographer for Mac is the only program able to create MM fonts. The new FontLab version is said to include Multiple Master features for Windows.

4.7.2 Creating a Logo Font.
An existing company logo, a symbol, or an icon often has to be inserted into documents. If you use different letterheads or forms, using preprinted paper means that you have to load the printer with the right paper or choose the right paper tray before printing. If the background with a company logo, etc., is also done using PostScript one kind of paper is enough for different forms. Creating a logo font has several advantages over embedding EPS graphics:

- ▸ The screen display is noticeably better and quicker, as (which is the case with EPS graphics) there is no need to rescale a low resolution version of the picture; instead ATM rasterizes the font at all sizes and also makes use of hints. Font caching speeds up both screen display and printing.

- ▸ Logo fonts are easy to use: all you have to do is choose the font and size. A clever encoding (such as choosing the first letter for various logos) makes it even easier.

- ▸ One font can hold several versions of the logo. This means that the user does not have to remember the names of dozens of EPS files.

The typographer Luc(as) de Groot has perfected logo font encoding in a project for the Netherlands Transport Ministry: The letters ABCD in the font give the name of the ministry in Dutch, EFGH give the name of the first department, IJKL the second etc. Choosing the bold weight

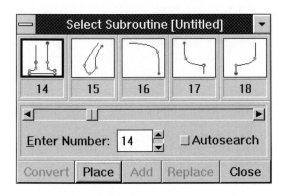

Fig. 4.35.
FontLab provides access to the subroutines which describe individual character elements within a font

gives the English version, italic the French version and bold-italic the German version!

In practice, when creating a logo font you assume that a paper version of the font exists, and that this is to be used as the model for a PostScript font. As well as a scanner you need image manipulation software and a font editor which can import and vectorize bitmaps. Proceed as follows:

- ► Firstly, scan the character. Be careful to align it exactly vertically, or it will sit wrongly in the font and have to be corrected later. Scan as large a version of the logo as possible at a resolution of 300 to 400 dpi. Generate a black and white picture (no colors or gray levels) and turn off interpolation (which simulates higher resolution).
- ► Import the scan into an image editor (if you did not scan directly from this software) and determine the size of the rectangle which surrounds each of the characters individually.
- ► Copy each character to the clipboard using a rectangular selection area of the size determined above.
- ► Paste the clipboard contents into the font editor, in the required character slot. If need be correct the position of this background picture. In the case of symbols, give them a descriptive name, if your font editor allows it.
- ► Activate the autotrace function of the font editor, to convert the bitmap character to an outline description. Check and if need be correct these outlines.
- ► Specify the character spacing (that is the white space to the left and right of the logo).

After you have repeated this procedure for all the characters you can create the font in the desired format and make some test prints which will probably show that further corrections are needed. The first choice of format is Type 1. In a few cases, if the template is too complicated, the number of control points may exceed an internal limit and you should switch to Type 3 format.

If you already have a digital version of the logo (for example, if it was designed with a graphics program) you can load it directly into the font file. Most font editors can load EPS files in AI format, so that scanning and vectorizing are unnecessary.

4.7.3 Hints. If you have read this far, you must indeed be very interested in fonts! As a reward you will learn here about the most important types of hints and how they work. When designing or modifying a font in a font editor you will have access to some or all of these hints: some programs generate the hints automatically and do not allow manual corrections.

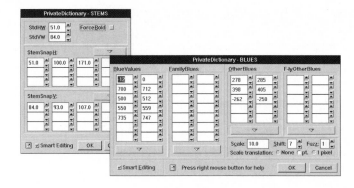

Fig. 4.36.
In FontLab the user can specify all desired stems and BlueValues

The hints in a Type 1 font supplement the outline definitions by describing important characteristics of an individual character or a whole font; for example, the thickness of the vertical stems of the upper case letters B, D, E, F, H, etc. Maintaining these typographic characteristics is more important for a good representation of the font than the exact translation of the outlines to a whole-pixel grid. At small font sizes or on a low resolution output device the transfer is always subject to rounding errors. The rasterizer (that is the PostScript interpreter or ATM) takes note of the hints and alters outlines by amounts smaller than one pixel. These – deliberate – small deviations make the characters look more regular and improve the readability of the font.

Global hints. This type of hint describes characteristics which affect all (or many) characters in a font. The first of these is the normalization of stem widths. Through errors in digitizing or deliberate variations in the shaping of the characters, it can be that the main stems of similar letters (such as *T* and *P*) are not the same width, but do not quite overlap. Assuming that one stem of a 10 point character has a theoretical width of 1.4 pixels and the other 1.6 pixels, they must be rasterized with either one or two pixels. However, this is a difference of 100 percent, which is not tolerable. If however the same characters are to be printed at 100 points, then the stems are 14 or 16 pixels wide; this difference can (and should) be noticeable. Some sort of logic is needed to ignore the differences at small font heights but convert them at large sizes. To do this, you specify the most often used widths for horizontal and vertical stems in the font (the *StdHW* and *StdVW* parameters) as well as up to 12 further commonly used stem widths (*StemSnapH* and *StemSnapV*). In the case of automatic hinting (for example, Fontographer) the font editor sorts all of the stems which appear according to width and determines the most commonly occurring values. It then uses these for the above parameters. In addition, Fontlab allows you to enter stem width values directly.

The alignment zones called BlueZones are related to overshoots: round letters like *O* or *p* are usually a little larger than those which are flat (*T, x*) and extend a little below the baseline. This way type designers compensate for an optical illusion: if they were the same size, the eye would give the impression that the rounded letters were a little too short! Overshoots ensure optical equality, although the sizes are actually different. However, you should not overdo things: the overshoot cannot be smaller than one pixel. If it is, and the corresponding arc is itself only one pixel wide, an overshoot of one pixel would be too much. In a case like that it's necessary to dispense with the overshoot. So that the rasterizer recognizes overshoots as such and can if need be suppress them, special hints – for historical reasons called *BlueValues*[1] – mark the limits of the alignment zones. As many as seven different zones can be defined. In addition, all members of a font family can have their own blue zones.

Character level hints.   Apart from global hints, there are hints which affect the appearance of individual characters only . They determine the positions and weight of horizontal or vertical strokes, including serifs or roundings. In font editors, these hints usually show as arrows or bars in the letters.

The rasterizer treats them as follows (using the example of a horizontal hint, represented by a vertical arrow or bar): if a point on the outline has the same y coordinate as the beginning of the arrow, it is nudged to a grid point. All the points with the same y coordinate as the end point of the arrow are moved to a grid point (by an amount of at most half a pixel). The *StemSnapH* and *StdHW* parameters are also used here.

---

1. At the beginning of the 1980s, a graphics tablet was used at Adobe for digitizing fonts. A puck with four color coded buttons was connected to the tablet. The blue button was used for marking the important horizontal characteristics of a character, including the overshoots.

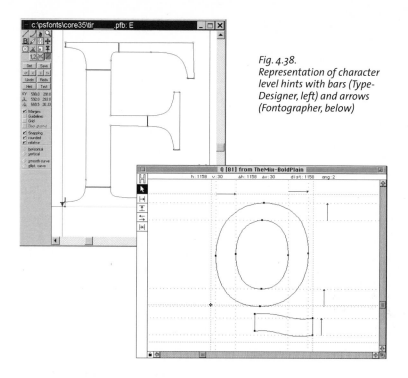

Fig. 4.38.
Representation of character level hints with bars (Type-Designer, left) and arrows (Fontographer, below)

The *flex mechanism* handles very flat curves which run exactly horizontally or vertically. Such flat curves occur in some fonts as the end of serifs, for example the Palatino and Garamond fonts. Such curves are absolutely critical, as without extra controls they can easily be overexaggerated at low resolutions. The flex mechanism replaces – depending on the size of the character and the resolution – both stretches of the curve with a single straight line to avoid too strong an overshoot. The corresponding hint designates points to be taken into account by the flex mechanism.

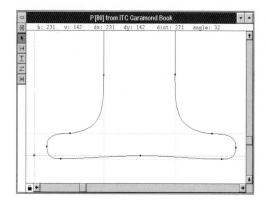

Fig. 4.39.
Garamond's serifs are typical candidates for the flex mechanism

PostScript Level 2

5

In 1990, Adobe published the second edition of the "Red Book" containing the Specification of PostScript level 2. Soon after, the first level 2 devices were available. Although software developers supported level 2 only reluctantly in the beginning and even today driver support for level 2 could be better, most new PostScript devices are level 2 capable. So what's the big deal with level 2 anyway?

5.1 The Goals of Level 2

5.1.1 Standardization.
An important goal when defining Level 2 was to "catch" existing language extensions and to fix a unified standard. This was necessary because Adobe had to extend the PostScript language several times in order to keep up with the printer hardware development:

- ▸ The first color printers brought the PostScript color extension containing, among others, the CMYK color model (see Section 6.5) and new operators for colored raster images.
- ▸ Connecting hard disks to printers for storage of fonts and system files demanded new operators for file input/output.
- ▸ Composite fonts were introduced for the Asian market. They are intended mainly for Japanese with its large character set and complex glyphs.
- ▸ Display PostScript extended PostScript to computer monitors. This way, PostScript is no longer restricted to static page descriptions but is also suited for dynamically driving window systems.

All of these extensions were only implemented on the respective devices. This jeopardized the de facto standard PostScript: drivers could not create uniform PostScript code for all devices but had to be configured for the respective device, or try to find out which operators the device supported. Adobe tried to unify these extensions in Level 2 in order to ensure a clearly defined and permanent standard. Obviously, this new standard had to be compatible to Level 1 so that one could use existing PostScript files and software on Level 2 devices. In order to profit from the Level 2 innovations, however, modified software is necessary (i.e. Level 2 savvy PostScript drivers and applications).

5.1.2 Optimization.
Even in Level 1, the PostScript graphics model is very exhaustive and there are only a few desirable extensions (transparent objects, for example). Therefore it is not very surprising that Level 2 does not expand the basic graphics model. Simply put, PostScript Level 2 doesn't allow any other printouts than Level 1, but facilitates their creation. This means print files are smaller, need less memory, and print faster. Adobe gained these optimizations by extending the language itself and by implementing the PostScript interpreter more effectively, so that even Level 1 programs execute faster on a Level 2 interpreter. Contrary to Level 1 interpreters, in Level 2 the components of the interpreter (stacks, font cache, path storage etc.) are no longer assigned fixed amounts of the available memory, but the memory allocation is being adapted dynamically. This way, with the same amount of memory installed, there is for example

more font storage available if the graphics are not too large or one can borrow RAM from the stacks. Additionally, the rigid memory management model (with the save/restore operators) is expanded on with the distinction between local and global memory. This allows to effectively store and delete font definitions. Thanks to this dynamic memory allocation, a page description using only Level 1 operators producing a *limitcheck* error on a Level 1 device may be processed without problems on a Level 2 device with the same amount of RAM installed!

Useful optimization strategies are realized by operators for data compression and decompression. Above all, raster images create huge amounts of data which may take considerable time on the relay channel and then on the interpreter. With Level 1, a PostScript driver developer had to implement his own compression schemes if he wanted to reduce the amount of data. Often, the longer processing time in the interpreter ate up the time saved in data transmission because decompression had to be implemented with (slow) PostScript commands. Level 2 offers several compression and decompression techniques which are considerably faster than equivalent PostScript programs because they run internally on the interpreter.

Binary token encoding in addition to the usual ASCII encoding is another optimization concerning data transmission time and memory usage. With this encoding, PostScript commands are no longer identified by their plain text names but by numbers. Binary encoding results in more compact PostScript files and speeds up printing. The Adobe driver for Windows and LaserWriter 8.0 for Macintosh support binary PostScript data (see Section 2.1). Another binary encoding method called *binary object* is used in Display PostScript systems. It is not as compact as *binary token* but can be generated and interpreted very quickly. Binary encoding may only be used in restricted environments because it needs a transparent relay channel. Note that binary encoding is not related to the *binary control protocol* used for transmitting 8-bit data over 7-bit channels (see Section 2.3.2).

5.1.3 Device Independence.   One of the most important aspects of PostScript is its device independence: a page description can be executed on arbitrary devices and always delivers the highest possible output quality, independent of the device's resolution, color capabilities or other properties. (Only color reproduction brings device properties into the game, see Section 6.5.) However, there are device properties a driver needs to know in order to offer them to the user or to reasonably make use of them. This includes different paper sizes and trays, duplex printing, or functions such as sorting, punching, and stapling. Such device specific functions had to be controlled with

statusdict operators in Level 1. These operators are only available on devices with the respective functionality. On other devices, they result in an error message so that print files containing statusdict operators are indeed device *dependent*. In Level 2, Adobe engineers mastered to activate device dependent functions in a device independent manner. In order to achieve this, they introduced a mechanism that may request arbitrary printer functions – even those that were not available at the time Level 2 was defined! A printer on which the respective function is not implemented does not produce an error message but simply ignores the request. For requests that may not safely be ignored (e.g., a certain paper size), the printer may be configured to behave differently (e.g., scale the pages and print on another paper size).

Another important aspect is the so-called device independent color, which receives more and more attention with the increasing deployment of color printers. The goal is to achieve identical color reproduction on different devices (ranging from monitor and color printer to offset printing machines), and the calibration of these devices. This topic is covered more detailed in Sections 5.2.2 and 6.5.

5.1.4 Integration Philosophy.

Many advantages of Level 2 are obvious in everyday use, others may only be acknowledged from a different point of view: Adobe does not only position PostScript as a page description language for printers and imagesetters but also pursues larger goals:

- ► Introduction of PostScript fax brought compression and decompression of fax data. In Level 2 this is handled by filter operators.
- ► Exchanging PostScript data plays an increasing important role. The EPS and DSC standards are, strictly speaking, not part of the PostScript *language* but no doubt belong to the PostScript environment and are documented in the red book along with Level 2.
- ► There are some points in Level 2 which allow compatible extensions, e.g., the resource facility discussed in the next section. Deploying PPD files also facilitates the integration of new printer specific features.
- ► The PostScript interpreter is no longer restricted to the printer controller or imagesetter RIP but works in many constellations. The configuration and extension features of Level 2 make it easy to use the interpreter in changing environments or to drive several different devices with the same interpreter.
- ► Level 2 prepared the ground for many elements found in the PDF document format, e.g., compression filters and ASCII85 encoding.

5.2 Main Extensions in Level 2

Following an overview of Level 2 we now discuss the main extensions in more detail. In Section 5.4 we will see how to profit from these features in everyday use.

5.2.1 Filters and Compression Techniques.
Compression techniques play an important role in modern computer applications: they help reduce the amount of data, speed up data transmission (via network or modem), and save storage. Given the significance of compression techniques – especially in image processing applications – the idea of integrating compression operators into the PostScript language suggested itself. The language extension bases on the remarkably elegant concept of so-called filters. A filter is a PostScript operator that changes data in a certain way. The source of the data may be a conventional disk file, a relay channel, a data generating procedure, or even another filter (because filters may be combined). A program can use a filtered file similar to the original data source, the only difference being the filtered data. For reasons of symmetry, Level 2 contains compression filters as well as decompression filters for each supported scheme *(Encode/Decode)*. A page description will however normally only contain decompression filters, the compression has to be carried out in the driver.

The two simplest filters do not carry out any (de-)compression but convert binary data to an ASCII representation suitable for 7-bit relay channels (see Section 2.3.1). ASCIIHEX encoding represents the data using only 16 ASCII characters (0–9 and A–F). The disadvantage of this 7-bit encoding is the amount of data produced: ASCIIHEX doubles the data size.

ASCII85 encoding is a cleverer technique. It originates from Unix systems and uses almost all printable ASCII characters (85 characters). This way ASCII85 encoding achieves 7-bit representation while only enlarging the data size by a factor of 1.25. The algorithm packs the bytes in groups of four and reads them as a four-digit number to the base of 256. It converts this number to a five-digit number to the base of 85 and represents this number with the characters "!" (the value 0) to "u" (the value 85).[1]

The RunLength, LZW, CCITTFAX, and DCT filters are real data compression and decompression filters. Of course, Adobe did not choose these filters haphazardly – they represent the most important compression schemes used in many hardware and software products as well as approved standards (see next section). The most prominent use is the compression of image data which are transmitted in com-

---

1. *This only works because* $256^4 < 85^5$!

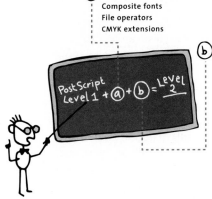

Fig. 5.1.
PostScript Level 2
language extensions

(a) Display PostScript
Composite fonts
File operators
CMYK extensions

(b) Device independent color (CIE)
Color separation
Patterns
Device independent functions
Forms
Resource management
Font rasterization with ATM algorithms
Speed and memory optimizations
Compression and decompression filters
New screening functions (AccurateScreens)

pressed format to the printer and decompressed by the PostScript interpreter. Compression carried out by the PostScript interpreter is only suitable for special cases, e.g., storing compressed data on the printer's hard disk.

All compression techniques generate binary data which are not suitable in certain environments. In this situation, the above-mentioned combination of filters helps: as a filter produces another file for its output, this new file may again be filtered. This way it is possible to compress data with the LZW scheme and then encode them "7-bit clean" with the ASCII85 method. In the interpreter, the ASCII85-Decode filter regenerates the binary data which are then decompressed by the LZWDecode filter. The decompressed data may be used as appropriate, e.g., for describing a raster image.

In Section 5.4 you will find hints on using the decompression filters of PostScript Level 2.

5.2.2 Color Spaces and Device-Independent Color. When
PostScript Level 1 hit the market in the mid-1980s, color devices didn't play any role. Nowadays, we have thermal transfer printers, dye sublimation devices, ink jet printers, and the new color lasers, all of which bring cost-efficient color output to the graphics and office market. However, the first color printers that included the CMYK extensions for PostScript Level 1 made clear what the main problem with computer color was: the RGB electron guns of a monitor produce certain colors, a color printer using the same color data generates completely different colors, and printed matter using PostScript imagesetter and offset machine still looks different. There was definitely no reliable color processing on the PC; professional color cali-

bration of all devices involved in the production process was difficult, if not impossible.

This issue is called *device-independent color.* The goal is to achieve identical optical impression of an image, say a scanned photo, on all devices, be it, monitor, printer, or offset printing machine. In order to achieve this, one not only needs image color information but also color data characterizing the device in use. Both sets of data together with suitable software set the grounds for device-independent color processing.

InPostScript Level 2, the first step in this direction is the distinction between the actual color specification ("which colors does the image contain?") and the reproduction of these colors on a certain device ("How are the colors generated on this device?"). To specify the color, one has to choose a suitable color space and then identify the color values with respect to that color space. There are three groups of different color spaces:

- Device-dependent color spaces are related to a certain output technique for generating color. This includes the familiar RGB color space, named after the three electron guns of a monitor for red, green and blue, and the CMYK color space, named after the basic colors *cyan, magenta, yellow,* and *black* of four-color process printing (*k* for black in order to avoid confusion with blue).

- Device-independent color spaces. As early as 1931, the CIE (*Commission Internationale de l´Éclairage*) defined a device-independent color specification method. It is not related to a certain output technique but to the human eye's perception of color. The CIE color space is best suited for specifying colors in a device-independent manner.

- Special color spaces in the PostScript language simplify the programming of certain features. This includes patterns (an area is not filled with a color but instead tiled with a pattern), color separations, and color specification using a small and limited number of colors (palette). Patterns are supported by many graphics applications and sometimes realized with the Level 2 pattern feature when printing. Color palettes make it possible to choose a limited number of colors (often 256) which the PostScript interpreter can process very effectively. This plays an important role for screen output using Display PostScript.

Device-independent color processing in the PostScript interpreter is however only one of several components for exact color reproduction. Other components are necessary which are ideally integrated into a color management system (CMS). In Section 6.5 you can find more details concerning color spaces, CMS and the respective functions in PostScript Level 2.

Level 2 makes it possible to produce color separations directly in the imagesetter RIP. But this is not widely used; most color separations are still generated by application software.

Another Level 2 extension is related to scanned image data: each color component can be encoded with 12 bits, which means there are for example 4096 levels of gray. In Level 1, image data could only use 8 bits per color component which limited the number of possible gray levels to 256.

A technique called *AccurateScreens* is intended to improve half-toning and to avoid the shortcomings of the Level 1 halftoning mechanism (which is called RT screening). AccurateScreens needs more memory and CPU horsepower but produces significantly better half-tones than RT screening. In real life, however, AccurateScreens has to compete with frequency modulated screening implemented by several RIP manufacturers. More details on these halftoning techniques may be found in Section 6.3).

5.2.3 Forms.
A particular shortcoming of PostScript Level 2 mainly shows up in office usage: consider printouts each containing the same graphic (e.g., a logo on company stationary). In this case, the interpreter unnecessarily rasterizes the image for each page. For complex images this poses a severe bottleneck for printer performance. In Level 1, the only solution was to define the logo as a font in order to make use of the text output optimizations in the interpreter (font cache) for the logo as well. In Level 2, the caching technique has been extended to the so-called forms. A form is a graphic that can be cached between pages. The interpreter has to rasterize the graphic only on the first page; all following pages take advantage of the graphic stored in the forms cache. There are more detailed remarks on form usage in Section 5.5.

5.2.4 Composite Fonts.
PostScript fonts are based on 8-bit character sets which means there are at most 256 different characters. This is sufficient for most western languages. Far Eastern writing systems (Chinese, Japanese, and Korean, CJK), however, need several thousand glyphs. Because of the inability to handle these fonts efficiently in PostScript Level 1, Adobe implemented specialized versions of their PostScript interpreter for the Japanese market which are capable of processing the so-called Composite Fonts. These are font structures consisting of many "normal" fonts. This makes it possible to process many thousand glyphs efficiently. Because of the huge number of characters in a font, Japanese printers and the Japanese edition of Adobe Type Manager (ATM-J) need significantly more memory than the standard version.

Composite Fonts are not only suited for Asian scripts but also for creating a Unicode font. Unicode is a standardized 16-bit character set which combines all writing systems of the world in a huge collection of glyphs. It may well play the role of a "universal ASCII standard" some day. Unicode contains more than 60 000 glyphs. Although many important manufacturers are members of the Unicode consortium, today there are only few Unicode implementations, among them Windows NT. Suitable applications are however missing.

Composite Fonts are an integral part of PostScript Level 2. However, Adobe has introduced still another font technique known as CID fonts. The CID font format is compatible to composite fonts and is intended to make handling of large fonts still more effective (see Section 4.5.3).

5.2.5 PostScript Resources.

The resource mechanism proves the integration philosophy and extensibility the Adobe engineers had in mind when developing Level 2. Though not directly visible to the user, it simplifies the task of generating PostScript commands that do not rely on printer specific functions. In this context, resources are objects needed by the PostScript interpreter, but – depending on the environment – may have to be accessed in different ways, e.g., fonts, prologs, encoding vectors, or forms.

A good example are fonts treated as resources. From the interpreter's point of view, fonts may stem from different sources: some are stored directly in the printer on EPROM chips, others are loaded residently from the computer to the printer's memory. If a hard disk is attached to the printer or the interpreter runs on the same computer as the application programs, fonts may as well be loaded from disk. Alternatively, a network font server may supply all printers in the LAN with PostScript fonts. Although these possibilities are quite useful, a driver has a hard time deciding which fonts are available on a given device.

In Level 1 there is no satisfactory solution to this problem. The *findfont* operator searches the printer's memory for (built-in and dynamically loaded) fonts, but for searching the hard disk additional program statements are necessary which may even vary among devices. Contrarily, Level 2 contains an operator for searching resources regardless of their location. This operator looks for a resource of a certain type (a font, for example) by its name (Garamond, for example). If the interpreter can somehow access this resource, it is made available without the driver knowing the exact origin.

Storing one's own resources is not only important for fonts but also for procedures (prologs or *ProcSets*) which are needed for each printout and should not be loaded along with each single print file.

5.3 Excursus on Compression Techniques

Compression techniques play a major role not only in PostScript Level 2 but also in most raster graphics file formats (e.g., TIFF of GIF), freely available archiving and compression programs (e.g., pkzip, Stuffit) as well as in diverse hardware and software products such as hard disk compressors (e.g., Stacker) or fax machines (CCITT standard). In practice, the variety of known compression schemes reduces to only a couple of algorithms.

5.3.1 RunLength Compression.
RunLength Compression uses a simple algorithm that replaces a number of identical bytes (a *run*) with two bytes. The first byte indicates the length of the run, the second byte the actual byte value to be repeated. In case there are no identical bytes, the first byte indicates how many of the following bytes are to be copied without any change. To distinguish the two cases "shortened run of identical bytes" and "complete sequence of different bytes", the sign of the first byte is used.

Obviously, the RunLength algorithm can only achieve good compression if there are many runs of identical bytes in the input data. This is normally the case for black and white image data. RunLength can be implemented very easily and is used in many graphics file formats, e.g. TIFF, BMP, and PCX.

RunLength compression is the only technique that may reasonably be implemented using PostScript operators directly. Some programs for converting raster graphics to EPS compress the image data via RunLength and include Level 1 PostScript code for decompression in the EPS file. Examples are the *pbmtops* program (part of the PBM-PLUS package) and Ghostscript's *psmono* device driver (which produces PostScript output from PostScript input).

5.3.2 LZW Compression.
The LZW algorithms (there are dozens of variations; the group is named after Abraham Lempel, Jacob Ziv, and Terry A. Welch) "remember" repeated input sequences in a table which is constructed in a very clever way from the input data, and replaces these sequences by dynamically created abbreviations of variable length. The main point of the LZW technique is that the table containing the abbreviation codes doesn't need to be stored or transmitted along with the compressed data but can be reconstructed during decompression. The algorithm adapts to the input data and achieves good compression ratios while being suited for a broad range of applications.

LZW algorithms are not limited to a certain type of input data but compress black and white images, color images, text, or program files. Many general purpose compression programs use some LZW variant (e.g., *pkzip, compress, gzip*). LZW compression is implemented in the TIFF and GIF graphics file formats as well as in modems employing V42bis compression. Although programming the compression algorithm itself is relatively straightforward, an efficient (read: fast) implementation requires considerable programming effort.

There is one snag with LZW: the LZ78 variant used in the GIF graphics format and in PostScript Level 2 is subject to several U.S. and foreign patents owned by the Unisys Corporation. They license this patent in exchange for a one-time fee. Modem manufacturers are the most important licencees. Adobe licensed the algorithm for use in their own products. Strictly speaking, every software manufacturer using LZW in a PostScript Level 2 driver has to pay such a fee too.

In early 1995 Unisys started charging fees for using GIF compression as well. This initiated the quest for a patent-free LZW alternative. The LZ variant of *gzip* is seen as a plausible substitute, employed in the Portable Network Graphics (PNG) file format.

5.3.3 CCITT Compression.   The CCITT compression scheme is named after the postal standardization committee CCITT (*Comité Consultatif International Telegraphique et Telephonique*, now *International Telecommunication Union*, ITU). It is intended to speed up fax transmission. As with LZW, CCITT designates several algorithms. Group 3 compression is supported by most fax machines. A newer technique, called Group 4 compression, roughly doubles the compression rate of Group 3. CCITT is a static scheme (it does not adapt to different kinds of input data) and is optimized for typical fax documents that consist of black and white low resolution (100–200 dpi) raster data with small numbers of black pixels. Huffman encoding, often mentioned in connection with CCITT, is a simple compression scheme published by David Huffman in 1952. CCITT Group 3 compression is a special case of Huffman encoding.

Contrary to the standardized compression *algorithm* there is no standardized file format for CCITT compressed data. For this reason, fax modem manufacturers developed their own file formats for storing fax data, which are – needless to say – incompatible.

5.3.4 DCT or JPEG Compression.   DCT (discrete cosine transform) compression forms the core of the JPEG compression standard *(Joint Photographic Experts Group)* for gray-level and color images. JPEG is an approved ISO standard and contains several compression algorithms for different application fields. The most important one is called *baseline* process. Contrary to the other algorithms discussed above, this is a *lossy* algorithm. This means that after compressing

and decompressing an image the result may differ from the original image. Obviously, this is intolerable for text or program files but makes sense for compressing raster images with large color depth. In this case, JPEG allows to fine-tune the tradeoff between image quality and compression ratio (see examples). The idea is to choose the JPEG

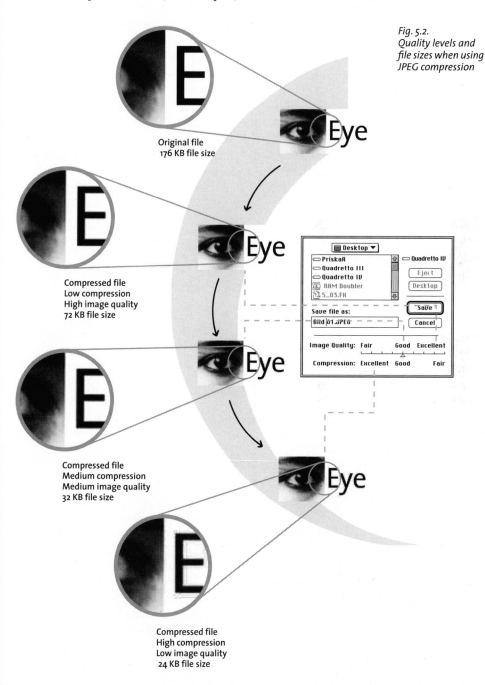

Fig. 5.2.
Quality levels and file sizes when using JPEG compression

Original file
176 KB file size

Compressed file
Low compression
High image quality
72 KB file size

Compressed file
Medium compression
Medium image quality
32 KB file size

Compressed file
High compression
Low image quality
24 KB file size

parameters so that the loss in image quality is not evident on a given device (because of the device's output resolution) or may be tolerable for a certain application.

JPEG compression combines the discrete cosine transformation with a process called quantization which is responsible for the difference between compressed data and original data. The last stage is a backend employing the Huffman encoding mentioned above. The DCT filter in PostScript level 2 supports JPEG baseline compression only. There are extended JPEG algorithms which do also achieve lossless compression, but they are not widely used.

JPEG compression achieves enormous compression ratios up to 1:50 but implementing it requires much effort. While JPEG compression is very useful for continous tone images (mainly photos of realistic scenes), it should not be used for images containing abrupt color changes, e.g., line art drawings. JPEG compression for screenshots is definitely the wrong choice as one can clearly see compression artifacts. In the same spirit, JPEG should not be used for images containing only a small number of colors, e.g., converted GIF files with 256 colors.

5.4 Level 2 in Practice

5.4.1 Level 2 Hardware.
In the first place, you may ask yourself whether or not your printer, imagesetter, or previewer contains a Level 2 interpreter. The PostScript program *info.ps* on the accompanying CD-ROM may be used to check the interpreter's language level. Simply transfer this file to the printer or imagesetter like a regular print job or open it with the previewer. The program informs about the language level of the PostScript implementation as well as some other characteristics of the interpreter.

If you have a PPD file for the device, you can recognize Level 2 devices by the entry

```
*LanguageLevel: "2"
```

Generally we can assume that most new printer makes are Level 2 capable, regardless whether an Adobe interpreter or a compatible clone is used. Similarly, the Display PostScript implementation in NEXTSTEP 3.0 and higher is based on PostScript Level 2. Ghostscript, as well, reached full Level 2 compatibility with version 3.0. The RIPs for imagesetters suffered some years of delay regarding Level 2 but nowadays it may also be considered standard for new models.

Regarding the exact implementation of the language standard and therefore Adobe compatibility of clones, the current situation is similar to the mid-1980s with respect to Level 1: several manufacturers offer their own Level 2 implementation to get round paying Adobes license fees. Market demands Level 2 compatibility for almost every new PostScript device in order to protect investments. However, in some cases you find Level 2 compatibility in the manual only instead of in the interpreter. When we tested several printers for a computer magazine, it turned out that not a single clone implemented Level 2 completely and accurately! (All tested printers appeared on the market in 1994 or later.) In the test we checked core Level 2 algorithms such as compression.

In professional use, a printer which is not completely Level 2 compatible resembles a time bomb: it may work as expected for some time, but installing a new driver or changing the operating system show that the printer's Level 2 compatiblity is no great shakes. There's no point in arguing that not every driver supports Level 2 yet – the manufacturer might as well position the device as a Level 1 printer instead...

However, it may be assumed that Level 2 clones – similarly to Level 1 clones – get more stable over time and implement the language extension exactly. This improvement will take place faster and faster with more Level 2 capable software available.

5.4.2 Level 2 Drivers.

Until recently, Level 2 capable software was very rare. Software developers didn't accept Level 2 as enthusiastically as Adobe might have thought. One can only speculate about the reasons. One reason is that there were only few Level 2 devices in the beginning. Another reason is the complexity that Level 2 burdens on driver developers.

Not surprisingly, Adobe themselves took care for the long-awaited Level 2 drivers for Windows and Macintosh. Apple integrated the Adobe driver as LaserWriter 8.0 into MacOS; the Windows driver was available bundled with certain printers and with application software.

The PostScript drivers of newer systems such as OS/2 3.0 (Warp) and Windows 95 are Level 2 capable. The same holds true for modern Unix applications with an integrated PostScript driver such as FrameMaker. Although with some drivers the user can click a checkbox to enable Level 2, this should rarely be necessary as the driver should already be configured for a certain printer type. In this case, the driver knows about the printer's features from its PPD file. Additionally, most drivers generate "conditional code" that checks the language level at run time and automatically calls Level 1 or Level 2 operators. Although it's possible to emulate many Level 2 operators using Level 1, this doesn't work for all Level 2 features.

Level 2 capability of several PostScript drivers and applications

PostScript driver/system/application	Level 2 capable?
Windows 3.x, standard driver	no
Windows 3.x, Adobe driver (AdobePS)	yes
Windows 95, standard driver	yes
MacOS, LaserWriter 8.0	yes
OS/2 3.0 (Warp)	yes
FrameMaker 4.0/5.0 for UNIX	yes
Adobe Illustrator file format	no
Adobe Photoshop	yes

5.4.3 Applications Creating Level 2 Code.

As explained in Section 2.1, some programs generate the PostScript code for printer output themselves without the help of a system-level driver. Modern software of this kind may also generate Level 2 this way. One example is the PostScript output of the Acrobat programs: because of the structural similarity between PostScript Level 2 and the Portable Document Format (PDF) it's reasonable to convert PDF to Level 2 directly. There are some examples in the next section.

Graphics applications often create EPS files containing self configuring PostScript code. On a Level 2 device Level 2 operators are used, (less efficient) Level 1 operators otherwise. If you import such an EPS file into your document, you may get Level 2 code without ever knowing it. In Section 5.5 you can find hints on converting existing raster graphics files to PostScript Level 2 EPS files.

5.4.4 Level 1 Compatibility.

Each software or hardware extension poses the question of backward compatibility in order to protect investments. Because of this important point Adobe took great care to make sure existing drivers work well with Level 2 devices: the "official" Level 1 language is completely contained in Level 2. But what does "official" really mean? As explained in Section 2.1.1, some PostScript operators are implemented on certain devices only because they drive device specific functions. If a PostScript file contains device specific functions (especially the *statusdict* operators, e.g., for selecting a paper tray), the document may only be printed on certain devices, i.e., those with an implementation of the operator in question. It is possible, however, to generate "cautious" PostScript code which first checks for the existence of those operators before actually using them. If a PostScript developer does not use this technique he risks PostScript output that generates an *undefined* error when printing. Many users experienced problems of this kind when switching to a Level 2 device. They didn't know that it was not the language level that caused the problems but the software they used, because it generated device-dependent PostScript output.

Obviously, the best solution is to upgrade to a software version which takes into account device specific functions. A workaround is to define dummy definitions that cancel the offending commands. Unfortunately, a general recipe for this kind of bugfix cannot be given and one has to examine the error in detail.

What about new software that is supposed to generate PostScript Level 1 as well as Level 2? We have to distinguish between software with direct access to the interpreter and a PostScript driver creating a print file without knowing on which device it will be printed.

In the first case, the driver checks the language level of the printer and accordingly creates Level 1 or Level 2 code. If the target device is unknown, there are several possibilities:

▶ The application doesn't need Level 2 features or isn't able to generate Level 2 code at all. In this case, the file contains Level 1 code only and works on any PostScript device.

▶ The application is able to generate Level 2, but can also emulate Level 2 features using Level 1 code. In this case one uses self-configuring code: the PostScript program checks the interpreter's language level and uses Level 1 or Level 2 accordingly. This is the safest approach to the language level issue.

▶ The application definitely needs a Level 2 device, e.g., for CIE color spaces or JPEG compressed image data. In this case emulation with Level 1 commands is not possible and printing has to be stopped if only a Level 1 device is available. A well-programmed PostScript prolog should also handle this case. It's much easier for the user if she sees a note concerning PostScript Level 2 instead of a succinct message *Error: undefined; OffendingCommand: filter!*

5.4.5 Converting Level 2 to Level 1.

If you want to print files of the last type (PostScript code that definitely needs Level 2) on a Level 1 device, you have to change back the file to Level 1. There are two possibilities to achieve this:

Method 1: Rasterization with Ghostscript. Rasterize the file with Ghostscript's *psmono* device driver. Contrary to other drivers, this driver does not generate code for a certain device but creates Level 1 PostScript from the input file. The new file contains a black and white version of the input file in which the image data is RunLength compressed. Although compressed, *psmono* files can get quite large (depending on the resolution used for rasterization). In any case, they allow printing Level 2 files on Level 1 devices. With the help of Ghostscript, this conversion is quite easy to achieve. However, you should be aware of the fact that object oriented graphics are converted to raster graphics. This may or may not be acceptable as it can degrade image quality. In appendix B you will find more details on the necessary Ghostscript options.

Method 2: Distilling to PDF.   To use this method you need Acrobat Distiller which converts the PostScript file to a PDF file. This is possible because Distiller contains a Level 2 interpreter. Now you can open the generated PDF file with Acrobat Reader or Exchange and print the file again (or create a PostScript file). In the print dialog you can specify whether to generate Level 1 or Level 2.

Note that there are some inherent limitations in PDF with respect to PostScript. These limitations are listed in Section 8.2.1.

5.5 Using Level 2 Without a Driver

In this section we present some ways to make use of Level 2 features even if you don't have a Level 2 capable printer driver. Requirements and applicability of these hints vary considerably – simply pick the ones that are suitable for your situation!

5.5.1 Compressed Raster Graphics in Level 2.   Although the same compression techniques found in Level 2 are part of many raster graphics file formats (e.g., TIFF, GIF, JPEG), existing PostScript drivers don't explore this fact. Since in many cases the relay channel (e.g., serial or parallel port) forms the printing bottleneck it's reasonable to convert the image data to EPS with a suitable utility. These EPS files should contain the compressed image data along with Level 2 operators for decompression. In principle, such a utility is not one of the usual converters but only "wraps" the compressed image data in a different way. These compressed PostScript files replace the original TIFF or JPEG file. This method is advantageous in situations where large amounts of image data have to be transmitted to the printer over a slow link, especially for printers with a fast CPU (because decompression takes place in the printer).

The JPEG wrapper.   To realize this idea, I wrote a JPEG "wrapper" called *jpeg2ps* which you can find on the accompanying CD-ROM. *jpeg2ps* takes a JPEG compressed image file, determines some image parameters (e.g., width and height) and generates an EPS file containing the JPEG data and the according Level 2 operators for decompression. To be on the safe side, the prolog checks whether the file is being printed on a Level 2 interpreter. If this is not the case, it prints an error message and stops processing. The EPS file may be printed standalone or embedded into another document. The image is scaled to fit on a letter size page in portrait or landscape format. This makes it easy to print the file without further embedding. By default, *jpeg2ps* also converts the JPEG data to ASCII85 representation to allow printing over 7-bit links. If the file is to be printed over a binary proof channel, ASCII85 is no longer necessary. In this case you can generate binary data with the *-b* command line option.

Let's not conceal a disadvantage of the JPEG wrapper: the generated EPS files don't contain screen previews so that after embedding in a DTP program only a gray rectangle is visible. (But you can fix this, see Section 3.5.2).

You can create similar JPEG compressed EPS files in Adobe Photo-Shop using the "Export", "EPS-JPEG" function.

While writing *jpeg2ps*, I came up with a little by-product called *viewjpeg.ps*. This utility turns Ghostscript or any other Level 2 capable previewer into a JPEG viewer (see Appendix B for more details).

Other Ghostscript utilities called *viewgif.ps* and *viewpbm.ps* employ the same principles and makes it possible to view GIF and PBM files directly in Ghostscript.

TIFF files.   Another program related to compression and Level 2 is *tiff2ps* which you also can find on the CD-ROM.[1] Similar to the JPEG wrapper, *tiff2ps* reads TIFF graphics files and wraps the compressed image data as Level 2 EPS in ASCII85 representation. Optionally, the program decompresses the image data for use on a Level 1 device. In this case ASCIIHEX representation is used which even a Level 1 interpreter understands. *tiff2ps* accepts TIFF files compressed with the RunLength, LZW, fax (CCITT) Group 3 and 4 compression algorithms as well as uncompressed TIFFs.

Fax formats.   Analogous to *jpeg2ps* and *tiff2ps* it would be possible to write a similar wrapper program for fax compressed image data. This is however doomed to failure because there is no standard file format for fax compressed data. This means one had to implement each file format of the fax modem manufacturers separately.

5.5.2 Printing PDF files.   Because of the close relationship between PostScript Level 2 and PDF it is possible to make use of the compression features in Level 2 when printing PDF files. Since Acrobat Software largely bypasses the printer driver and produces its own Post-Script output, this offers a possibility to create Level 2 code.

1. *Due to licensing issues the CD-ROM only contains executable versions of tiff2ps for MS-DOS and several Unix systems. Unfortunately, I cannot make available the C source code in this case.*

The usage is really simple – you only have to check the Level 2 box when printing from Acrobat. If the PDF file contains compressed images, these are sent to the printer in compressed format. Since most raster graphics in PDF files are compressed, the advantage is obvious: print files are smaller than Level 1 files and are transmitted faster to the printer.

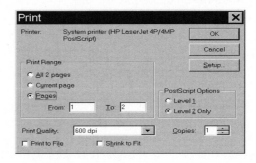

Fig. 5.3.
In the print dialog
of Adobe Acrobat
you can choose
between Level 1
and Level 2

5.5.3 Accelerated Printing of Fax and Other Image Data.

The technique described above can be further expanded on. If you use a fax modem and often need to print faxes received on the computer, you probably know the problem: printing a fax on a slow PostScript printer may take considerably longer than receiving the data in the first place! The reason for this is that the printer driver generating the data has no clue about Level 2 and CCITT compression.

The following method may sound like a deviation but in many cases speeds up PostScript fax printing considerably. It is not limited to fax data but may be used with other applications as well, e.g., printing from image processing software.

The method requires PDF-Writer (this is the Acrobat printer driver that generates PDF output). First you have to configure PDF-Writer's compression features. Choose the dialog window containing the compression options. In this window, activate LZW compression for text and graphics. For optimized fax printing, choose "CCITT Group 4" for black and white images, "LZW" for other applications. Optimum compression settings for color and gray level images depends on your quality requirements: as JPEG compression may degrade image quality, start with medium JPEG compression. If you still gain acceptable print quality with the highest compression level, you can further reduce the file size this way. If you generate PDF files with Distiller instead of PDF-Writer, you have to choose the appropriate compression options in Distiller's menu.

Next, simply "print" your document (fax, raster image, etc.) from your fax or image processing software to a PDF file using PDF-Writer.

Now start Acrobat Reader or Exchange, open the new PDF and print with the Level 2 option checked as described above.

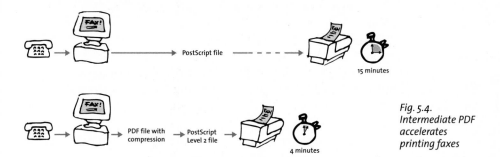

Fig. 5.4.
Intermediate PDF accelerates printing faxes

The small performance penalty of starting another program (Adobe Acrobat) may well speed up the whole process: In one case a fax page that took 15 minutes on a slow PostScript printer when printed directly from the fax software was finished after 4 minutes when printed as PDF! The size of the print files was 230 KB and 78 KB respectively. Although it's difficult to generalize these numbers, you'll probably get the picture. In many cases the PDF deviation accelerates printing.

You should not use this method, however, if there is a chance of losing document properties when converting to PDF, for example, customized halftone screens. Also take care of Acrobat's font substitution mechanism.

5.5.4 Forms.

I am currently not aware of any standard application that makes use of Level 2's forms feature. For this reason let's sketch how a customized PostScript environment can boost print performance. Institutional users such as large companies and governmental offices who print a large number of copies on a relatively small number of forms or stationery are prime candidates for forms. But even with spezialized applications such as CAD (*computer aided design*) or architecture the forms feature may bring advantages. For example, in a CAD application electronic components are defined as forms, which are repeatedly printed as part of a circuit printout, or house symbols in architectural software.

In most cases, the graphic in question is available as EPS: In the first step, an experienced PostScript programmer has to change the file so it may be executed as a procedure from an arbitrary point in a PostScript file. (According to the size of the graphic, this may or may not be difficult to achieve.) Now the modified logo gets installed in the printer permanently. This may be achieved by loading to the printer's memory residently (see Section 2.3.3) or, still better, by storing it on the printer's hard disk. In the first case the logo has to be reloaded after each startup or reset of the printer.

In the second step a new EPS file for the logo is created. It no longer contains the actual PostScript code but only a link to the logo form lurking in the printer's memory or on disk. Ideally, this dummy EPS file contains the same screen preview as the original file so that users are able to see it on their screens. Additionally, the EPS should first check for the existence of the logo form and print an error message if it wasn't loaded.

There are two optimizations in this technique:

▸ Individual print jobs do not contain the complete EPS data but only a small EPS dummy. According to the size of the EPS and the relay channel's bandwidth this may be a big win. Up to this point, the trick works identically on Level 1 devices.

▸ The Interpreter has to process the logo only when it is encountered for the first time. The results are not only printed but also cached in the interpreter's forms cache. All succeeding logos need not be processed again, but can be fetched from the cache instead. The performance gain depends on the logo's complexity and size. This second optimization may only be achieved on Level 2 devices because of the forms cache feature.

There are really some pearls worth exploring in Level 2!

5.5.5 BeginPage/EndPage Procedures.
BeginPage/EndPage procedures are a rarely known Level 2 feature. They allow a user-defined PostScript procedure to be installed at the beginning or end of each page of a document. These procedures need not be part of the print file but may also be added to an existing document afterwards. A BeginPage procedure is executed before the page contents are rasterized, an EndPage procedure is called when the page is completely rasterized but not yet transferred to paper or film. Both procedure types can can place additional text or graphics elements on the page. The interpreter supplies the procedures with the actual page numbers. With some imagination, there are many applications for such procedures, some of which (but not all) are also offered by application software. Using BeginPage procedures in some cases also simplifies print automation. Here are some examples:

▸ Thumbnails or *n*-up printing: individual pages are scaled down and printed in rows or columns on a single page. Many DTP programs and several drivers help saving trees with offering such a thumbnail function – but this doesn't help for existing PostScript files.

- Duplex printing: the BeginPage procedure may well print only every other page. This is useful if you want to print both sides of each sheet of paper and your printer doesn't have a duplex unit. first print the PostScript file with a BeginPage definition that prints only even pages, then the pages already printed are stacked into the printer's tray a second time (possibly face-down, according to page ordering in the output tray) and to print the odd pages.
- Margins for stapling: even and odd pages are shifted sidewards differently in order to create margins on one edge of the paper.
- Watermarks: Sometimes documents receive sort of a "watermark", i.e., constant text appearing on the background of each page (common examples are the words "Confidential" or "Draft" printed diagonally on each page). Using a BeginPage procedure, it's possible to create such watermarks regardless of the application used for creating the PostScript files.
- Page numbering: for documents with low layout requirements (program listings, for example) it may be reasonable to create and print page numbers directly in the printer.
- Banner page: Users sharing a single printer often run the risk of mixing up individual print jobs. In this situation a banner page is useful. It is printed before or after a print job and contains additional information, e.g., user name or number of pages printed.
- Printing crop marks, if this is not possible with the originating software (or for already existing PostScript files).

In PostScript Level 1, there is a makeshift solution for "mounting" a certain procedure at the end of each page. To achieve this, the *showpage* operator is redefined, which is executed at the end of each page. The operator is replaced by a manually programmed procedure that prints a watermark, for example. But this technique has the disadvantage of overprinting existing text on the page; also, it doesn't work with all print files or PostScript prologs. In this case it's better to use Level 2's BeginPage or EndPage procedures. Contrary to the *showpage* method, they work with all kinds of PostScript files and are very flexible because they can be executed before and after each page is being constructed.

To make use of such procedures a method is needed to conveniently integrate (and disable) these procedures in the printing process. This of course depends on the operating system in use and the respective printing environment. Embedding is easiest if the generating application offers "hooks" for integrating custom PostScript code. Embedding the procedure code as EPS doesn't help because EPS files cannot make any global changes affecting the whole document.

If you work on a Unix system, it may be possible to configure the spooling system so that it transmits the procedures to the printer when a certain command line option is given. If PPD files are used, it's possible to "invent" a new printer feature and add an entry in the printer's PPD file. Printer drivers that interpret all PPD entries present the new feature to the user in the print dialog.

In Windows NT, it's possible to misuse the separator pages to smuggle PostScript code into the print files. The user only has to choose the necessary separator page.

Since BeginPage/EndPage procedures are not supported in standard software, PostScript programming experience is necessary to make use of them. Obviously, this is not helpful for most users. According to the scope of the applications, it may be reasonable to invest in PostScript programming to optimize the overall print performance or quality.

For example, I wrote a special BeginPage procedure for a particular customer who does database publishing: They use software that creates PostScript files for catalogs directly from the database entries. Unfortunately, the software isn't able to embed the company logo. For this reason, they had to manually strip in the logo – on several hundred pages each month! The BeginPage procedure now automatically prints the logo on each page.

5.5.6 Hidden Characters in a Font. In Section 4.5.1 we ran into the following problem: How can we determine a font's character set, that is the complete list of character glyphs in the font (regardless of encoding vectors)? Since character output in Level 1 is bound to a specific encoding vector, which in turn is limited to 256 characters, some clever PostScript programming is required to perform this task.

In Level 2 it's possible to print single characters only by using the respective glyph name (without any encoding vector involved). The PostScript program *allglyph.ps* on the accompanying CD-ROM implements this idea for Type 1 fonts. Simply enter the name of the font in question on the last line of this program. It prints a sorted list containing all character glyphs of a font, along with their glyph names.

Gray Levels and Color

6

Gray levels and color are very extensive topics – many books deal with them exclusively, from theoretical foundations to the intricacies of real world application. This chapter is meant to provide a short introduction to the topic and cannot substitute the manuals and the experience of the printing industry. The following sections give an overview of the methods employed in PostScript as well as tips for practical usage.

6.1 Simulating Gray Levels and Color

Regard the image on the very first page of this book. You will see a somewhat pale photograph. If you take a closer look, you will recognize tiny little characters which together make up the image. These characters are taken from the monospaced font ThesisMono and provide the illusion of smooth gray levels building an image when viewed from a distance.

This image symbolizes this chapter's main topic: simulating gray levels with restricted output means. I created the image with a Post-Script program which I called *alpha device*. Using the alpha device you can reproduce arbitrary PostScript images on devices that only have alphanumeric characters such as non-graphical terminals or even typewriters.

Several reproduction techniques allow continuous-tone gray levels or colors, i.e., smooth transitions between dark and light or between different colors, to be created. These include photographic film and computer monitors attached to a TrueColor graphics adapter. But the most important printing techniques are binary: most laser printers can only darken a pixel or leave it alone, in offset printing you can either put ink on the paper or leave the paper's color unchanged.

Commercial printers and lithographers, who have been dealing with the gray level problem for a long time, came up with solutions to this problem very early. Developed at the turn of the century, *screening* has since become an integral part of the art of printing. You can easily check how screening works by taking a closer look at a newspaper photograph: gray levels are being simulated by dark spots of varying size. At normal reading distance you can hardly discern the spots but instead get the illusion of certain gray levels (the gray level depending on the size of the spot). Only at closer scrutiny or with the help of a magnifying glass do the tiny dark spots show up.

Halftoning or screening makes use of a property of the human visual system called spatial integration. If we look at some area from a large enough distance, the human eye averages the details contained in this area and transmits this average intensity only. The eye's spatial resolution is approximately one minute of arc ($=^1/_{60}$ degrees). Using high-school math, it's easy to calculate the distance at which it is impossible to distinguish isolated objects, and spatial integration begins.[1] Figure 6.1 graphically depicts this relationship. For later reference, the diagram not only gives the object's size but also object fre-

---

1. *If you went to the beach while your math teacher talked about trigonometry, consider the following: Let d be the object's diameter, s the distance from object to spectator, and α the viewing angle. Then $\tan \alpha = d/s$; using $\alpha = 0°1'$ yields $s = d/0.0003$ (approximately).*

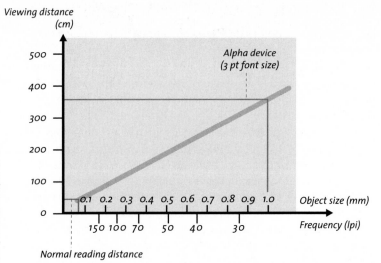

Fig. 6.1.
The line shows the
relationship
between object
size and the
viewing distance
at which you
cannot recognize
an individual
object anymore

quency, i.e., the number of objects per inch. Example for reading the diagram: the characters in the alpha device image are less than 3 pt in height, or about 1 mm. This means you have to step back about three meters in order to no longer recognize the characters them- selves. Try it!

By the way, the diagram doesn't tell the whole truth. While it's hardly possible to recognize objects of 1/300 inch diameter, 300 dpi resolution is not at all sufficient for high-quality output. This not only holds true for halftoning – which reduces the usable resolution, as we will see shortly – but also for black-and-white objects, fonts, for example. The reason is the human eye's sensitivity to irregularities. Even if you can't recognize a single pixel, you can see the difference in width between a one-pixel and a two-pixel line.

Another interesting question relates to the number of gray levels the human eye is able to distinguish. The numbers given in scientific literature vary because they depend on certain environmental condi- tions. These include illumination as well as the medium's dynamic range, that is the ratio of lightest and darkest reproducible tone. Generally, we may assume that 200 levels of gray are sufficient to produce the impression of continuous shading. Accordingly, in PostScript Level 1 color depth is restricted to 8 bits, which gives 256 levels of gray. In Level 2, color depth may as well take 12-bit values, which means 4096 levels of gray, but applications hardly ever use this feature.

The classical halftoning technique employed for conventional printing creates the differently sized spots with a simple arrange-

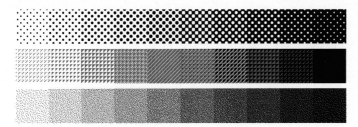

Fig. 6.2.
Simulating gray
levels using
clustered dot
dithering, pattern
dithering and
diffusion dithering

ment. It involves a specialized camera and a glass screen with engraved lines.[1] The original is photographed through the screening
plate. According to the laws of light diffusion, the size of each dot on
the film relates to the darkness of the image at the respective point in
the photograph. Depending on quality aspects and reproduction
technique, different screening parameters are used, the most important being the number of engraved lines per inch *(lpi)*, also known as
screen frequency. Conventional halftoning is not only simulated by
digital means, as we will see, but also the source of the technical
terms *halftoning, screening* and *lines per inch* – although in digital
reproduction we no longer use screening plates nor engraved lines.

Simulating gray levels is based on several pixels being lumped together to a larger halftone spot, this way yielding the impressing of
gray levels. The gray value is determined by the dot density, that is,
the ratio of the halftone spot's size related to the overall size of the
particular grid area. If all pixels are darkened, we have 100% black. If
no pixel at all is darkened, we get paperwhite, i.e., 0% black. If i out of
n available pixels are darkened, this area yields the impression of the
gray value i/n.[2]

How should the individual pixels in a halftone cell be darkened?
There are many ways, several of which are important in PostScript
screening. Generally, simulating gray levels on devices with limited
gray level capabilities is called *dithering* in computer graphics.

Clustered dot ordered dithering simulates photographical screening by lumping together individual pixels to larger dots. The pixel
group forms a larger spot that grows from the center of the halftone
cell outwards until it fills the whole cell. The clustered pixels imitate
the photographical spot. This is the predominant PostScript screening technique. We will cover it in more detail in the next section.

---

1. *I use a worn-out screen of this kind (two feet diameter, 150 lpi) as a tabletop. A friend of mine
saved it from an old lithography house waiting for demolition.*
2. *Often confusion results from the fact that in PostScript gray levels are specified by brightness,
not darkness: A value of 0 means black, a value of 1 means white. This difference comes from the
additive color model (black = no light = 0) and is relevant only if you manually edit PostScript
files.*

Dispersed dot ordered dithering or *pattern dithering* doesn't group together individual pixels but distributes (or disperses) them over the whole halftone cell. Each gray level is represented by a certain pixel pattern. This technique is mainly used at low resolutions, such as in monitors, and is featured in most image processing programs. It is also used by some printer manufacturers to improve laser printer halftones (HP Enhanced Halftone in the LaserJet 4M Plus, for example). The above-mentioned alpha device also belongs to this class, as its raster cells don't grow from the center but use fixed patterns (i.e., characters). Pattern dithering cannot normally be used in PostScript.

    Dispersed dot diffusion dither uses individual pixels which are not lumped together but are instead dispersed over the whole halftone area in a random manner. This makes the halftone cell less visible.

Fig. 6.3.
Several dithering techniques. Viewed from a distance, (b)–(d) appear similar, although they lack (a)'s detail resolution

(a) Original photo, screened for printing with clustered dot dithering (but with a much finer line screen)

(b) Clustered dot dither

(c) Pattern dither

(d) Diffusion dither

In Contrast to *ordered dithering* a certain gray level is represented by different pixel patterns each time it is reproduced. These individual calculations require significant processing power. Diffusion dithers have entered the world of PostScript recently by the name of stochastic or frequency modulated screening (FM). The term *stochastic screening* is derived from the random (stochastic) pixel distribution. Frequency modulated means that in contrast to clustered dot dithering not the amplitude (size) of the halftone spots varies but instead their frequency (number of spots per cell – not to be confused with the number of cells per inch). The spots' size remains constant. There are several proprietary drivers for color ink jet printers that implement this kind of dithering.

The techniques mentioned above are not only used for simulating gray levels, but also for color output. Commonly, in four-color printing the color components, cyan, magenta, yellow and black – CMYK in short – are halftoned separately and printed one after the other. When the individual colors merge together on paper, we have the impression of continuous color.

6.2 Frequency, Angle, and Spot Function

The vast majority of PostScript interpreters simulate gray levels and color with *clustered dot dither*ing, i.e., halftone spots that gradually increase in size until they fill the whole halftone cell. This halftoning technique is controlled by the frequency, angle, and spot function parameters. These parameters affect output quality but may not be chosen arbitrarily.

6.2.1 Frequency.
Frequency is the number of halftone cells per distance unit, for historical reasons called lines per inch (lpi). The larger the frequency, the smaller the resulting halftone cells. In order to achieve continuous gray levels – as opposed to a collection of discernible individual halftone spots – the frequency needs to be as high as possible. However, increasing the frequency also means reducing the number of pixels per halftone cell available for building the halftone spot. This number relates to the number of possible gray levels. Therefore we have to trade the number of different gray levels for a higher frequency. It's easy to calculate the relationship between the

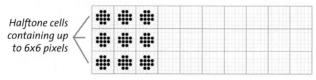

Halftone cells containing up to 6x6 pixels

Fig. 6.4.
Resolution and size of halftone spots

two entities: a square halftone cell with n pixels on each side yields $n^2 + 1$ different gray levels, as we may darken $0, 1, 2, \ldots , n^2$ pixel. For example, if the halftone cell is four pixels wide, between 0 and $4^2 = 16$ pixels may be darkened, which means 17 possible gray levels. The side of the cell in turn may easily be calculated as the resolution in dots per inch (dpi), divided by the number of halftone cells per inch. This yields

$$\text{Number of gray levels} = \left(\frac{\text{Resolution in dpi}}{\text{Frequency in lpi}} \right)^2 + 1$$

Figure 6.5 shows some examples for a halftoned image using different frequency values. Lower frequencies not only result in coarse halftone cells but also limit the usable detail resolution. Figure 6.6 plots the above formula for the relationship between the number of available gray levels and the frequency at resolutions of 300, 600, and 1200 dpi. The staircase characteristic relates to standard RT screening

Fig. 6.5.
Halftoning at 40,
60, 80, and 120 lpi

(rational tangent), the dotted line to Adobe AccurateScreens. We will examine both techniques in more detail shortly.

Different applications and printing techniques require or allow different frequency values:

Laser printer 300 dpi	50–80 lpi
Newspaper	75–90 lpi
Photocopier	50–90 lpi
Laser printer 600 dpi	70–110 lpi
Offset printing	70–110 lpi
Offset printing with coated paper	125–150 lpi
Offset printing with double coated paper	150–200 lpi

The table makes it clear why imagesetters use resolutions of several thousand dpi: if we demand 256 levels of gray at 150 lpi, applying the above formula shows that a resolution of 2400 dpi must be used!

The PostScript interpreter has to calculate a pixel pattern for each gray level the cell is to simulate. To speed up this calculation, the interpreter determines the pixel patterns for all available gray levels only once and store these patterns in a special cache memory. With decreasing frequency the number of pixels per halftone cell increases and therefore also the number of possible pixel patterns. The lim-

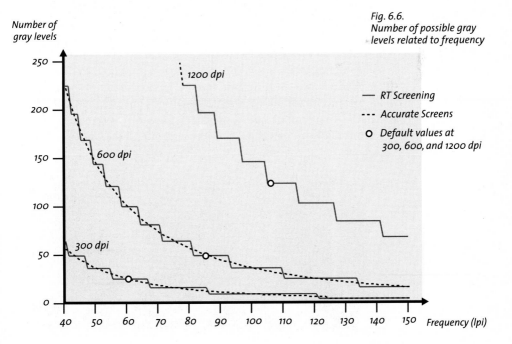

Number of gray levels

Fig. 6.6.
Number of possible gray levels related to frequency

—— RT Screening

- - - Accurate Screens

O Default values at 300, 600, and 1200 dpi

1200 dpi

600 dpi

300 dpi

Frequency (lpi)

ited screen cache memory poses a lower limit on the frequency. On many devices, the frequency cannot be lower than about 10 lpi.

6.2.2 Angle. If you examine halftoned images very closely, you will realize that the halftone cells are not aligned in a horizontal and vertical grid but with an angle of 45°. There are two reasons for choosing this screening angle. Firstly, human perception is optimized for recognizing horizontal and vertical features – most objects in everyday life are aligned this way: chairs, tables, houses, and even most people themselves. This means that diagonally oriented halftone cells make it easier to hide the screening structure and to withdraw attention from the halftone cells. Secondly, many objects contained in the image are aligned vertically or horizontally as well. Using diagonally oriented halftone cells reduces ugly interactions between image content and halftone grid.

If you only have to simulate gray levels using black ink, choosing an appropriate screening angle is easy: In most cases the halftone cells are aligned at 45°. But in four-color printing, choosing screen angles is more difficult. For technical reasons it's impossible to print four colors exactly one on top of the other; instead, one has to use different screen angles for each ink. When regular grids (or oscillations) are superimposed, a phenomenon called interference may occur. With acoustic oscillations – colloquially known as sounds – interference shows up as beat frequency: two sound overlap to create a third sound whose frequency equals the difference of the original sounds. It's easy to depict interference patterns of printed grids. Figure 6.8 shows two grids rotated by 5°, 15°, and 45°, respectively. In some cases, halftone spots cluster together to form a flowerlike shape. This is called a rosette. Interference produces strange patterns which are known as moiré. Since moiré patterns are often recognizable in the final printed matter, the goal is to prevent moiré patterns by technical means. To achieve this, the screening angles for the

Fig. 6.7.
Halftoning at
0°, 15°, and 45°
(at 85 lpi)

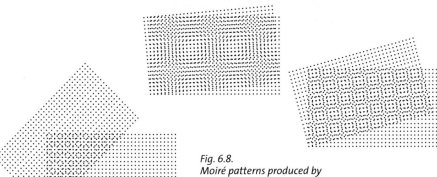

Fig. 6.8.
Moiré patterns produced by superimposing regular grids rotated by 5°, 15°, and 45°, respectively

process colors should be chosen as far apart from one another as possible. The following combination of angles has proven to be practical: Black, being the dominant color, is printed at 45°, which is least visible to the eye. Cyan and magenta are turned at 30° each with respect to black, i.e., 75° and 15°, respectively. Finally, yellow is printed at 0° because with such a light color even horizontal halftone cells are not easily spotted.

There are many many combinations of screening angle and frequency which are supposed to suppress moiré patterns. However, when exploring suitable combinations one has to face a fundamental problem with the clustered dot halftoning technique: the integer grid doesn't allow arbitrary angles but only certain rotations with an integer width/height ratio. Mathematically, the tangent of the rotation angle must be a rational number (i.e., ratio of integers). For this reason, the above method is called RT Screening (*rational tangent*). With RT Screening, a PostScript program may request arbitrary screening angles and frequencies but the interpreter in many cases has to adjust these values in order to fit the rectangular integer grid. This also explains the staircases in Figure 6.6: only certain numbers of gray levels are possible – the interpreter cannot produce in-between values. The same holds true for the frequency and angle values.

Screen angles on cash bills. As a side remark, there are completely different applications for varying the screening angle. If you happen to have some cash bills from European countries, you may be able to recognize one of several features to defeat money forgery.[1] For example, take one of Germany's 100 DM bills. If you can't find one, you can

1. *U.S. Dollar bills are a primary target for counterfeiters as they don't exhibit such features.*

Fig. 6.9.
"Secret writing"
by using different
screening angles

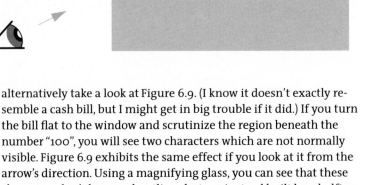

alternatively take a look at Figure 6.9. (I know it doesn't exactly re-semble a cash bill, but I might get in big trouble if it did.) If you turn the bill flat to the window and scrutinize the region beneath the number "100", you will see two characters which are not normally visible. Figure 6.9 exhibits the same effect if you look at it from the arrow's direction. Using a magnifying glass, you can see that these characters don't have real outlines but are instead built by a halftone screen whose angle is turned at 90° with respect to the surrounding area's halftone screen. The characters and the surrounding area have the same brightness. They are only visible because of varying light reflection caused by the rotated line screen.

6.2.3 Spot Function.

Up to now, we regarded the halftone spot as a circular black blob that gets bigger with increasing gray levels until it merges with its neighbors. However, in PostScript as well as in con-ventional screening it's possible to use other dot shapes instead of the circle. Elliptical, diamond, and other spots may not only be used for special effects (remember the line screen on cash bills) but more importantly for improving gray levels. In practice, the round dot has some disadvantages which are related to the printing ink's or toner's characteristics. When the edges of the tiny circles meet, the remain-ing white areas form little stars that tend to fill up with color, thereby darkening the image. Prepress experts talk about the remaining white area "plugging" with ink. At the light end of the gray scale the small dots may not keep the color, thereby lightening the image. With a round spot shape, the dots start joining at around 78% gray. This happens on four sides of the dot simultaneously. This dot join results in tonal jumps which are visible as shade-stepping, especially in blends.

The phenomenon of halftone spots not representing the gray value that in theory corresponds to the area covered is called *dot gain* and depends on the environment, e.g., on the type of ink or toner used and the characteristics of the paper.

Simple round dot:
{dup mul exch dup mul add 1 exch sub}

Euclidean spot:
{abs exch abs 2 copy add 1 gt {1 sub dup mul exch 1 sub dup mul add 1 sub} {dup mul exch dup mul add 1 exch sub} ifelse}

Line spot:
{pop}

Elliptical spot:
{dup mul 0.7 mul exch dup mul add 1 exch sub }

Fig. 6.10. Several halftone spot functions. The blends were printed at 15 lpi, the photographs at 110 lpi

In their first PostScript implementations, Adobe used the simple round halftone spot. After discovering its disadvantages, they switched to the so-called Euclidean spot in newer versions of the PostScript interpreter. This spot resembles a dark circle in the light tones, changes to a checkerboard pattern at 50%, and finally uses a white circle on dark background.

Figure 6.10 demonstrates the classical round spot and the Euclidean spot as well as two other spot functions. These spot functions are shown in a high-frequency photograph and a low-frequency blend which clearly shows the shape of the dots. Since in several programs you may manually enter PostScript code for spot functions (see Section 6.2.5), the appropriate PostScript statements are also included. We saw the line screen earlier when we discussed the security feature of cash bills. The elliptical spot has an advantage over the round spot in that adjacent spots only join at two places simultaneously. This reduces tonal jump artifacts. But the longish form may produce unwanted lines in the image.

6.2.4 Dot Gain and Transfer Function.

An ideal device behaves linearly, i.e., the output exactly resembles the gray value requested by the input (=PostScript program). In practice however, dot gain provides a nonlinear characteristic for most devices. Figure 6.11 shows a typical laser printer output curve, in which the gray levels in the mid-tones are too dark.

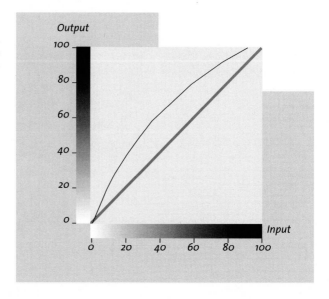

Fig. 6.11.
A typical laser
printer transfer
curve

In order to correctly reproduce the midtones, the gray values have to be adjusted to compensate for the output curve. It's clearly impractical to change the gray values of all objects in a PostScript file accordingly. Instead, PostScript has the concept of a *transfer function*. Using this function, a PostScript file adjusts all gray levels in one go. Each gray value has to pass this function, which may for example compensate for the dot gain in the midtones by decreasing the gray values accordingly. Making a device behave linearly by adjusting the input values is called gamma correction (especially with monitors).

To find the right amount for adjusting the gray values it's necessary to calibrate the device. This includes printing test pages which contain certain gray or color plates and then measuring the actual printed gray values. This is accomplished with a special device for measuring densities accurately (called a densitometer). However, you can also calibrate your printer without buying a densitometer (see below).

When calibrating a device it's important to realize that the calibration results heavily depend on the environmental conditions. This not only includes paper stock and toner or ink but also the halftone type and frequency. This is because dot gain depends on the size of the halftone spots and therefore on frequency and spot function. This means that each density measurement is only valid for the exact conditions under which the measurement was performed.

The transfer function may also be (mis-)used for special effects. Inverting the curve yields inverted output (black and white reversed). If you use asymmetric dot shapes, however, the result does not exactly resemble a negative version of the image. Another "misuse" is simulating the economy mode built into several printers: The transfer curve is changed in a way that every gray level is substituted by half its value. This is meant for test prints that don't need to be printed with the full amount of toner.

Calibrating a printer without a densitometer. Using a little trick it's possible to exactly measure gray values and calibrate a device without a densitometer. This may be helpful if laser-printed photos appear too dark but you can't afford a densitometer. As noted above, dot gain depends on the halftone spot size. By constructing a huge "halftone spot" that consists of a large black square and some surrounding white space, it's possible to reproduce exact gray values, provided you look at the image from a large enough distance. On the accompanying CD-ROM you will find test pages for simulating gray levels from 10% to 90% in this way (see Figure 6.12). The left-hand side of the page simulates a certain gray level with black squares, the

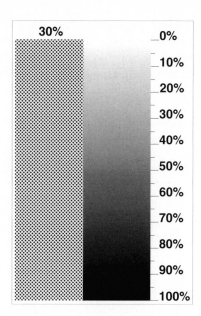

30%	0%
	10%
	20%
	30%
	40%
	50%
	60%
	70%
	80%
	90%
	100%

Fig. 6.12.
Test page for
measuring
density

right-hand side prints a gray blend using PostScript's standard spot function which is subject to the usual device inaccuracies (dot gain).

To perform the measurement, print all nine test pages and look at each from a distance of 10–20 feet with good illumination and a light background. For each page, find the area on the right side whose gray level resembles that of the left side and note its percentage value. It may not be easy to find this area, but it's possible to achieve a 5 percent accuracy. Watch the line in the middle where the left and right sides meet: at the top, the right side is clearly lighter than the left side, at the bottom it's darker. Somewhere in between you can hardly recognize the frontier line because both sides appear equally gray. This is the area whose percentage you are looking for.

Using the values "measured" in this way you can draw your printer's calibration curve. The percentage values you noted for the right side resemble the input, the exact values of the left side resemble the output. Using this transfer curve, you can correct the PostScript data in your application programs (see next section).

6.2.5 Controlling Halftone Parameters. Up to now, you have
learned that PostScript halftoning is controlled by frequency, angle, spot function, and transfer function. Quite naturally, you may ask how to change these parameters without doing PostScript programming. Once again, the answer is: it depends. Similar to the font download, application programs, drivers, and device offer several possibili-

ties which sometimes cancel each other out. If you want to produce complex pages or use rather esoteric halftoning parameters to achieve some special effects, make sure everything works as expected by doing a test print or a test page on the imagesetter. Always remember that (by definition) halftoning is device dependent!

Applications. The halftoning options of application programs vary with their PostScript capabilities. The forerunner is Adobe Photoshop: in its page setup dialog you can adjust all four halftoning parameters. Photoshop knows several standard dot shapes (=spot functions). If you are not satisfied with these, you can also hack your own PostScript code for custom halftone dots. Enter the appropriate PostScript code between curly braces in the "Shape", "Custom..." dialog of the "Halftone Screens" panel. The halftoning parameters are stored along with the image if you save it in the Photoshop or EPS formats. The "Transfer Functions" dialog allows to enter the results of your printer calibration. The table can hold the measured or estimated output gray value for several fixed input values.

While Adobe Illustrator is only able to globally change halftone parameters, in Macromedia FreeHand you can individually set each of the halftoning parameters for each object in a drawing.

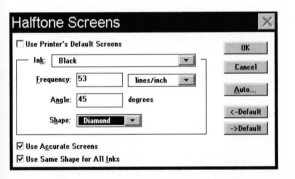

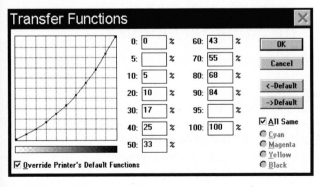

Fig. 6.13.
While most applications give the user global control over halftone parameters (left: Photoshop), FreeHand (above) allows to set them individually for each object in a drawing

PostScript drivers. In some drivers you can adjust halftoning parameters, in others you can't. While the Adober drivers for Windows
and Macintosh (LaserWriter 8) don't say anything about halftoning
and completely rely on the applications, the Microsoft driver for
Windows 3.1 accepts frequency and angle values in the "Options",
"Advanced..." menu (see Figure 2.8). The Windows 95 driver also
accepts these parameters in the "Graphics" tab (see Figure 2.12).

Device settings. Each PostScript device has default settings which
make the halftone process work even you don't specify any halftone
parameters yourself. These defaults are optimized for plain vanilla
applications which means they will produce acceptable results in
many cases, but not in all. If you have any special requirements
concerning halftoning, you have to take care of the appropriate
parameters yourself.

Take special care of the screen filters implemented in some imagesetter RIPs. These are operators that trap every attempt to modify
halftone parameters and changes them to what the manufacturer
thinks are better parameters. In some cases, they completely drop the
whole request. As we will see in the next chapter, this makes sense for
frequency modulated screening since this technique doesn't have a
notion of halftoning angle and frequency.

What takes precedence? Inside a PostScript file you can change
halftoning parameters as often as you like. In the following hierarchy,
if one step doesn't make any settings the one below takes precedence:

- Object-level settings (e.g., produced in a graphics program).
- Settings for embedded EPS files.
- Application program settings.
- Driver settings.
- Values adjusted by screen filters.
- Device defaults.

The screen filter is the only instance that may override other settings.

6.3 Improved Halftoning Techniques

PostScript's standard halftoning technique inhibits two major shortcomings:

- At low resolutions (laser printers especially), it achieves only a
  limited number of gray levels.
- High-end DTP has problems with moiré patterns caused by
  unfavorable frequency/angle combinations.

To solve the first problem, some manufacturers developed proprietary solutions to improve laser printer halftoning. Apple's Photo-

Grade technique varies individual pixels' size which in turns gives better control of the halftone spots' size. This yields as much as 91 gray levels at 300 dpi and a 106 lpi frequency. As you may see in Figure 6.6, this a large improvement on standard 300 dpi halftoning.

Hewlett-Packard's *Enhanced Halftoning* technique, which is used in the LaserJet 4M Plus printer, yields 122 levels of gray at 600 dpi and 106 lpi. Gray levels are simulated by *pattern dithering*.

Aside from such custom solutions, there are two important techniques to improve PostScript halftoning: supercell screening and frequency modulation.

6.3.1 Supercell Screening.
Each digital system is susceptible to quantization effects – informally known as stairstepping or jaggies – because digital entities can only achieve fixed values instead of arbitrary values. These effects are so common that we hardly notice them in many cases: A graphics program cannot draw slanted lines on the screen but only approximates them with little jaggies. With laser printing, we try to hide the jaggies by increasing the resolution. In digital halftoning, all entities are subject to quantization errors: the number of possible gray levels achieves only fixed values (see Figure 6.6) because the halftone spots in turn can only cover a certain percentage of the whole cell as they have to use an integer pixel count. Frequency and angle may be freely chosen – but how the interpreter uses them is a different story. The diagrams in Figure 6.14 show

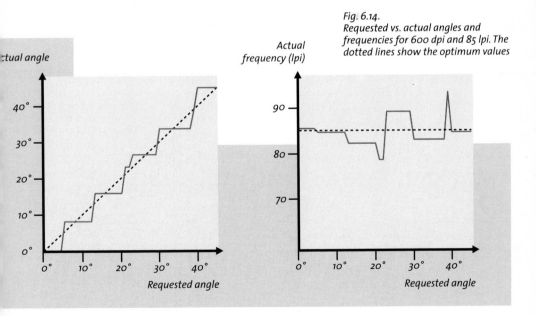

Fig. 6.14.
Requested vs. actual angles and frequencies for 600 dpi and 85 lpi. The dotted lines show the optimum values

which angle and frequency you'll get when you request angles between 0° and 45° on a 600 dpi device. The interpreter clearly has a hard time to deliver the requested values exactly.

While such inaccuracies are not directly visible to the eye, they can however cause the dreaded moiré patterns in multi-color printing. In order to prevent these, the frequency must be within 0.01 lpi and the angle within 0.001° of the optimum values. Using conventional screening, it's hard to keep tolerances this tight.

RT screening. The reason for the stepping artifacts is asy to understand. In our simplified screening model we regarded the halftone spot as a square that can be rotated at arbitrary angles. In the real world, however, the halftone cell has to be aligned to the pixel grid because we can't cut pixels as we can cut a cake. Even the square shape of the halftone cell can only be achieved in special cases, e.g., at an angle of 0°. Figure 6.15 shows halftone cell alignment at 45°. When rotating halftone cells, the corners of the cell must "snap" to the pixel grid. This means we can only achieve angles for which each corner has an integer vertical and horizontal distance from the lower left corner. As in math the ratio of these distances is called the tangent and the ratios of integers are known as rational numbers, conventional PostScript halftoning is also called *rational tangent* (RT) screening. With RT Screening all halftone cells have the same size and shape, and only a limited set of angles and frequencies is possible.

Supercells. The larger the halftone cell, the more accurate a certain angle is to achieve. Large cells, however, have the disadvantage of being easily discernible as such and of reducing usable resolution, resulting in less image detail. The supercell principle not only increases cell size but also combines individual cells to larger units or supercells (see Figure 6.16). In such a unit, individual cells may have

Fig. 6.15. The grid of half-tone cells at 45°

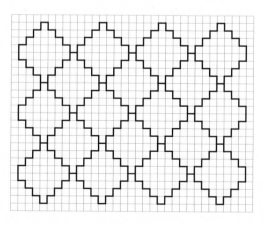

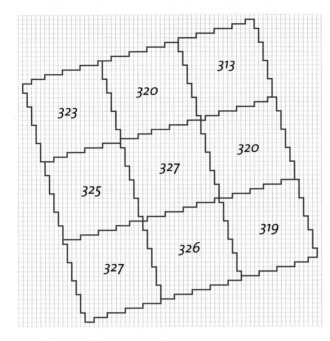

Fig. 6.16.
Combining several individual halftone cells in a supercell. The numbers indicate the number of available pixels in each cell

different sizes and shapes. These differences are accounted for in the supercell. Supercells make it possible to achieve the requested values much more exactly (see also Figure 6.6).

With RT Screening, the interpreter has to calculate the shape of the halftone dots only once since all cells have the same size and shape. Calculating supercells, however, requires much more interpreter horsepower. Each halftone cell has a different shape and has to be calculated individually, which needs much more processing power and memory.

Adobe integrated supercell screening under the name of *Accurate-Screens* in some Level 1 interpreters (Emerald RIP) and all Level 2 interpreters. Since AccurateScreens may heavily increase processing time and not every application needs the additional accuracy, it is not activated by default. Interpreters with AccurateScreens support have the following line in their PPD file:

```
*AccurateScreensSupport: True
```

AccurateScreens is activated by special PostScript operators which have to be generated by the application program (e.g., PhotoShop's "Halftone Screen" dialog, see Figure 6.13). AccurateScreens not only needs more processing time but also more memory. This may cause problems when less memory is available for the interpreter.

To reduce supercell processing time, Adobe developed special hardware for screening calculations. The PixelBurst coprocessor teams up with the RIPs CPU and not only calculates halftone cells but also carries out several other tasks which run very quickly because they are implemented in hardware.

Other vendors offer their own supercell solutions. In Linotype-Hell's RIPs it is called HQS Screening, Agfa markets Balanced Screening. In the real world, supercell screening had to make room for frequency modulated imaging which drew much attention in recent years.

6.3.2 Frequency Modulated Imaging.

While the supercell technique tries to closely approximate a given halftone angle and frequency, *frequency modulated* or *stochastic screening* completely eliminates halftone angles. We already encountered the basic principle in Section 6.1 when we took a look at *diffusion dithering*. Small spots are distributed over the available area so that they average the gray value. Contrary to classical halftone screening, the distribution is completely random. This random distribution accounts for the term *stochastic* screening. (In fact, one should talk about stochastic imaging as there are neither real nor conceptual screens.) While in conventional RT screening the distribution of the halftone spots remains constant and only their size or amplitude varies, in frequency modulated imaging the spots always have the same size, though they are unevenly distributed, i.e., their frequency varies (not to be confused with line frequency). The small spots have the nice side effect of improving detail resolution. But the smaller spot size makes the whole plate copying and printing process more demanding.

RIP manufacturers have developed several variations based on this principle. They differ with respect to the stochastic distribution of spots. Examples are BrilliantScreens (Adobe), CrystalRaster (Agfa), MezzoDot (Berthold), Diamond Screening (Linotype-Hell), ESCOR-VM (Varityper).

Generally, frequency modulated imaging is activated directly at the imagesetter's RIP which means the user doesn't have to prepare any special PostScript instructions to make use of it. Halftoning parameters set in the PostScript file (angle, frequency, spot function) are meaningless, however, and are disregarded by the interpreter.

6.4 Color Separation

As already noted, in offset printing the primary colors cyan, magenta, and yellow are used. In theory, combining the three colors at maximum intensity yields black. In the real world. however, a muddy brown results. This makes it necessary to add some black ink. The fourth color not only accounts for "real" black, but also enhances contrast (which is important for type) and deepens shadow areas. Additionally, the whole process consumes less ink since three colors are substituted by black ink. This saves money because black ink is cheaper than colored inks. Another reason for substituting equal amounts of primary colors with black is the speed of today's offset presses[1] – the paper cannot take large amounts of four inks quickly enough.

Splitting a colored image into its primary colors is called color separation. For each printing color, a separate film has to be produced from which the respective printing plate is copied. Printing colors are not only the process colors cyan, magenta, yellow, and black (CMYK) but also additional colors called *spot colors* or *custom colors*. These represent colors that may not be produced by combining process colors but need special ink. Spot color is used, for example, for printing a company letterhead in the corporate color. Using four colors in this case would result in exorbitantly high printing costs. There are some colors such as bright gold and silver tones that cannot be produced at all by mixing CMYK components.

Traditionally, to create color separated films, the lithographer had to photograph the original using several color filters. In the realm of PostScript, there are several possibilites for generating color separations:

- ▶ The application programs creates a separate PostScript file for each color component, thereby performing color separation itself.
- ▶ The application program creates a single PostScript file containing all color information (composite file). Additional separation software takes this file to create a single file for each separated color.
- ▶ PostScript level 2 interpreters are capable of generating color separations internally. This feature is not yet widely used, however.

An example for separation software is Adobe Separator. It redefines the PostScript color operators so that they only produce the separated color and leave the others alone. The redefined color operators are contained in a modified PostScript prolog. The actual page descriptions don't have to be modified. For this reason, separation software need not contain a complete PostScript interpreter. Separation software blows up the data volume: CMYK color separation produces four times as much PostScript data compared to a composite file. Hopefully, in the long run color separation software will be replaced by sepa-

---

1. Newspaper printing has been compared to putting kerosene on toilet paper at 200 miles per hour.

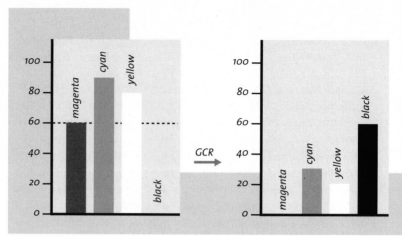

Fig. 6.17.
Equal amounts of
cyan, magenta and
yellow are replaced
with black (gray
component
replacement)

ration carried out in a Level 2 interpreter. Also note the related Section 3.3.6.

In order to reduce the amount of ink printed on the paper, equal amounts of cyan, magenta, and yellow are replaced by the same amount of black. This is done in two steps. *Gray Component Replacement* (GCR) or *Black Generation* determines the amount of black to be added. The black contribution can at most reach the minimum of the CMY amounts (see Figure 6.17). In the extreme case, one or more colors completely vanish so that the paper has to hold no more than two primary colors plus black at any one place. Since this technique may produce sharp color transitions, generally not the maximum possible amount of color is removed but slightly less.

Secondly, *Undercolor Removal* (UCR) reduces the CMY components to compensate for the amount of black ink added in the first step.

PostScript Level 2 includes two operators for controlling GCR and UCR. In practice, however, they are rarely used, since most software creates its own color separations and in modern image processing programs the user can exactly control black generation.

6.5 Exact Color Reproduction

The number of color PostScript devices has greatly increased over the last few years. In professional use, thermal transfer printers, color copiers, dye sublimation printers, and color lasers are in most cases PostScript-powered. Cheap hardware and powerful software brings color to the desktop. However, it cannot be taken for granted that the final printed product appears in the same colors seen on the monitor.

The fundamental differences in color reproduction on screen (additive color model, RGB primary colors) and printing press (subtractive color model, CMYK primary colors) often yield ruddy skin tones, poison green apples, or other artifacts in printing – although on the screen everything looked perfectly alright.

The situation somehow resembles that of digital typography ten years ago: PostScript offers important aids for solving everyday problems, but current software doesn't use them optimally. In the late 1980s, there were Type 1 fonts, but font supply and system integration were still too bad. Color reproduction today is similar: PostScript Level 2 offers device-independent color (shortly we will see what this means), but only few applications make use of it. Only recently has device-independent color been integrated in the main operating systems.

The following sections will give an overview of the problems related to exact color reproduction and solutions offered by color management systems.

6.5.1 Color Spaces.

The most important goal when working with color is to achieve constant color reproduction. The colors shown on the monitor should exactly match the printed colors. In order to understand why such a seemingly simple goal requires much effort we have to take a look at the problem of specifying and measuring colors.

Device-dependent color spaces. Most computer users and programmers are accustomed to at least two systems for quantitatively describing colors (so-called color spaces). The RGB color space starts out with black and combines red, green, and blue light to mix colors. Its technical implementation can be found in any color monitor equipped with three electron guns firing at red, green, and blue phosphors located near the screen. For each pixel, phosphor atoms are excited which emit light in one of the primary colors. In-between colors are generated according to additive color mixing: if there is no primary color, all color is missing and the screen remains black; all three primaries fired together at maximum intensity produce white light.

In the printing process, however, we have subtractive color mixing: starting with white paper, colored ink particles are added which absorb certain colors from the surrounding white light. If there is no color, we have white (or the color of the paper); maximum ink for each primary color completely absorbs the light which yields black. As described above with color separation, the primary colors cyan, magenta, and yellow as well as black are used.

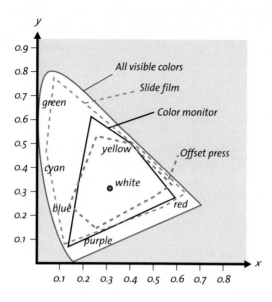

Fig. 6.18.
The CIE chromaticity diagram and the color gamuts of slide film, monitor and offset press

In theory, it's possible to convert RGB and CMYK colors with simple formulas. At first sight it seems that color specification is exact. However, it is easy to understand that this is not true: the darkest black a monitor can produce depends on the surrounding illumination, the colors it can create depend of the type of phosphor used. In four-color printing, the tone of the paper determines the brightest white, color combinations depend on the inks in use. The subject is further complicated by other artifacts. For example, not every color can be reproduced by mixing three or four primary colors.

Even if we have formulas to convert between RGB and CMYK values, this doesn't guarantee identical color on monitor and paper. Why in the world should the combination of three colored phosphors exactly match the paper's white? The RGB and CMYK color spaces (and several others) are related to a certain class of output device. For this reason, they are called device-dependent color spaces. Color spaces which are not suitable for comparing colors with absolute fidelity are called non-calibrated.

Device-dependent CIE color spaces.   In an attempt to allow device-independent and therefore portable color measurement, as early as 1931 the Commission Internationale d'Éclairage (CIE) defined color spaces which are not related to a certain output device. Instead, they are based on a mathematical model of human color perception. In CIE color spaces (there are several variants), colors are specified by three abstract coordinates which are derived from human color perception. When graphically depicting these color spaces, the brightness coordinate is usually ignored which results in the two-dimensional diagram shown in Figure 6.18. This CIE chromaticity diagram (colloquially also known as a horseshoe diagram) contains all visible colors. The spectral (or rainbow) colors from purple, blue, cyan, green, and yellow to red are located along the perimeter of the horseshoe, white is located close to the center. Figure 6.18 also shows the color areas that may be reproduced using slide film, color monitor, and offset press. The set of colors that may be achieved on a certain device is called its gamut. These gamut areas make it clear that we definitely cannot print all visible colors. Additionally, a monitor is able to display colors which are not possible in print – and vice versa.

Several variations of the CIE color space have been developed which are related to the original CIEXYZ color space – named after its coordinates – by mathematical transformations. The most important extensions are the L*a*b* (also called CIELAB) and L*u*v* (also called CIELUV) color spaces. L*a*b* separates luminance and two color components, arbitrarily called a and b.

6.5.2 Gamut Compression.

"Exact" color reproduction on different devices is related to a fundamental problem which may not even be solved by the most exact device calibration. If you cannot reproduce every color, the best thing to do is to convert one device's gamut into another device's gamut. This conversion is called gamut compression.

According to the type of image several strategies are used: With *colorimetric gamut compression* every color contained in the output device's gamut is reproduced exactly, colors outside its gamut are approximated by the "nearest" color (however that may be defined). Different colors in the original may happen to be mapped to the same output color. Colorimetric gamut compression is mainly useful for photographs of real scenarios.

With *perceptual gamut compression* the original's gamut is compressed into the output device's gamut. White is mapped to the brightest color the output device can reproduce, black is mapped to the darkest, and the colors are adjusted accordingly. This may change all colors involved; however, color differences (or "distances") rarely vanish. This technique is mainly used for computer graphics and machine-generated images.

Output device variations. Exact color reproduction is not only made worse by the color characteristics, which not only vary among output techniques in general, but also among several printer makes and even among several samples of the same printer make. This is caused by aging effects and manufacturing tolerances which both may change the color characteristics over time.

6.5.3 Color Management Systems.

We have identified two main problems in color reproduction: The color specification in device-dependent color spaces is inaccurate, and gamut compression distorts the colors. In order to handle these difficulties, several measures are necessary:

- ▶ The color data of the original have to be defined in a device-independent manner.
- ▶ Each device involved needs an appropriate color profile describing its color behaviour exactly.
- ▶ At each input (scanner) or output (monitor, printer) operation the image data have to be converted according to the device's color profile.

The first topic is up to the application software. Adobe Photoshop, for example, internally handles colors in the device-independent L*a*b* color space and allows color image data to be stored in a device-independent format. Additionally, this allows calibrated color data to PostScript Level 2 printers to be directly transmitted (see next section).

To create color profiles, device characterization and calibration is necessary. Characterization means the relationship between the device color space and a CIE color space and is performed by the manufacturer. Calibration is necessary to compensate for the color shifts caused by aging and other effects. For monitors, this means determining the color values of the used phosphor, the white point, and the gamma curve (nonlinear relationship between signal voltage and

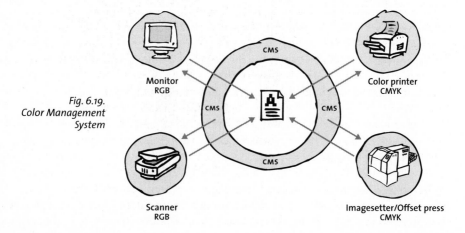

Fig. 6.19.
Color Management
System

ouput intensity). For scanners the values delivered for reference plates are determined. For printers white point and black point (the brightest and darkest possible color) as well as the available primary colors are measured in order to determine the printer's color gamut. In addition, dot gain curves (halftoning and color shifts) are needed which often means measuring thousands of color patches.

Converting color data between device-dependent color spaces and CIE color spaces as well as managing device profiles is optimally done by a *Color Management System* (CMS) built into the operating system. A CMS knows the properties of all involved devices and performs the appropriate conversions. Standardization and integration into the operating system are necessary to give application programmers and device driver developers a well-known interface for controlling the devices. To integrate a new scanner, monitor or printer, the manufacturer has to provide the appropriate device profile. Alternatively, the user may create the profile himself with the help of calibration software.

The color data may be treated in one of two different ways. Either all color data is converted to a CIE system immediately before any further processing, or it is stored in a device-dependent color space and additionally tagged with an appropriate device profile which allows color conversions to be performed at a later time. This second method saves a lot of calculations, since color space conversions are very compute-intensive. The conversion routines are called *Color Matching Methods* (CMM) and are part of the CMS. As described above, they may convert colorimetrically or perceptually.

Standardization of Color Management Systems (CMS).   The practical use of a CMS depends on its integration into the operating system. Ideally, the color profiles used for device characterization can be exchanged between different operating systems. In 1993, several major players in the hardware and software business (among them Agfa, Apple, Adobe, Kodak, Microsoft, Sun, and SGI) formed the International Color Committee (ICC) to promote standardization. Apple once again was the forerunner and integrated the ColorSync CMS into MacOS. ColorSync includes default color matching methods which already achieve good results. Additionally, color matching methods (conversion routines) of other manufacturers may be integrated.

While Apple bought its conversion algorithms at Linotype-Hell, other operating system vendors licensed color technology from Kodak. Microsoft integrated the Kodak scheme in Windows 95 by the name of ICM (Image Color Matching). The device profiles of ICC members are said to be compatible among operating systems. While color processing on the Mac is an important factor, on Windows it is still in its infancy. We may well expect applications that make use of color management in Windows 95 to appear very soon.

6.5.4 Color Processing in PostScript Level 2.

Color processing in PostScript Level 2 was completely revamped with respect to Level 1 color devices which only support device-dependent color spaces. Having in mind the previous section on color management systems, Adobe's vision in implementing color processing in Level 2 is remarkable. This especially holds true when we recall that the specification of Level 2 is several years old while color management systems only recently make use of its functions.

Color processing in Level 2 is performed in two strictly separated phases (see Figure 6.20). *Color specification* first describes the input data. This includes the type of color space in use as well as additional parameters. While the interpreter internally uses the device-independent CIEXYZ color space, it accepts device-dependent color spaces (such as RGB or CMYK) as well as device-independent color spaces. By cleverly choosing the parameters a wide range of color spaces is possible. This range includes the internally used XYZ, calibrated RGB, standard CIEL*a*b* and the video systems YIQ and YUV used in the NTSC, SECAM, and PAL television standards. Additionally, one-dimensional color spaces may be used, for example, calibrated grayscale.

For specifying a color space, conversion functions to the internally used CIE system must be given as well as the gamut of the image data to be printed. To achieve this, the color specification includes the white point (the brightest color used) and optionally the black point (the darkest color). This first phase of color processing is in no way related to the device but only depends on the image data.

All the device-dependent operations in color processing take place in the second phase called *color rendering*. This means converting the colors specified in the first step in values suited for the output device.

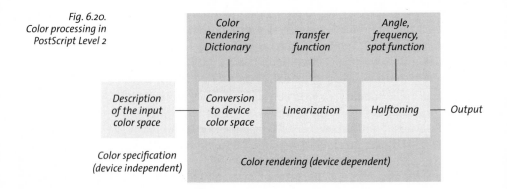

Fig. 6.20.
Color processing in
PostScript Level 2

If the input data were specified in a CIE color space, gamut conversion has to be performed and the modified CIE values have to be transformed to final color data (CMYK, for example) by means of the *color mapping function*. As described above, for the gamut conversion to be successful both the input data's gamut and the device's gamut must be known. While the former is part of the color specification, the latter is (along with the color mapping function) contained in a special data structure called *Color Rendering Dictionary* (CRD).

The color rendering dictionary contains all device-specific properties relating to color output, that is the color gamut, white point, and black point as well as routines for converting CIE color spaces to the device's color space. CRDs don't belong in regular PostScript files but are meant to adjust color output and to calibrate a device. Each Level 2 interpreter is shipped with a default CRD which contains suitable conversion routines and parameters for the device. Using PostScript instructions, it's possible to replace the default CRD with another one representing new device calibration data or new conversion routines. This is analogous to the parameters describing transfer function, halftone angle, frequency, and spot function: All these parameters are device-dependent and should only be changed for a certain device or to achieve special output effects. The application software has to provide means to change these parameters.

Contrary to the halftoning parameters, entering a few numbers in a dialog box is not sufficient. The implementation of device-independent CIE color spaces in PostScript Level 2 forms the basis of calibrated color output. The CRD resembles an interface for supplying calibration data from the CMS to the PostScript interpreter. Ideally, the device profiles managed by the CMS (which already contain calibration data and conversion routines) can be packaged as CRD and sent to the PostScript device. For example, AppleSync is able to convert device profiles to CRDs in order to provide calibration data for Level 2. This allows the processing power needed for color correction to be distributed: Either the image data are being adjusted on the workstation using the device profile, or they are sent unaltered to the printer which adjusts it for output using a suitable CRD.

The employment of CIE color spaces, the strict division between device-dependent and device-independent phases, and the flexibility provided by CRDs make PostScript Level 2 an important building block of exact color reproduction.

Display PostScript

PostScript's success in the printer and imagesetter business suggested implementing the page description language for computer monitors also. This extension is called Display PostScript (DPS) and is used on Workstations with the X Window System (X11) and NEXTSTEP.

7.1 Overview

7.1.1 Advantages of Display PostScript.   As early as 1985, when the first LaserWriter printers hit the market, Adobe startet developing a PostScript extension for computer displays. This extension was jointly developed at Adobe and NeXT and first implemented in the NEXTSTEP operating system. Several years later, when the X Window System (X11) blossomed into an accepted standard for graphical Unix workstations, Adobe integrated Display PostScript into X11 with the help of the Unix manufacturer DEC.

Using a single graphics language for both monitor and printer eliminates many format conversions which on other systems are necessary for printing and often introduce rounding errors and degrade quality. When printing, both Microsoft Windows and Macintosh need to convert from their intrinsic graphics model (GDI and QuickDraw, respectively) to an appropriate printer language. Using Display PostScript, converting a screen representation to a PostScript printer representation is straightforward. Display PostScript even improves screen output quality:

- ▶ When creating compound documents, imbedded EPS graphics are directly displayed on the screen; it's no longer necessary to supplement the PostScript data with preview bitmaps.
- ▶ The available wealth of PostScript fonts may be used on the screen. Text is being displayed in arbitrary size and orientation, text effects such as shearing, outline fonts, etc., are as easy as plain text.
- ▶ On a monochrome screen, DPS automatically simulates gray levels by means of dithering. Screening and dithering are used for all graphical objects (image data, line art, or text).
- ▶ Color representation is optimized for the respective device. This ensures optimal color output. Display PostScript simulates colors that are not available on the screen by dithering.
- ▶ Bitmaps may be arbitrarily scaled, rotated, and color-changed.

At first sight, it may sound a little bit strange to integrate Display PostScript as screen control language into an existing window system (NEXTSTEP and X11, respectively). However, the window system was an important prerequisite, because Display PostScript only offers a graphics model and operators for implementing it. It does not have any interactive functions such as window management or handling of mouse events. For this reason, Display PostScript always cooperates with another layer implemented in the operating system or the X Window server.

Fig. 7.1.
Display
PostScript in
NEXTSTEP

7.1.2 Language Extensions in Display PostScript.

The Post-Script interpreter in a printer processes static page descriptions only: it reads statements describing the page from the relay channel, the interpreter generates the page in memory, and finally the print engine produces the printed page.

Display PostScript, however, operates in a dynamic environment in which a user may use multiple windows simultaneously. The contents of a window are not related to the rest of the screen – windows overlap each other, are visible again and have to be partially redrawn. Today's low screen resolution of about 72 to 100 dpi make it necessary to optimize text output for legibility.

To meet these requirements Adobe implemented several language extensions in Display PostScript, many of which made their way into PostScript Level 2. Some concepts and operators are however only reasonable in interactive systems and are therefore missing in printer implementations.

Window management. When moving windows on the screen, it often happens that parts of a window are obscured and others need to be redrawn. It would be very inefficient to redraw the whole window contents only to make a previously hidden part of it visible again. With the *view clipping* operators the programmer can tell the interpreter which parts have to be redrawn. A program may use *hit detection* features to determine whether a given pixel lies inside or outside of an object (to decide, for example, whether a mouseclick hit an object or a menu). Finally, adjusting the halftone phase eliminates ugly artifacts that may occur when the user scrolls a dithered or halftoned window area and multiple halftones don't align any more.

Bitmap fonts. Low resolution is a big obstacle for high-quality screen output. This is especially true for text at small point sizes. If only a few pixels are available for each glyph, the characters are not only ugly, but also rounding errors in the character width may occur which affect legiblity. Manually created bitmap characters, which must be drawn by a type designer in addition to the outline font, improve legibility but may also differ from the exact character width. In Display PostScript it is possible to integrate such hand-tuned bitmap fonts into the system. Application software can decide whether to use bitmap fonts for small point sizes or to always use automatically generated characters.

Contexts. A printer processes the contents of several pages one after the other. On the contrary, a DPS system must be capable of dealing with several independent windows simultaneously (i.e., manage several "pages" at the same time). In order to achieve this, DPS associates a context with each window. A context pretends to be a separate PostScript interpreter; in reality a single interpreter handles all contexts and multitasks their operations – much the same way modern operating systems handle multiple applications simultaneously.

Normally, a single context suffices for the screen output of a particular program. There are situations, however, in which a single program may as well use multiple contexts, e.g., for drawing embedded EPS graphics.

Efficient operator encoding. In order to meet the performance requirements of an interactive system, DPS applications accelerate output by means of a compact binary enconding called *encoded user names*. This technique supplements other binary encodings available on all PostScript Level 2 systems.

7.1.3 Availability of Display PostScript. The somewhat orphaned NEXTSTEP operating system set aside, Display PostScript is mainly used in combination with the X Window System on several Unix Workstations. DPS is however not part of the X11 core system; each manufacturer has to license it with Adobe and offer it as part

of their own X11 implementation. Unfortunately, DPS did not make a standard for graphical workstations up to now. Nevertheless, the number of Display PostScript machines increases steadily.

Users of other manufacturers' workstations need not do without Display PostScript: the DPS/NX agent, part of Acrobat Reader 1.0 and delivered with several Adobe applications, enables DPS on arbitrary X servers (see Section 7.2.1).

While early Display PostScript implementations contained only Level 1 operators plus several DPS specific enhancements, newer DPS systems are based on PostScript Level 2 (NEXTSTEP started Level 2 compatibility with version 3.0). The following table gives an overview of Display PostScript systems manufacturers:

Manufacturer	Operating system	Window system
NeXT	NEXTSTEP	NEXTSTEP
DEC	OSF/1, Open VMS, ULTRIX	X Window System, DECwindows
IBM	AIX	X Window System, AIX windows
SGI	IRIX	X Window System
SunSoft	Solaris 2.3 and above	X Window System
ICS	SunOS extension	X Window System

7.2 Display PostScript in the X Window System (DPS/X)

7.2.1 DPS/X Architecture.
The X Window System is based on a strict division of labor. The X server handles screen, mouse, and keyboard, processes user input and generates screen output. Application programs are called clients and cannot access the hardware directly. Instead, they communicate with the server. Client–server communication is done via the X protocol. This protocol is LAN capable (TCP/IP in most cases) which means that client and server may run on different machines in the network.

X Server with DPS extension. In the original configuration, DPS/X was implemented as an extension to the X Window System. The PostScript Interpreter is part of the X server, applications send PostScript commands to the server via the X protocol. The *xdpyinfo* program, used to display general information about the server in use, indicates a DPS extensions with the following line:

```
Adobe-DPS-Extension
```

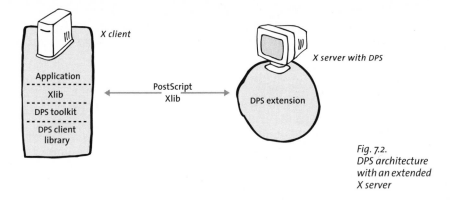

Fig. 7.2.
DPS architecture
with an extended
X server

There is an X library function which a client can use to decide whether the server is DPS powered or only accepts conventional X calls.
Since DPS is implemented as an X11 extension without sacrificing the
original functionality, it is fully compatible with existing applications that do not use PostScript for screen output.

DPS/NX agent. In many cases it is impossible to upgrade a workstation to use Display PostScript, either because the manufacturer
doesn't offer DPS or the X server is integrated into an X terminal. In
this case, the DPS/NX agent allows screen output via PostScript. In
such a configuration the interpreter isn't implemented as part of the
X server but runs as a "regular" program on the same machine as the
application. The NX agent accepts DPS calls from the program, interprets them, and translates them to plain old X calls which it sends to

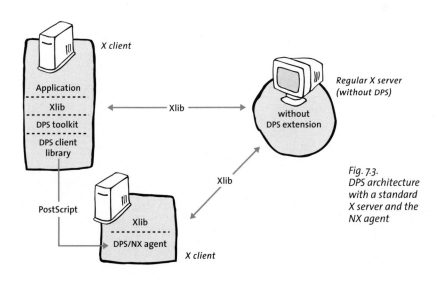

Fig. 7.3.
DPS architecture
with a standard
X server and the
NX agent

the server via the X protocol. This way the NX agent DPS-enables arbitrary X servers. The application checks at startup time whether the X server in use contains the DPS extension. If not, it launches the NX agent.

Extensions for X clients.   X Clients must be modified in order to take advantage of Display PostScript. This is simplified by several components which fit into X11's layered programming model:

- ► The Client Library allows the client to send PostScript commands to the server. The Client Library starts the DPS/NX agent if necessary (invisible to the client).
- ► The *pswrap* utility translates PostScript procedures to C functions which may be called in an application program. This enables application developers to integrate their own PostScript procedures.
- ► The DPS toolkit contains several programming aids on a higher abstraction level, e.g., a file previewer, a dialog box for choosing fonts, and the font sampler which shows samples of all installed fonts (see Figure 7.4).

One of the X Window System's biggest advantages is its platform independence. Applications may run on a certain machine and output over the network on a second workstation (probably driven by a different operating system) or an X terminal. This cross-platform capability would be lost if one could only develop and launch Display

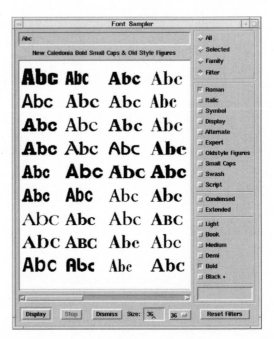

Fig. 7.4.
The font sampler
in the DPS toolkit
simplifies font
selection in
application
programs

PostScript applications on DPS systems. For this reason, Adobe donated the Client Library and the pswrap utility as a contribution to the X Window System. Using these, it is possible to develop and launch Display PostScript applications on any X11 machine (with or without DPS). Of course the applicaton has to send its output to a DPS capable X server. The client components of Display PostScript are freely available, whereas the server with the PostScript interpreter isn't. The NX agent, which also contains an interpreter, is also freely available (with Acrobat Reader 1.0). Not surprisingly, it is configured to cooperate with Acrobat only.

7.2.2 PostScript Resources.

A PostScript interpreter and applications need access to several kinds of data which are called resources (similar to Level 2). This includes fonts and metrics files, encoding vectors, PostScript prologs (*procsets*) and more. In Unix, these resources are configured with ASCII files. They use the file name suffix *.upr* (*Unix PostScript resource*). The following example shows part of the NX agent's UPR file:

```
PS-Resources-1.0
FontAMFM
FontExtra
FontAFM
FontAxes
FontBlendMap
FontBlendPositions
FontFamily
FontOutline
.
FontAFM
AdobeSansXMM-BlackCn=AdobeSansXMM.font/AdobeSansXMM-BlackCn.AFM
...
Times-Roman=Times-Roman.font/Times-Roman.afm
ZapfDingbats=ZapfDingbats.font/ZapfDingbats.afm
.
FontFamily
...
ITC Zapf Dingbats=Medium,ZapfDingbats
Symbol=Medium,Symbol
Times=Bold Italic,Times-BoldItalic,Bold,Times-Bold,Italic,
Times-Italic,Roman,Times-Roman
.
FontOutline
AdobeSansXMM=AdobeSansXMM.font/AdobeSansXMM
AdobeSerifMM=AdobeSerifMM.font/AdobeSerifMM
Courier=Courier.font/Courier
Courier-Bold=Courier-Bold.font/Courier-Bold
...
```

```
Times-Roman=Times-Roman.font/Times-Roman
ZapfDingbats=ZapfDingbats.font/ZapfDingbats
```

The sections of a UPR file are separated by periods and describe the following types of resources:

Keyword	Meaning
FontOutline	Font definition files
FontPrebuilt	Prebuilt bitmap font files supplementing outline fonts
FontAFM	Metrics files in AFM format
FontAMFM	Metrics files in AMFM format for multiple master fonts
FontAxes	Axis names for multiple master fonts
FontExtra	Additional information for multiple master fonts
FontBlendMap	Equivalent to the BlendMap entry in multiple master fonts
FontBlendPositions	Equivalent to the BlendPositions entry in multiple master fonts
FontBDF	Bitmap fonts in BDF format
FontBDFSizes	BDF font parameters (point size, x and y resolution)
FontFamily	Characteristics and names of each member of a font family
Form	Form definition files
Pattern	Pattern definition files
Encoding	Encoding files
ProcSet	PostScript prolog files

Creating UPR files with makepsres.   If you want to install additional resources (mainly fonts), you have to extend the UPR files according-ly. This is most easily accomplished with the *makepsres* utility, which is installed along with Display PostScript or the NX agent. When it creates a new UPR file, this tool honors PostScript resources from several origins:

▸ Resource files contained in directories specified on the command line.

▸ Resource files whose names are contained in UPR files, whose names have in turn been specified on the command line.

▸ Resource entries from UPR files directly specified on the command line.

makepsres recognizes several types of resource data automatically (fonts, for example). Unknown resource files must start with a line of the form

```
%!PS-Adobe-3.0 Resource-<resource-type>
```

Alternatively, the user can specify the resource type interactively. The default file name for resource files is *PSres.upr*.

The man page of makepsres contains more information and a list of command line options.

Search path for UPR files. The system administrator or a user can use the PSRESOURCEPATH environment variable to specify one or more directories which Display PostScript or the NX agent should search for UPR files. Multiple directory names are separated by the familiar colon character. Two successive colons instruct the programs to search their respective (program dependent) default directories. The listed directories are first searched for a file named *PSres.upr*. If it is found and starts with the line

```
PS-Resources-Exclusive-1.0
```

the search process is finished. If the keyword *Exclusive* is missing or *PSres.upr* doesn't exist at all, every file named *.upr* in that directory is examined.

7.2.3 Installing Additional Fonts.
Including additional fonts is the most important reason for customizing the default resource configuration. This not only relates to Display PostScript and commercial Adobe applications but also to Acrobat Reader 1.0: installing often used fonts speeds up font rendering and improves display quality. If Acrobat Reader has access to a font's outline definition, it is unnecessary to simulate the font with Acrobat's Multiple Master mechanism.

If you want to install a font, you need the font's ASCII file containing the outline definition and the metrics file in AFM format (check out Section 4.6.3 if you have to convert from other formats). If you converted fonts from other platforms, rename the font files with the name of the font. This makes it easy to identify the font files.

Let's assume font and AFM files are contained in the */home/thomas/fonts* directory. Use the following shell commands to configure the fonts for use in Acrobat Reader (according to your particular type of shell you might have to adapt these commands accordingly):

```
cd /home/thomas/fonts
makepsres
PSRESOURCEPATH=/home/thomas/fonts::
export PSRESOURCEPATH
acroread&
```

The easiest way is to define the PSRESOURCEPATH environment variable in the shell's initialization file (*.cshrc, .login, .profile* or whatever). To make fonts available to all Acrobat users on a system, the system administrator may include the line

```
SITE_PSRESOURCEPATH=/home/thomas/fonts
```

in the file <installdir>/AcroRead_1.0/custom/SITE_PSRESOURCEPATH.
Acrobat Reader automatically reads this file at startup time.

Font directory names. The fact that each DPS system manufacturer installs fonts in another directory structure doesn't really facilitate multi-platform system management. The following table contains the names of the default font directories. For comparison, the table also contains some non-DPS systems which use Type 1 fonts for screen display.

System	Default directory for PostScript fonts
DEC OSF/1	/usr/lib/X11/fonts/Type1Adobe
DEC Ultrix	/usr/lib/DPS/outline/decwin
HP-UX 9.0	/usr/lib/X11/fonts/type1.st/typefaces
IBM AIX	/usr/lpp/DPS/fonts/outlines /usr/lib/X11/fonts/Type1/DPS
NEXTSTEP	/NextLibrary/Fonts/outline (default fonts) /LocalLibrary/Fonts/outline (additional fonts)
SGI IRIX	/usr/lib/DPS/outline/base /usr/lib/X11/fonts/Type1
Solaris and SunOS	/usr/openwin/lib/X11/fonts/Type1/outline
Ultrix	/usr/lib/DPS/outline/decwin
Unix SVR4.2	/usr/lib/X11/fonts/type1 (additional fonts) /usr/lib/X11/fonst/mitType1 (fonts from the MIT distribution)
VMS	SYS$COMMON:[SYSFONT.XDPS.OUTLINE]

Adobe Acrobat and PDF

8

Adobe Acrobat and the Portable Document Format (PDF) promise to simplify universal document exchange, regardless of the operating system and application software. Thanks to hypertext capabilities, PDF documents are even superior to their paper counterparts. This chapter explains the basics of PDF and how it is related to PostScript, presents typical PDF/Acrobat applications, and gives practical hints for using Acrobat software.

8.1 The Roots of Acrobat

8.1.1 The Paperless Office – Mere Fiction?   The cliché of the paperless office is as old as it is false: The employment of computers in offices and homes enormously pushed paper consumption. While formerly a letter produced on a typewriter was certainly good enough, people nowadays demand elaborate DTP documents which have to be printed several times in order to try different fonts or to correct minor typos.

In many application areas paper is indeed essential. Legal aspects aside (validity of contracts and signatures), psychological aspects play a major role: who wants to read his newspaper in the subway on a notebook computer instead of printed on paper? In the offices ergo-nomics are important: a real desktop offers much more space than a virtual one. Also, papers lying on the real desk are much more com-fortable to read, since they have resolution and contrast values which in the near future cannot be matched by computer monitors.

A more complex society demands more communication means. Every small office tries to network computers and peripherals, on the national and global level online services (e.g., Internet, CompuServe) grow at an enormous rate. In some application areas e-mail is much more important than conventional mail (fondly called "snail mail") and fax.

While digital communication obviously has its advantages, it also suffers from some limitations: it's not sufficient merely to network the computers – all participants have to agree on the operating sys-tems and application software used for information interchange. At first glance this may not seem to be a major obstacle. But consider an engineer who wants to send a technical drawing that he created on his workstation to the marketing department which uses only Macs. Even if sender and receiver of a document use the very same system and program, the receiver can only open a document if he or she has installed the necessary fonts.

Online publishing, i.e., digital publication of books, magazines, and other documents, is another example. Which kind of file format should be used in order to make the data accessible to as many poten-tial users as possible? Of course, one could confine oneself to pure text files, but these can't fulfil today's graphics design requirements (corporate identity created by special fonts and demanding graph-ics). Let's summarize the requirements on a universal file format for data exchange:

> ▸ It is independent from a certain operating system, application program, or manufacturer.

- It doesn't suffer from limitations regarding graphical and layout features.
- It solves the font problem.
- The files should be very space-efficient to save storage space and network bandwidth.
- The files should be editable.
- The format should be open and extensible.
- The format should seamlessly integrate into the existing work-flow.

8.1.2 The PostScript Experience.

In order to understand PDF's details, it helps to recall the pros and cons of PostScript which developers as well as users have got used to in the course of more than ten years.

PostScript's often-told advantages regarding output satisfy some of the above requirements: its graphics capabilities and typographic quality as well as independence from programs, character sets, and operating systems are important properties. Even so, a number of severe disadvantages impede the use of PostScript as a file exchange or archiving format for digital documents:

- PostScript files can get very large.
- A PostScript interpreter is needed to process PostScript files.
- PostScript files cannot be edited (to change individual objects on a page).
- It's difficult to manipulate the pages in a document, e.g., change the page order or extract single pages.
- Searching for text phrases in PostScript files is impractical, if not impossible.
- The linear page ordering makes it difficult to access arbitrary pages in the document.
- "Font not found, using Courier": a document is unusable if the necessary fonts are not available.

Since these disadvantages are not only very tiresome when exchanging documents but also when using PostScript as a page description language for driving output devices, PostScript's inventor, Adobe, tried to create some remedies: Level 2's compression algorithms reduce file size; the Illustrator file format (AI) is compact, doesn't require an interpreter for processing, and is editable; PostScript files may be structured by the use of DSC comments.

8.2 Key Elements of the Acrobat Technology

8.2.1 The Portable Document Format (PDF). The Portable Document Format (PDF) is the basis of Acrobat. When developing PDF and Acrobat, Adobe could build on their experience with PostScript and platform-independent software. PDF exhibits many components discussed in various chapters in this book: PostScript's graphics capabilities, the Illustrator file format, Level 2's compression and device independent color as well as Type 1 and Multiple Master fonts. This mixture is spiced up by hypertext techniques (such as links) popularized by the World Wide Web. From a programmer's point of view, object oriented programming had its influence, too.

The next couple of pages give an overview on PDF's most important features and attributes. Several of these features were introduced with PDF 1.1 which is implemented in Acrobat Software versions 2.0 and higher (see next section). The PDF 1.1 extensions are marked as such in the description.

There's still more to come: PDF 1.2, announced for mid-1996, will further extend PDF to accommodate some changes for linking Acrobat to the World Wide Web, and for using PDF in the print production workflow. You can find an overview of PDF 1.2 at the end of this section.

Graphics capabilities. PDF contains all graphical capabilities of PostScript (Level 1 and 2). This includes path operators for constructing line and curve segments, instructions for drawing lines and fill-ing areas with color, text output and raster graphics. Similarly to PostScript, these operators are not tied to a specific device resolution.

While PDF uses PostScript's graphics model, it doesn't offer the flexibility of a programming language. There are no loops, conditionals, or other control structures. This makes PDF less flexible compared to PostScript, but much more efficient. The resulting files are smaller and easier to process.

Compared to PostScript, there are several limitations in PDF:
- PDF doesn't support user-defined spot functions and transfer curves for simulating gray levels, but always uses a default spot function.
- The (rarely used) fill patterns, useful for patterning areas in PostScript Level 2, are not available in PDF.
- Spot colors have to be converted to a conventional color space (RGB or CMYK) or device-independent CIE color.

Hypertext features. Digital documents are not only meant to imitate their paper counterparts but should also extend the classical

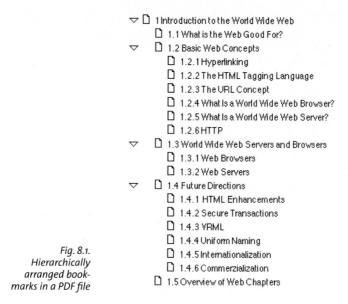

*Fig. 8.1.
Hierarchically
arranged book-
marks in a PDF file*

usage possibilities. This includes technical aspects such as copying
without quality loss, fast worldwide transmission, etc., as well as con-
tent-related features. PDF's hypertext features are meant to fulfil
these requirements. First of all, they make it easy to navigate online
documents on screen.

Bookmarks characterize fixed positions in the document by
means of cleartext descriptions. The user can jump to the desired
destination in the document by clicking on the respective bookmark.
The author of the document may even specify the zoom factor for
displaying the destination. The bookmark text itself is not tied to a
fixed document position but is displayed next to the actual document. Bookmarks may be arranged in a hierarchical way, e.g., to label
several levels of chapter headings. The Acrobat software displays
bookmarks with subordinate bookmarks with a small triangle (like
folders on the Mac).

Cross-references or hypertext links further aid in navigating the
document. Such a link consists of source and destination. The source
is simply a rectangle on a page. Clicking on the rectangle displays the
target which may be an arbitrary page of the document. This makes it
easy to follow cross-references or related topics in the text (e.g., "see
also..."). In PDF 1.1, links may not only point to another location in the
same document, but also to completely different documents. They
may even launch another application.

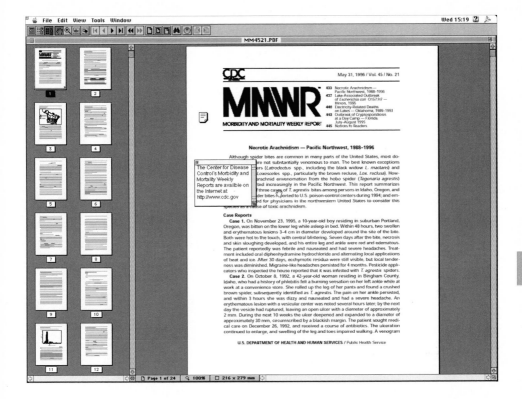

Fig. 8.2.
Acrobat Reader displays a document with thumbnails (to the left of the main window) and two annotations (one is open, the other closed)

Thumbnails (named after their size) are miniature representations of a page. They allow for an easy overview over the document. Clicking a page's thumbnail displays the page in the main window (such as with links).

Using notes (or annotations) it's possible to embed small amounts of text into a PDF file. On screen they appear similar to the well-known Post-Its. A mouse click on a note opens it and makes its text content visible. PDF 1.1 allows for notes in different colors. They may also be charaterized by an individual title, e.g., the name of the person who created it, and the current date.

Font issues. The font problem cannot be solved by the PDF text output operators alone: if the receiver of a document hasn't installed the necessary fonts, the dreaded "Font not found, using Courier" message could occur. Acrobat solves this dilemma by using Multiple Master fonts: Acrobat substitutes missing fonts by MM fonts, using generic serif and sans serif fonts. In order to save a document's formatting (line and page breaks), the PDF file contains a font descriptor for each font used. Such a font descriptor characterizes a font's met-

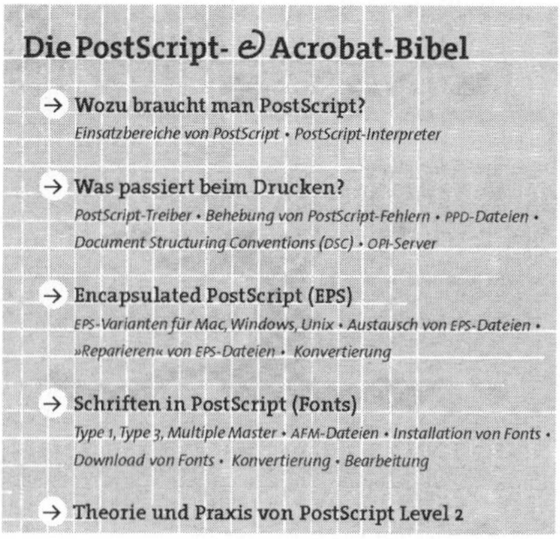

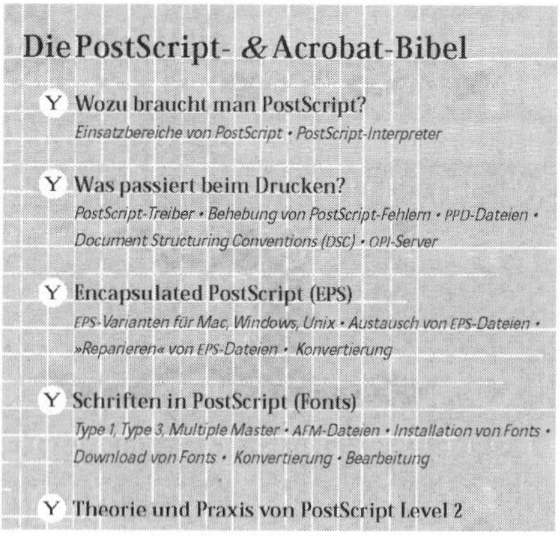

Die PostScript- ℰ Acrobat-Bibel

→ **Wozu braucht man PostScript?**
Einsatzbereiche von PostScript · PostScript-Interpreter

→ **Was passiert beim Drucken?**
PostScript-Treiber · Behebung von PostScript-Fehlern · PPD-Dateien ·
Document Structuring Conventions (DSC) · OPI-Server

→ **Encapsulated PostScript (EPS)**
EPS-Varianten für Mac, Windows, Unix · Austausch von EPS-Dateien ·
»Reparieren« von EPS-Dateien · Konvertierung

→ **Schriften in PostScript (Fonts)**
Type 1, Type 3, Multiple Master · AFM-Dateien · Installation von Fonts ·
Download von Fonts · Konvertierung · Bearbeitung

→ **Theorie und Praxis von PostScript Level 2**

Die PostScript- & Acrobat-Bibel

Y **Wozu braucht man PostScript?**
Einsatzbereiche von PostScript · PostScript-Interpreter

Y **Was passiert beim Drucken?**
PostScript-Treiber · Behebung von PostScript-Fehlern · PPD-Dateien ·
Document Structuring Conventions (DSC) · OPI-Server

Y **Encapsulated PostScript (EPS)**
EPS-Varianten für Mac, Windows, Unix · Austausch von EPS-Dateien ·
»Reparieren« von EPS-Dateien · Konvertierung

Y **Schriften in PostScript (Fonts)**
Type 1, Type 3, Multiple Master · AFM-Dateien · Installation von Fonts ·
Download von Fonts · Konvertierung · Bearbeitung

Y **Theorie und Praxis von PostScript Level 2**

Fig. 8.3.
Font substitution in Acrobat. Above: all neces-
sary fonts are available in the system. Right:
fonts are substituted with generic MM fonts.
Though character metrics are retained, a
font's characteristics may get lost (e.g. the
shape of the "&" character.

rics data and some general properties (e.g., serif or sans). Using the metric descriptor, Acrobat generates a substitute MM font. While this font doesn't exactly resemble the original (missing) font, at least the character widths and formatting are retained. A complete font requires 30–60 KB of storage, a font descriptor only 2–4 KB.

Obviously, this simulation only works for "regular" fonts based on the latin script for which the glyph complement is covered by the two generic substitute fonts. Symbol fonts or characters from foreign scripts are never substituted but have to be completely embedded in the PDF file.

Embedding the complete font data in the PDF file is also a requirement for applications in which exact font representation (instead of substitution) is desirable. To achieve this, the familiar Type 1 font format is used. This way, embedded fonts can be used for ATM screen display or PostScript printing. Also, PDF files may contain Type 3 and TrueType fonts.

PDF 1.1 introduced *font subsets* as further enhancement. *Subsetting* a font means only embedding the characters of a font which are actually used in the document. This not only reduces file size but also circumvents the problem of font pirating – the receiver may extract embedded fonts from a PDF file and re-use them illegally. It's easy to recognize subsetted fonts by their name, which always contains six random characters and a plus sign in front of the original font name, e.g.,

```
DDJGKA+MinionMM_590_47
```

File size and compression.   File size is a big conern for online docu-ments. Service bureau operators are used to dealing with PostScript files the size of several dozens of MB. Such a big chunk is completely unsuited for disk or network file transfer. In comparison to Post-Script, PDF tries to reduce the file size by several means:

- ► PostScript Level 2's compression techniques (CCITT, LZW, Run-Length, and JPEG; see Section 5.3) not only reduce the storage re-quirements of bitmap images, but also compress vector graphics and even text. Generally, PostScript files do not contain com-pressed text.
- ► Optimized drawing instructions allow for compact representation of all graphical elements.
- ► Downsampling raster images, i.e., reducing their resolution, cuts down the amount of data in situations where high resolution isn't needed, e.g., if a document is exclusively used on screen.[1]
- ► Due to the standardized drawing instructions and the missing programming constructs a separate prolog isn't necessary. In PostScript files, the prolog often accounts for 50 KB of data.
- ► When embedding fonts, font subsetting achieves significant stor-age savings by only including the character descriptions actually used in the document.

File structure.   PostScript files are organized sequentially – the pages are contained in the original order from the file's beginning to the end. This means a program has to scan through the whole file in or-der to access a certain page. PDF files, however, are optimized for fast and efficient access to random pages of the document. The elements comprising a page are contained in the file as separate objects and may be re-used on different pages (e.g., fonts or repeated graphics). A table at the end of the file (the *cross reference* or *xref table*) describes each object's position in the file. A special object (called the *catalog*) defines the document's contents, i.e., its pages and bookmarks. If a program wants to process the file, it only has to load the cross-refer-ence table into memory and use it to access arbitrary pages and their

---

1. *Strictly speaking, downsampling is not a feature of the PDF file format but one of the software used for creating PDF files.*

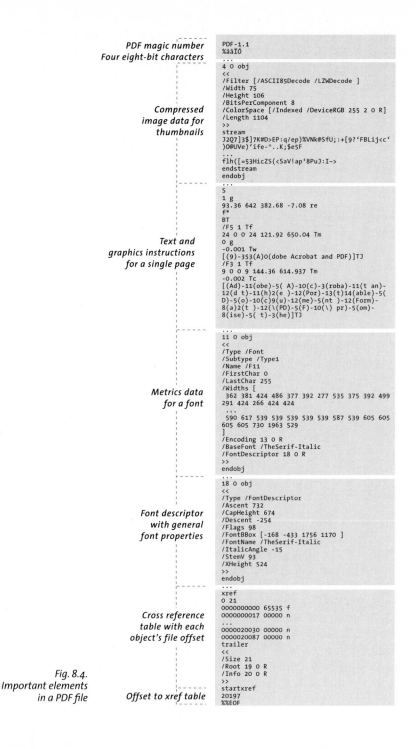

PDF magic number
Four eight-bit characters

Compressed
image data for
thumbnails

Text and
graphics instructions
for a single page

Metrics data
for a font

Font descriptor
with general
font properties

Cross reference
table with each
object's file offset

Fig. 8.4.
Important elements
in a PDF file

Offset to xref table

```
PDF-1.1
%àáÏÓ
...
4 0 obj
<<
/Filter [/ASCII85Decode /LZWDecode ]
/Width 75
/Height 106
/BitsPerComponent 8
/ColorSpace [/Indexed /DeviceRGB 255 2 0 R]
/Length 1104
>>
stream
J2Q7]3$]7K#D>EP:q/ep)%VNk@SfU;:+[9?'FBLij<c'
)0@UVe)'ife-^..K;$e5F
...
flh([=53HicZS(<SaV!ap'8PuJ:I~>
endstream
endobj
...
S
1 g
93.36 642 382.68 -7.08 re
f*
BT
/F5 1 Tf
24 0 0 24 121.92 650.04 Tm
0 g
-0.001 Tw
[(9)-353(A)0(dobe Acrobat and PDF)]TJ
/F3 1 Tf
9 0 0 9 144.36 614.937 Tm
-0.002 Tc
[(Ad)-11(obe)-5( A)-10(c)-3(roba)-11(t an)-
12(d t)-11(h)2(e )-12(Por)-13(t)14(able)-5(
D)-5(o)-10(c)9(u)-12(me)-5(nt )-12(Form)-
8(a)2(t )-12(\(PD)-5(F)-10(\) pr)-5(om)-
8(ise)-5( t)-3(he)]TJ
...
11 0 obj
<<
/Type /Font
/Subtype /Type1
/Name /F11
/FirstChar 0
/LastChar 255
/Widths [
 362 381 424 486 377 392 277 535 375 392 499
291 424 266 424 424
...
 590 617 539 539 539 539 539 587 539 605 605
605 605 730 1963 529
]
/Encoding 13 0 R
/BaseFont /TheSerif-Italic
/FontDescriptor 18 0 R
>>
endobj
...
18 0 obj
<<
/Type /FontDescriptor
/Ascent 732
/CapHeight 674
/Descent -254
/Flags 98
/FontBBox [-168 -433 1756 1170 ]
/FontName /TheSerif-Italic
/ItalicAngle -15
/StemV 93
/XHeight 524
>>
endobj
...
xref
0 21
0000000000 65535 f
0000000017 00000 n
...
0000020030 00000 n
0000020087 00000 n
trailer
<<
/Size 21
/Root 19 0 R
/Info 20 0 R
>>
startxref
20197
%%EOF
```

graphical and hypertext contents. This is especially significant for large files, since the time required for opening the file is no longer related to file size. The cross-reference table is a crucial component; damaged PDF files with the last part missing are unusable (contrary to PostScript files).

In order to avoid rewriting the complete file even for small changes, PDF files can be updated incrementally. Extensions or changes to the file can be appended at the end of the file. This leaves existing components in the file, but marks them invalid if they are to be replaced by newer objects. This technique has several consequences:

- ▶ The time required for writing the changes to the hard disk is not related to the file size but only to the order of magnitude of the changes.
- ▶ Changes can be undone since the old objects still physically exist in the file.
- ▶ Paradoxically, PDF files may increase in size instead of decrease if you delete pages. Deleted elements remain part of the file and are only marked as invalid at the end of the file.
- ▶ PDF is perfectly suited for WORM storage devices ("write once, read many") since the data need not be changed, but only appended.

PDF takes care of the tiresome line-end problem: MS-DOS, Mac, and Unix use different conventions for marking the end-of-line character. This matters because the line ends may be changed when PDF files are mailed in ASCII format or transferred to another system on floppy disk. In this case the mailer software or disk driver sometimes change the line-end characters. This behavior changes all file offsets, thereby destroying the cross-reference table. PDF 1.1 introduced binary files, which cannot be transferred as text files anyway. Therefore, line-end characters are not of much concern in PDF 1.1.

It's easy to recognize PDF files and the PDF version by looking at the first few characters in the file. These are either %PDF-1.0 or %PDF-1.1.

PDF is an extensible format. It's possible to write PDF processing software that ignores unknown objects to a large extent. One possible extension, introduced with Acrobat 2.1, is the integration of multimedia components such as video and audio data.

Also, PDF files may contain general information about the document itself, including its title, subject, author, and content keywords. This information simplifies searching large document collections.

The only structural limit in PDF is related to file size. PDF files may reach a maximum of 10 GB, i.e., 10 000 MB.

The following features were introduced in PDF 1.1 and version 2.0 of the Acrobat software.

Security and encryption.   PDF 1.1 allows documents to be encrypted and safeguarded with a password. Anyone trying to open such an encrypted document needs the password. Also, documents may only be partially secured, e.g. to prevent printing, copying text and graphics, or adding annotations. While most PDF 1.1 extensions may silently be ignored by older software, this is obviously not the case for encryption (if the encryption is to be of any use).

PDF encryption is based on the RC4 algorithm designed by Ron Rivest, who is a well-known cryptographer and co-founder of RSA Data Security, Inc. This company grants licenses on RC4 encryption but has never published the detailed specification of the algorithm. Choosing an undocumented encryption scheme for PDF has the disadvantage that third party developers or authors of public domain software are unable to write programs which can deal with encrypted PDF files. Note that this issue is not related to illegitimately accessing secured PDF documents, since the password is needed for opening a file anyway.[1]

In order to comply with the restrictive U.S. export regulations for cryptographic software, Acrobat uses a key length of 40 bits. This at least makes sure that encrypted documents cannot be cracked by your neighborhood college hacker over the weekend. However, using a brute force attack it's possible to break RC4 encryption at such a small key length. Indeed, the well-known Web browser Netscape Navigator uses the same algorithm and the same key length (at least in the export version) – and this exact combination has recently been proven to be susceptible to an attack using a cluster of workstations cooperating via the Internet. Keep in mind that Acrobat's encryption may well keep your private or corporate data somehow confident, but is too weak to protect national or really valuable data.

Reading aids.   Reading documents on screen can be very tiresome, especially for multi-column text – the user must constantly employ the scroll bar to see the next portion of text. In PDF 1.1, Adobe introduced *article threads* to facilitate on-screen reading. An article in this sense consists of several rectangular areas that define the flow of text. When the mouse cursor is located in such an area, it changes its shape. Clicking in an article results in the next text portion of the flow being displayed. Also, the zoom factor is adjusted to use the full screen width. This way it's much easier to read longer text passages arranged in columns.

---

1. *In September 1994, technical details of the RC4 algorithm were anonymously posted on the Internet. However, since Adobe uses an internal password in addition to the user-supplied password it's still impossible to write public domain programs for opening encrypted PDF files.*

Device independent color.   PDF 1.0 allows only the device-dependent color spaces gray level, RGB, and CMYK for color output. PDF 1.1 introduced the device-independent color spaces which are also available in PostScript Level 2. These enable PDF files to accurately reproduce color on each kind of output device. A PDF document may specify one of several optimization goals related to color output which have to be implemented in the PDF reading software (see also Section 6.5.2):

- Absolute color fidelity with respect to a reference color.
- Relative color fidelity with respect to the output device, e.g., paper white.
- Approximation of all used colors with colors available on the respective device.
- Saturation fidelity, e.g., for business graphics.

Device-independent color was one of the remaining requirements for high-quality output. PDF files using device-independent color specification can only be produced with Acrobat Distiller 2.0 and higher.

Disadvantages of PDF.   The PDF file format has some inherent drawbacks:

- PDF files are always optimized for a certain output device. Adjusting a document for different devices requires several versions of the document. A well-designed online document (small amounts of text per page, large font size) doesn't look very well in print, whereas good print documents are tiresome to read on screen (you need to scroll often, screen redraw may be slow).
- PDF doesn't contain information about the logical structure of the document, for example chapter division, section, headings, etc. Although Adobe promised to integrate SGML features, these depend on the application software used for generating the documents.
- There are only a few possibilities to edit or change a PDF file's contents. However, this may change in the future when more application programs are capable of directly processing PDF.
- It's impossible to do color separations with PDF; PostScript must be used instead. This flaw is not really related to the PDF format itself but to missing PDF separation software.
- PDF must be completely transferred before even the first page is visible (unlike HTML, PDF is not a stream format that contains all the information in sequential order). Especially when downloading a file from the Internet, this is a major drawback since you have to wait for the whole document to be transferred.

- PDF's internal text storage isn't suited for text search and retrieval tasks. Heavy use of kerning, for example, may prevent hits when searching for text.
- PDF, being a *portable*, i.e. device-independent format, lacks device-dependent features such as spot functions and user-defined transfer curves. These are crucial for using PDF as a high-end prepress production format.

PDF 1.2 extensions. Adobe tries to remedy some of the above limitations with the PDF 1.2 extensions which will be implemented in the Acrobat 3.0 software. The most important enhancements are:

- "Optimized" PDF files which accelerate PDF download over the Internet. This is coupled with features of the Web browser and server and is covered in more detail in Section 8.4.5.
- Extensions for production printing: Adobe announced the integration of features for high-end production printing which enables PDF to be used as a delivery format even for the most demanding print documents. The extensions include device-dependent features such as color separation, transfer curves and halftone functions, as well as OPI 1.3 and 2.0 comments for image replacement. Note that the Acrobat viewers disregard most of these features for screen display.
- Double-byte character encoding: PDF 1.2 will make use of the CID font technology (see Section 4.5.3 for an overview) for Asian scripts such as Chinese, Japanese, and Korean.

8.2.2 Acrobat Reader and Exchange. If a manufacturer wants to introduce a new format and expect it to resemble a widely accepted standard, solving the technical issues is only half the battle; the availability of software supporting the new format is crucial as well. The manufacturer has to avoid a vicious circle: third-party developers don't want to support a format which is not widely used, and users don't bother with a format not supported by their standard software. Adobe avoided this deadlock by several clever moves:

- The software for viewing and printing PDF documents (Acrobat Reader) is freely available for several operating systems.
- Acrobat Distiller and PDFwriter PDF-enable a huge base of existing software (see below).
- Adobe documented the PDF file format to allow other manufacturers to integrate PDF features into their software.
- Adobe opened up major application areas by signing several strategic alliances.
- Acrobat software includes communications means which allow a tight integration into existing software.

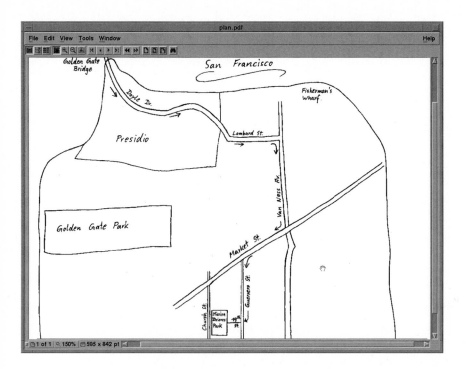

The window shows a title bar "plan.pdf" with menu items File Edit View Tools Window and Help. A hand-drawn map of San Francisco is displayed including labels: Golden Gate Bridge, San Francisco, Doyle Dr., Fisherman's Wharf, Lombard St., Presidio, Van Ness Av., Golden Gate Park, Market St., Church St., Mission Dolores Park, 19th St., Guerrero St. Status bar reads "1 of 1 150% 595 x 842 pt".

Concerning the free Reader software, Adobe had to learn their lesson, though: the first version wasn't free but was sold for $ 50. This clearly hindered the large-scale employment of PDF.

Fig. 8.5.
Acrobat Reader
under Unix
with a fax in
PDF format.

Acrobat Reader. The reader is used for screen display and print-out of PDF files. It may be freely copied and redistributed. You can find Acrobat reader installation software for several operating systems on the accompanying CD-ROM. Acrobat Reader includes all functions for displaying and navigating PDF files. It interprets the page descriptions, follows the links, and displays bookmarks and annotations. The Reader also converts PDF files to printable PostScript, making use of Level 2 if the device supports it.

Note that there is no logical page numbering in PDF: the first page in a document is always numbered 1, other pages being numbered sequentially. Especially for large documents consisting of multiple individual files this is tiresome since the logical page number doesn't match the page number displayed in Acrobat Reader.

In an attempt to emphasize the platform-independent character of PDF, Adobe implemented Acrobat Reader on several system platforms. On the accompanying CD-ROM you will find versions of Acrobat Reader for the following operating systems (I produced the screen snapshots for this chapter on several of these):

System	Variant	Notes
Macintosh	68K and PowerPC	Doesn't run on old 68000 Macs; Both versions contain ATM-LE
Windows	3.x, 95, NT 3.5 and above	Doesn't require ATM
MS-DOS	all	Includes drivers for diverse graphics cards and VESA. Only Acrobat 1.0 available.
OS/2	Warp or Warp Connect	
Unix	Solaris 2.3 and above	Not compatible to OpenWindows 3.0
	SunOS 4.1.1 and above	Includes DPS/NX
	SunOS 4.1.3 and above	DPS/NX no longer required
	HP-UX 9.0.3 and above	
	SGI IRIX 5.3 and above	Includes DPS/NX
	IBM AIX 4.1 and above	Acrobat 3.0

On systems with installed Adobe Type Manager (ATM) Acrobat Reader uses it for font rendering. The ATM version must be Multiple Master capable. Acrobat Reader for Mac comes with a slim version of ATM which only works with Acrobat but not with other programs. Acrobat Reader 2.1 for Windows contains the font rendering software internally. Unlike version 2.0, it also works under Windows (3.x, 95, and NT) without ATM.

Screen output of Acrobat Reader 1.0 for Unix was based on Display PostScript. Since an DPS-extended X Server is not always available, the Reader distribution contained the NX agent which translates Post-Script instructions to plain X11 operations (see Section 7.2.1). Version 2.1 no longer requires Display PostScript, nor does it contain the DPS/NX agent.

Acrobat uses the generic Multiple Master fonts AdobeSans and AdobeSerif for substituting unavailable fonts. The Mac and Windows Reader use any installed system printer driver for printing PDFs. However, if PostScript output is to be produced, Reader bypasses the printer driver almost completely. Taking the similarities between PDF and PostScript into account, this shouldn't be much of a surprise. For this reason, Reader makes use of a Level 2 device, even if the installed system printer driver doesn't support PostScript Level 2.

Acrobat Exchange.   Exchange is the "grown up" version of the Reader and is distributed as a commercial product. It offers all the features of the Reader plus the capability of editing PDF documents. This doesn't mean you can change the original contents of the pages (e.g., fix typos) but you can insert annotations and bookmarks, insert or delete pages, change the page size, create thumbnails and links as well as import and export annotations.

Plug-ins and programming interfaces. Acrobat Exchange offers several communications means and programming interfaces which are meant to keep the Acrobat software suite flexible and extensible. Plug-ins (modelled after Photoshop) are separate modules which expand the functionality of the basic software. The plug-in interface specification is available from Adobe, so interested third-party software developers are able to write their own modules. Starting with version 2.1, plug-ins are no longer limited to Exchange but also work in Acrobat Reader. The Acrobat API (Application Programming Interface) offers means of process communication via AppleEvents, AppleScript, OLE2, and DDE. Developers may obtain a special SDK (Software Development Kit) from Adobe.

Full text retrieval and Acrobat Catalog. Acrobat Reader and Exchange contain a simple search tool which may be used for searching isolated text fragments in PDF files. This tool, however, is not very powerful. It has to reconstruct semantic entities from the layout information. Many text and DTP programs don't output the text word by word but instead character for character in order to fine-control character spacing. This means that when searching for a word Acrobat has to calculate and compare character and word spacing values since there are no blanks as word separators. This technique is not sufficient for large amounts of data or complex search tasks. To rectify this, Adobe licensed Verity's Topic Search Engine, a full text search and retrieval software, and integrated it as a plug-in in Exchange 2.0.

Acrobat Catalog (available for Mac and Windows) is an indexing program which generates full text indexes for an arbitrary number of PDF files. Acrobat uses sophisticated index and retrieval algorithms similar to those used in database systems: relevance ranking (or score) according to the number of occurrences of a word in the document and the proximity of multiple words; stop list with words to be

Fig. 8.6.
Search results for a query using an indexed Acrobat file. The circles indicate the relevance ranking of the documents

ignored when indexing a document (for example: *About about Above above After after Also also Although although An an And and As as At at Be be Because because...*); search using boolean operators and generation of a hit list sorted by relevance ranking. If the creator of a document collection – say a CD-ROM publisher – runs Acrobat Catalog on his files, users who installed the search plug-in can easily search for keywords and combinations of keywords, and can quickly access the search results.

Acrobat 3.0 enhancements. At the time of writing, beta versions of Acrobat 3.0 were already available. The following are the most important enhancements in Acrobat 3.0, either announced or already available in the beta releases:

- ► Acrobat Exchange "optimizes" PDF files for page-at-a-time download (see Section 8.4.5 for details).
- ► Progressive display ("font blitting") speeds up page rendering. First the text is displayed in a substitution font, then the images, and finally embedded fonts replace the substitution fonts.
- ► Anti-aliased text improves screen display.
- ► New page views are available: continuous scrolling scrolls adjacent pages in a single column, 2-up page view displays double-page spreads.
- ► The capture module is implemented as a plug-in for Exchange.
- ► More operating system platforms are supported.
- ► The "Save As EPS" feature will allow to transform PDF pages to files which may be embedded in other documents using standard DTP software.

8.2.3 Creating PDF Documents.
In order to make the Acrobat technology widely accepted, Adobe had to offer easy ways to generate PDF files. They offer several techniques which differ in scope. The most important PDF generating programs – called Acrobat PDFwriter and Distiller – PDF-enabled thousands of application programs at one stroke.

PDFwriter. Acrobat PDFwriter is a printer driver for Mac or Windows which doesn't drive any printer but instead generates PDF files. "Tapping" the printer interface of application software is a well-known trick, also used for example in drivers for fax modems. This technique PDF-enables each program provided it is capable of printing its data. This of course includes almost every software dealing with documents of one or another kind – word processing, DTP, graphics and image processing, spreadsheets, presentations software and many more.

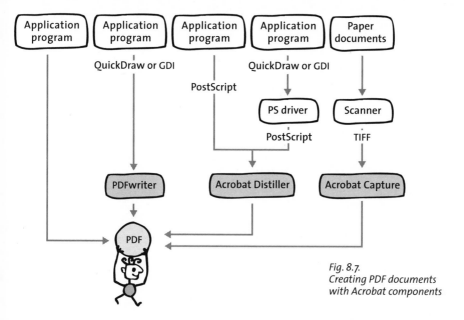

Fig. 8.7.
Creating PDF documents
with Acrobat components

PDFwriter is tied to the system printer interface (GDI or QuickDraw) and is therefore subject to some limitations. Since it doesn't contain a PostScript interpreter, it has to ignore the PostScript instructions of embedded EPS files and only uses the preview section. This obviously degrades the quality of the generated PDFs. Also, PDFwriter only obtains printable data from an application and therefore cannot be used for generating hypertext elements.

Distiller.   In situations where there is no system-wide printer driver (e.g., under MS-DOS or Unix), or when a program generates complex PostScript output, PDFwriter is not adequate. In this case, Acrobat Distiller is a much more powerful tool for generating PDF. This software includes a full-blown PostScript Level 2 interpreter for processing arbitrary PostScript files and converting them to PDF documents. Distiller accepts all files suited for output on a PostScript device. Contrary to PDFwriter, there are no restrictions in Distiller concerning graphical features or PDF output. Distiller is preferable to PDFwriter in the following situations:

▸ The original documents contain embedded EPS graphics.
▸ The application program generates PostScript code itself, bypassing the printer driver.
▸ The resolution of raster images is to be reduced in the process of generating PDF (downsampling).
▸ The document contains complex graphics, e.g., color blends.

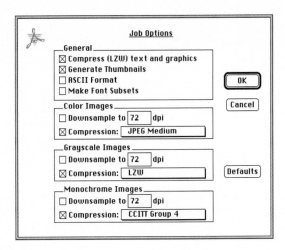

▸ Multiple-Master fonts are to be embedded in the file.

▸ The PDF documents should contain hypertext features.
Generating hypertext features is possible either by using applica-
tion-level support or manually (see Section 8.6).

There are two important groups of user-selectable options when
distilling PostScript files – image compression and downsampling,
and font embedding.

In Section 5.3 you can find some hints on choosing the best compression algorithm for several application scenarios. With the exception of JPEG compression, all algorithms are lossless. This means that
in the worst case (if you are messing with the compression options
without knowing what you're doing) the files get larger. However, if
you select JPEG compression inappropriately, image quality degrades.
JPEG compression should only be used for scanned black and white or
color images. The quality settings allow the tradeoff between image
quality and file size to be controlled. Never use JPEG compression for
pencil artwork or screenshots. From time to time printed screenshots
appear in books or magazines with visible pixel distortions – typical
artifacts of inappropriate JPEG usage.

Font embedding is another tradeoff between file size and output
quality. If you are sure that the receiver has installed all necessary
fonts (e.g., if you circulate documents among your workgroup) or the
PDF document uses only Acrobat's standard fonts, it's not necessary
to embed any font description. However, if exact document reproduction is an issue and you are unsure about the receiver's font configuration, it's better to embed all necessary fonts (assuming you can
still handle the file size). Using the "font subset" feature further reduces PDF file size.

Finally, a warning related to font processing in Distiller: Multiple Master font substitution only works for displaying or printing PDF files, but not for distilling. Therefore Distiller needs access to all fonts used in the PostScript file to be distilled!

Converting paper documents with Acrobat Capture.   Distiller and PDFwriter are suitable for new documents created on the computer. Many organizations, however, have tons of legacy documents in printed form. These are not only cumbersome in handling, but also need a lot of storage – in this case not in megabytes but in feet of shelf length! Scores of software companies have developed OCR programs (*optical character recognition*) which try to convert scanned documents back to text files. However, the recognition part never works perfectly, so the digitized documents have to be checked and corrected manually which requires much effort. Alternatively, one could store the scanned bitmap version of each page along with the OCR-generated text file.

PDF with its graphical and typographical features is perfectly suited for storing such documents. Adobe offers Acrobat Capture (for Windows) as an OCR package for generating PDF files. Capture differs from other OCR software in how it deals with characters that couldn't be reliably identified. Such characters are copied into the generated PDF as a bitmap. This way the page completely resembles the scanned original. However, a large proportion of the document is stored in textual rather than bitmapped format. This has big advantages in terms of searching and indexing the documents, as well as smaller file size. Capture tightly integrates bitmap and text information in a document. The program not only tries to identify individual characters but also recognizes several kinds of font. To achieve this, typographical parameters such as x-height and stem width are analyzed according to an internal database and used to pick a suitable font for the text representation in the PDF file. Capture scans the original documents and allows wrongly identified characters to be corrected before storing the file as PDF.

Acrobat Capture is subject to two limitations. Firstly, Capture only accepts line art or gray scale files for input, but not colored files. This may not be much of a problem in the business sector with large amounts of black-and-white documents lurking in the basement. The second limitation is much more severe, at least for typographically aware users or those dealing with European languages – Capture only deals with English text. This is a limitation in the OCR module, since it contains language-dependent grammar and hyphenation features. Capture doesn't use Windows' ANSI character set but is restricted to the 7-bit ASCII code. Missing umlauts and special characters render the program unusable for certain applications.

Creating PDF directly from application programs.   Since the technical details of PDF are fully specified and published, it's not necessary for application programs to rely on Distiller or PDFwriter; a program can generate PDF files directly. We may expect a number of software manufacturers to take advantage of this fact in the near future.

It shouldn't be too much of a surprise that Adobe is also the forerunner in this case: starting with version 5.5, Adobe Illustrator is capable of opening, editing and saving PDF files. The same holds true for Macromedia FreeHand 5.5, and possibly more graphics programs soon.

8.3 PDF Usage Examples

PDF as a platform-independent document format offers many applications which previously were either impossible or could only be realized with specialized software (if at all). In the following sections, we take a little tour of Acrobat usage examples. The examples are meant as appetizers and emphasize useful aspects of Acrobat and PDF.

Online documents.   In many cases PDF only serves as a transport vehicle for files which the receiver wants to reproduce in printed form. A real online document, however, does not emphasize the printed form but is intended to be consumed on screen. The easy conversion of PostScript data to PDF tempts to re-use the layout of printed documents for online products. But you should resist this temptation and redesign your documents for online consumption, taking the idiosyncrasies of typical computer monitors into account.

This includes the trivial fact that most paper documents are oriented in portrait format whereas most monitors have landscape format. Also, the amount of information presented on a single page should be adapted to the monitor's size and resolution. If you re-use the layout of the printed version, you may save some effort but do not necessarily satisfy your readers. It'scertainly no fun using Acrobat to tediously scroll through a multi-column newspaper layout. If you definitely want to use multi-column layout (perhaps paper and online version have to be produced from the same source), you should facilitate reading the resulting PDFs by using the article thread feature.

A good online document may even be used on a notebook computer without the need for a magnifying glass. If your budget doesn't

Fig. 8.9.
Online document vs.
paper-oriented layout

allow two different document versions to be produced in parallel, you can compensate for this by making good use of the index and hypertext features. These interactive elements are by definition meant to facilitate using the document on screen. For the sake of your readers, make use of hyperlinks and bookmarks wherever possible. In Section 8.6 you can find several possibilities to generate hypertext elements manually or automatically.

The creator of a PDF document also influences the important characteristics screen redraw speed and file size. The resolution (and therefore size) of embedded raster images may be reduced using Distiller's downsampling option. This significantly reduces file size without severely affecting screen output in most cases. Computer monitors rarely have more than 100 dpi resolution; typical office printers have 60–80 dpi (since with grayscales the physical resolution of the print engine cannot be fully used, see chapter 6).

Also, the number and kind of fonts used in the document have an influence on file size. If you are experiencing severe file size problems, consider refraining from font embedding and only use substitute fonts or Acrobat's standard fonts (I know – that's not exactly what typographically aware designers want).

Workgroups.   Creating, exchanging, and reading documents plays a crucial role in business life: a memorandum for colleagues, an offer for the customer, a report for the department head and the like. Especially for workgroups which are already networked, Acrobat is a good solution to everyday communications problems. Clever use of Acrobat technology can save thousands of trees being cooked to copier paper. Independently from their respective software, all participants can create documents with the PDFwriter and send them to their colleagues. For large amounts of documents – say your combined customer database or the shared company archive – it's reasonable to index the PDF files with Acrobat Catalog to accelerate and facilitate access to the data. If your data have to be updated regularly, put the files on the server and run Catalog every night to update the index files.

Copy-editing and proofreading cycle.   Generally, many people are involved in generating large documents. This is especially true for technical documents. The author or editor write the copy text, the graphics designer or layouter create the illustrations and put it all together. All parties involved have to swap their document versions and incorporate each other's changes. Even if a single person is responsible for contents and layout, a proofreading cycle is necessary in most cases. For example, the author sends the manual draft to an engineer who checks it and communicates his change requests and corrections to the author.

Often, a host of operating systems is involved in this scenario – the author works under Windows, the graphics designer on a Mac, and the engineers have their beloved Unix workstations. Such a heterogenous environment is perfectly suited for using Acrobat:

- ▸ The creator of the document generates a PDF version and sends it (via network, disk, or whatever) to his customer, copy-editor, etc.
- ▸ The copy-editors read the document with Acrobat Exchange and insert annotations into the document which contain their change requests.
- ▸ To reduce network traffic (or save disks), annotations are exported from the document ("Edit", "Notes", "Export...") to a separate PDF file which is sent to the original creator. This avoids the main document being sent back to the creator who already has it.
- ▸ The author imports the notes into his version of the PDF file and incorporates the necessary changes into the original document (using whatever software he uses to create the document).

If more than one copy-editor is involved, each can use a different color for his notes. This makes it easy to recognize which department

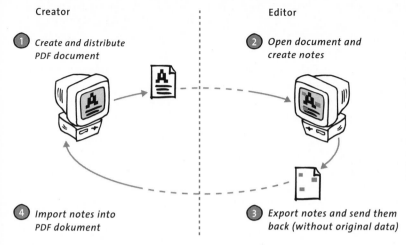

Creator

① *Create and distribute PDF document*

Editor

② *Open document and create notes*

③ *Export notes and send them back (without original data)*

④ *Import notes into PDF dokument*

*Fig. 8.10.
Copy editing with Acrobat: PDF files are sent to the customer or copy-editor who incorporates annotations with Acrobat Exchange. These notes are exported and sent back to the creator*

had to say what about the new manual or whether the notes relate to content or layout.

Presentations. PDF is also suited for preparing computerized presentations. Illustrations, diagrams, etc., are prepared with arbitrary software and converted to PDF with PDFwriter or Distiller. The generated file may be transferred along with Acrobat Reader. Acrobat software supports computer presentations with two features:

▸ Using "View", "Full Screen" the whole screen estate may be used for the document without wasting precious screen space for menus and similar material. Each mouse click advances the document view by one page.

▸ Acrobat can automatically browse all pages without user interference. Simply enter the desired viewing time for each page in the "Edit", "Preferences", "Full Screen..." menu, and start browsing the document with "View", "Full Screen".

A new technology called Acrobat Player facilitates PDF presentations for a wider audience. Acrobat Player is a device that contains dedicated PDF software. It accepts PDF files on floppy or hard disk and displays it using a beamer, similar to a conventional overhead projector. Adobe developed the Player core technology, third-party manufacturers incorporate it in their own devices.

The drag & drop feature described in Section 8.5 makes it easy to assemble a presentation from several documents.

Telephone directories and building maps. Most companies regularly print phone directories and building maps which give information about staff, office and phone numbers. Often, the new release is already out of date when it hits the desks. Using Acrobat, the same information may be distributed and updated more easily. A PDF file lists all employees and their phone numbers, as well as a map of the building. If you click on an employee's name, the respective office is displayed. Hypertext links are used to achieve this effect.

Sending PDF to the service bureau.   PDF may also substitute Post-Script as the format of choice for sending page descriptions to the service bureau for driving an imagesetter or printer. The creator of the documents needs Acrobat Distiller, the service bureau operator only needs Acrobat Reader.

The client creates print-to-disk PostScript files (see Section 9.2.3) and distills them to PDF. PDFwriter should not be used in this situation since it offers only limited functionality. Also, deactivate JPEG compression and image downsampling in the distiller in order to avoid image quality degradation. Furthermore, you don't want the imagesetter to use substitute fonts for your document. For this reason, embed all fonts in the generated PDF or make sure they are already installed on the imagesetter's RIP.

The service bureau operator opens the files in Acrobat Reader or Exchange and generates PostScript data for the imagesetter via the system driver as usual. Sending PDF to the service bureau instead of PostScript has several advantages for the service bureau operator:

- ► Distiller works as a preliminary check point that catches Post-Script errors possibly contained in the file.
- ► Generally, PDF files are much smaller than PostScript files, thereby simplifying transport and handling.
- ► In most cases, laser printer proofs are no longer necessary since the document can be checked on screen.
- ► The service bureau operator can use his familiar PostScript environment (drivers, PPDs, etc.) and doesn't have to install each new version and plug-in of all software packages or to rely on the customer to choose all the correct settings for his device (in the case of PostScript files).
- ► If there are problems, single pages are easily extracted and imaged separately.
- ► Using suitable software (see Section 8.5.4) it's possible to do last-minute edits shortly before imaging the file. This is generally not possible with PostScript files.

There are however some cases in which you shouldn't use PDF as a substitute for PostScript. This especially relates to the couple of Post-Script features that don't have a PDF counterpart, i.e. user defined spot functions and Level 2's fill patterns. Color separations are another critical point – software to directly separate PDF is not yet available. You have to create a PostScript file from Acrobat and separate it using conventional PostScript separation software. Acrobat 3.0 will enable PDF for use in the high-end production environment.

Distiller as a software RIP.   Cleverly used, Acrobat Distiller and Reader, combined with a suitable printer driver, may function as a software RIP for rendering PostScript files on an arbitrary (non-Post-Script) printer. Firstly, use Distiller to convert the PostScript file to PDF. Open the file in Reader or Exchange and print using a previously installed system driver. Due to the missing system printer drivers, this technique doesn't work under Unix.

Printing and storing computer faxes.   How to quickly print raster data on Level 2 devices has already been discussed in Section 5.5.3. Especially for fax data received via a fax modem on the computer, PDF is suited as a storage format. It's much easier to deal with PDF files than with the native formats of most fax programs.

Acrobat in the World Wide Web.   PDF complements HTML very well and seamlessly integrates to the World Wide Web. The next section is devoted to an in-depth discussion of integrating Acrobat to the Web.

8.4 Acrobat in the World Wide Web

8.4.1 The Document Languages HTML and PDF.   The Internet witnessed long discussions on the issue whether PDF would replace the Hypertext Markup Language HTML – which is used to create documents for the World Wide Web (WWW) – and whether or not this is desirable. However, the question is posed in the wrong matter: PDF and HTML have been developed for different purposes and, accordingly, have their own strengths and weaknesses.

While both formats support hypertext features, HTML and PDF differ in their content philosophy. PDF exactly reproduces the graphical contents of the original document and doesn't care for content structure (semantics), whereas HTML contentrates on content categories – such as headings and paragraphs. This is also emphasized by the fact that HTML is derived from SGML (Standard Generalized Markup Language). The author of an HTML document has only few layout controls. Each user may configure her Web browser according to taste and available resources (screen size, fonts, color, etc.). HTML is much simpler in structure than PDF. As its name implies, it simply marks up portions of text and offers only restricted means of graphic and page layout. The following table compares HTML and PDF with respect to several criteria which are relevant to creators and users of documents.

Property	HTML	PDF
Standardization of the format	international groups	Adobe (by means of specification and implementation)
Viewer software	free and commercial viewers for all platforms	free viewers for all platforms (Acrobat Reader and Ghostscript)
Software for generating the format	free and commercial products for all platforms	commercial, only for Windows, Mac and some Unix systems
Converting existing documents	requires much effort	easy via PostScript output
Editing the files	with text or HTML editor	only with commercial software
Document structuring	very good	bad
Search features	very good	medium; very good for indexed documents
Hypertext features	very good	very good
Output quality	low	very high
Display speed	high	low for complex documents
Who decides on the document layout?	viewer	author
Suitability for screen representation	very high	only if document is designed accordingly
Layout and typography	bad	very good
Format complexity	simple tags (instructions in the text)	complex document format
File size	small	large
Pages can be displayed before the whole document is transferred to the reader	yes	only with optimized PDFs of Acrobat 3.0 and "byteserving" Web server

8.4.2 PDF as a MIME Type.

Every Web browser is capable of displaying several file types itself (in most cases text, HTML, GIF, and possibly more). For each file type the browser does not "understand" it launches external utilities or helper applications. These are often called viewers, although they are not restricted to screen display but may as well play a sound file, for example. Files in the World Wide Web are classified according to MIME types (Multipurpose Internet Mail Extension). MIME types and the corresponding viewers can be configured for most Web browsers via a configuration file or menu. This also applies to PDF files which nicely complement HTML. PDF files have a MIME type of

```
application/pdf
```

Configuring a Web browser for PDF.   Using the Windows version of the widely used Netscape Navigator browser as an example, let's step through the configuration process:

- ▶ Launch Netscape Navigator.
- ▶ Choose "Options", "General Preferences...", and the "Helpers" tab.
- ▶ Click "Create New Type..." and create MIME type *application*, subtype *pdf*. The extension also becomes *pdf*. In the "Action" field click "Launch the Application" and enter the directory path to Acrobat Reader (or Exchange), e.g., *c:\acroread\acroread.exe*.
- ▶ Click "OK" and "Options", "Save Options".
- ▶ Launch Acrobat Reader or Exchange and choose "Edit", "Preferences", "General...". Deactivate "Display Open Dialog at Startup". This instructs Acrobat to immediately display the file (whose name is provided by Netscape) instead of prompting for a file name.

Under Unix, MIME types are generally configured in the *.mailcap* file. The entry for Acrobat Reader is as follows:

```
application/pdf; acroread  %s
```

Finally, the correspondence between MIME types and file extensions has to be configured in the *.mime.types* file. Insert the following line:

```
application/pdf    .pdf
```

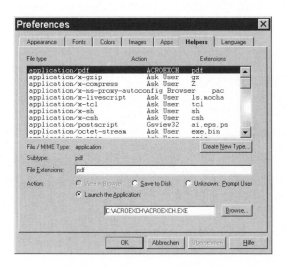

Fig. 8.11.
Configuring
Acrobat Exchange
as a viewer for PDF
files in Netscape
Navigator

Compatibility of PDF documents. A Web publisher should ensure that her Web pages are accessible to a large user community and don't exhibit unnecessary limitations. With Acrobat, compatibility is hardly an issue because older software (e.g. Reader version 1.0) ignores most newer extensions and silently displays PDF 1.1 documents. The encryption feature is one notable exception to this rule: it's impossible to open a password-protected document with Reader 1.0. For this reason, Web publishers shouldn't offer documents in which for example printing is disabled via the security feature because users of older software cannot open the file at all!

8.4.3 WWW Links in PDF Files.

Configuring PDF as a MIME type allows embedding URLs (Universal Resource Locators) as links to PDF files in HTML documents. The Weblink plug-in – installed as a standard part of Acrobat Reader 2.1 for Mac, Windows and Unix – supports links in the opposite direction, i.e., embedding URL links as part of PDF files. Clicking such a PDF link that points to a PDF file on the Internet instructs Reader or Exchange to launch a previously configured Web browser (via "Edit", "Preferences", "WWW Link..."). The browser transfers the file from the server to the local machine and presents it to Acrobat for screen display. If the URL doesn't point to a PDF document but to another Internet resource, the web browser itself handles the data returned by the server.

Communication with the browser is implemented with DDE and AppleEvents and uses different drivers ("Connection Type"). Currently, the standard driver for web browsers works with Spyglass Enhanced Mosaic 2.0 and Netscape Navigator 1.1 and higher. Apart from following a link by clicking on it, the Weblink plug-in also allows to directly open an URL by typing it into a dialog box. Also, a base URL

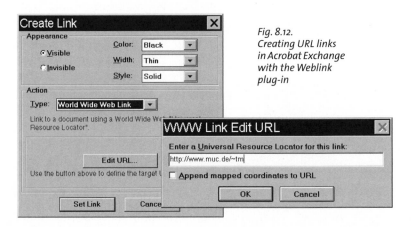

Fig. 8.12.
Creating URL links in Acrobat Exchange with the Weblink plug-in

can be defined that describes the location of the document in which it is contained. Acrobat and the Web browser use it for relative URLs.

You can create URL links similar to regular PDF links with Exchange's link tool. Assuming the Weblink plug-in is installed, choose "World Wide Web link" as link type and enter the URL. The option "Append Mapped Coordinates to URL" works similarly to the ISMAP attribute in HTML: before requesting the file, Acrobat appends the mouse cursor's coordinates in points (relative to the upper left corner of the link). This instructs the Web server to send position-dependent data, for example, if you click on a map. This kind of interactive graphics is called image map in Web speak. While classical image maps can only contain raster images (mostly in GIF format), PDF documents allow arbitrary mixtures of raster and object graphics. As an example, Figure 8.13 shows an Internet "map" which contains the URLs of Web servers. Clicking the URL in Acrobat launches the Web browser for displaying the data sent from the server.

8.4.4 Tightly Coupling Acrobat and Web Browser.

When Adobe developed Acrobat and PDF, they couldn't foresee the enormous success the World Wide Web would have. The engineers in Mountain View/California reacted very quickly and offered the Weblink plug-in for integrating Acrobat and WWW. The fast availability of Weblink and its implementation as a plug-in prove the extensibility of Acrobat as well as the flexibility of PDF. Since HTML and PDF com-

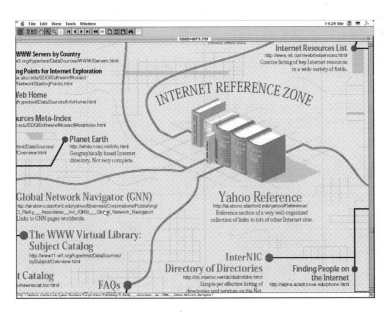

Fig. 8.13.
The roadmap contains a map in PDF format containing Internet servers along with their URLs embedded in the PDF file

plement each other very well, many Webmasters around the world adopted PDF. They (and their users) however realized a disadvantage of PDF already mentioned at the end of Section 8.2.1: PDF is not a stream format, i.e., a file must be completely transferred from server to client before the first page can be displayed. Since in general PDF files are much larger than HTML files, this property slows down web surfing significantly. Also, it's somehow clumsy to always launch Acrobat Reader as external viewer.

For these reasons, Adobe developed several extensions for Acrobat 3.0. They are aimed at accelerating PDF display and integrating Acrobat and Web browser more tightly. The necessary file format extensions are incorporated in version 1.2 of the PDF specification.

Integrating Web browser and Acrobat viewer. As long as a Web browser has to launch an external viewer for PDF files, these appear somewhat alien to the world of HTML. To remedy this, Adobe pushed the tight integration of Web browser and Acrobat viewer. In a joint effort with Netscape Communications, they made use of both the plug-in technique and the APIs (application programming interface) of Netscape Navigator and Acrobat Reader to seamlessly combine both programs. Clicking a PDF link in an HTML file instructs Netscape

Fig. 8.14.
Netscape or
Acrobat? Acrobat
3.0 tightly couples
both programs:
Acrobat displays a
document in
Netscape's window
and also docks its
toolbar in Netscape

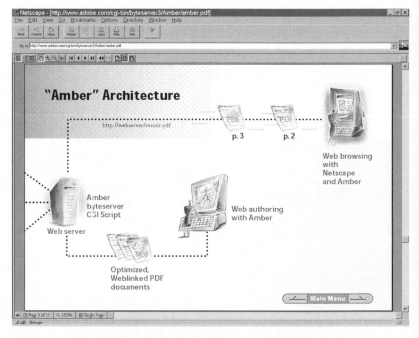

to launch the Reader that requests the document parts from the server (using the browser for communication) and displays it in Netscape's window. The Reader's menu items and tool bar are also visible in Netscape's window. This eliminates the need to use two different programs and deal with separate document windows. In order to further blur the difference between PDF and HTML, PDF files are listed in the browser's history list just as any other visited HTML file. This means you can use the forward/backward buttons to jump to HTML as well as PDF files. These features are implemented in Netscape 2.0 and higher. Adobe announced similar support for Microsoft's Internet Explorer.

Embedding PDF in HTML documents.   Netscape defined a new HTML tag which lets you reference data for a Netscape plug-in in the HTML file. This works similar to embedded GIF or JPEG files. Contrary to image files, however, the plug-in data is not only statically displayed as part of the HTML page, but can be interactively processed by the plug-in module. It may, for example, play a sound or video file, or, in our case, display and browse a PDF document.

In order to see how the EMBED tag works, let's take a look at the HTML code I used to generate Figure 8.15:

```
<EMBED SRC="http://www.lunatix.com/PDFs/pdfspec.pdf"
WIDTH=430 HEIGHT=532>
```

The URL may point to an arbitrary PDF file located on the user's hard disk or somewhere on the Internet. Netscape uses the file name suffix to determine the appropriate MIME type and the kind of plug-in to launch, retrieves the data from disk or off the net and feeds it to the plug-in registered to that particular MIME type. In the case of PDF, Acrobat Reader displays the PDF in a rectangular subpart of the HTML page. The size of this area in pixels is determined by the WIDTH and HEIGHT parameters. If the user clicks on the displayed PDF page, the Acrobat plug-in takes over the complete browser window for displaying the PDF document as well as bookmarks or thumbnails and the Acrobat toolbar. Using the toolbar, the whole PDF document may be browsed. Unlike embedded EPS graphics in a DTP document, an embedded PDF may consist of more than one page.

There's one catch related to the WIDTH and HEIGHT arguments for the EMBED tag. These parameters determine the size of the display area for the embedded PDF regardless of the PDF document's original size. While the page may be deliberately scaled down, changing the width/height ratio results in the PDF being distorted. To avoid this, use Acrobat Exchange or Reader to determine the document's page size in points (the values displayed in the status bar at the bottom of Exchange's window). Either use these size values as pixel size for the

EMBED tag, or change both values by the same factor, e.g., divide both by two to save screen estate.

8.4.5 Optimized PDFs and Byteserving.

The display "speed" of a document does not only depend on measurable variables such as network bandwidth, processor clock, etc., but also on cleverly exploring the available bandwidth. For Web browsers, some sort of "psychological accelerator" is state of the art: the browser first loads the document text, then low resolution graphics. While the user already reads the text, the browser downloads higher resolution image data (this is mostly accomplished via the "interlaced" feature of GIF images). Since the Web surfer can already read the text even if downloading is not completely finished, the download process appears to be faster.

Fig. 8.15.
Embedding a PDF document inside
HTML. Assuming the Acrobat plug-
in is installed, the first page of the
PDF is displayed in the browser's
window. Clicking on it makes the
complete PDF document accessible

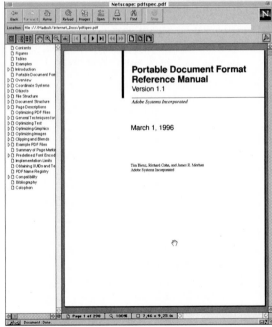

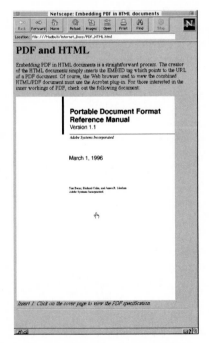

Optimized PDF files.   Adobe extended this principle to PDF files. Normally, the cross-reference table at the end of a PDF file is needed to access the individual pages' contents (text, images, fonts, etc.). New optimized PDF files contain an additional table at the beginning . ("hint table"). The Reader software decides, according to this table, which elements are needed to display the first page. Progressive display subjectively accelerates the download: first the text is displayed, then the graphics follow. Text rendering is accelerated by "font blitting" – the text is first displayed using a substitution font. Only when the missing outline fonts are loaded from the server is the preliminary text representation replaced by the "real" font.

You can optimize existing PDF files with Acrobat Exchange 3.0. Simply check the "Optimize Document" button in the "Save As..." ´dialog box. Using the "File", "Document Info", "General..." menu it's easy to find out whether or not a given file is already optimized. To optimize many PDF files in one go, use Exchange 3.0's "Batch Optimize..." feature.

Byteserving PDFs.   Optimized PDF files alone, however, couldn't achieve significant improvements since Web servers always transfer documents as a whole. For this reason, Adobe makes use of an extension to the basic Web server protocol HTTP (hypertext transfer protocol) that allows to transfer files partially. This *byteserver protocol* HTTP extension enables the Web browser to request only parts of a file from the Web server. The server sends a set of byte ranges of the file as a multi-part MIME response. This allows Acrobat software to request (via the Web browser) only those parts of a PDF file which are necessary to render a given page.

Obviously, this page-at-a-time download only works for optimized PDF files. Non-optimized files may of course also be linked to the Web

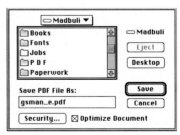

Fig. 8.16.
You can optimize PDF files with Acrobat Exchange 3.0's "Save as" feature (below), and check for optimization in the "General Info" box (left).

but must be completely transferred to the browser before they can be displayed.

There is a draft standard for the (relatively simple) byteserver protocol extension. It is already implemented in several Web server products (Netscape Enterprise Server, Open Market Secure WebServer 2.0, O'Reilly & Associates' WebSite 1.1, QuarterDeck Corporation's WebStar, Microsoft's Internet Information Server). If a particular server program doesn't support the protocol, it can easily be implemented via the server's CGI interface. Adobe provides a byteserver perl script to achieve this.

8.4.6 CGI Scripts for Dynamically Creating PDF.

The success of the World Wide Web is partly based on the ability to integrate new data types. In many cases, however, static (fixed) files are not satisfactory because the information has to be dynamically generated or to be extracted from a database and further processed before being presented to the user.

To work around this restriction, a Web server can be extended by the *Common Gateway Interface* (CGI). CGI and the forms feature of HTML open huge possibilities. Consider the following typical scenario: the user selects a "normal" Web page containing a form with several input fields. In these fields he enters data describing the information requested, e.g., search expressions for a database query. The Web server sends these data to a separate program called a CGI script. The script processes the input and, for example, queries the database. The query results are further processed in the script and sent to the Web server (often as HTML code). The web server in turn sends the returned data to the browser. This makes it possible to dynamically create HTML pages according to user input.

A well-known example for dynamically created Web pages are access statistics which are used on many servers to display the number of user accesses for a particular page. To create such a statistic, the protocol data are used to generate a diagram in GIF format which is then sent to the browser. Since HTML doesn't directly support object oriented graphics, this scheme only works with raster images. But it would be nice to use PDF files instead because of their graphics capabilities. Also, PDFs can be scaled to arbitrary size without loss of quality.

In theory, there are several ways to achieve such a dynamic integration of PDF in the World Wide Web. For example, one could use a program to create a graphics file from the data, convert it to PostScript, and launch Acrobat Distiller to produce a PDF. However, Distiller's launch time and processing speed object to this solution. Also, many Web servers run on platforms for which Distiller is not avail-

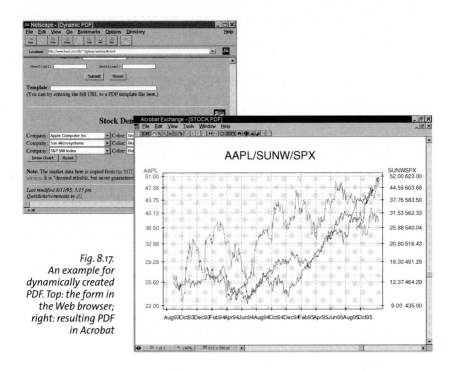

Fig. 8.17.
An example for
dynamically created
PDF. Top: the form in
the Web browser;
right: resulting PDF
in Acrobat

able. Another solution might be a program for directly generating
PDF from the data. Though quite reasonable, this approach requires
large development efforts if the program is to support PDF completely.

Even so, there is yet another variation developed by Dave Glazer
who presents it on his home page (*http://www.best.com/~dglazer/
adobe*) from which Figure 8.17 is derived. The basic observation is that
the generated PDF files are similar to each other, e.g., a constant background upon which variable data are placed. Therefore it is sufficient
to create a PDF as a template and use a CGI script, which simply adds
the variable parts to the PDF template.

As an example, let's take a look at a Web server which presents
stock data in PDF format. The user enters the name of the company in
whose stock values he's interested. The web server transfers the company name to a CGI script which queries the information from a database (or another Internet server, or whatever). The script then enters
the data in a PDF template. Finally, the server sends the PDF to the
browser which displays it using Acrobat software. Ideally, the PDF is
displayed directly in the Browser using the Acrobat plug-in.

This sort of dynamic PDF also requires some programming effort,
but shows how to reasonably integrate Acrobat to the World Wide

Web. Also the effort required is not as high as completely implementing a PDF interface (instead of only the template).

8.5 Tips and Tricks for Acrobat and PDF

8.5.1 Using PDF Documents

Arranging pages in Exchange. A little-known feature of Acrobat Exchange is the drag & drop function for arranging pages. To use it, enable thumbnails (you have to create the thumbnails first if the document doesn't contain any) and enlarge the thumbnail area by dragging the separator line (see Figure 8.18). Now you can rearrange the thumbnails (and therefore the pages) by clicking in the page number at the bottom of a thumbnail and dragging the page icon to the desired location. This feature is not restricted to the same document; you may, for example, be used to arrange pages from different documents into a PDF presentation file.

A similar drag & drop feature allows several PDF documents with the Windows version of Exchange to be combined: open the first document in Exchange, then drag the other from File Manager onto Exchange's window. A dialog box pops up asking where to insert the second document's pages.

Fig. 8.18.
You can rearrange the pages in a PDF document or drag them to another document using Exchange's drag & drop feature

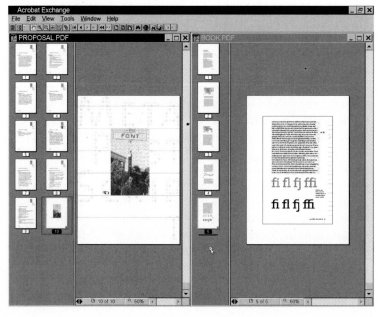

File size after deleting pages. The details of PDF have it that documents may increase in size instead of decrease after deleting pages because the deleted data remains part of the file, only the cross-reference table at the end of the file is updated. However, if you use "Save as..." to save the file under a new name, the internal file structure is completely rebuilt, and only the actual page descriptions are stored in the file. This makes the file smaller than the simple "Save" function.

Extracting text from PDF files. You can extract text from PDF files by selecting it with the text selection tool in Acrobat and copying it to the clipboard. This method has its disadvantages: you cannot copy the whole text contents of a document at once but have to deal with each page individually. Also, the text is copied to the clipboard without linebreak characters. That's OK for text to be reformatted, but unacceptable for copying program listings or tables.

In this situation Ghostscript and the *ps2ascii.ps* utility can help. It extracts text not only from PostScript files but also from PDF documents. Contrary to Acrobat, the whole document is processed, and line breaks are retained. More details on using this utility can be found in Section B.6.3.

Under Windows, there's another possibility to extract text from a PDF file: print it to file with the "Universal/Text only" printer driver.

PDF files on the Mac. PDF files are intended for exchanging data between different systems. However, if a Mac user receives a PDF file from another system via e-mail, the file often lacks the Mac-like reference to the creating software. This means the Finder can't open the file by launching Acrobat. It's easy to fix this problem by opening the PDF file in ResEdit and changing the file creator field to "CARO" (!) and the file type to "PDF " (four characters, the last is a blank).

Damaged PDF files. If a PDF file was damaged during network transfer Acrobat Reader or Exchange complain with the following notice:

```
This file is damaged but is being repaired.
```

Whether or not the file can be successfully repaired depends on the nature of the damage: if the cross-reference table is missing Acrobat cannot open the file. If the offset entries in the table are slightly incorrect, the file may however be opened. This may happen when a file is transferred between Mac or Unix and Windows and the line end characters are converted by some involved software component. In this case, the page descriptions are OK but the file positions are wrong. Acrobat is able to fix this kind of problem.

This allows you to edit a PDF file's content with a text editor if need be; to fix a typo, for example. However, the file should only contain ASCII characters. If this is not the case, you can convert it back to Post-Script and re-distill the file using Distiller's ASCII-only option.

Acrobat Reader under Unix. The Unix Reader extracts PDF documents from mailbox files and also accepts files encoded with *uuencode*. Simply launch Acrobat Reader with the name of the mailbox file as a command line argument.

8.5.2 Printing PDF Documents

Faster printing with Level 2. Because of the close relationship between PDF and PostScript Level 2 Acrobat explores Level 2 features to speed up printing and keep the print files small. For this reason, you should definitely enable the Level 2 option in Acrobat's print dialog if your device is Level 2 capable.

Problems when printing PDF files. Some printers cannot reliably print Multiple Master fonts and choke on PDF, especially when substitute fonts are involved. This problem relates to, for example, NeWS-print devices and even some printers equipped with an Adobe interpreter, e.g., Apple LaserWriter NT. In some cases you can still print the document by installing the required fonts, thereby disabling the font substitution mechanism.

If the PostScript printer is short on memory, printing a PDF document may result in the *VMerror* message. Sometimes you can fix this problem by only allowing a single substitution font (instead of two) in the "File", "Preferences", "General preferences..." dialog.

Batch printing under Unix. The Unix versions of Acrobat Reader and Exchange are capable of batch printing (in addition to interactively starting the printing process). You can convert PDF files to Post-Script without displaying them on screen with the following command line:

```
acroread -toPostScript file.pdf > file.ps
```

If you want to convert several PDF files at once you can specify a target directory:

```
acroread -toPostScript file1.pdf file2.pdf <directory>
```

An additional command line option forces Level 2 output:

```
acroread -toPostScript -level2 file.pdf > file.ps
```

Acrobat Reader and Exchange 1.0 need an X server for printing. This means the DISPLAY environment variable should be set. In version 2.1 this restriction has been lifted.

8.5.3 Creating PDF Documents

Distilling EPS files.   In Chapter 3 we discussed the differences between PostScript and EPS files. These are also relevant for Acrobat Distiller. Generally, it's not possible to convert EPS files with Distiller. Possible reasons for this include an optional binary preview in Windows EPS files, graphic positioned outside the page, or the missing *showpage* operator. While it's possible to fix each of these problems, it's much easier to place the EPS graphic on an empty page using a suitable program and then create a new PostScript file as input for Distiller.

Page orientation.   Wrong page orientation of landscape pages often causes grief. While it's easy to rotate a page printed in landscape format, this is quite troublesome on the screen (you can rotate the PDF pages in Exchange, rotate your 20 inch monitor, or crick your neck). An undocumented operator in the PostScript file may help in this situation. It is interpreted by Distiller and allows you to fix the page orientation:

```
statusdict /CTMOrientation 0 put
```

The values 0, 1, 2, and 3 rotate the pages by 0°, 90°, 180°, and 270°, respectively. This instruction may be used with different parameters for each page.

Page size.   The size of PDF pages may be adjusted in Acrobat Exchange. Alternatively, the following instruction can be inserted at the beginning of the PostScript file to be distilled (or in Distiller's startup file):

```
<</PageSize [width height]>> setpagedevice
```

Width and height values must be inserted in points.

Color in PDF files.   If your PDF contains black-and-white only instead of color after distilling, you have to configure a color printer as target device in the original application before creating the PostScript file. Some programs don't emit color information otherwise.

Distiller error messages.   Distiller, being a PostScript interpreter, issues the usual PostScript error messages if there is some reason to complain about the input files. Generally, all kinds of PostScript errors discussed in chapter 2 may be triggered. In Section 2.5.3 you find hints on troubleshooting such cases. PJL (Printer Job Language) instructions for HP printers are a particular tricky source of error. If Distiller issues the error message

```
%%[ Error: undefined; OffendingCommand: @PJL ]%%
```

you must configure the printer driver to not generate PJL instructions. Also, Distiller doesn't accept Type 42 fonts (TrueType fonts wrapped as PostScript). The common Ctrl-D character – present in many PostScript files – doesn't cause any harm in Distiller.

If you often want to switch between printing on a PJL (HP) device and preparing PostScript files for Distiller and don't want to reconfigure the printer driver each time, you can cancel the dreaded PJL instructions with the following definition in Distiller's startup file:

```
/@PJL { currentfile //=string readline { pop } if } bind def
```

Bitmap fonts.   If a document is displayed very slowly in Acrobat Reader or Exchange, and the fonts appear jaggy even in large magnification, the distilled PostScript file probably contained Type 3 fonts. This is often the case for converted TeX documents and files created with the Windows driver configured to convert TrueType fonts to Type 3. Bitmap fonts not only slow down rendering the PDF file on screen or printer but also increase the file size. In these cases it's preferable to install Type 1 outline fonts or configure the driver to emit Type 1 directly and to re-distill the file. Distiller always embeds Type 3 fonts.

8.5.4 Editing PDF Documents.   Generally, PDF is a one-way format for documents. In most cases, PDF documents only have to be displayed or printed but the contents remain unchanged. The only editing functions available in Acrobat Exchange are rearranging pages and inserting bookmarks, hypertext links, or annotations. This is sufficient for many applications in which the PDF files need not be changed. In some situations however it's desirable to edit or change PDF documents without accessing the original document or application and re-creating the PDF. For example, a typo has to be fixed, an image replaced, or even larger changes to be accomplished. Currently there are only few software packages that allow one to directly open and edit PDF files or to convert them to some other editable format.

Graphics programs.   Some newer graphics applications are capable of opening, editing and saving PDF files without any prior conversion. These include Adobe Illustrator 5.5 and higher (for Mac, Sun, and SGI) and Macromedia FreeHand 5.5 (for Mac). Expect other manufacturers to PDF-enable their software soon.

When opening a PDF file, Adobe Illustrator displays the thumbnail representation of the pages (if there are no thumbnails, opening a large document is a chore). You can use the familiar graphics and text tools to manipulate the document's contents. Afterwards it can be saved as PDF again. Since the AI file format doesn't directly support raster images, Illustrator extracts raster images embedded in PDF files and stores them in separate files. Double-clicking an image launches Photoshop for editing (if it is available).

There are some limitations since Illustrator doesn't implement all features of Acrobat Exchange. It's not possible to edit hypertext links; existing links are retained when saving a PDF file again. Also, there is no Multiple Master font substitution available in Illustrator. All fonts used in the document must be installed on the system since Illustrator cannot make use of embedded fonts. Finally, Illustrator refuses to open encrypted PDF files.

Tailor. Tailor was developed by the software manufacturer First-Class NV (located in Belgium). It uses Display PostScript under NEXT-STEP and allows editing PostScript and PDF files (the Mac version currently only accepts PostScript). Similar to Illustrator, you can edit and change single elements in a PDF document. Storing a file as PDF isn't possible – Tailor converts to PostScript before saving the file. You can find more information on Tailor's features in Section 9.3.3.

Transverter Pro. The software PostScript RIP Transverter Pro was developed by TechPool Software (Cleveland, Ohio) and is available in Windows and Mac versions. It displays PDF files on screen and converts them to Illustrator format in which they may be opened using any AI compatible program.

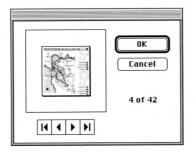

Fig. 8.19.
Adobe Illustrator
displays the
thumbnails when
opening a PDF file.

ePScript. The ePScript software package also runs under NEXTSTEP and developed by the German company OneVision. ePScript opens PostScript as well as PDF files and offers a wealth of editing functions. More information on ePScript can be found in Section 9.3.5.

8.5.5 PDF Software on the CD-ROM.
There is some free software available for displaying and printing PDF files. Acrobat Reader is freely available but doesn't support all platforms. This is mainly a concern for users of Unix workstations who want to deal with PDF files and have an operating system not supported by Adobe. You can find all programs discussed in this section on the accompanying CD-ROM.

Ghostscript (all systems). The PostScript interpreter Ghostscript is capable of processing, displaying, and printing PDF files. This makes Ghostscript the only software for PDF which is available for all major (and some minor) platforms. In addition to displaying PDF files on screen and printing them to non-PostScript printers, Ghostscript also allows PDF to be converted to PostScript Level 2. Though Ghostscript tries to choose suitable substitution fonts for missing fonts, it doesn't match Acrobat's font substitution mechanism with Multiple Master fonts. However, since Ghostscript adjusts the substitute fonts' metrics, the results are much better than when substituting Courier for all missing fonts (as happens in the printer). Therefore, the best document rendering is achieved if all necessary fonts are either installed in Ghostscript or contained in the PDF file. Another limitation relates to the hypertext features. Ghostscript only processes the layout-related instructions in a PDF file and doesn't follow hypertext links or display bookmarks and thumbnails.

Ghostscript also includes a small batch file/shell script for converting PDFs to PostScript Level 1 or Level 2 from the command line. Starting with version 4.0, Ghostscript is even capable of converting PostScript to PDF, i.e., it serves as a replacement for Acrobat Distiller. Although this features suffers from some limitations, it makes Ghostscript the only free program for distilling PostScript files to PDF on virtually any platform. You can find more details on Ghostscript's PDF features in Section B.6.2.

Perl script pdf2ps. The *pdf2ps.pl* script needs the Perl interpreter. It converts PDF files to PostScript Level 2 and can also create a separate PostScript file with the PDF's thumbnail images. Like Ghostscript, this script suffers from some limitations with respect to handling missing fonts. pdf2ps is the only program to extract thumbnails from a PDF file (if present) and allows to print an overview of the whole

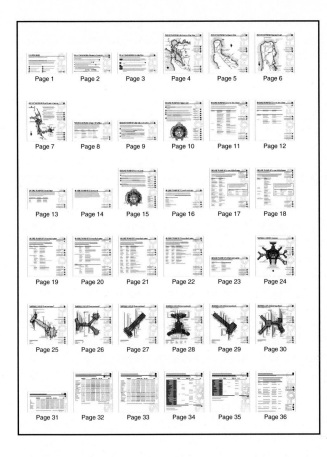

Fig. 8.20.
The pdf2ps Perl
script prints an
overview with a
PDF file's
thumbnails

document (see Figure 8.20). Also like Ghostscript, it doesn't accept
encrypted documents.

Converting text to PDF with Gymnast (Windows). The shareware
program *Gymnast* for Windows converts text files to simple PDF files.
While its practical use is limited, it may be helpful in understanding
the structure of PDF files. Since Gymnast creates simple structured
files without binary data the generated files may be examined in a
text editor.

PDFViewer for NEXTSTEP. PDFViewer displays PDF files under NEXT-
STEP. It makes extensive use of Display PostScript for screen output.
PDFViewer supports links, bookmarks, and annotations and also tries
a simple sort of font substitution.

XPDF (Unix/X Window System). XPDF is a PDF viewer for the X Window System for which C source is available. Though not as sophisticated as Acrobat Reader, XPDF supports more platforms and is a very lightweight program. XPDF displays PDF documents on screen and can also convert them to PostScript Level 2. XPDF also follows embedded links, but doesn't display bookmarks or annotations. The package includes a utility program for converting PDF files to PostScript Level 2 from the command line.

8.6 How to Create Links in PDF Documents

8.6.1 Acrobat-Savvy Applications.
Since Distiller converts arbitrary PostScript files to PDF it's child's play to use any document creation software – word processors, graphics and presentation software, etc. – for preparing PDF files. However, there's more to Acrobat support than only converting printable parts of a document since PDF also sports hypertext features. Although these may be generated using Acrobat Exchange, it's much more comfortable to have the original application take care of this. For this reason, Adobe defined special PostScript operators which Distiller uses to create hypertext elements automatically. By embedding these operators in the PostScript output the original application software – which contrary to Distiller knows about the logical structure of the document – can instruct Distiller to generate hypertext elements. Which elements can be generated depends on the scope and functionality of the application. Here are some examples:

- ► A word processor which automatically generates a table of contents for a book may create bookmarks and links for all entries contained in the table of contents.
- ► A DTP program that arranges text in multiple columns may generate instructions for PDF article threads which follow the text flow according to the column layout.
- ► An index may also be enhanced by hypertext links: clicking an entry's page number jumps to the respective page.
- ► General document information such as author, title, subject, etc., are prime candidates for the info dictionary contained in the PDF file.
- ► Presentation software may generate bookmarks for each slide or insert comments into annotations.

Some DTP systems such as FrameMaker, PageMaker, and Corel Ventura already implement such features. The software generates the instructions necessary for the PDF hypertext features, according to document contents and user preferences. If your particular software is not (yet) PDF-savvy, there are still means to embed the hypertext instructions in the PostScript output:

- ▶ The instructions are written to a file which is distilled along with the actual PostScript data. This technique is limited to instructions at the beginning of a document.
- ▶ In some application programs you can define the PDF instructions directly on a page and have the software insert them into the PostScript output stream.
- ▶ As a bad "hack", the hypertext instructions may be included in an embedded EPS file, camouflaged as an ordinary graphics file.

Let me clearly state that these are only makeshift solutions which are meant to bridge the gap to real PDF-savvy software. In the following sections the necessary operators are presented and several examples are given for the above-mentioned techniques. The examples are slightly more technical than the rest of this book and are intended for readers who have at least seen some pieces of PostScript code already.

8.6.2 PostScript Operators for Hypertext Links.

PostScript instructions only describe the printed page; there are no provisions for hypertext features such as annotations, links, and bookmarks. To solve this problem, Adobe defined the new *pdfmark* PostScript operator which Distiller recognizes and processes. This operator allows hypertext features to be generated at the time the PostScript code is distilled to PDF. This avoids re-inserting the links every time a new document version is distilled.

The *pdfmark* operator is only evaluated in Distiller but not in PDF-writer. Since pdfmark isn't implemented in PostScript printers, it's a good idea to conditionally cancel it using the following code at the beginning of the PostScript file:

```
/pdfmark where
{pop} {userdict /pdfmark /cleartomark load put} ifelse
```

This code "neutralizes" pdfmark in the printer but doesn't affect the distiller. This allows to use the same PostScript files for printing and distilling.

pdfmark instructions always start with a square bracket, different pairs of keywords and values, and the name of the hypertext element to be created. The keywords are always introduced by a slash, "/", the value's data type depends on the kind of keyword. Let me give some examples.

The following instruction defines title, author, and keywords for the document. These data are displayed in Acrobat Reader or Exchange via "File", "Document Info", "General...".

```
[      /Title (Annual review)
       /Author (Thomas Merz)
       /Keywords (Annual review, revenue, business development)
       /Creator (DocuSystem 5.0)
/DOCINFO pdfmark
```

The following instruction defines a rectangle for an annotation and the text contained in the annotation. Double-clicking the annotation in Acrobat makes the text visible.

```
[      /Rect [ 75 586 456 663 ]
       /Contents (Let's check colors on this page again)
/ANN pdfmark
```

The following instruction defines a link from the current page to page 3. The coordinates describe the active area of the link, i.e., the rectangle in which a mouse click triggers the hypertext jump.

```
[      /Rect [ 70 650 210 675 ]
       /Page 3
       /View [ /XYZ null null null]
/LNK pdfmark
```

The table lists the most important pdfmark instructions. The complete specification can be found in the *pdfmark Reference Manual* (see bibliography).

Starting with Acrobat 2.1, the /LNK key is supported for compatibility reasons only, but its use should be discontinued. Links should instead be created with a special form of the /ANN key. The following pdfmark code creates a rectangle which leads to page 14 of the PDF document.

```
[      /Rect [70 100 170 130]
       /Page 14
       /Subtype /Link
/ANN pdfmark
```

Specifying URL links requires yet another form of the /ANN instruction:

```
[      /Rect [70 100 170 130]
       /Action << /Subtype /URI /URI (http://www.muc.de/~tm) >>
       /Subtype /Link
/ANN pdfmark
```

All coordinates have to be entered in points in the usual PostScript coordinate system; strings have to be surrounded by parentheses. If a string contains parentheses or line breaks these have to be "escaped" by a preceding backslash character, "\". For all strings PDFDocEncoding is used which is widely identical to ISO Latin 1 (and therefore the

```
```

Name	Possible keywords	Remarks
/LNK (link)	/Page pagenum	target for a hypertext jump: integer: page number /Next: next page /Prev: previous page no entry: same page
	/View destination	position and zoom factor of target page [/XYZ null null null]: same zoom factor /Fit: fit page to window /FitW: fit page width to window
	/Rect [llx lly urx ury]	rectangle describing the link's active area
/ARTICLE (article thread)	/Title string	article's name
	/Rect [llx lly urx ury]	rectangle for the article
	/Page pagenum	page number
/DEST (jump destination)	/Dest name	defines the current page as a named destination for use in hypertext jumps
/DOCINFO (general document information)	/Author string	name of the person who wrote the document
	/CreationDate string	creation date of the document
	/Creator string	name of the program used to create the original document
	/Title string	title of the document
	/Keywords string	keywords describing the document's contents
/PAGE	/CropBox [llx lly urx ury]	crop current page
/PAGES	/CropBox [llx lly urx ury]	crop all pages of the document
/ANN (annotation)	/Contents string	contents of the annotation
	/Rect [llx lly urx ury]	rectangle for the annotation
	/Open boolean	true: annotation is open false: annotation is closed no entry means false
	/Title string	title of the annotation
	/Color colorspec	color of the annotation
/OUT (bookmark)	/Page pagenum	number of the page the bookmark points to. 0 means no jump, the bookmark has subordinal bookmarks
	/View [destination]	see /LNK
	/Title string	text of the bookmark
	/Count int	number of subordinal bookmarks; not necessary if there are no subordinal bookmarks; negative numbers mean bookmark is closed

Unix and Windows character set). Mac users should enter octal codes to ensure portability for all non-ASCII characters.

A final note on the page numbers used for links and bookmarks: these always relate to the physical page number which is also displayed in Reader. Every document starts at page 1, regardless of the page numbers which may be printed on the document's pages.

8.6.3 Distilling Multiple Files at Once.
Sometimes it's necessary to distill multiple PostScript files to a single PDF file. The complete document may consist of several chapters in their own files, or special pdfmarks have to be inserted (see examples in the next sections). Combining multiple PostScript files in one PDF file also cuts down the file size because fonts and other resources have to be put in the file only once.

To generate a PDF document from multiple PostScript files, use a text editor to create a small batch file for Distiller which looks similar to this:

```
/prun {
        /mysave save def
        dup = flush
        RunFile
        clear cleardictstack
        mysave restore
} def

(c:\\ps\\file1.ps) prun
(c:\\ps\\file2.ps) prun
```

The last lines contain the names of all files to distill. The example above is meant for Windows. On other platforms the file name conventions have to be obeyed, for example on the Mac:

```
(volume:folder:file1.ps) prun
(volume:folder:file2.ps) prun
```

The batch file containing the file names is processed with Distiller. The *prun* procedure is responsible for memory management and opens each file in turn.

8.6.4 PDF Documents with FrameMaker.
FrameMaker offers a wealth of hypertext commands for designing online documents. The similarity between Frame's hypertext features and those of PDF suggests to convert the links contained in Frame documents to PDF links automatically.

PDF documents with FrameMaker 5. FrameMaker 5 is one of the programs mentioned above that are able to derive suitable pdfmark instructions from the document's contents and embed them in the PostScript output stream. The following table lists the relationship between a Frame document's contents and Acrobat elements:

FrameMaker	Portable Document Format (PDF)
cross-reference	link
hypertext command	link
hypertext alert	annotation
heading	˙ bookmark
text flow (text frame)	article thread
launch external program	(although possible in PDF 1.1, FrameMaker doesn't create the respective instructions)
(no equivalent)	general document information (subject, author, keywords, etc.)
(no equivalent)	Uniform Resource Locator (URL)

FrameMaker completely translates cross-references and hypertext commands to PDF elements. Their existence in the original document justifies the PDF equivalent. Similarly, text columns in the Frame document are translated to a PDF article thread. Bookmarks are a different case: the user must decide which types of paragraph (e.g., different heading levels) should define a new bookmark and what their hierarchical relationship is. Frame 5 offers a configuration dialog in the advanced print setup menu where you can specify the hierarchy of bookmarks (see Figure 8.21).

As you can see from the table, not all Frame or PDF attributes can be generated automatically. The following sections explore some tricks which not only PDF-enable older Frame versions but also allow to generate document information and URL links automatically from Frame 5 documents. I hear you asking "what's wrong with adding this stuff in Acrobat Exchange?". The answer is simple: many documents change very frequently, and the resulting PDF not only has to be re-generated every time but also the URLs added manually. It may save much work to create the URLs directly from within the document.

pdfmark operators in a PostScript column. The first technique makes use of Frame's ability to embed user-defined PostScript code in a text column in the document. Simply insert the PostScript instructions in a text column just as it were regular text, select the text frame and choose "Format", "Text Flow" (in Frame 5: "Format", "Customize Layout", "Customize Text Frame...") to assign the "PostScript code" attribute to the text column. When printing the document,

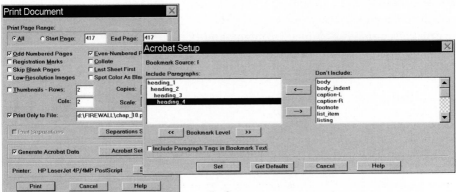

Fig. 8.21.
When creating a PostScript file in FrameMaker 5, you can define the relationship between paragraph types and bookmarks as well as the hierarchy of bookmarks.

FrameMaker inserts the column's contents into the PostScript output stream without changing it. Before Frame outputs this code it transfers the text column's coordinates to the PostScript stack. These are superfluous and have to be removed using four *pop* commands before issuing the pdfmark instructions. Seems complicated? Take a look at the following example which inserts general document information into the resulting PDF file:

```
pop pop pop pop
/pdfmark where
{pop}{userdict /pdfmark /cleartomark load put} ifelse
[     /Title (Annual report)
      /Author (Thomas Merz)
      /Keywords (Annual report, revenue, business development)
      /Creator (FrameMaker 5.0)
/DOCINFO pdfmark
```

Note that the PostScript column should be transparent or located aside from regular text columns so it doesn't obscure other text. If you want to edit the PostScript code again, you have to deactivate the "PostScript code" attribute and assign it again when you're done editing.

Frame 4 also creates bookmarks. The second method (besides pdfmark in a PostScript column) for generating pdfmark instructions in Frame was developed by Charles Poynton and simplifies automatic generation of bookmarks. You can find a detailed description in his document "Making Acrobat Bookmarks using FrameMaker" on the accompanying CD-ROM. The basic idea is to use FrameMaker to create a list of all instructions for the bookmarks and to feed these data into Distiller before the actual PostScript file is processed. If chapter headings are to be used as bookmark text, you can simply create a table of contents which doesn't contain the usual chapter numbers, heading text, and page numbers, but instead pdfmark instructions for the corresponding bookmarks. The following is a template that achieves this effect. It must be used in an appropriate text flow on a reference page in the Frame document:

```
[      /Page <$pagenum>
       /View [/XYZ null null null]
       /Title (<$paranum> <$paratext>)
/OUT pdfmark
```

The magic trick is to pull the variable parts of the instruction (in this case page number and bookmark text) from FrameMaker variables. When generating the table of contents (which in fact does no longer deserve this name), FrameMaker generates a pdfmark for each heading. The pdfmark contains chapter number and heading text. Save this pseudo table of contents as a text file and either insert its contents at the beginning of the document's PostScript code, or process both files at once in Distiller (see Section 8.6.3).

As an alternative to using chapter headings for bookmarks, you can resort to a special marker. In this case the bookmark text is derived from the <$markertext> variable (instead of <$paranum> and <$paratext>). Instead of generating a table of contents you have to generate a marker list which creates the necessary pdfmark instructions.

Note the PDF string syntax has to be obeyed for the marker text. Also, with large documents consisting of several files carefully check the page numbering – distill all PostScript files to a single PDF as described above.

Embedding URL links via pdfmark. The first example using pdfmark in a PostScript column is very simple because there has no location or rectangle to be defined to which the information is tied. URL links, on the other hand, are defined within a single active rectangle. Generating this rectangle makes the pdfmark code slightly more complicated, but not much.

Again, the basic procedure involves inserting pdfmark instructions in a PostScript column. Fortunately, FrameMaker supplies the text frame's coordinates on the PostScript stack, so the pdfmark code has access to the size and location of the text frame. Instead of disposing the coordinates as we did above, we will use them for defining the URL link's rectangle. If you're not fluent in PostScript, don't worry.

Simply insert the following piece of code into a PostScript column, replacing the URL with your favorite web site's address:

```
[      /Rect [ 7 -4 roll 4 -2 roll pop pop 0 0 ]
       /Action << /Subtype /URI /URI (http://www.muc.de/~tm) >>
       /Subtype /Link
/ANN pdfmark
```

The PostScript gobbledywobble in the first line uses the column's co-ordinates to define the link rectangle. URI refers to Uniform Resource Identifier which is a slightly different concept from URL (Uniform Resource Locator); we can however disregard the differences in our context. After assigning the "PostScript code" attribute to the text frame, you can arbitrarily resize it to resemble the size of the hot spot you want to use as an URL link. It doesn't matter if parts of the code disappear after resizing the column – the PostScript code will be allright.

To make the active area visible you can either assign a color to the text column's border in FrameMaker, or insert the additional pdfmark key /Color after the /Action line above to specify the rectangle's color.

You may have noticed that it's rather clumsy to assign and remove the "PostScript code" attribute to the text column several times. To simplify this process, you can use FrameMaker variables that hold your URLs. Using these variables both in the actual text column and in the PostScript column it's much easier to incorporate changes.

Remember that for the URL links to work in Acrobat Reader or Exchange the Weblink plug-in has to be installed and that URL pdfmark instructions only work in Acrobat Distiller 2.1 and above.

8.6.5 Creating Links Automatically in Microsoft Word.

It's easy to create PostScript output with Microsoft Word and feed it to Distiller. However, using Word's print fields you can insert your own PostScript code in the output file. This technique is perfectly suited for interspersing pdfmark instructions. Firstly, use "Tools", "Options", "View" to activate screen display of fields. This makes life easier in the following steps. Using "Insert", "Field...", "Field name print" you can insert pdfmark instructions (surrounded by double quotes) in a dialog box. The \p option tells Word to define some variables which we can use for defining a link's active area. The manual doesn't say anything about print fields and PostScript variables. You have to place the cursor in a print field and activate the help button to get some information.

Defining symbolic names for each link destination frees the links from the page numbering and makes them work even when the document's formatting changes. For example, to jump to the beginning of chapter 1, use the following instruction inside the chapter 1 heading to define a link destination called C1 (the underlined part is contained in the print field):

```
{print "[/Dest /C1 /DEST pdfmark"}Chapter 1: Introduction
```

Defining the actual link is somewhat more complicated. The Post-Script option \p and the para *keyword* coax the definition of a rectangle out of Word. This rectangle surrounds the current paragraph; its definition is contained in the *wp$box* variable. This rectangle is suited for serving as the link's active area. The symbolic name /C1 defined above serves as link destination:

```
{print \p para "[/Rect [wp$box pathbbox] /Dest /C1 /LNK
pdfmark"}Jump to chapter 1
```

The Microsoft Word documentation demands the paragraph containing the print field to be at least one inch tall, although I found this not a strict requirement in practise. This can be achieved by choosing appropriate font size or inserting empty lines. The pdfmark instructions are transferred to the PostScript file and processed by Distiller (don't forget that pdfmark triggers a PostScript error in the printer if you don't take the precautions mentioned at the beginning of Section 8.6.2).

If you label all link destinations with print fields you can prepare automatic generation of links completely in the Word document without having to change the PDF file every time the original document's contents changed.

Similarly to FrameMaker, you can also generate URL links automatically with Microsoft Word. Use the following print field to embed URLs:

```
{print \p "[ /Rect [wp$box pathbbox] /Action << /Subtype /URI
/URI (http://www.muc.de/~tm) >> /Subtype /Link
/ANN pdfmark"}Click here to jump to my Web site.
```

Note that this instruction makes the current paragraph the active area for the link, not only the URL's text.

8.6.6 pdfmark Operators in EPS Graphics.
The following trick is meant for programs which – unlike FrameMaker and Microsoft Word – don't allow embedding PostScript code. It only requires the ability to import EPS files. The embedded EPS "graphic", however, does not contain an illustration but pdfmark instructions instead. This technique is not really gentleman-like but until PDF support is as widespread as is PostScript support today, the end justifies the means...

For the embedding to work, the dummy EPS file must obey the formal rules discussed in Chapter 3. We'll make the graphic as small as possible to prevent it from disturbing the layout. However, the graphic's size mustn't be zero because otherwise division by zero may occur in the embedding program's PostScript code. Since embedding changes the coordinate system this trick is best suited for coordinate-independent pdfmark instructions, e.g., creating bookmarks or general document information. The following example embeds document information in an EPS file:

```
%!PS-Adobe-3.0 EPSF-3.0
%%BoundingBox: 0 0 1 1
%%EndProlog
/pdfmark where
{pop} {userdict /pdfmark /cleartomark load put} ifelse
[       /Title (Annual report)
        /Author (Thomas Merz)
        /Keywords (Annual report, revenue, business development)
        /Creator (ReportMaker 2.5)
/DOCINFO pdfmark
%%EOF
```

The two lines immediately after %%EndProlog prevent PostScript errors when printing the document. The space needed by the graphic is so small (one point in each direction) that it can be ignored. Since the fake EPS doesn't contain any preview it is displayed as a gray box on screen. Don't worry.

The final example shows how to create a special sort of bookmark using the EPS technique. Double-clicking the bookmark in Acrobat doesn't jump to another document location but instead launches an external application (Windows' PaintBrush program in the example):

```
%!PS-Adobe-3.0 EPSF-3.0
%%BoundingBox: 0 0 1 1
%%EndProlog
/pdfmark where
{pop} {userdict /pdfmark /cleartomark load put} ifelse
[       /Action /Launch
        /Title (Launch Paintbrush)
        /DOSFile (c:/windows/pbrush.exe)
/OUT pdfmark
%%EOF
```

Details on this variant of the OUT instruction and the syntax for other operating systems can be found in the pdfmark documentation.

Miscellaneous

9

This chapter covers several topics that don't quite fit in any of the other chapters. Even so, it contains many links and cross-references to other sections and to the software on the CD-ROM. Firstly, we explore ways to speed up printing and to prepare PostScript data for the service bureau. Next, we look at how to edit PostScript files. The last two sections cover conversion of text and graphics files from and to PostScript.

9.1 Optimizing Print Performance

Hardware and software are locked up in a sort of arms race: even for the most advanced computer there is an application that demands too much of the machine. Up-to-date software packages – already suffering from the "featuritis" disease – get bigger and bigger with each release number because memory and CPU chips decrease in price from year to year. For printers the situation is similar. The processing power of a current PostScript printer equipped with a RISC CPU would have been enough for a department mainframe not so long ago. Conversely, the first LaserWriter printers' main memory is just enough today for a pocket calculator.

If you don't want to take part in this arms race, or can't buy a new printer because your hardware budget is already exhausted, you may speed up printing without new hardware. There are different ways to achieve this; they depend on application, environment, and operating system. An office that prints several hundred single-page letters each day has totally different requirements from a graphics designer who is fed up with waiting 15 minutes for his layout proof to emerge from the printer.

The optimization tips in the following sections are meant to suggest several methods from which you can pick those that are appropriate for your situation. The tips in the first section can be implemented using standard software components, the other sections cover advanced techniques, up to PostScript programming. Of course, the latter is not perfectly suited for every man and his dog. For large organizations, however, it may well pay off to invest in some days of PostScript development in order to optimize print performance for many end users. The table at the end of this section gives an overview of the proposed methods and how to implement them on Windows, Mac, and Unix.

9.1.1 Optimization Using Standard Software.

The first tips can be implemented with standard software and do not require any programming experience. The required software is listed as well as typical application scenarios in which these tips may be useful.

Download fonts permanently. If every printed document uses the same download fonts, e.g., the corporate type, and these fonts are not built into the printer's memory, you should permanently load them in the printer. Permanently loaded fonts persist from one print job to another until the device is reset or powered off. Since a font family with four or six typefaces already consumes several hundred KB, this technique can significantly speed up printing. To implement it, you need a font downloader. For printers shared by several users this is best accomplished in the morning when computer and printer are being powered on. Under MS-DOS and Unix it's possible to load the fonts automatically. This way, users are not bothered with font management. They only have to configure their printer driver or application software to not download the PostScript fonts used in the document. In Section 2.3.3 you can find further information on permanently downloading fonts.

Download the PostScript prolog permanently.   The prolog containing PostScript definitions may be treated similar to download fonts. Normally, the prolog is contained in the print job and uses 30–50 KB. For small documents it is not uncommon that the prolog is larger than the actual page description. Since the prolog never changes, several MB of superfluous data may be transferred to the printer every day. You can prevent this by permanently downloading the prolog. The Windows driver (all versions) has a simple check box to achieve this. Load the prolog to the printer once, and the size of all subsequent print jobs will decrease by 30 KB. If you forget to download the prolog, an error message is printed that describes the problem – no document can be printed without the prolog. Permanently downloading the prolog is most effective when many short documents are printed as separate print jobs.

Transfer compressed image data.   If you have a printer with a fast CPU that is connected to the host computer via a slow link (e.g., serial interface), the size of the data transmitted to the printer is a crucial parameter with regard to printing speed. If image data (raster images) are to be printed in such a configuration, compression can boost print performance. In Section 5.5.1 several compression features of PostScript Level 2 are explored. In practise, there are several possibilities to make use of these features:

- ► JPEG compressed EPS files can be generated via Photoshop's Export function.
- ► Using the *tiff2ps* and *jpeg2ps* programs on the accompanying CD-ROM you can generate compressed PostScript from TIFF and JPEG graphics files.
- ► Take a "deviation" via PDF and print from Adobe Acrobat.
- ► Newer drivers have integrated bitmap compression features, e.g., AdobePS for Windows 3.x or the standard PostScript driver in Windows 95.

PostScript Level 1 allows bitmap compression only with the Run-Length algorithm, which is implemented in the Windows 95 driver as well.

Obviously, you should try to minimize the amount of print data in the application program already. Check for color images that should only be printed black and white – in this case it's better to switch from color to b/w before printing. Also, be careful to select image resolutions suited to the output device: excess resolution doesn't help image quality but only slows down printing.

Optimize transfer speed. If you already took measures to reduce the amount of print data, you can additionally try to increase data transfer speed. This seems to imply additional hardware, but in some cases doesn't require much effort. For example, only use the serial interface if absolutely necessary (if cable length is an important factor). Try to find out the maximum serial transfer speed possible in your environment. Windows 95 and most Unix systems allow 57600 baud reliably, which is not possible under Windows 3.x. This is at least half the speed of a parallel interface.

By networking your printer you can further accelerate data transfer. Since several printer models include a network interface by default, Windows for Workgroups, Windows 95, or Mac users only need cables and possibly a cheap network card for the computer in order to take advantage of printer networking. Ethernet support in the printer definitely pays off for Mac, Windows, or Unix workgroups which are already networked.

You can find more details on the characteristics of interface types in Section 2.3.1.

Use binary protocols. Under Windows and Unix most PostScript printers are driven using the standard protocol which is incapable of transferring binary data. Binary data, e.g., raster images, have to be converted to ASCII format which doubles file size. If your printer supports *(Tagged) Binary Control Protocol* (TBCP or BCP), you can prevent the size doubling using suitable software. This is achieved most easily using the PostScript drivers of Windows 95 or AdobePS for Windows 3.x. These drivers directly implement the newer protocols. In Unix, smart system administrators can integrate the *quote* program from the CD-ROM.

On the Mac this optimization isn't necessary since AppleTalk is by default capable of transferring binary data; the driver usually generates binary data. More details can be found in Section 2.3.2.

9.1.2 Optimization Requiring More Effort. Implementing
the tips in this section requires more effort, either in terms of additional software (font editor) or PostScript programming experience

(or consulting). However, the larger the scope of the optimization – and therefore the potential savings – the faster the effort will pay off.

Define repeated graphics as a font.   In many situations an EPS graphic is printed unaltered on every page, e.g., a company logo printed on the letterhead. In this case defining the logo as a character in a special font brings a big performance boost. Such a logo font not only accelerates output through faster rendering and the font cache's benefits, but also enhances output quality. On screen, the logo isn't represented as a low-resolution TIFF or QuickDraw image but accurately rendered by ATM. For low and medium resolution printing, hints enhance the logo's output quality. In Section 4.7.2 you can find a description on how to build your own logo font using existing EPS graphics or scanned originals. The advantages of the Type 1 font format pay off for black and white pictograms for which the outlines are not too complex. However, bitmaps, multi-color logos and very complex outlines require Type 3 fonts which are often difficult or impossible to create in a font editor.

You can easily combine this method with the above mentioned tip on permanently downloading fonts in order to reduce PostScript data transmission time.

Permanently load EPS graphics.   This tip and the next one are heavy stuff since they require a solid background in PostScript programming. The mechanism for permanently downloading not only applies to fonts but also to arbitrary PostScript instructions. The problem is to store the contents of an EPS graphic as a compact data structure in the printer's memory so it can repeatedly be executed without side effects.

This is best achieved by defining the graphic as a single PostScript procedure which is permanently downloaded to the printer. Next, you define dummy EPS files for use in your text processing or DTP application. These dummies contain the required data (BoundingBox comment, possibly screen preview), but instead of the PostScript code they only contain a call to the previously defined procedure parked in memory. Programmers who take their job seriously will check the availability of the procedure at the beginning of the EPS file and print an appropriate error message if it is not available.

The main problem with this technique is that it is not at all trivial to "procedurize" arbitrary EPS files. For small files it may suffice to simply put procedure brackets around the instructions and to define a name for the procedure. For more complex graphics, however, internal limitations of the PostScript interpreter apply (e.g., the number of elements on the stacks). Image data for raster images has to be placed in the memory correctly. While it's possible to solve these problems, they require a good deal of PostScript programming experience.

This technique may drastically increase your throughput, especially if data transfer is a major bottleneck. Instead of the EPS file only a single instruction consisting of a few bytes is transferred to the printer.

Take advantage of PostScript Level 2 forms. This trick extends the idea of permanently downloading EPS graphics by means of PostScript Level 2's forms feature (explained in more detail in Section 5.5.4. If you already managed to define a procedure for your graphic, you can also define it as a so-called form (assuming a Level 2 device is available). This makes the interpreter store the rendered version of the graphic in a temporary buffer. Next time the same graphic is printed in the same size, it need not be rendered again but instead can be taken from the buffer. While the tip above saves transmission time, the instructions are not executed at all in this case! However, this only works if the graphic is to be output in the same size and orientation, and if the printer has enough memory available. The interpreter places the rasterized graphic in the forms cache, where (like the rendered characters in the font cache) it is stored in the printer's *Virtual Memory.* According to the available memory and the amount of memory used by permanently loaded fonts it may be reasonable (or necessary) to invest in memory expansion.

9.1.3 Summary

Optimization	Macintosh	Windows	Unix
Load fonts permanently	With downloader	With downloader	In most cases only manually
Load prolog permanently	Not possible via driver	Driver configuration	Depends on application software
Compress raster images	EPS-JPEG, Acrobat	EPS-JPEG, Acrobat, tiff2ps, jpeg2ps	EPS-JPEG, Acrobat, tiff2ps, jpeg2ps
Optimize transfer speed	EtherTalk instead of AppleTalk	Ethernet or fast parallel interface	Ethernet
Binary transmission	Automatically	With AdobePS or Windows 95	Suitable backend or quote
Graphics as Font	Create logo font with a font editor		
Permanently load EPS graphics	PostScript programming		
Forms	PostScript programming		

9.2 Preparing Data for the Service Bureau

Most prepress professionals know from painful experience that when fighting with an imagesetter almost all the problems covered in this book may arise: missing fonts are replaced with Courier, complex graphics yield a *limitcheck* error, screening parameters or page sizes are screwed up.

Using the foundations presented in this book and preparing your data carefully, you can bring down the number of erroneous imagesetter outputs to a minimum. This not only decreases your chances of a heart attack, but also saves time and money.

While most graphics designers and service bureaus traditionally use Macs as their workhorses, the number of DTP addicts increases who use cheap Windows machines to compose ads, fan club magazines or books. Some problems occurring with imagesetters are related to general PostScript issues (e.g., missing fonts), while others are caused by some of Windows' idiosyncrasies or the differences between the Mac and Windows platforms.

9.2.1 General Remarks.
You can choose several ways to send your data to the service bureau. If you create your document with standard software that is also available in the service bureau, you can send them the data in your application's native file format, e.g., as a Quark Xpress, PageMaker, or Microsoft Word file. The service bureau operator opens the files with the very same program and uses his printer driver to generate PostScript data which are directly sent to the imagesetter RIP.

Alternatively, the creator of the document can generate the Post-Script data on his own by redirecting her PostScript printer driver to disk (print-to-disk file). The operator transfers this data to the RIP using a PostScript downloader program. Both methods have their own traps and pitfalls which we will take a look at shortly.

Recently, a third method showed up which is not yet widely in use: sending the data in the *Portable Document Format* (PDF). This is covered in more detail in Section 8.3.

In case you're preparing your first imagesetter job, cooperate with a new service bureau, or have changed your configuration (operating system, driver, application, etc.), you should first talk to the imagesetter operator and discuss the following topics:

- ▸ Do they prefer native application files or PostScript files (see below for criteria).
- ▸ Which fonts are already available in the service bureau?
- ▸ Which resolution and screening parameters are required for the job? These are related to the contents of the document (text only,

or high-resolution graphics?) and the printing technique (e.g., silk-screen or offset printing).

- ▸ Are crop marks required? Ask the printer (the person, not the machine) to clarify this point.
- ▸ If you send native application files: compare your software equipment with that available in the service bureau.
- ▸ If you send PostScript files: talk about page formats and film size as well as page orientation on the film.

Many service bureaus offer a form on which customers can supply all relevant information.

9.2.2 Sending Native Application Files.
This technique is the easiest one for the customer. It requires both creator and service bureau operator to have the same software equipment. It is crucial to supply all elements necessary to print the document. This includes:

- ▸ All document components, i.e., separate chapter files or partial documents.
- ▸ All graphics files linked to the document but not directly embedded in it (EPS, TIFF, etc.). Forgetting graphics files is a major source of errors!
- ▸ The RIP must have access to all fonts used in the document. Depending on the font vendor's licensing conditions, the fonts may or may not legally be sent to the service bureau.

Problems may arise even if both parties use the same software. Check the following details:

- ▸ Software versions: most software packages are "upwards compatible". However, sometimes changing the program version results in different line and page breaks because the formatting algorithms differ. This means your documents look different on the imagesetter than on your proof printer.
- ▸ Language version and dictionaries must be identical on both sides since they drastically affect the formatting, especially automatic hyphenation.
- ▸ Many programs can be extended by additional modules called extension, addition, plug-in, or whatever. Some plug-ins not only affect the creation of documents but are necessary for opening and printing the file. In this case the plug-ins are required in the service bureau, too.

9.2.3 Sending PostScript Files.
PostScript files contain a final-format description of a document and generally cannot be edited (see next section for hints how to defeat this point). Contrary to native application files, the formatting of PostScript files cannot change. However, the responsibility for creating correct PostScript

data shifts to the creator of the document. If complete and correct PostScript files are sent to the service bureau, only stubborn Post-Script errors can thwart successful creation of films.

If you want to create PostScript data yourself, you have to redirect the printer driver's output to a file and check the following issues:

- ▸ Most imagesetters require special PostScript instructions for set-ting page size and orientation. For this reason, you should con-figure your PostScript driver for the respective device.
- ▸ If the fonts used in the document are not installed on the RIP, they must be contained in the PostScript file or delivered separately. The exact mechanism to control font download depends on your operating system and driver (see Section 4.4).
- ▸ Do not send pure EPS files since problems may arise due to the dif-ferent EPS flavors (screen preview, *showpage* operator). Additional-ly, EPS files do not contain instructions for setting the page size; in most cases, fonts are also not contained. Load the EPS file to a graphics or DTP program and create a print-to-disk PostScript file. Do not use EPS export.
- ▸ If you have a large imagesetter job, you should do some test pages. It's better to invest some money in test output than to create sev-eral hundred pages of trash.
- ▸ According to page format and film size you can possibly save film by producing landscape (rotated) output.
- ▸ Include laser printer proofs with your PostScript data so that the service bureau operator has a chance to check the films.

Windows idiosyncrasies.   Chapter 2 lists some idiosyncrasies of the Windows PostScript drivers and the protocols which are generally in use. These make it necessary to obey several precautions:

- ▸ Control characters and protocol functions have nothing to do in a PostScript file! For this reason, deactivate Ctrl-D and special proto-cols such as BCP (see Sections 2.4.1 and 2.4.2).
- ▸ Configure your driver to include the necessary fonts in the Post-Script output file (if they are not installed in the RIP). For the Microsoft Windows PostScript driver this is a critical point since the font configuration depends on the printer interface – and this changes when you redirect the printer driver to a disk file!

Checking PostScript files (preflight).   It's impossible to tell the results (or trouble) by looking at a PostScript file from the outside. If – for good reasons – you refuse to examine PostScript files in a text editor, you can check your PostScript files with a software RIP. This is sometimes calles "preflight". Alternatively, you can send your file to a PostScript printer using a downloader program. However, this is not always possible, e.g., when your printer doesn't support the necessary page size.

You can check your PostScript files on screen with GSview/Ghostscript, Acrobat Distiller or one of the available software RIPs. If you want to use GSview/Ghostscript, note the following:

▸ Use a resolution that makes the whole page appear on screen. To explore details, you can increase the resolution.

▸ Keep an eye on Ghostscript's messages in the console window. There you can see whether Ghostscript has to load fonts from disk or had to substitute it – the latter is not exactly what you want to happen in the service bureau!

Preflighting a PostScript file on screen can help discover common problems. However, some faults are invisible on screen, e.g., wrong screening parameters.

9.3 Editing PostScript Files

In this section we explore some ways to edit existing PostScript files, i.e., change their contents without using the application in which the file originally was created. This includes much more than the usual EPS manipulation (scaling, rotation, clipping). Let's recall our example of a translator who receives EPS files of unknown origin and has to translate the captions contained in the graphics. If he can't make the EPS files editable again, they are quite useless. In the best case, he can import the file and "glue" another text box on top of the existing characters. As you have learned from this book, processing PostScript files generally requires a full-blown PostScript interpreter. This makes editing PostScript files a rather complicated task.

Software for editing PostScript files is of particular interest to service bureaus in order to fix typos caught a few minutes before sending the file to the RIP even if they don't have the original application software at hand.

9.3.1 Converting to Illustrator Format.
Converting to Adobe Illustrator's native file format is an important means to make PostScript files editable again. AI files can be opened and read by many graphics programs. As the AI format does not directly support raster images, this technique usually only works for object oriented graphics and text. There are several ways to convert PostScript files to Illustrator format:

▸ The shareware program *epsConverter* for the Mac.

▸ The *ps2ai.ps* utility program which can be found on the accompanying CD-ROM. It requires a PostScript interpreter and can be used with Ghostscript or a PostScript printer with bidirectional communication channel (see below).

- ▶ Several commercial software RIPs, e.g., Transverter Pro.
- ▶ Newer versions of some graphics applications are capable of processing arbitrary PostScript files. Examples are CorelDraw 5 or Illustrator 6.0 which includes a PostScript Level 1 interpreter.

Converting to AI format with ps2ai.ps.   The *ps2ai.ps* utility, which is included in the Ghostscript distribution, realizes a seemingly simple idea. It redefines the PostScript operators for graphics output so that they don't produce real graphical elements, but instead write a textual representation in AI format to a file. This tool can most easily be used with Ghostscript or with a printer's PostScript interpreter, provided it is connected to the host computer via a bidirectional communication line. A description of the process using Ghostscript can be found in Section B.6.1.

Although ps2ai.ps doesn't completely convert some kind of files, it works quite well.[1] There are some details to take care of after the conversion: the files usually contain a bounding rectangle which can be deleted in the graphics program. Additionally, the elements of the graphic are grouped. This grouping can also be removed in the graphics program.

Future Ghostscript releases will probably include a driver for directly generating Illustrator format, thereby eliminating the need for *ps2ai.ps*.

9.3.2 Distilling to PDF.   If Acrobat Distiller is at hand, you can convert your PostScript file to PDF format, thus making it editable again. In Section 8.5.4 you can find a description of programs capable of editing PDF files.

Note that with respect to PostScript, PDF has some restrictions related to its graphics features (see Section 8.2.1).

9.3.3 Tailor.   Tailor is a PostScript editor which has been successfully marketed for the NEXTSTEP platform since 1993. Tailor makes use of the Display PostScript interpreter included in the NEXTSTEP operating system to make PostScript files editable again (see Figure 7.1).

A Mac version of Tailor has been available since spring 1996. Since there is no Display PostScript for the Mac, the program must include its own PostScript interpreter. Instead of re-inventing the PostScript

---

1. I was able to test-drive this technique while I was working on the German translation of the book "Introduction to Computer Graphics" by Foley et al. Naturally, this computer graphic classic contains hundreds of illustrations which were delivered in EPS format. After converting them with ps2ai.ps, I could open the files in Adobe Illustrator and translate the English captions to German.

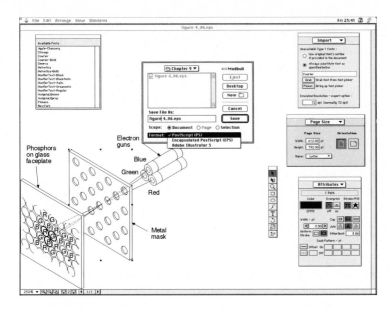

Fig. 9.1.
Tailor for NEXTSTEP and Mac allows to edit PostScript files and convert them to Adobe Illustrator format

wheel, Tailor's developer FirstClass fell back to a well-known buddy: Ghostscript.

Tailor is capable of opening PostScript files (Level 1 and 2) from arbitrary sources, be it EPS files with or without preview, single or multipage. The files may be generated with arbitrary drivers from arbitrary operating systems.

Tailor's user interface is similar to a graphics program. The Inspector displays the attributes of a selected text or graphics element. You can alter these attributes directly in Tailor, e.g., text font, color, or line width. The text is separated into individual fragments that relate to the driver's output entities (words in most cases). These entities may be changed and edited. For large amounts of text, however, Tailor is not suited because there is no automatic line wrap or justification. If you want to do larger edits, you can save the file in Illustrator format and open it with a graphics program.

A feature which is quite useful once you get used to it is Tailor's automatic grouping. The software recognizes an embedded EPS graphic and automatically treats its contents as a group. This grouping may be cancelled and reactivated (to make single edits).

9.3.4 Commercial Software RIPs.

Several commercial software RIPs not only drive a variety of printer models, but are also able to generate object oriented graphics formats. Which RIP to use obviously depends on the platform it runs on, the supported graphics formats and the price tag. Even if you want to buy a Software RIP to Post-Script-enable a printer, making EPS files editable may be a useful side-effect.

Windows RIPs capable of converting PostScript files to object oriented graphics formats include Transverter Pro by TechPool Software (creates AI and WMF) and ZScript by Zenographics (WMF).

9.3.5 ePScript.

Prepress professionals probably wonder why the world of PostScript seems to be so complicated. Each individual task is handled by a different program; layout software, image manipulation tools, graphics programs have to be paid for (and mastered), additionally an OPI server and color separation software is needed. The whole gobbledywobble is topped by the PostScript interpreter, either sitting in a hardware RIP or implemented as software.

If you're interested in a *real* integrated solution, take a look at the ePScript software developed by the German company OneVision. This software is an integrated package for opening arbitrary Post-Script files and allows to edit and manipulate all kinds of objects that may be contained in a print-to-disk or EPS (or PDF) file. It offers tools for image manipulation, drawing, and text handling. These tools aren't makeshift programs but full-blown modules of their kind. ePScript makes use of the genuine Adobe PostScript Level 2 inter-

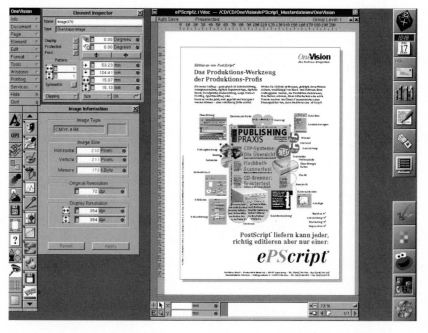

Fig. 9.2.
ePSscript is a complete system for opening Post-Script files and editing their image, graphics, and text contents

preter contained in Display PostScript systems. For this reason, it requires the NEXTSTEP system as an operating system basis (supported hardware includes NeXT, Sun Sparc, HP-PA, and Intel). The forthcoming OpenStep for Windows NT will allow ePScript to run on this Microsoft platform too (an NT version of ePScript is scheduled for autumn 1996).

ePScript is a complete production environment for the prepress industry and has a rather high price tag. However, you need to consider that on a single platform you can deal with all sorts of strange input files your customers may deliver. You can check the "quality" of PostScript files as well as perform last-minute changes, and use the system for both creative and production work. OneVision's suite is especially interesting for the newspaper market and ad agencies as a tool for validating and correcting incoming PostScript files created on arbitrary operating systems with diverse application programs. What's more, the suite adds basic functionality such as separation, OPI services, and process calibration.

What I liked best about ePScript's PostScript editing features is the fact that it automatically detects text columns and, unlike other systems, does not split the text into single words but creates the familiar text flow boxes containing text of different sizes and fonts.

Such a PostScript editing system not only serves as a prepress repair kit, but gains more and more importance as digital print techniques (computer to plate) are introduced. By cleaning up the input files, ePScript may save much time formerly wasted by trying to process ill-behaved PostScript.

9.4 Converting Raster Graphics Formats

There are two basic formats for storing computer graphics: vector and raster formats. Vector or geometric formats contain a "mathematical" definition of the graphic consisting of objects such as lines, circles and colored areas. Raster formats describe an image as a rectangular pixel array. Each pixel can take on one of several color values. PostScript files may contain vector images as well as raster data.

Both techniques have their pros and cons. Vector graphics (typically created with drawing software) may be scaled without loss of quality. However, they are not suited for reproducing natural scenes or photographs that require raster graphics. These in turn degrade in quality if enlarged.

In many situations converting raster graphics to PostScript or vice versa is necessary, e.g., for printing a raster file on a PostScript printer or to manipulate PostScript files with pixel based filters.

9.4.1 Converting Raster Graphics to PostScript.

Converting raster graphics data to PostScript is necessary if you want to print a file on a PostScript device as well as for importing raster graphics in a DTP program which doesn't support that particular format but only accept EPS.

Image processing software.   The easiest way to convert raster data to PostScript (or EPS) is opening the file in a suitable image processing program and saving it in EPS format. This applies to many public domain and shareware programs – e.g., PaintShop Pro for Windows or XV and ImageMagick for Unix – and of course to major commercial products such as Photoshop, Painter, or PhotoStyler. If you have to convert a large bunch of files, the interactive process is very time-consuming. In this case the batch conversion mode offered by some programs (e.g., PaintShop Pro) helps to automatically convert a large number of files. The graphics converters discussed below are another solution.

Graphics converters.   Conversion programs for graphics file formats are quite common on Unix systems. With such a converter you can transform a graphics file to another format with a single command line. On the accompanying CD-ROM you will find the PBM tools which are widely used on Unix systems. Internally they use three formats, namely PBM (Portable Bitmap, black and white), PGM (Portable Graymap, 256 shades of gray), and PPM (Portable Pixmap, 24 bit color). The three formats are often referred to as PNM (Portable Anymap). The PBM package contains converters for transforming many common graphics formats to PNM and vice versa, as well as tools for image manipulation (rotation, inversion, scaling, etc.). The package consists of many single programs which may be "concatenated" via pipe for more complex tasks.

As an example, let's take a look at converting an X11 screen dump to PostScript format. The following command line generates a screen dump in XWD format, converts it to PPM, transforms from PPM (color) to PGM (gray level), and finally creates a PostScript file:

```
xwd | xwdtopnm | ppmtopgm | pnmtops > screendump.eps
```

The *pnmtops* program creates PostScript Level 1 files and optionally compresses the image data using the RunLength algorithm. Since the generated PostScript contains the necessary EPS comments the file may be embedded in a document. Normally, landscape raster graphics are rotated, but you can change this behaviour via a command line option.

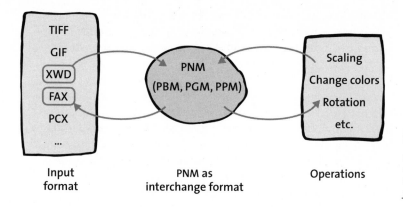

Input format	PNM as interchange format	Operations
TIFF GIF XWD FAX PCX ...	PNM (PBM, PGM, PPM)	Scaling Change colors Rotation etc.

Fig. 9.3.
The PBM tools can be used to convert between many graphics formats

There are of course several commercial conversion packages available for all platforms, e.g. ImageAlchemy or Debabelizer, which convert dozens of common (and uncommon) graphics file formats.

"Wrapper" for PostScript Level 2.   In Chapter 5 we took a look at Level 2's compression schemes. One interesting aspect of these algorithms is the fact that they allow to convert compressed image data to PostScript without decompressing the pixel data. Actually, the only sort of wrapping the image data is required. You can generate such wrapped image data in Photoshop by exporting in the EPS-JPEG format. There are two wrappers on the accompanying CD-ROM which implement this technique for the JPEG and TIFF graphics file formats. More details can be found in Section 5.5.1.

Screen or printer output without conversion.   It was already noted that PostScript is a full-blown programming language. It allows you to write programs that analyze a raster graphics file's internal structure and extract the image data contained in the file (without explicitly converting it previously to PostScript). The Ghostscript distribution contains the *viewgif.ps, viewjpeg.ps,* and *viewpbm.ps* utility programs which can display or print GIF, JPEG, and PBM files using Ghostscript's Level 2 filters. They analyze the file and decompress the raster data contained in it. These tools do not use any Ghostscript-specific instructions; in principle, they also work on other interpreters. However, they need access to the file system. You can find more information on these tools in Section B.6.1.

9.4.2 Converting PostScript to Raster Graphics.   This conversion requires much more effort since a full-blown PostScript interpreter is needed to process PostScript files (the limited Illustrator

format is an exception to this rule). This explains why for a long time it was impossible to convert PostScript files to raster formats. Nowadays we have several possibilities at hand, among them – who wonders? – Ghostscript.

Converting from PostScript to TIFF, GIF, or another raster format is useful if you want to manipulate a PostScript graphic with the pixel oriented tools available in image processing software. Another important application are screen presentations which you want to produce using standard DTP software and PostScript. Concerning screen display, there are some advanced rendering options such as anti-aliased fonts. These compensate for low resolution by making use of gray levels (see Figure 9.4)

The most important variable when converting PostScript to raster data is the resolution, i.e., the number of pixels per unit of length. While in the other direction (raster to PostScript) the number of pixels is already determined by the raster data, in this case resolution, number of gray levels, and color can be controlled in the interpreter. Higher resolution yields better image quality, but also larger files.

Adobe ScreenReady.   ScreenReady is a Mac program for converting PostScript (or EPS) files to PICT. It contains a PostScript interpreter and offers several rendering options such as color depth, image resolution, and anti-aliasing. Adobe positions the program for creating multimedia presentations and other on-screen work. As its name implies, ScreenReady is only suited for files to be displayed on the monitor since the image width and height are limited to 4096 pixels each. This translates to a resolution of around 400 dpi for letter size pages – certainly not enough for using ScreenReady as a software RIP for high-resolution output.

Rendering Illustrator files.   As explained in chapter 3, processing Illustrator files doesn't require a full-blown PostScript interpreter.

Fig. 9.4.
Rendering a PostScript file: the vector description containing lines and curves of a font (above) is converted to the pixel grid (middle). If the device is capable of directly reproducing gray levels, the output may be enhanced by anti-aliasing

Rendering

Rendering

Rendering

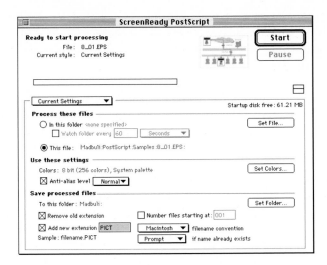

Fig. 9.5.
Adobe ScreenReady renders PostScript files for screen representation

Adobe Illustrator and other programs may be used for exporting an image in several raster formats. However, to achieve better results, you can use Photoshop's AI import feature. Photoshop offers several options for controlling the conversion from vector to pixel format (see Figure 9.6). You can select the resolution as well as the color mode used in the conversion. This makes it easy to optimize the results for certain applications (e.g., screen presentation). The "anti-aliased" option in most cases improves screen display by using gray levels.

Rasterizing Illustrator files, which are already "reduced" PostScript, is subject to some other limitations in Photoshop: the program does not support fill patterns, filled outline text, nor embedded EPS files.

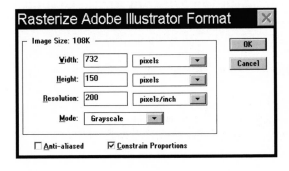

Fig. 9.6.
You can set the resolution when importing Illustrator files in Photoshop

Ghostscript drivers.   For each PostScript page, Ghostscript determines a raster representation which may not only be output on screen or printer but may be stored in one of several bitmap file formats as well. The Ghostscript distribution contains drivers for the BMP, PCX, TIFF, PBM/PGM/PNM , and PNG (*Portable Network Graphics*) raster formats. Since the standard version does not contain all drivers, you may have to compile your own Ghostscript version (see Section B.3.3). Ghostscript also offers font anti-aliasing to enhance image quality. In Section B.6.1 you can find some examples for using Ghostscript's bitmap drivers.

Since Ghostscript processes PDF as well as PostScript files, this technique also allows to convert PDF files to raster formats.

Software RIPs.   Many commercial software RIPs are able to convert PostScript files to raster formats. This includes Freedom of Press and Transverter Pro. The latter, for example, generates TIFF output with a resolution of up to 720 dpi.

Exporting Graphics with Adobe Acrobat.   If you have Acrobat Distiller, you can convert your PostScript file to PDF and open it in Acrobat Reader or Exchange. These programs allow to export images via the clipboard as they are displayed on screen. From the clipboard you can further process the images. The downside of this technique is that the screen display also determines the image quality. This means the method is simply a more comfortable way of doing a screenshot.

Hacker's way.   There is a special case in which you can convert PostScript data to a raster format without an interpreter. If you extract the image data from the PostScript file with a text editor, you can convert it to PGM with one of the Unix PBM tools. The program is called *psidtopgm* (*PostScript image data to PGM*) and requires the image size in pixels to be given on the command line. These numbers can be found in the PostScript file in front of the actual image data.

9.4.3 Converting PostScript to PostScript Raster Graphics.
Though you probably think the idea crazy, there are indeed some applications for converting vector PostScript to raster PostScript! This means rasterizing all elements contained in a PostScript file, but generating a PostScript bitmap file instead of saving the resulting image as TIFF or PCX.

You can achieve this by combining several of the techniques described above (PostScript to raster, raster to PostScript). However, Ghostscript includes the *psmono* driver which directly produces PostScript bitmap files. This driver may be configured for a certain resolution and converts arbitrary PostScript files to black and white Post-Script Level 1 bitmaps, compressed via RunLength.

Don't see any application for that? Consider this: your PostScript device doesn't accept a certain file whereas Ghostscript renders it just fine. Convert it to bitmap PostScript via Ghostscript, send it to the device, and bingo! This may happen, for example, if the printer runs out of memory or doesn't support a certain feature (e.g., Multiple Master fonts). Take care, however, to set the resolution high enough so your file's image quality doesn't degrade.

9.5 Converting Text Files

9.5.1 Converting Text Files to Postscript. Under Windows or

on the Mac, if you want to print a text file on a PostScript printer, you open it with a text editor and generate PostScript output via the printer driver. The same is of course possible under Unix with a suitable text or DTP program. However, system administrators and programmers are often facing the problem of printing large system files, database excerpts or program listings and manual pages. In most cases, these files should be printed without any bells and whistles – simple layout, monospaced font. While dot matrix printers accept pure text files, a PostScript printer rejects text files with an error message because it expects to receive PostScript data. As an exception, printers with automatic emulation sensing recognize text files and automatically do the right thing.

If the printer doesn't distinguish text from PostScript data, plain text must be converted to PostScript before it can be printed. Such text-to-PostScript converters are widely used under Unix. They transfom a PostScript device to a simple line printer.

Such a converter doesn't do any formatting (e.g., calculate line breaks) but only preserves existing indentation (spaces and tabs). For this reason the converters use a monospaced font, mostly Courier.

Commerical products – such as Adobe's TranScript suite – put aside, there are myriads of freely available converters. However, not all of them fulfill some basic requirements:

▸ PostScript output should be DSC compatible to allow additional processing of the file or positioning on a certain page when Ghostscript/Ghostview are used to display the file on screen.
▸ European users demand their native page formats, e.g., A4.
▸ If the text uses more characters than are contained in pure ASCII, the extended ISO Latin 1 character set is desirable.

On the accompanying CD-ROM you can find several converters for text files that fulfill these requirements (with the exception of *emulate.ps* which doesn't support Latin 1). In choosing a suitable program, not only its features are important but also the implementation language. The converters may be implemented in the C programming language, as a Perl script or with plain PostScript instructions.

Lineprinter emulation in PostScript. The most basic solution to the lineprinter problem doesn't require any auxiliary programs. The PostScript file *emulate.ps* on the CD-ROM demonstrates the power of PostScript as a programming language. It contains a short PostScript prolog which is already capable of printing text files. To use it, the text file has to be appended to the PostScript code. The emulator instructions loop through the text line by line, printing each line and simultaneously calculating the next line's position on the page. When the end of the page is reached, a *showpage* command is issued to eject the current page and the printing postion is moved to the beginning of the next page. Since the program determines the printable area automatically, it works with different paper sizes.

At the beginning of the file *emulate.ps* you can adjust several parameters for fine-tuning the output. These parameters include font size or additional margins. To print a text file, you must transfer the PostScript instructions and the text as a *single* print job to the device. Under MS-DOS, use the command

```
copy /b emulate.ps+file.txt lpt1:
```

Under Unix, use the following shell command:

```
cat emulate.ps file.txt | lp
```

Since Macintosh and Windows don't offer means to combine two files, one would have to open the text file in a editor and insert the contents of *emulate.ps* at the beginning. However, if you have the file in the editor already, you could just as well issue the editor's print command.

a2ps. The *a2ps* C program is suitable as a system administrator's work horse. It prints portrait and landscape pages, truncates long lines or optionally folds them on multiple lines. *a2ps* interprets the tab, backspace, and formfeed control characters. The backspace feature is especially useful for printing Unix manuals, since *nroff* uses it to simulate underlined text (character, backspace, underscore). On the CD-ROM you will find the C source as well as a version of *a2ps* compiled for MS-DOS.

textps. Another C program called *textps* is contained in the *lprps* package used to drive PostScript printers on BSD Unix systems. *lprps* is configured as input filter in the file */etc/printcap* and is responsible for communicating with the printer and interpreting error messages.

```
TEXTPS(@MAN1EXT@)                              TEXTPS(@MAN1EXT@)


NAME
       textps - text to PostScript filter

SYNOPSIS
       textps [ -cn ] [ -ln ] [ -mn ] [ -tn ] [ -vn ] [
       filename... ]

DESCRIPTION
       textps is a simple text to PostScript filter.  It is usu-
       ally  invoked automatically by a spooler.  Input files can
       use ISO Latin-1.  Two or more identical overstruck charac-
       ters  are rendered using a bold font.  Tabs are assumed to
       be set every 8 character positions.  textps is designed to
       produce  good output with lpr -p or pr | lpr; if you print
       unpaginated text, you will need to increase the -t  option
       and decrease the -v or -l option.

OPTIONS
       The arguments for all options except -l are floating-point
       numbers.  The argument for -l must be a positive  integer.

       -cn    Use n characters to the inch.

       -ln    Use n lines per page.

       -mn    Use a left margin of n points.

       -tn    Position  the  baseline of the first line of text n
              points below the top of the page.

       -vn    Use a vertical spacing of n points.

       The default behaviour is -c12 -l66 -m18 -t8 -v12.

SEE ALSO
       psrev(@MAN1EXT@), lprps(@MAN8EXT@), psif(@MAN8EXT@)
```

Fig. 9.7.
*textps formats
and prints its own
manual page as
an example*

It also distinguishes text from PostScript print data by looking at the
first two characters of the file. Text files are redirected to the filter *textps* before sending them to the printer. This filter may as well be used
as a standalone program. It prints A4 or letter pages and interprets
tab and backspace characters. It even recognizes the combination
character, backspace, character – used to simulate bold text in some
manual pages – and prints it in a bold font. This makes textps an ideal solution for man pages (see Figure 9.7).

i2ps. *i2ps* doesn't require a C compiler but consists of a Perl script
which is processed by the Perl language interpreter. *i2ps* offers everything a demanding user needs: A4 or letter size, two- or three-column
output, optionally numbered lines, portrait and landscape pages, and
selectable font size. Long lines can be truncated or folded. Since *i2ps*
doesn't do any special handling for the backspace character, it isn't
suitable for certain manual pages.

Ghostscript and gslp.ps. The lineprinter emulation *gslp.ps* contained in the Ghostscript distribution is another means for printing

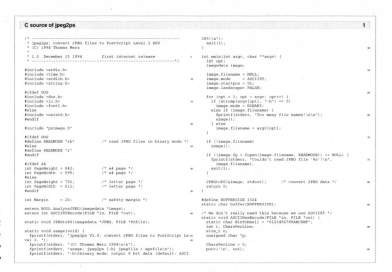

```
C source of jpeg2ps                                                                                    1

/* --------------------------------------------------------          I85)\n");
 * jpeg2ps: convert JPEG files to PostScript Level 2 EPS               exit(1);
 * (C) 1994 Thomas Merz                                              }
 *
 * 1.0  December 15 1994      first internet release         5      int main(int argc, char **argv) {
 * --------------------------------------------------------- */         int opt;
                                                                       imagedata image;
#include <stdio.h>
#include <time.h>                                                      image.filename = NULL;
#include <stdlib.h>                                          10         image.mode     = ASCII85;
#include <string.h>                                                    image.startpos = 0L;
                                                                       image.landscape = FALSE;
#ifdef DOS
#include <dos.h>                                                        for (opt = 1; opt < argc; opt++) {
#include <io.h>                                               15           if (strcmp(argv[opt], "-b") == 0)
#include <fcntl.h>                                                           image.mode = BINARY;
#else                                                                      else if (!image.filename) {
#include <unistd.h>                                                          fprintf(stderr, "Too many file names!\n\n");
#endif                                                                       usage();
                                                             20           } else
#include "psimage.h"                                                        image.filename = argv[opt];

#ifdef DOS
#define READMODE "rb"        /* read JPEG files in binary mode */      if (!image.filename)
#else                                                        25         usage();
#define READMODE "r"
#endif                                                                 if ((image.fp = fopen(image.filename, READMODE)) == NULL) {
                                                                        fprintf(stderr, "Couldn't read JPEG file '%s'!\n",
#ifdef A4                                                                  image.filename),
int PageHeight = 842;           /* a4 page */                            exit(1);
int PageWidth = 595;            /* a4 page */                 30       }
#else
int PageHeight = 792;           /* letter page */                      JPEGtoEPS(&image, stdout);     /* convert JPEG data */
int PageWidth = 612;            /* letter page */                      return 0;
#endif                                                       35       }

int Margin   = 20;           /* safety margin */                   #define BUFFERSIZE 1024
                                                                   static char buffer[BUFFERSIZE];
extern BOOL AnalyzeJPEG(imagedata *image);
extern int ASCII85Encode(FILE *in, FILE *out);               40    /* We don't really need this because we use ASCII85 */
                                                                   static void ASCII85Encode(FILE *in, FILE *out) {
static void JPEGtoPS(imagedata *JPEG, FILE *PSfile);                 static char BinToHex[] = "0123456789ABCDEF";
                                                                     int i, CharsPerLine;
static void usage(void) {                                            size_t n;
   fprintf(stderr, "jpeg2ps V1.0: convert JPEG files to PostScript Le  unsigned char *p;
vel 2. ");                                                    45
   fprintf(stderr, "(C) Thomas Merz 1994\n\n");                     CharsPerLine = 0;
   fprintf(stderr, "usage: jpeg2ps [-b] jpegfile > epsfile\n");      putc('\n', out);
   fprintf(stderr, "-b\tbinary mode: output 8 bit data (default: ASCI
```

Fig. 9.8.
i2ps prints
program
listings space
efficiently

text files. Using this auxiliary program, Ghostscript either creates PostScript instructions or renders the text for a certain output device. *gslp.ps* offers several formatting options such as headers and footers or page numbers. You can read more about using this tool in Section B.6.3.

pstree. The *pstree* Perl script is a nice solution for a special problem. It prints a clear representation of the directory tree on a hard disk or other storage device. The script automatically determines placement and scaling of each directory name in order to fit the whole tree on a page. This is useful to get an overview over large file systems. As an example, Figure A.1 (see Appendix A) – produced with *pstree* – depicts the directories on the accompanying CD-ROM. On the left side , the top directory is printed, to the right the "leafs" of the file tree are arranged.

The script generates all necessary EPS comments so that you can embed its ouput in another document. However, *pstree* does not create a screen preview section.

9.5.2 Extracting Text from PostScript Files. Sometimes the

problem arises of extracting the text contents from a PostScript file. For example, only the PostScript version of a document may be available and the text contents are to be used separately (instead of being printed). One could print the file and re-type the text (or scan it and use OCR software), but this is error-prone and expensive. It's much easier to extract the text directly from the PostScript file. The problem, however, is that most PostScript drivers don't output the text as a whole, but position each character or word individually. The single characters have to be combined to reasonable entities afterwards. In rare cases it is possible to easily locate the text in the PostScript file and copy it. The PostScript interpreter has a much easier job to achieve this since it executes all text output instructions anyway. Generally, some postprocessing will be necessary, e.g., hyphenation cannot be undone but yields both parts of the word along with the hyphen.

Ghostscript and ps2ascii.ps.   The *ps2ascii.ps* PostScript program contained in the Ghostscript distribution extracts the text contents from a PostScript file by redefining the text operators and sending the text to the standard output instead of printing it. (This technique is similar to the one used in *ps2ai.ps* to create Illustrator compatible output.) According to what you intend to do with the text, you can choose between two variations. The first creates pure text data, while the second additionally yields the position of individual strings on the page and the font used to print the text. The program also works with PDF files. More details on using this tool can be found in Section B.6.3.

Converting to PDF.   Still another possibility to extract text from a PostScript file is converting to PDF format with Acrobat Distiller and opening the PDF file in Acrobat Reader or Exchange. These viewers have a selection tool that can be used to select text on a page and

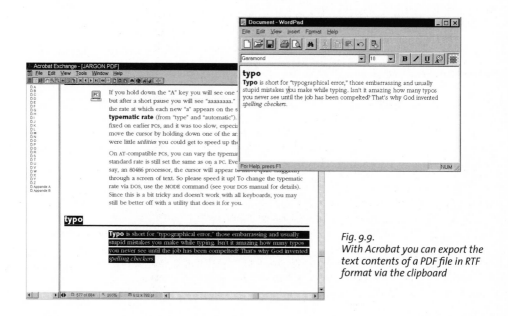

Fig. 9.9.
With Acrobat you can export the text contents of a PDF file in RTF format via the clipboard

export it to the clipboard. Using the RTF clipboard type, information on font name and size can also be exported. This way it's possible to transfer the text to an RTF capable text editor. The missing text structure in PDFs shows up as a disadvantage. If, for example, you want to extract three-column-text from a page, the text is selected using the whole page width. You can prevent this by pressing the Ctrl key (Windows) or Alt key (Mac) while selecting the text. This makes Acrobat draw a rectangle which is used to select only the text contained within the rectangle.

Contents of the CD-ROM

A

This appendix tells you how to use the accompanying CD-ROM, which compression and archiving methods were used, and how the software is organized on the CD-ROM.

Here, installation and usage of the software are touched only briefly; more details can be found in the respective chapters in the book and in the text files that come along with the programs.

A.1 Using the CD-ROM

A.1.1 General

Format.   The accompanying CD-ROM is formatted according to ISO 9660. This format is largely identical to the so-called High Sierra standard. ISO 9660 forms the least common divisor of CD-ROM formats and is used on many operating systems. A CD-ROM using ISO 9660 is therefore perfectly suited for a platform-independent book like this. However, the format also has disadvantages, which mainly show up on Mac and Unix systems. There are only short file names, lowercase/uppercase is not significant, and file names may not contain special characters. If you're already familiar with using CD-ROMs on your system, you won't have any problems. If not, you'll find some hints for several operating systems in the following sections.

Physical data access aside, each platform has its own conventions concerning line end characters and compression and archiving methods. I tried to obey existing standards and common usage as far as possible. In Section A.1.5 there are hints on decompressing and converting files.

License conditions.   All software packages, documentation, and other files on the accompanying CD-ROM are free. Even so, some are subject to certain copyright or license conditions. You have to check the respective author's conditions which are in most cases contained in some text files (often *readme, license.txt*, etc.). You may arbitrarily copy the complete CD-ROM contents but you are responsible for complying with the license conditions yourself. In particular, this relates to commercial software usage and sales.

A.1.2 Using the CD-ROM under MS-DOS, Windows, OS/2

Under MS-DOS, Windows, and OS/2 a CD-ROM is represented by a separate drive letter (assuming a CD-ROM driver is correctly installed). You can use the additional drive much like a hard disk, with the exception that it is read-only. Since the ISO file system is nearly identical to the DOS file system, you shouldn't have any trouble accessing the CD-ROM.

Many programs on the CD-ROM can directly be launched under MS-DOS. Often, source code is also available which you can use to build your own program versions if you have a C compiler.

A.1.3 Using the CD-ROM on the Macintosh

Since the CD-ROM doesn't contain a Macintosh file system (HFS) you have to install the system extensions *Foreign File Access* and *ISO 9660 File Access* (or *High Sierra File Access*) before you can use the CD-ROM. Sometimes you have to deactivate other file system extensions such as *AccessPC*.

The limitations of the ISO file system are clearly evident on the Mac: there are only short file names, all files have default icons in the finder, and they don't have extended file informations, e.g., file creator. For this reason, you can't open a file by double-clicking on it but only using a program's "File", "Open" dialog (e.g., Acrobat Reader for PDF files).

The Binhex format (suffix *.hqx*) allows both data and resource fork of a Mac file to be stored in a "flat" file and deliver Mac files on an ISO formatted CD-ROM. Binhex format is often combined with a compression scheme like *StuffIt* (suffix *.sit*). Applying both techniques results in the *.sit.hqx* suffix which had to be shortened to *.hqx* on the CD-ROM. To unpack the Mac files on the CD-ROM you need the *StuffIt Expander* program or a similar decompression utility for *.sit.hqx* files. Since it's impossible to store executable Mac programs on an ISO CD-ROM, you have to get StuffIt Expander from somewhere else. There are numerous shareware suppliers and online services where you can get the program. Using the *unsit* program for MS-DOS you can also unpack *.sit* files on other systems.

A.1.4 Using the CD-ROM Under Unix

On Unix systems you have to mount the CD-ROM as a readonly file system using the *mount* command. On newer systems (e.g., Solaris) this may be accomplished automatically by a demon when inserting the disk. Since mount options and device file names vary greatly among Unix derivatives you have to consult your system documentation. Most systems require the *root* password for mounting a file system. Ask your system administrator if you don't have the password for *su root*. To successfully mount a CD-ROM you have to supply the readonly and file system command line options. Common file system designations are ISO 9660 (*iso9660*) and *High sierra file system (hsfs)*.

Some systems append a semicolon character ";" and a version number to CD-ROM file names. This is very inconvenient since you also have to supply these when referring to a file. The colon, however, is a shell special character and therefore has to be "escaped" with a backslash character "\". Most systems offer a special mount option for suppressing the file version numbers. This greatly simplifies CD-ROM usage.

The *mount* command mounts the CD-ROM in a directory which must already exist in the file system. The following examples show the commands for mounting the CD-ROM under several Unix derivatives. In most cases the device file names contain the SCSI address of the CD-ROM drive and therefore have to be adjusted accordingly. After mounting the CD-ROM you can *cd* to the /cdrom directory (or whatever you called the mount point).

System	mount command
SunOS	/etc/mount -r -t hsfs /dev/sr0 /cdrom
Solaris	/etc/mount -r -F hsfs /dev/sr0 /cdrom
IBM AIX	/etc/mount -r -v cdrfs /dev/cd0 /cdrom
HP-UX	/etc/mount -r -t cdfs /dev/dsk/c201d2s0 /cdrom
SGI IRIX	/sbin/mount -o ro,notranslate -t iso9660 /dev/scsi/sc0d5l0 /cdrom
SCO	/etc/mount -r -fHS,intr,soft,novers /dev/cd0 /cdrom
Linux	/etc/mount -r -t iso9660 /dev/cdrom /cdrom

With some exceptions the CD-ROM doesn't contain executable Unix programs but C source code instead. You need a C compiler to build the programs. Most software packages contain prebuilt makefiles. For some packages (or more esoteric Unix flavors) you'll have to adapt the makefile to your system before you can build the programs.

A.1.5 Compression and Archive Formats

The software on the CD-ROM was packed with several compression and archiving programs. Taking the large capacity of a CD-ROM into account, compression may seem unnecessary. However, there are some severe limitations of an ISO file system: Unix and Mac files usually have longer names, and many file names contain special characters which are not allowed in ISO 9660. In Section A.3 you can find descriptions of the compression and archiving programs used. The *tools* directory on the CD-ROM contains decompression programs for most formats and for several operating systems. A notable exception are the Macintosh Binhex and Stuffit formats, for which the CD-ROM doesn't contain decompression programs (due to the ISO format's limitations).

A.2 CD-ROM Directories

demo.   This directory contains some demo versions of commercial software. The demo versions are restricted in some way, and may be redistributed.

doc.   This directory contains some PDF files with additional information which are not covered in detail in this book. To view PDF files on screen you need Acrobat Reader or Ghostscript (both of which are supplied on the CD-ROM).

> - *details.pdf* contains technical details for selected topics (only relevant for programmers).
> - *framepdf.pdf* contains instructions for automatically generating Acrobat bookmarks with FrameMaker 4 (see Section 8.6.4).
> - *gsman_e.pdf* contains the Ghostscript manual from Appendix B.

example.   This directory contains several examples of file formats mentioned in this book.

fonts.   This directory contains several PostScript fonts. These are not intended to compete with the large available public domain font collections but only serve as samples.

ps.   This directory contains several PostScript files, some of which are mentioned in book chapters to solve application problems.

software.   This is the main directory which contains many utility programs, most of which are covered in the respective book chapters. Since most programs are available for several platforms and many book readers use more than one operating system, the software isn't grouped according to platform. Instead, a program's directory contains subdirectories relating to the target system. The *dos/windows/ mac* directories contain executable programs for the respective platform. Small programs often only consist of a single executable file, large packages either have to be decompressed or configured using a separate installation program. Most Unix programs are supplied as C source code. You can consult the table in Section A.4.1 to find out whether a certain C source is suited for Unix. The *compress* subdirectory often contains the package in compressed format (even if it is also contained in non-compressed form) to facilitate software transfer.

tools.   This directory contains tools for diverse compression and archiving formats (again, for several platforms). These programs are

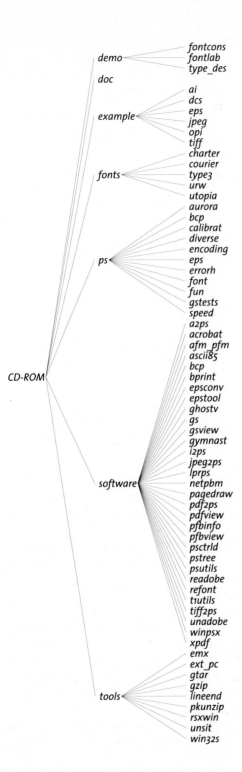

Fig. A.1.
Overview of the CD-ROM's
directory structure

not directly related to this book's contents but complement the programs in the *software* directory.

A.3 Auxiliary Software ("tools" Directory)

The following sections detail the CD-ROM's directory contents. For many programs an Internet FTP server address is also given where you can find the most current version.

emx: run time support for 32-bit programs under MS-DOS and OS/2
Platform: MS-DOS, OS/2
Directory: emx
Internet: ftp-os2.nmsu.edu/os2/unix/emx09a/emxrt.zip

emx is needed to run the epstool utility under MS-DOS or OS/2 on 386 processors (and higher). More information can be found in the epstool description below.

extract: Decompressing Compactor Pro files
Platform: MS-DOS
Directory: ext_pc

extract decompresses files compressed on a Mac with *Compactor Pro*.

gunzip: Dekompression
Platforms: MS-DOS, Unix, C source code available
Directory: gunzip
Internet: prep.ai.mit.edu/pub/gnu

GNU zip (*gzip*, suffix *.gz*) is a freely available compression program for which C source is available; the same holds true for the *gunzip* decompression companion program. The C source for both is suitable for all Unix systems. An executable MS-DOS version is also contained on the CD-ROM. gzip uses the same algorithm as pkzip but can only compress a single file at a time. For this reason gzip is often combined with tar or gtar/gnutar to pack several files into an archive which can be compressed (see below).

gtar: File archiving
Platforms: MS-DOS, Unix, C source code available
Directory: gtar
Internet: prep.ai.mit.edu/pub/gnu

The tar archiving program is standard on all Unix systems. tar doesn't compress files but packs multiple files (or directories) into a single archive. It is often combined with a compression program. The result of *tar* and *gzip* usually has the *.tar.gz* suffix, under MS-DOS and the accompanying CD-ROM shortened to .tgz. To unpack a tar archive under MS-DOS you find a gtar executable on the CD-ROM as well as C source code for Unix. However, *gtar* is compatible with the widely used Unix *tar* (but has a much larger functionality).

lineend: Convert line end characters
Platforms: MS-DOS, Unix, C source code available
Directory: lineend

The line-end program converts line end characters in text files according to several operating systems' conventions: MS-DOS uses the CR/NL combination, MacOS a single CR, and Unix a single NL character. The program may be useful when transferring text or PostScript files from one system to another.

pkunzip: Dekompression
Platform: MS-DOS
Directory: pkzip

pkzip (suffix .*zip*) is a widely used shareware program for compressing files on MS-DOS. You can find the pkunzip decompression program on the CD-ROM.

rsxwin: Run time support for 32 bit programs under Windows
Platform: Windows
Directory: rxswin
Internet: ftp-os2.nmsu.edu/os2/unix/emx09a/rsxwin2a.zip

rsxwin is needed for running the epstool program under Windows (enhanced mode). More information can be found in the epstool description below.

unsit: Dekompressing StuffIt files
Platform: MS-DOS
Directory : unsit

unsit decompresses files compressed on the Mac with StuffIt.

win32s: 32 bit Windows system extension
Platform: Windows 3.x
Directory: win32s
Internet: ftp.microsoft.com/softlib

win32s is a Windows 3.x system extension which is necessary for running 32 bit programs. To install it, start the *setup* program in the */tools/win32s/windows/disk1* directory.

A.4 PostScript and PDF Utilities ("software" Directory)

A.4.1 Overview

The following table gives an overview of the *software* directory's contents. The table lists the directory name, key words describing the program's purpose, and the availability on different platforms. More details on individual packages can be found in the next section.

Overview of the CD-ROM's software directory.

Directory	key words	MS-DOS	Windows	Unix	Macintosh	source code
a2ps	convert text → PostScript	x		x		x
acrobat	Adobe Acrobat Reader	x	x	x	x	
afm_pfm	convert PFM ←→ AFM	x		x		x
ascii85	ASCII85 protocol	x		x		x
bcp	Binary Control Protocol	x		x		x
bprint	download PostScript to the printer		x			
epstool	manipulate EPS files	x	x	x		x
ghostvie	Ghostview for X11			x		x
gs	Ghostscript	x	x	x	x	x
gsview	GSview for Windows		x			x
gymnast	convert Text → PDF		x			
i2ps	convert Text → PostScript	x		x		x
jpeg2ps	convert JPEG → PostScript Level 2	x		x		x
lprps	PostScript backend for BSD systems			x		x
netpbm	graphics converters for many formats			x		x
pagedraw	PageDraw graphics program		x			
pdf2ps	convert PDF → PostScript Level 2	x		x		x
pdfview	view or print PDF files			x		
pfbinfo	read PFB font files	x				
pfbview	view PFB font files		x			
psctrld	Windows Ctrl-D problem		x			
pstree	print a directory tree	x		x		x
psutils	several PostScript utilities	x		x		x
readobe	"pack" PostScript fonts for the Mac				x	
refont	convert Mac fonts	x				
t1utils	several tools for Type 1 fonts	x		x		x
tiff2ps	convert TIFF → PostScript Level 2	x		x		
unadobe	"unpack" PostScript fonts for the Mac				x	
xpdf	display and print PDF files			x		x
winpsx	font downloader for Windows		x			

A.4.2 Program Descriptions

a2ps: Convert text files to PostScript
Platforms: MS-DOS, Unix, C source available
Directory: a2ps
Internet: ftp.germany.eu.net/pub/comp/applications/textproc/
PostScript/a2ps

a2ps converts text files in ASCII or ISO format to PostScript. More
details can be found in Section 9.5.1.

Adobe Acrobat Reader
Platforms: MS-DOS, Windows, Windows NT, OS/2, Macintosh, SunOS,
Solaris, HP-UX, SGI, IBM AIX
Directory: acrobat
Internet: ftp.adobe.com/pub/adobe/Applications/Acrobat,
http://www.adobe.com/acrobat

Acrobat Reader displays and prints PDF files. If you want to use the
PDF files on the CD-ROM you should install Acrobat Reader on your
system if you haven't done so already. For Windows, Mac, Solaris,
SunOS, HP-UX, and SGI-IRIX version 2.1 of Acrobat Reader is supplied
on the CD-ROM, for MS-DOS there's only version 1.0 available. More
information on Acrobat and PDF can be found in Chapter 8.

Installing Acrobat Reader under MS-DOS.   Acrobat Reader needs a
graphics card with a VESA compatible driver. The installation package, however, contains a universal VESA driver for many graphics
cards. The installation requires ca. 4 MB of hard disk space. *cd* to the
/software/acrobat/dos directory and start *acrodos*.

Installing Acrobat Reader under Windows.   Acrobat Reader runs
under Windows 3.1, Windows 95, Windows NT, and OS/2. The software
requires ca. 2.5 MB of hard disk space, a 386 processor or higher, and
4 MB RAM. Select the */software/acrobat/windows* CD-ROM directory in
Program Manager or Explorer and double-click *acroread.exe*. The install program asks for an installation directory and decompresses the
necessary files.

Installing Acrobat Reader on the Macintosh.   The Mac installation
contains 68K and PowerPC versions and automatically installs the
appropriate version. Acrobat Reader requires 4 MB of hard disk space
and a minimum of 2 MB RAM (3.5 MB on PowerMacs). Use StuffIt
Expander to decompress the file *acroread.hqx* in the *software:acro-
bat:mac* folder and double-click *Acroread.mac*.

Installing Acrobat Reader under Unix. The Unix version of Acrobat Reader needs 8 MB hard disk space. You need to mount the CD-ROM in the file system first (see Section A.1.4). Change to the appropriate Unix directory and start the installation script. More details can be found in the accompanying online documents. Installation commands for IBM AIX, SunOS, Solaris, and HP-UX:

```
# cd /cdrom/software/acrobat/<system>
# ./install
```

The install script first displays the usage license which you have to confirm, and than prompts for some parameters interactively (e.g., the installation directory). Adhere to the script's instructions. After successfully installing Acrobat Reader you can launch it with the *acroread* script which is placed in Acrobat's *bin* directory. The help file is supplied as man page as well as in PDF and can be accessed like this:

```
acroread -help
```

Acrobat Reader uses several dynamic (shared) libraries which must be accessible in the system's default directories. If this isn't the case you must set some environment (shell) variables. For example, in our test installation on HP-UX 9.0.1 Acrobat Reader didn't find the *libXext.sl* library. Using *find*, we located this library file in the */usr/lib/X11R5* directory. Therefore, we added this directory to the SHLIB_PATH variable in the *acroread* shell script:

```
SHLIB_PATH=...existing values...:/usr/lib/X11R5
```

Converting AFM to PFM and PFM to AFM
Platforms: MS-DOS, OS/2, Unix, C source code available
Directory: afm_pfm

The afm2pfm and pfm2afm utilities convert AFM to PFM metric files and vice versa. This is helpful when you want to exchange fonts among Unix, Windows, or OS/2. More details can be found in Section 4.6.

ascii85: 7 bit encoding according to ASCII85
Platforms: MS-DOS, Unix, C source code available
Directory: ascii85

The *bto85* and *85tob* utilities convert binary data to ASCII85 encoded text files, and vice versa.

bcp: Binary Control Protocol
Platforms: MS-DOS, Unix, C source available
Directory: bcp

The *quote* program converts PostScript files according to the *Binary Control Protocol* (BCP). BCP allows to transmit binary data to a Post-Script printer via serial or parallel interface and can accelerate printing of image data. The *unquote* companion program converts in the other direction, i.e., it interprets control characters sent from the PostScript printer to the computer. It is useful only in rare cases. More information on BCP can be found in Section 2.3.2. If you want to use BCP note that you also need two PostScript programs for activating/deactivating BCP. These PostScript programs can be found on the CD-ROM in the *postscript/bcp* directory.

bprint: Download PostScript files to the printer
Platform: Windows
Directory: bprint

BinaryPrinting transfers PostScript and other print files to the printer port (bypassing Print Manager). This allows to print existing Post-Script files without copying the files to lpt1:. More details can be found in Section 2.4.1.

epstool: Manipulating EPS files
Platforms: MS-DOS, Windows, Unix, C source code available
Directory: epstool
Internet: ftp.cs.wisc.edu/pub/ghost/rjl

epstool extracts the PostScript or preview section from an EPS file or uses Ghostscript to create a preview section. Information on its usage can be found in Section 3.5 and the epstool documentation.

To run epstool under MS-DOS on 386 processors and higher you need the emx 32-bit runtime support. Launch the program as follows:

```
emx epstool.exe <epstool options>
```

If epstool isn't contained in one of directories contained in the PATH variable you must supply its complete path name.

Under Windows on 386 and higher epstool needs the rsxwin 32-bit runtime support which supplies a window for epstool. Launch epstool as follows from Program Manager or a MS-DOS window under Windows 95:

```
rsxwin epstool.exe <epstool options>
```

The above remark on complete path names holds true for the Windows case, too.

Ghostscript: PostScript and PDF interpreter
Platforms: MS-DOS, Windows, Windows NT, Macintosh, Amiga, Atari,
Unix, C source code available
Directory: gs
Internet: ftp.cs.wisc.edu/pub/ghost/aladdin
http://www.cs.wisc.edu/~ghost/index.html

Ghostscript is an interpreter for PostScript Level 2 and PDF. It drives
numerous displays and printers and runs on many operating systems. You will find detailed information in the Ghostscript manual
contained in Appendix B "GhostScript".

Ghostview/GSview: Ghostscript front end
Platforms: Windows, Windows NT, Unix, C source code available
Directory: gsview (Windows and OS/2); ghostv (Unix)
Internet: ftp.cs.wisc.edu/pub/ghost/rjl (GSview)
prep.ai.mit.edu:/pub/gnu (Ghostview)

GSview is a Ghostscript front end that greatly simplifies using Ghostscript under Windows. It is based on the Unix/X11 program Ghostview. Both are covered in more detail in the Ghostscript manual contained in Appendix B "GhostScript".

gymnast: Convert text files to PDF
Platform: Windows
Directory: gymnast

Gymnast converts text files to PDF. Its layout options are rather limited; the user can select font and font size. Additionally, Gymnast allows to embed special instructions in the input file for creating PDF
hypertext links.

i2ps: Convert text files to PostScript
Platforms: all systems with Perl interpreter (mainly Unix)
Directory: i2ps
Internet: ftp.germany.eu.net/pub/comp/applications/textproc/
PostScript

i2ps is a Perl script which converts text files in ASCII or ISO format to
PostScript. More details can be found in Section 9.5.1.

jpeg2ps: Print JPEG files with PostScript Level 2
Platforms: MS-DOS, Unix, C source code available
Directory: jpeg2ps

jpeg2ps converts images in JPEG format to EPS files which make use of
PostScript Level 2's compression features. The resulting EPS files are
considerably smaller than corresponding Level 1 files and therefore

can be transmitted faster. They require a Level 2 device, of course. More details can be found in Section 5.5.1.

lprps: PostScript backend for BSD Unix systems
Platfroms: SunOS, BSD based Unix derivatives, C source code available
Directory: lprps
Internet: ftp.jclark.com/pub/lprps

lprps is a package to drive PostScript printers under Unix. It comprises several programs: *lprps* is a PostScript backend which relays the printer's error messages via the *syslog* facility; *psrev* reverts a document's page ordering; *psif* automatically distinguishes between text and PostScript files; *psof* prints banner pages; *textps* converts text files to PostScript.

PBM tools: Graphics converter for Unix
Platform: Unix, C source code available
Directory: netpbm
Internet: ftp.stanford.edu/class/cs248/netpbm

The PBM tools are a set of converters for converting many common graphics formats. They use PBM, PGM, and PPM as intermediate formats. In Section 9.4.1 you can find an example of how to use these tools.

PageDraw: Windows drawing program
Platform: Windows
Directory: pagedraw
Internet: http://www.wix.com/PageDraw

PageDraw is an object oriented drawing program for Windows. It saves the drawings in Illustrator compatible format. Since PageDraw implements only the Illustrator 88 format it cannot open all AI files.

pdf2ps: Converting PDF to PostScript
Platforms: All systems with Perl interpreter (mainly Unix)
Directory: pdf2ps
Internet: peanuts.leo.org/pub/comp/platforms/next/Unix/text

The *pdf2ps.pl* Perl script converts PDF files to PostScript Level 2. It doesn't simulate missing fonts with Multiple Master fonts and can't open encrypted files. If the PDF document contains thumbnails the script generates an additional PostScript file with a thumbnail overview. You can control via command line options whether to generate binary files or to use hex or ASCII85 encoding for 7-bit clean output.

PDFViewer: View and print PDF files

Platform: NEXTSTEP 3.1 and higher (3.3 recommended), every hardware variant
Directory: pdfview
Internet: peanuts.leo.org/pub/comp/platforms/next/Text/apps

PDFViewer is a program for viewing and printing PDF files on NEXT-STEP. It displays the document in zoom levels between 10% and 800%, follows links, and displays bookmarks, notes, and thumbnails. PDF-Viewer can print the whole document or selected pages only. Missing fonts are replaced by adapted Times-Roman and Helvetica fonts. Screen and printer output require PostScript Level 2.

PFBdir and PFBinfo

Platform: MS-DOS
Directory: pfbinfo

The *PFBdir* and *PFBinfo* programs read general information from a font's PFB file. This may be useful for example to find out a font's exact PostScript file name.

PFBview: Display Type 1 fonts

Platform: Windows
Directory: pfbview

pfbview displays all characters contained in a Type 1 font file. Contrary to other programs of its kind, *pfbview* doesn't resort to ATM for font rendering but directly opens the font file and interprets it. For this reason pfbview isn't limited to the Windows character set but displays all characters defined in the font. More details can be found in Section 4.5.1.

PSctrlD: Ctrl-D problem under Windows

Platform: Windows 3.x
Directory: psctrld

With *psctrld* you can instruct the PostScript printer driver whether or not to generate the Ctrl-D control character. This is only reasonable for the Microsoft PostScript driver since it doesn't offer any option apart from editing the win.ini file.

pstree: Print directory trees

Plattfoms: All systems with Perl interpreter (mainly Unix)
Directory: pstree
Internet: ftp.csc.ncsu.edu/perl/scripts

pstree is a Perl script for generating a graphical representation of a directory tree in PostScript format. Figure A-1 is an example of an image generated by pstree. More details can be found in Section 9.5.1.

PostScript utilities
Platforms: Unix, MS-DOS, C source code available
Directory: psutils
Internet: ftp.dcs.ed.ac.uk/pub/ajcd/psutils.tar.Z

The PostScript utilities offer many possibilities for manipulating DSC compliant PostScript files:

- *psselect* extracts single pages or page regions from a PostScript file; *psnup* scales down and prints several pages on a single sheet of paper (n-up-printing);
- *epsffit* shrink-wraps EPS graphics to a certain size;
- *psbook* arranges several pages on one sheet of paper;
- *pstops* arranges the pages in a PostScript file, e.g., change page ordering, scale up or down, translate, and rotate pages;

The package also contains several Perl scripts for special tasks, e.g., fix incompatibilities between different PostScript prologs.

readobe: Generate Macintosh fonts
Platform: Macintosh
Directory: readobe

readobe converts Type 1 fonts in ASCII format to the Mac's resource format. More details can be found in Section 4.6.

refont: Converting Mac fonts
Platform: MS-DOS
Directory: refont

refont converts Type 1 Fonts from the Mac to Windows fonts. The program also converts TrueType fonts from the Mac for Windows. The package also takes care of transforming AFM files to PFM format. More details can be found in Section 4.6.

Type 1 utilities
Platforms: Unix, MS-DOS, C source code available
Directory: t1utils

The Type 1 utilities convert several flavors of Type 1 fonts. They transform PostScript fonts in PFA, PFB, and Mac/resource format in one another. Also, they decode fonts to pseudo PostScript code (and vice versa). More details on *t1ascii*, *t1binary* and *unpost* can be found in Section 4.6.

tiff2ps: Print TIFF files with PostScript Level 2
Platforms: MS-DOS, Unix, C source code not available
Directory: tiff2ps

tiff2ps (similar to *jpeg2ps*) converts image data in TIFF format to EPS files which make use of PostScript Level 2's compression features. The resulting EPS files are considerably smaller than corresponding Level 1 files and therefore can be transmitted faster. They require a Level 2 device, of course. More details can be found in Section 5.5.1.

Due to licensing issues the C source code of this program cannot be made available. The CD-ROM contains executable versions for MS-DOS and several Unix systems.

unadobe: "Unpack" Mac fonts
Platform: Macintosh
Directory: unadobe

With *unadobe* you can convert PostScript fonts from the Mac's resource format to ASCII format. More details can be found in Section 4.6.

xpdf: Display and print PDF files in X11
Platform: Unix, C source code available
Directory: xpdf
Internet: http://www.contrib.andrew.cmu.edu:/usr/dn0o/xpdf/xpdf.html

xpdf displays PDF files in the X Window System and is able to convert PDF to PostScript Level 2. The package also includes a utility for converting PDF to PostScript from the command line.

winPSX: Windows font downloader
Platform: Windows
Directory: winpsx

WinPSX is a downloader for loading PostScript fonts to the printer permanently.

A.5 PostScript Files ("ps" Directory)

The programs in the *ps* directory are pure PostScript files and are therefore suitable for all operating systems.

Aurora: Color separation
Aurora is a PostScript package for generating color separations on Level 1 devices. It redefines all color PostScript operators so that they print a previously defined color (in black) instead of all colors.

Binary Control Protocol (BCP)

binary.ps activates the binary protocol BCP; *standard.ps* activates the standard protocol, i.e., it deactivates BCP. More details on BCP's properties and advantages and its availability in printer makes can be found in Section 2.3.2.

Diverse

ctrld only contains the Ctrl-D control character which is used for separating PostScript jobs when using serial or parallel transmission.

emulate.ps is a little PostScript prolog for a line printer emulation (printing ASCII files). For more details, see Section 9.5.1.

info.ps prints some information about the PostScript interpreter in use. This includes the manufacturer, PostScript level, version number, available RAM etc.

still.ps is Glenn Reid's distillery. This program "distills" PostScript progams to a simpler format which nevertheless produces the same output but in most cases is smaller and runs more quickly. Don't confuse distillery with Acrobat Distiller.

resident.ps contains the PostScript instructions for permanently loading code or fonts in a printer's interpreter.

Character sets and encoding

The *encoding* directory contains PostScript encoding vectors for several character sets: MS-DOS codepages 437 and 850, Windows ANSI, ISO Latin 1 and Latin 2, Macintosh, NEXTSTEP, Adobe StandardEncoding, and PDFDocEncoding. You can find printed tables of these characters sets in Appendix C.

allglyph.ps prints all characters contained in a font (its glyph complement) in alphabetical order. The program needs a PostScript Level 2 interpreter.

reencode.ps is the standard procedure for changing a font's encoding vector. More details can be found in Section 4.5.1.

EPS

The *eps* directory contains some utilities for working with EPS files:

epsfinfo.ps uses PostScript instructions to determine a graphic's BoundingBox, and prints the BoundingBox's coordinates on its standard output. For this reason, the program only works with a Software RIP or printers with a bidirectional channel.

grid.ps prints a PostScript coordinate grid which can be used for estimating a graphic's BoundingBox. More details can be found in Section 3.5.

PostScript error handler

The *errorh.ps* file contains a PostScript error handler which traps PostScript errors. It prints the kind of error and some additional information. More details can be found in Section 2.5.2.

Font tools

diskload.ps can be used for storing a font on a printer's or RIP's hard disk. To use it, you must enter the name of the font at the beginning of the file and append the font data in ASCII format to the file.

makepfm.ps creates PFM files for using a font under Windows. To use it, read the comments and insert the requested information in the file. Now you must run the program on a PostScript interpreter with binary-proof communications channel (preferably Ghostscript). More details can be found in Section 4.6.1.

mm.ps is the Multiple Master Analyzer. It analyzes a Multiple Master font's design axes and prints its coordinate range, parameter curves, and some font samples. More details can be found in Section 4.2.4.

Fun

This directory contains some more or less useful PostScript samples:

animate.ps is a small PostScript animation which generates a short film strip which is meant for screen display using a PostScript interpreter (there's no point in printing it!). The animation's graphics are not really great but it is very well suited as an optical speed test for comparing computers or PostScript RIPs.

calender.ps prints a plan for a polyhedron. Its sides are printed with a calender, a month each side. You can enter the year at the beginning of the file.

spiral.ps contains PostScript code for spiraling text.

Ghostscript test files

The *gstests* directory contains some test files for checking Ghostscript or other PostScript interpreters.

Test pages for printer calibration

The PostScript files in the *calibrat* directory print test pages which can be used for manually calibrating a printer. More details on the files and the process can be found in Section 6.2.4.

PostScript interpreter speed test

Internet: http://www.achilles.net/~jsg/ppst/

The *speed* directory contains the *PostScript Processing Speed Test* (PPST). This test prints seven pages with the results of diverse performance tests. The table accompanying the PostScript file lists the performance values of many common printer makes for comparison.

Additionally, PPST determines general information about the printer, e.g. size of the printable area, version number of the PostScript interpreter, available RAM, number of pages printed so far, etc.

A.6 Demo Versions ("demo" Directory)

Font Consultant
Platform: Windows
Verzeichnis: fontcons

Font Consultant (Vardas, UK) manages fonts under Windows. The demo version is fully functional. However, it is restricted to a maximum of 20 fonts.

FontLab
Platform: Windows
Directory: fontlab

FontLab (SoftUnion, St. Petersburg, Russia) is a powerful PostScript and TrueType font editor. More details on FontLab can be found in Section 4.7.

Type-Designer
Platform: Windows
Directory: type_des
Internet: http://www.dtpsoft.de

Type-Designer (DTP-Software Manfred Albracht, Aachen, Germany) allows one to create and edit PostScript and TrueType fonts. More details can be found in Section 4.7.

Ghostscript

B

Ghostscript is an interpreter for PostScript Level 2 which displays PostScript and PDF files on all common operating systems. Ghostscript can be found on the accompanying CD-ROM. Ghostscript offers many configuration options and is able to do many uncommon format conversions. This appendix contains the Ghostscript user manual and is provided to aid in Ghostscript installation, usage, and trouble-shooting.

B.1 What is Ghostscript?

L. Peter Deutsch, founder of Aladdin Enterprises, Menlo Park, California, wrote the PostScript Level 2 and PDF interpreter *Ghostscript* in the C programming language. The program runs on most operating systems, including MS-DOS, Windows 3.x, Windows 95, Windows NT, OS/2, Macintosh, Unix, and VAX/VMS and has been available free of charge ever since its introduction 1988. With the help of many users and programmers on the Internet Ghostscript has become a high-quality and versatile PostScript interpreter. Peter Deutsch also distributes a commercial version with customer-specific enhancements and support. Ghostscript's capabilities include:

Screen output. Ghostscript displays PostScript data on the screen. This is useful to examine PostScript graphics or for saving a few trees if you want to browse some product documentation which is available in PostScript format only. Ghostscript checks PostScript files before you transfer them (e.g., to a service bureau): Are all the necessary fonts there? Are the graphics okay? Do the files contain all pages?

Ghostscript also helps with PostScript trouble-shooting: A faulty page can be rendered on screen revealing which graphics element yields an error message. Ghostscript provides the usual PostScript error messages. A separate frontend to the interpreter, called GSview (for Windows and OS/2) or Ghostview (for the X Window System), simplifies the handling of PostScript files with a user-friendly GUI interface: with these frontends the user can access random pages in the document. Without them, Ghostscript displays the pages one after another, from the beginning to the end of the file.

Printer output. Another important task of a PostScript RIP is to render PostScript data for output on a graphics-capable printer. The Ghostscript distribution contains a wealth of drivers for a wide range of printer models, from the more popular to the more esoteric. A list of all drivers is found in Section B.3.3. These drivers are an integral part of Ghostscript and are not related to Macintosh or Windows system drivers.

Ghostscript can even help optimize the output of a PostScript-capable printer: if the computer's CPU is significantly faster than the printer's, Ghostscript can in many cases speed up PostScript output. PostScript printers with too little RAM sometimes cause trouble. Ghostscript can remedy this by making use of your computer's main memory (and a swap file or swap partition). Ghostscript has proven to be a robust and reliable PostScript-RIP that is superior to many commercial PostScript clones.

PDF on every platform.   Beginning with version 3.33, Ghostscript also contains an interpreter for the *Portable Document Format* (PDF), the foundation of Adobe Acrobat. Large parts of Ghostscript's PDF interpreter are written in PostScript. It displays and prints PDF files and even converts them back to PostScript. This makes Ghostscript the only program that displays Acrobat files on all Unix platforms, although it only interprets layout-related information and currently ignores hypertext links or annotations.

Starting with Ghostscript 4.0, the program is also capable of converting PostScript files to PDF, i.e., it offers Distiller functionality. Though this feature, called the pdfwrite device, still has some shortcomings, it is certainly an important milestone since Ghostscript is the first and still the only free program that converts PostScript to PDF.

Utilities and converters.   A complete PostScript interpreter together with suitable drivers and utilities makes it possible to carry out many of the operations covered in this book. These include displaying graphics files in the formats GIF, JPEG, or PBM; extracting textual data from PostScript or PDF files; rasterizing PostScript to raster graphics formats such as TIFF, PBM, PNG; converting EPS graphics to the editable Illustrator format, and many other useful features.

License conditions for the end-user.   Although Ghostscript is available free of charge, it is still subject to certain license conditions. These are always contained in the Ghostscript program package. Until 1994, Ghostscript was subject to the GNU Public License (GPL). Under the terms of this license, the originator retains the copyright for his work. The use and further distribution of the program, however, are not restricted significantly. Starting with version 3.0 in 1994, Peter Deutsch replaced the GPL with the more restrictive Aladdin Ghostscript Free Public License (AGFPL). Under the terms of the AGFPL, no payment is required for private and commercial use of the program. The sale of Ghostscript is explicitly prohibited, however. Exempted from these conditions are BBSs, or servers for which users pay access fees independent of the downloaded software, and CD-ROMs whose contents may be reproduced and distributed without any payment involved. Anyone interested in commercially licensing Ghostscript should contact Aladdin Enterprises or one of its distribution partners. The complete text of the AGFPL is found in the file named *public* which is part of the Ghostscript distribution fileset.

B.2 Installing Ghostscript

B.2.1 Installation on MS-DOS, Windows, and OS/2

Requirements and versions. The Ghostscript installation (not including fonts) uses 3 MB hard disk space. There are several flavors of Ghostscript for PC systems:

System	File name	Notes
MS-DOS	gs.exe	Limited to 640 KB; little support
MS-DOS, 80386 and higher	gs386.exe plus dos4gw.exe	Version with DOS extender; very fast.
Windows 3.x	gswin16.exe plus gsdll16.dll	16-bit version; it consists of a DLL and a (small) EXE program.
Windows 3.x with Win32s; Windows 95 and NT	gswin32.exe plus gsdll32.dll	32-bit version with enhancements for Windows 95 and NT; it consists of a DLL and a (small) EXE program
OS/2	gsos2.exe plus gsdll2.dll	Uses gspmdrv.exe as display driver for the presentation manager

Setup program for Ghostscript and GSview. Under Windows and OS/2 the user frontend GSview facilitates using Ghostscript by supplying a handy interface to the interpreter. With the GSview setup program you can install both Ghostscript and GSview comfortably. In the */software/gsview/windows* directory on the CD-ROM, launch the program *setup.exe* (for Windows) or os2setup.exe (for OS/2). The required ZIP files for Ghostscript and GSview are already contained in that directory. After displaying some information, the setup programs asks for the name of the directory to which the software is to be installed, and decompresses the ZIP archives. Then it creates a program group (Windows 3.x) or a start menu entry (Windows 95).

After launching GSview you have to choose "Options", "Configure Ghostscript..." to the enter the path name of the Ghostscript DLL, the include path, and possibly some Ghostscript options (see Figure B.1).

Note that *GSview* requires the 32-bit version of Ghostscript. With "File", "Open" you can open PostScript files. GSview then passes these files on to Ghostscript for rendering. Using the menu sequence "Media", "Resolution" you can adjust the screen size: larger resolution values yield a larger screen representation. Use smaller resolution if you want to see the entire page at a time without scrollbars. With the "Media" menu you can adjust the page size (media format).

Installing Ghostscript manually. If you don't use Windows, don't need GSview, or can't stand setup programs, you can install Ghost-

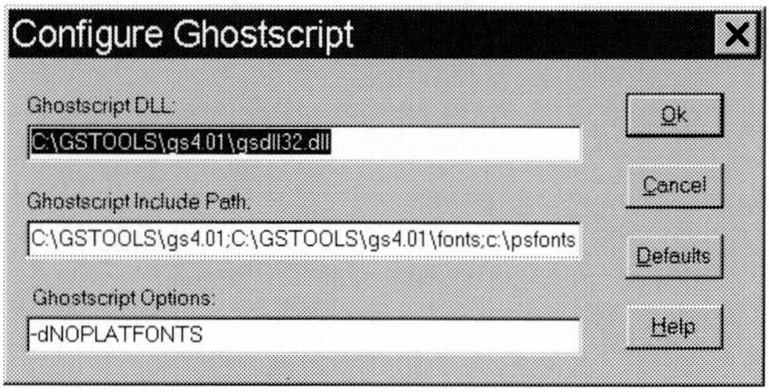

Configure Ghostscript

Ghostscript DLL:
`C:\GSTOOLS\gs4.01\gsdll32.dll`

Ghostscript Include Path:
`C:\GSTOOLS\gs4.01;C:\GSTOOLS\gs4.01\fonts;c:\psfonts`

Ghostscript Options:
`-dNOPLATFONTS`

Ok   Cancel   Defaults   Help

Fig. B.1.
Configuring Ghostscript
path names in GSview.

script manually. All of the files contained in the archive *gs401ini.zip* plus one of the executables listed in the table above are necessary for using Ghostscript. However, the CD-ROM already contains complete file sets (excluding fonts) in the directories *dos, win, win32*, and *os2*. To install Ghostscript, simply copy the files from the suitable directory on the CD-ROM to a directory on your hard disk (e.g., *C:\gs*). To use the 32-bit version for Windows 3.x, you need the *win32s* system extension in addition to the Ghostscript files. Win32s can be found on the CD-ROM in the *tools/win32s/windows* directory and has to be installed separately. (Note: many software packages use win32s, so it may already be installed on your system.)

If you're short on disk space, you can run Ghostscript directly from CD-ROM. The MS-DOS version of Ghostscript uses the environment variable GS_LIB to locate the initialization files if they cannot be found in the current directory or the standard directory *c:\gs*. It's best to include the following statements in your *autoexec.bat* file (assuming you installed Ghostscript in *d:\progs\gs*):

```
set GS_LIB=d:\progs\gs
set PATH=...other path entries...;d:\progs\gs
```

Alternatively, the command line option *-I* can be used to tell Ghostscript where to find its files:

```
gs -ID:\progs\gs
```

Launching and testing Ghostscript.   On MS-DOS, you start Ghostscript by typing the program name as usual. With Windows, it's easier to double-click on Ghostscript's icon in the file manager or to create an icon in the program manager. The file *tiger.ps* (part of the Ghostscript distribution) is perfectly suited to test your installation. Start Ghostscript and type in the following command at Ghostscript's prompt:

```
GS>(tiger.ps) run
```

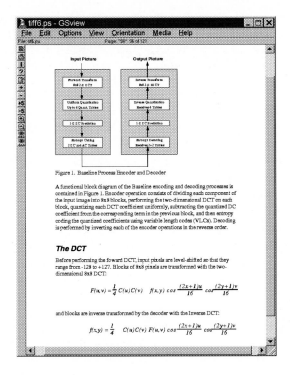

Fig. B.2.
GSview simplifies Ghost-script usage under Windows and OS/2. It also offers additional possibilities, e.g., dealing with EPS files

Ghostscript should now display the test file on screen. Having finished the page, Ghostscript asks you to

```
>>showpage, press <return> to continue<<
```

If the file contains more than one page, Ghostscript renders the next page after the return key is pressed.

Caution: The installation is not yet complete! To complete the installation, font access for Ghostscript needs to be configured. This is covered in Section B.2.4. If you want Ghostscript to use the same command line options every time, you can use the environment variable GS_OPTIONS. Ghostscript evaluates this variable before checking the "real" command line options. Especially with Windows 3.x this is much more convenient than the rather clumsy call by way of the program manager and "File", "Run..."

Double-clicking PostScript files. In Windows 3.x you can simplify opening PostScript files: first, use the registry editor RegEdit to register GSview for opening ("gsview32 %1") and printing ("gsview32 /p %1", not reasonable for PostScript printers) PostScript files. Then, using "File", "Link" in file manager, link file type "PostScript" and program GSview to the extension *.ps*. Having done this, double-clicking on a PostScript file automatically launches GSview.

In Windows 95 you can link GSview to PostScript files with a somewhat lengthy menu sequence in the Explorer: "View", "Options...", register card "File types", file type "PS file", "Edit...", action type "Open", "Edit...". In the last dialog box enter the path to GSview. Double-clicking on a PostScript file now launches GSview.

Additional features of GSview. GSview offers many additional Ghostscript functions which are described in several chapters of this book. This includes dealing with EPS files, randomly accessing the pages of DSC (*Document Structuring Conventions*) conforming Post-Script files, extracting selected pages to print parts of a document only, copying the bitmapped page contents to the clipboard, or selecting printer drivers in a convenient manner.

GSview uses temporary files for communicating with Ghostscript. These are either created in the current directory or in the directory specified in the TEMP environment variable. The TEMP variable must therefore point to a writable directory on disk, if GSview is run directly from CD-ROM.

B.2.2 Installation on the Macintosh

Requirements and versions. Ghostscript for the Macintosh is called *Mac GS Viewer*. It's available in three versions, one for Macs with Motorola CPU 68020 and higher, a native version for PowerPC's, and a version for Mac Classics with 68000 CPU (min. 3 MB available memo-

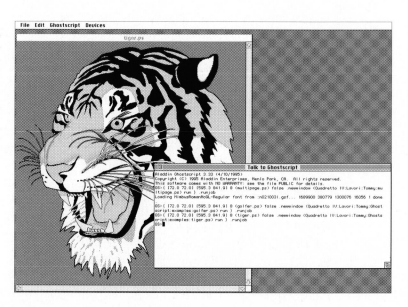

Fig. B.3. Mac GS Viewer displays the tiger test page. You can enter Post-Script commands in the console window and open files via "File"

ry). The installation needs approximately 6 MB disk space (including fonts). Mac GS viewer is based on Ghostscript 3.33. Contrary to Windows and OS/2, there is no equivalent of GSview for the Mac. Fortunately, this deficiency is compensated for by several extensions in Mac GS Viewer and its user interface. You can find the following compressed archive files on the CD-ROM:

gs_files.hqx	init files and documentation
gs_68k.hqx	executable for 68020 CPU and higher
gs_ppc.hqx	executable for PowerPC
gs_class.hqx	executable for Mac Classic
gs_fonts.hqx	standard fonts for Ghostscript
gsmacsrc.hqx	Mac specific C source files for Ghostscript

To install Mac GS Viewer you need the program Stuffit Expander which is not included on the CD-ROM. Decompress the archive *gs-files.hqx*. This places the contents of this archive in the *Ghostscript* folder. Decompress one of the executable files (*gs_68k.hqx*, *gs_ppc.hqx* or *gs_class.hqx*) along with the Ghostscript fonts from the archive *gs-fonts.hqx* into the same folder. The archive *gsmacsrc.hqx* is only needed for compiling an individual version of Ghostscript.

Launching and testing Ghostscript.   Launch Ghostscript by double-clicking on the Mac GS Viewer icon. After initialization, the console window ("Talk to Ghostscript") will appear with the Ghostscript prompt

GS>

Although you can type in PostScript commands in the console window, it's much easier to use Mac-style menu commands. The sequence "File", "Open" lets you open EPSF or TEXT files, e.g., the test

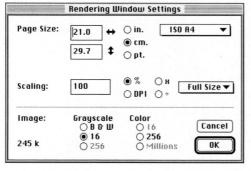

Fig. B.4.
The "Settings" panel changes page size, scaling factor, and color parameters

file *tiger.ps* in the Ghostscript folder. Activate balloon help to learn more about Ghostscript. After one page has been rendered on screen, the next page can be requested with "Ghostscript", "Next Page". The program can be closed with "Quit". The sequence "Edit", "Settings..." changes such internal settings as page size or the scaling factor of the window.

Device drivers and file output. By default, Ghostscript renders into a Macintosh window. It can also create instructions for other devices or graphics file formats. You can copy the bitmapped contents of a window to the clipboard, or save it as a PICT file with "File", "Save As...". In the "Devices" menu you can choose the output file. Although the Ghostscript source distribution contains many dozens of drivers, the Macintosh version only contains the screen driver, a few printer drivers, and drivers for the file formats PCX, PBM, and TIFF. This decision has been made in order to reduce storage requirements. Since it is not possible to dynamically load drivers, you have to recompile and link Ghostscript if you want to use additional drivers.

Font configuration. Ghostscript uses PostScript fonts in ASCII format. Since PostScript fonts on the Mac are usually stored in a compact resource format, Ghostscript cannot use them directly (this is planned for a future version). However, you can convert standard Mac PostScript fonts for use with Ghostscript with the *unadobe* utility on the CD-ROM. Execute the following steps for each font you want to use:

▶ Start *unadobe* and open the font file. *unadobe* doesn't change the font data, but instead converts the resource representation to a textual representation suitable for Ghostscript. Save the generated font file in the Ghostscript folder (using the old file name or a new one).

Fig. B.5.
In the "Devices" menu
you can choose a driver
for Mac GS Viewer

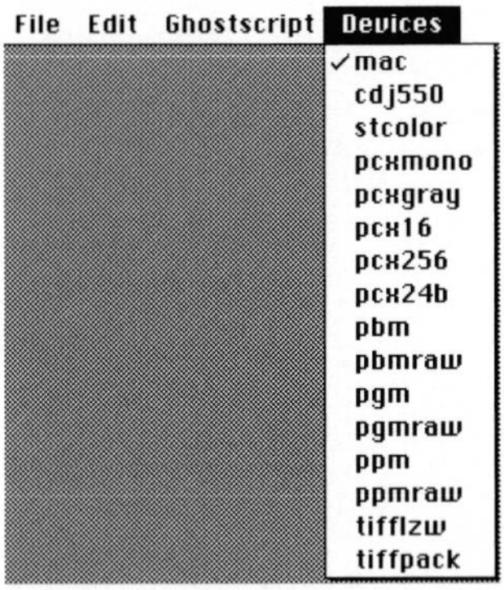

File Edit Ghostscript **Devices**

✓mac
cdj550
stcolor
pcxmono
pcxgray
pcx16
pcx256
pcx24b
pbm
pbmraw
pgm
pgmraw
ppm
ppmraw
tifflzw
tiffpack

- Edit the file *Fontmap* in the Ghostscript folder with a text editor (e.g., SimpleText or TeachText). Append a line similar to the following at the end of the file:

```
/TheSerifBold-Italic     (TheSerBol)
```

  This line contains the PostScript name of the font and the name of the font file that you used in the first step. The line must be terminated with a semicolon. If you're unsure about the exact PostScript name of the font, you can open the font file created by *unadobe* with a text editor and look for the entry /FontName.
- Launch Ghostscript to test the font. You can either use a suitable PostScript file or request the font manually in the console window:

```
/TheSerifBold-Italic findfont
```

Alternatively, you can install a fontmap file derived from another platform. For example, you can create the fontmap automatically on Windows (see Section B.2.4) and install it in the Ghostscript folder together with the font files. It's important not to change the font file names so make sure that they correspond to the fontmap entries. Naturally, you have to observe the font manufacturer's license conditions if the installed fonts originate from another system.

B.2.3 Installation on Unix

Precompiled executables. The complete C sources for Ghostscript are found on the CD-ROM. An individually configured version of Ghostscript can be built with these source files. This is described in Section B.3. To make your life easier, the CD-ROM contains precompiled Ghostscript executables for some common Unix flavors. The table below indicates operating system version and CPU platform on which the executables have been built. Check these to decide whether one of the precompiled binaries runs on your system. If so, the binary will save the hassle of building an individual version. Ghostview executables for these same systems are also found on the CD-ROM.

Operating system	CPU platform
Linux	x86
SunOS 4.1.1	Sparc
Solaris 2.3	Sparc
HP-UX 9.01	HP-PA
System V Release 4.2	x86
DEC OSF/1 V3.2	DEC Alpha
AIX 3.2	RS/6000

The installation of Ghostscript on Unix is controlled by the makefile. Therefore, you have to install the source package even if you can use one of the precompiled executables. The precompiled executables are configured with PostScript Level 2 and PDF support. They contain the most common device and file format drivers (see the table in Section B.3.3).

To install one of the precompiled versions first decompress the Ghostscript package in a newly created directory, copy the suitable program file (e.g., for Linux), and create a makefile (the tar command creates the directory gs4.xx, where 4.xx stands for the version number):

```
gunzip -c /cdrom/software/gs/compress/gs4xxsrc.tgz | tar xvf -
cd gs4.xx
cp /cdrom/software/gs/linux/gs gs
ln -s unix-gcc.mak makefile
```

Since you don't want to compile the C source (and use the precompiled binary instead) you have to adapt the makefile. Change the following line in the makefile (near the end of the file):

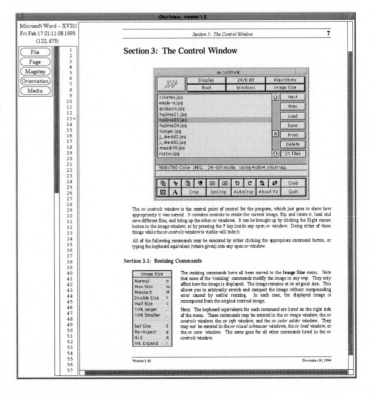

Fig. B.6.
With Ghostview for X11 you can easily control Ghostscript for screen and printer output. The page list allows quick access to random pages of DSC compliant documents.

```
install-exec: $(GS)
```

to

```
install-exec:
```

By default, the installation process copies files to the directories
/usr/local/bin and */usr/local/share/ghostscript/4.00*. If necessary, you
can change these in the makefile too (variable *prefix*). Now install the
files with the command

```
make install
```

(with *root* permission). You can delete the directory gs4.01 afterwards.
To finish the installation, install the Ghostscript fonts as described in
the next section.

Ghostview installation.   Like Ghostscript, Ghostview may be compiled from C source or installed from one of the precompiled versions on CD-ROM. To use one of these, copy the executable program
and the X resource file to a suitable directory on disk. On Linux, for
example, use the following commands to install the CD-ROM version:

```
install -s /cdrom/software/ghostv/linux/ghostv /usr/X11R6/bin/
    ghostview
install -m 0444 /cdrom/software/ghostv/linux/ghostv.ad
    /usr/X11R6/lib/X11/app-defaults/Ghostview
```

B.2.4 Font Configuration

This section applies to all operating systems except Macintosh. Font
configuration for the Mac differs from other systems and has been
covered with the Mac installation already. To apply the following
description for Unix, you have to adapt the syntax for environment
variables and directory paths appropriately.

For many years, the Ghostscript distribution contained only low
quality public domain fonts. In 1996, the German company URW++
contributed commercial-quality PostScript Type 1 fonts for use with
the Ghostscript package. These include look-alikes for the 35 Post-
Script core fonts found in most laser printers. The URW++ fonts are
distributed under the Aladdin and the GNU license.

You can find the URW++ fonts in the *urw* directory on the CD-ROM.
You can significantly enhance text representation on screen and paper by integrating high quality fonts.

Ghostscript uses all flavors of PostScript fonts and formats, i.e.,
Type 1, Type 3, ASCII, and binary. Ghostscript also is capable of processing TrueType fonts (see below). It is necessary for Ghostscript to

have access to the font file (installing the font in the operating system, ATM, or Display PostScript is not enough).

Static font configuration. There are two choices for the font configuration. If the installed font base rarely changes, put one or more font directories in the environment variable GS_LIB. For example, if you want to launch Ghostscript directly from CD-ROM on MS-DOS or Windows, use the following:

```
set GS_LIB=g:\fonts\urw
```

On Unix, you have to export the variable using the command

```
GS_LIB=/usr/local/share/ghostscript/fonts
export GS_LIB
```

Another difference for Unix systems is the colon ":" used as path separator instead of the semicolon ";". A typical hard disk installation on MS-DOS or Windows uses the following:

```
set GS_LIB=C:\gs;C:\gs\fonts
```

or on Unix:

```
set GS_LIB=/usr/local/share/ghostscript/fonts
export GS_LIB
```

Each directory in GS_LIB may contain the *Fontmap* file which defines the relation between font names and file names. To add new fonts, simply add a line similar to the following at the end of the *Fontmap* file:

```
/Fontname     (filename) ;
```

The file name in parentheses must be found in one of the font directories. In many cases you can save yourself the trouble of entering font and file names because there are prebuilt *Fontmap* files for several systems and font configurations. If you use one of the following, simply copy the appropriate file to the name *Fontmap*:

File name	Origin of fonts/name of operating system
Fontmap.atm	Windows with standard ATM fonts
Fontmap.atb	Adobe Type Basics font package
Fontmap.gs	URW++ fonts (standard fontmap)
Fontmap.os2	OS/2 with integrated ATM
Fontmap.osf	DEC OSF/1 with DPS
Fontmap.sol	Solaris 2.3 and higher with DPS
Fontmap.ult	Ultrix 4.3 and higher with DPS
Fontmap.vms	VAX/VMS with DECwindows/Motif and DPS

In order to let Ghostscript access the fonts in Display PostScript systems, you have to include the appropriate path name in GS_LIB. A list of these (quite varying) path names can be found in Section 7.2.3.

Dynamic font configuration. For large or frequently changing font installations the second method is preferable. Ghostscript checks the GS_FONTPATH environment variable to determine the available font files and scans these files to find out the names of the fonts they contain. Similar to GS_LIB above, this variable contains one or more directory names. Since Ghostscript automatically recognizes fonts, this method is much more flexible. However, since Ghostscript checks all font directories every time a new font is requested, this method increases startup time. To avoid inconsistencies, make sure there is no *Fontmap* file in one of the GS_LIB directories if you use GS_FONTPATH or launch Ghostscript with the -dNOFONTMAP option.

TrueType fonts. Starting with Version 4.0, Ghostscript contains a rasterizer for TrueType fonts. Note that Ghostscript supports two flavors of TrueType fonts.

Type 42 fonts: These contain TrueType data wrapped in PostScript instructions and can be directly processed by the interpreter. Type 42 capability is integrated in all Ghostscript configurations which include Level 2 support (which is the case for all default makefiles). Level 2 capable Ghostscript versions accept PostScript files with embedded Type 42 fonts (created, for example, by the Windows PostScript driver).

Native TrueType files: Files in TTF format (as installed under Windows) contain raw TrueType data which a PostScript interpreter cannot directly process. Ghostscript contains some additional code for interpreting raw TrueType files. This code is activated by the "ttfont" makefile option. Since TrueType plays an important role for Windows users, the Windows Ghostscript versions are configured with the "ttfont" feature by default. This means that the Windows TrueType font directory can be configured for use with Ghostscript just as any PostScript font directory. However, Ghostscript only recognizes TTF font files when searching font files via the GS_FONTPATH variable; it's not possible to process TrueType files via the "run" operator. You can work around this with the following instruction:

```
(file.ttf) (r) file .loadttfont
```

Platform fonts on Windows and X11. Ghostscript always needs access to all PostScript fonts used in a document. It rasterizes all the characters itself instead of delegating this task to the operating system, ATM, or the X server (like other programs do). However, to speed up processing, Ghostscript sometimes uses system fonts. This feature is called *platform fonts* and is used only for certain font sizes and horizontal or vertical text. Even so, the PostScript font name must exactly match the system font name.

For small font sizes, platform fonts generally improve screen font representation. In some situations, however, they make it worse – e.g., if PostScript and system font metrics don't match (which results in ugly formatting). Another problem affects fonts with unusual character sets (encodings). In both cases you can turn off platform fonts by launching Ghostscript with the -dNOPLATFONTS option. There is also a special X Window resource to achieve this:

```
Ghostscript*useExternalFonts:false
```

B.3 Building Ghostscript from C Source

Since the C source code of Ghostscript is readily available, you can build an executable version of the interpreter if you have a C compiler for your system (and some experience compiling C programs). This way, you can link in additional drivers that are contained in the Ghostscript distribution but that (due to memory restrictions) are not compiled into the standard versions. More adventurous programmers also have the chance to implement their own extensions to Ghostscript. The following sections will give an overview of the compilation process and the configuration options.

B.3.1 A Small Tour of Ghostscript Files

The Ghostscript source directory contains several hundred files. The compilation may even double this number, so you may well get lost in this multitude of files. The following table lists the most important file types contained in the Ghostscript distribution.

Files	Contents
readme, news	notes on the current version
new-user.txt	overview of Ghostscript
use.txt	information on using Ghostscript
make.txt	notes on compiling Ghostscript
other *.txt	additional documentation on special topics
public	"Aladdin Ghostscript Free Public License" (licensing conditions)
*.1	Unix-style manual pages
*.c, *.h, *.asm	source files
*.mak, *.def, *.rc, *.icx	auxiliary files for building the program

Files	Contents
*.sh, *.bat, *.cmd	scripts and batch files used in the build process; several special applications of Ghostscript
gs_*.ps	initialization files for Ghostscript
pdf_*.ps	initialization files for the PDF interpreter
other *.ps	auxiliary PostScript files and sample programs
Fontmap.*	Fontmap files for several systems

B.3.2 Compiling the Standard Version

Requirements. To build Ghostscript, you need approximately 15 MB disk space. The source is written in ANSI-C suited for most current C compilers. However, you can also use an old Kernighan & Ritchie compiler. The auxiliary program *ansi2knr* converts the source files to K&R syntax before compilation. Another auxiliary program called *genarch* automatically creates an include file which describes hardware and compiler architecture. This includes bit and byte ordering, word size and other system-specific information. Ghostscript can be compiled on MS-DOS, Windows, OS/2, Amiga, many Unix systems, Macintosh, and VMS. The C source is highly portable, so compiling it on new systems shouldn't be much of a problem.

Makefiles. The compilation process is controlled by makefiles which you can adapt as necessary. To improve legibility, the makefiles are split in parts:

gs.mak	Ghostscript "core" source
lib.mak	graphics library
int.mak	interpreter
devs.mak	device drivers
jpeg.mak	JPEG library
libpng.mak	PNG graphics file format library
zlib.mak	compression routines used for the PNG format

All other *.mak files are platform specific makefiles used to configure the development system. The compilation process for different platforms and the supported development systems are described in full detail in the file *make.doc*. The following description is not intended to replace this file, but to give you a jump start.

Compiling on MS-DOS, Windows, OS/2. First decompress the C source from the compressed archives *gs4xxsr1.zip* and *gs4xxsr2.zip*. The files in the other archives (*jpeg_6a.zip, lpng089c.zip,* and *zlib102.zip)* contain additional libraries used by Ghostscript. They are stored in subdirectories of the Ghostscript directory. The *-d* option of pkunzip creates the directory *gs4.xx* (*x:* represents the CD-ROM drive letter, 4.xx denotes the Ghostscript version number):

```
pkunzip -d x:\software\gs\compress\gs4xxsr1.zip
pkunzip -d x:\software\gs\compress\gs4xxsr2.zip
cd gs4.xx
mkdir jpeg-6a
cd jpeg-6a
pkunzip x:\software\gs\compress\jpeg_6a.zip
cd ..
mkdir libpng
cd libpng
pkunzip x:software\gs\compress\lpng089c.zip
cd ..
mkdir zlib
cd zlib
pkunzip x:software\gs\compress\zlib102.zip
```

The Ghostscript distribution contains makefiles for the Microsoft, Borland, Watcom, and other C compilers (see make.doc). For example, to create the 32-bit Windows version of Ghostscript using the Borland Compiler, you first have to create the makefile:

```
echo !include "bcwin32.mak" >makefile
```

Next, you can change some settings in *bcwin32.mak*, e.g., compiler and Ghostscript paths, optimizations for 386/486 CPUs or FPU, assembler accelerator modules, or debugging options. Finally, launch *make*. In an intermediate step you have to manually start the Windows program *genarch* to create a system specific include file.

Compiling on Unix. Decompress the C source for Ghostscript and the JPEG, PNG, and ZLIB libraries from the compressed tar archives into a suitable directory. The tar commands creates the gs4.xx directory and three subdirectories:

```
gunzip -c /cdrom/software/gs/compress/gs4xxsrc.tgz | tar xvf -
cd gs4.xx
gunzip -c /cdrom/software/gs/compress/jpeg_6a.tgz | tar xvf -
gunzip -c /cdrom/software/gs/compress/lpng089c.tgz | tar xvf -
gunzip -c /cdrom/software/gs/compress/zlib102.tgz | tar xvf -
mv libpng-0.89c libpng
mv zlib-1.0.2 zlib
```

The mv commands are necessary because the tar archives include directory names containing the version numbers.

The Ghostscript distribution contains makefiles for several operating systems and compilers (ANSI-C, Kernighan&Ritchie, and GNU-C). Choose the appropriate makefile from *.mak* and create a symbolic link with the following command (assuming you use the GNU compiler):

```
ln -s unix-gcc.mak makefile
```

Use *unixansi.mak* or *unix-cc.mak*, respectively, for an ANSI or K&R compiler. On some systems you have to adapt the search path for X11 specific include files and additional libraries. These are controlled by the XINCLUDE und LDFLAGS variables in the makefile which you can change before launching make. By changing the *prefix* variable in the makefile you can adapt the install directory. Now compile and install Ghostscript with the command

```
make install
```

Consult the make.txt file if you have trouble with the build process or experience compilation errors. The install process needs *root* permission on most systems. After compiling Ghostscript, the install command copies the executable program to */usr/local/bin* and the auxiliary files to */usr/local/share/ghostscript/4.xx*. To complete the installation, you have to install fonts for Ghostscript as described in the next section.

Now you should install and compile the Ghostview source. This is accomplished with the commands

```
gunzip -c gsview15.tgz | tar xvf -
cd ghostview-1.5
xmkmf
make
make install
```

If your system doesn't have the *xmkmf* program, you have to adapt the Ghostview makefile manually (this shouldn't be too hard if you have ever worked with makefiles).

Compiling on the Macintosh. In addition to the source code in MS-DOS or Unix format, you need the archive *gsmacsrc.hqx* to compile Ghostscript for the Mac. This archive contains some additional Macintosh-specific files. The source files end up in several folders. You'll find an overview of the build process in the *Mac GS Viewer Manual* (part of the Ghostscript files) and some hints for compiling with the MPW or CodeWarrior compilers in the file *worksheet*.

Compiling on other systems. The file *readme* contains some remarks on Ghostscript ports to other systems, including VMS, Amiga, Atari ST, Acorn Archimedes and NEXTSTEP.

B.3.3 Configuration Options and Drivers

You can adjust the Ghostscript makefile to build a version that suits your needs with several extensions and an individual assortment of drivers. The most important options are PostScript Level 1, PostScript Level 2, and PDF. Standard configurations for most systems include PostScript Level 2, and on 32 bit systems additionally PDF. You can use the FEATURE_DEVS variable in the makefile to control the interpreter's configuration.

The second configuration option relates to the set of included drivers. Since it is not possible to load Ghostscript drivers dynamically at runtime, you have to choose the driver set when building the program. In doing so, you trade functionality for memory efficiency: If all available drivers were included in Ghostscript, the program would need far too much memory. For this reason the standard configuration for each platform contains only the most important screen, printer, and file format drivers for the respective platform. You can check the list of available Ghostscript drivers using the command line

```
gs -?
```

You can also obtain the driver list with the following commands at the Ghostscript prompt:

```
devicenames ==
```

or

```
devicedict {pop ==} forall
```

If you want Ghostscript to use a driver for which C source is included in the distribution but which is not compiled into the executable by default, you have to build your own version by using a modified makefile.

Many Ghostscript drivers have been contributed by users and later became part of the Ghostscript distribution. If you want to write a new driver, read the remarks on Ghostscript/driver interaction in *drivers.doc*.

In addition to the file format drivers listed in the table below, previous Ghostscript versions contained one for the GIF graphics format. In reaction to the licensing problems around the LZW compression technique used in GIF, Peter Deutsch dropped support for this format from the Ghostscript distribution. If you have to create GIF files you can integrate the GIF driver from an older release. However, it's easier to render to another graphics file format (e.g., TIFF, or PBM) and convert it to GIF.

The table below lists all display, printer, and file format drivers available for Ghostscript 4.01. Each line lists the name of the device or format and the short name of the driver. The last column in the table tells you on which of the following platforms the particular driver is part of the standard configuration: MS-DOS 386 (D), Windows 32-bit (W), OS/2 (O), Unix (U),and Mac (M). The driver name is used in the makefile as well as for selecting a driver within Ghostscript. The makefile variables DEVICE_DEVS1 to DEVICE_DEVS15 contain the names of the drivers to be included in the program. If you don't supply a driver name at startup, Ghostscript uses the first driver in its list (which is a display driver on all platforms).

List of Ghostscript drivers available with version 4.01

Display drivers		
ATI Wonder SuperVGA, 256 colors	atiw	D
AT&T 3b1/Unixpc monochrome display	att3b1	–
Borland Graphics Interface	bgi	–
CRT sixels, e.g. VT240 compatible terminals	sxlcrt	–
EGA 640x350, 16 colors	ega	D
Hercules Graphics Display	herc	–
Linux PC with VGALIB	vgalib	–
Linux PC with VGALIB, 256 colors	lvga256	–
Macintosh window (QuickDraw)	mac	M
Microsoft Windows 3.1 DLL	mswindll	–
OS/2 DLL bitmap	os2dll	–
OS/2 Presentation Manager	os2pm	O
Private Eye display	pe	–
Sony Microsystems monochrome display	sonyfb	–
SunView window system	sunview	–
SuperVGA with S3 Chip 86C911	s3vga	–
SuperVGA 800x600, 16 colors	svga16	D
SuperVGA with Tseng Labs ET3000/4000 Chip, 256 colors	tseng	D
SuperVGA with VESA driver	vesa	–
Trident SuperVGA, 256 colors	tvga	D
VGA 640x480, 16 colors	vga	D
X Window System (X11), release 4 and higher	x11	U
X Window System as alpha device	x11alpha	U
X Window System as CMYK device, 1 bit per color	x11cmyk	U

List of Ghostscript drivers available with version 4.01

X Window System as b/w device	x11mono	U

Printer drivers

Apple Dot Matrix printer (also for Imagewriter)	appledmp	–
Apple Imagewriter, high resolution	iwhi	–
Apple Imagewriter, low resolution	iwlo	–
Apple Imagewriter LQ, 320 x 216 dpi	iwlq	–
CalComp raster format	ccr	–
Canon BubbleJet BJ10e	bj10e	DWOU
Canon BubbleJet BJ200	bj200	DWOU
Canon Color BubbleJet BJC-600 and BJC-4000	bjc600	DWOU
Canon Color BubbleJet BJC-800	bjc800	DWOU
Canon LBP-8II laser printer	lbp8	OW
Canon LIPS III laser printer with CaPSL	lips3	–
Mitsubishi CP50 color printer	cp50	–
DEC LA50	la50	–
DEC LA70	la70	–
DEC LA70 with low resolution extensions	la70t	–
DEC LA75	la75	–
DEC LA75plus	la75plus	–
DEC LJ250 Companion color printer	lj250	OW
DEC LJ250, alternate driver	declj250	OW
DEC LN03	ln03	–
Epson AP3250	ap3250	–
Epson-compatible dot matrix printer (9 or 24 pin)	epson	DWO
Epson-compatible 9-pin, intermediate resolution	eps9mid	OW
Epson-compatible 9-pin, triple resolution	eps9high	DWO
Epson LQ-2550 and Fujitsu 3400/2400/1200 color printers	epsonc	OW
Epson Stylus Color	stcolor	WOM
Epson Stylus 800	st800	WO
HP DesignJet 650C	dnj650c	–
HP DeskJet and DeskJet Plus	deskjet	DWOU
HP DeskJet 500	djet500	DWOU
HP DeskJet 500C, 1 bit per pixel	cdeskjet	DWOU
HP DeskJet 500C, 24 bit per pixel, also for DeskJet 540C	cdjcolor	DWOU
HP DeskJet 500C (same as cdjcolor)	cdj500	–
HP DeskJet 500C (not for 550C/560C), alternate driver	djet500c	OW
HP DeskJet 500C b/w, also for DeskJet 510, 520, 540C	cdjmono	DWOU
HP DeskJet 550C/560C	cdj550	DWOUM
HP LaserJet	laserjet	DWOU

List of Ghostscript drivers available with version 4.01

HP LaserJet Plus	ljetplus	DWOU
HP LaserJet IId/IIp/III* with TIFF compression	ljet2p	DWOU
HP LaserJet III* with delta row compression	ljet3	DWOU
HP LaserJet IIID with duplex function	ljet3d	–
HP LaserJet 4, 600 dpi	ljet4	DWOU
HP LaserJet 4 with Floyd-Steinberg dithering	lj4dith	–
HP PaintJet XL	pj	DWOU
HP PaintJet XL, alternate driver	pjetxl	–
HP PaintJet XL color printer	pjxl	DWOU
HP PaintJet XL color printer, alternate driver	paintjet	–
HP PaintJet XL 300 color printer, also for PaintJet 1200C	pjxl300	DWOU
HP 2563B line printer	lp2563	–
IBM Proprinter, 9 pin	ibmpro	DWO
IBM Jetprinter inkjet color printer (Modell #3852)	jetp3852	OW
Imagen ImPress	imagen	–
C. Itoh M8510	m8510	OW
Microsoft Windows system printer driver (DDB)	mswinprn	W
Microsoft Windows system printer driver (DIB)	mswinpr2	W
Mitsubishi CP50 color printer	cp50	–
NEC P6/P6+/P60, 360 x 360 DPI	necp6	OW
OCE 9050	oce9050	–
Okidata IBM-compatible dot matrix printer	okiibm	–
Okidata MicroLine 182	oki182	–
OS/2 system printer driver (only for OS/2 DLL)	os2prn	–
Ricoh 4081 laser printer	r4081	OW
Sony Microsystems NWP533 laser printer	nwp533	–
StarJet 48 inkjet printer	sj48	–
SPARCprinter	sparc	–
Tektronix 4693d color printer, 2 bits per RGB component	t4693d2	OW
Tektronix 4693d color printer, 4 bits per RGB component	t4693d4	OW
Tektronix 4693d color printer, 8 bits per RGB component	t4693d8	OW
Tektronix 4695/4696 inkjet plotter	tek4696	OW
Xerox XES 2700, 3700, 4045, and others	xes	–

Fax and file format drivers

BMP monochrome	bmpmono	WO
BMP 4 bits (EGA/VGA)	bmp16	WO
BMP 8 bits	bmp256	WO
BMP 24 bits	bmp16m	WO
CGM b/w, low level output only	cgmmono	–

List of Ghostscript drivers available with version 4.01

CGM 8 bits, low level output only	cgm8	–
CGM 24 bits, low level output only	cgm24	–
CIF file format for VLSI	cif	–
DigiBoard DigiFAX, high resolution	dfaxhigh	O
DigiBoard DigiFAX, low resolution	dfaxlow	O
Fax group 3, with EOLs, no header or EOD	faxg3	U
Fax group 3 2-D, with EOLs, no header or EOD	faxg32d	U
Fax group 4, with EOLs, no header or EOD	faxg4	U
ImageMagick MIFF format, 24 bit color (RLE compressed)	miff24	–
MGR devices, 1 bit monochrome	mgrmono	–
MGR devices, 2 bits gray scale	mgrgray2	–
MGR devices, 4 bits gray scale	mgrgray4	–
MGR devices, 8 bits gray scale	mgrgray8	–
MGR devices, 4 bits color	mgr4	–
MGR devices, 8 bits color	mgr8	–
PCX monochrome	pcxmono	DWOUM
PCX, 8 bits gray scale	pcxgray	DWOUM
PCX, 4 bits color	pcx16	DWOUM
PCX, 8 bits color	pcx256	DWOUM
PCX, 24 bits color	pcx24b	DWOUM
PDF (Portable Document Format)	pdfwrite	WU
Plain bits (raw format), monochrome	bit	DWOU
Plain bits (raw format), RGB	bitrgb	DWOU
Plain bits (raw format), CMYK	bitcmyk	DWOU
PBM (Portable Bitmap), ASCII format	pbm	UM
PBM, raw format	pbmraw	UM
PGM (Portable Graymap), ASCII format	pgm	UM
PGM, raw format	pgmraw	UM
PGM, optimizing to PBM ASCII if possible	pgnm	U
PGM, optimizing to PBM raw if possible	pgnmraw	U
PNG (Portable Network Graphics), monochrome	pngmono	WOU
PNG (Portable Network Graphics), 8 bits gray scale	pnggray	WOU
PNG (Portable Network Graphics), 4 bits color	png16	WOU
PNG (Portable Network Graphics), 8 bits color	png256	WOU
PNG (Portable Network Graphics), 24 bits color	png16m	WOU
PPM (Portable Pixmap), ASCII format (RGB)	ppm	UM
PPM, raw format (RGB)	ppmraw	UM
PPM, optimizing to PGM ASCII or PBM ASCII if possible	pnm	U
PPM, optimizing to PGM raw or PBM raw if possible	pnmraw	U
PostScript Level 1, monochrome bitmap	psmono	DWOU

List of Ghostscript drivers available with version 4.01

SGI RGB pixmap format	sgirgb	–
TIFF b/w, CCITT RLE 1-dim (fax group 3 without EOLs)	tiffcrle	DWOU
TIFF b/w, fax group 3 (with EOLs)	tiffg3	DWOU
TIFF b/w, fax group 3 2-D	tiffg32d	DWOU
TIFF b/w, fax group 4	tiffg4	DWOU
TIFF b/w, LZW (compression tag 5)	tifflzw	DWOUM
TIFF b/w, PackBits (compression tag 32773)	tiffpack	DWOUM
TIFF 12 bit RGB color (no compression)	tiff12nc	DWOU
TIFF 24 bit RGB color (no compression)	tiff24nc	DWOU

B.4 Ghostscript Primer

This section is meant to give you a jump start into directly using Ghostscript. If you use GSview or Ghostview to drive Ghostscript, you only have to configure the appropriate Ghostscript call; the rest is handled by the frontend.

B.4.1 Launching Ghostscript

In the following examples, *gs* always represents the name of the Ghostscript executable file. Depending on your platform, the actual name may vary.

File search path. First you have to make sure that Ghostscript finds its initialization and font files. When searching for files without an absolute file name, Ghostscript uses the following search order:

- ▸ The current directory.
- ▸ The directories listed at the *-I* command line option, e.g., on MS-DOS, Windows or OS/2:

      gs -Id:/gs4.xx;d:/gs4.xx/fonts

  or on Unix:

      gs -I/usr/local/lib/ghostscript:/usr/local/psfonts

- ▸ The directories listed in the GS_LIB environment variable.
- ▸ Predefined directories selected at build time using the GS_LIB_DEFAULT makefile variable (*C:\gs* on MS-DOS, Windows or OS/2; */usr/local/lib/ghostscript/4.xx* on Unix).

Watch the tiger. Ghostscript accepts the names of the PostScript files to display or print:

    gs file1.ps file2.ps ...

The interpreter processes the files one after the other. Then, Ghost-script prompts for PostScript commands:

```
GS>
```

At this prompt you can issue PostScript commands. If it is clumsy or uncommon to pass file names on the command line (e.g., on Windows), you can open files with the *run* command at the prompt. Try the *tiger.ps* sample file included in the Ghostscript distribution:

```
GS>(file.ps) run
```

On the Mac, it's even easier to use the "File", "Open" menu command.

Note concerning MS-DOS path names: Since the backslash "\" escapes the next character in PostScript strings, you have to use double backslashes in path names. However, a single Unix-style slash "/" also works as a separator in path names, for example

```
GS>(c:/gs/tiger.ps)run
```

The following command exits the interpreters:

```
GS>quit
```

Alternatively, you can append *-c quit* to the command line.

Selecting a driver. Usually, Ghostscript uses the first driver in its internal list (configured at build time). This driver outputs to the screen in the standard configurations on all operating systems. You can select another driver on the command line:

```
gs -sDEVICE=laserjet file.ps -c quit
```

This instructs Ghostscript to produces output for the particular device or file format (*laserjet* in the example above). Using the following commands at the Ghostscript prompt, you can change the driver at any time:

```
GS>(epson) selectdevice
GS>(file.ps) run
```

For printers with multiple resolutions you can also set the desired print resolution using the *-r* option:

```
gs -sDEVICE=epson -r60x72 -c quit
```

Redirecting printer data. On MS-DOS, Ghostscript sends printer data directly to the parallel port. On Unix, the printer data is sent to a temporary file. You can also redirect it to your own print file:

```
gs -sDEVICE=laserjet -sOutputFile=laserjet.prn file.ps -c quit
```

If the output file name contains the variable *%d* (e.g. *laser%d.prn*), Ghostscript produces one output file per page and replaces the *%d* with the page number. On Unix, you can also redirect the data to a pipe using the "\|" syntax:

```
gs -sDEVICE=laserjet -sOutputFile=\|lp file.ps -c quit
```

Finally, Ghostscript sends the printer data to its standard output with the following command line (the *-q* option suppresses messages):

```
gs -q -sOutputFile=- file.ps -c quit
```

On Windows and OS/2 the easiest way to redirect printer data is to use GSview. This frontend presents a menu for choosing the printer interface *after* Ghostscript rendered the document.

Page size.   Ghostscript uses U.S. letter size by default. To change this, use a text editor to locate the following line in the initialization file *gs_init.ps*:

```
% (a4) /PAPERSIZE where { pop pop } { /PAPERSIZE exch def }
    ifelse
```

In this line, remove the "%" comment sign at the beginning to use A4 format. You can also replace the "a4" in parentheses by any other known format. A list of all formats known to Ghostscript (and their dimensions) can be found in the *gs_statd.ps* file. Alternatively, you can change the page size on the Ghostscript command line:

```
gs -sPAPERSIZE=legal file.ps
```

B.4.2 Printing with Ghostscript

Printing on MS-DOS.   To reduce memory problems, you should use *gs386.exe* if possible. The following longish call processes a PostScript file for output on a Laserjet 4 printer connected to the parallel interface:

```
gs386 -q -dNOPAUSE -sDEVICE=ljet4 file.ps -c quit
```

The *-c quit* option is used to quit Ghostscript after the PostScript file is completely rendered. Due to the *-q* option, Ghostscript itself works quietly. However, the 386 MS-DOS extender still presents its copyright banner. You can suppress it with an environment variable:

```
set DOS4G=quiet
```

If your printer is not connected to the parallel interface or you want to bring the printer data to another machine, you can redirect it to a file:

```
gs386 -q -dNOPAUSE -sDEVICE=ljet4 -sOutputFile=ljet.prn
     file.ps -c quit
```

To print this file, send it to the printer interface with the *copy* command:

```
copy /b ljet.prn lpt1:
```

The */b* (binary) option is important because otherwise the copy command may not completely transfer the printer data.

Printing on Windows 3.x.   In Windows, it is easiest to use GSview for printing with Ghostscript. After installing this Ghostscript frontend correctly, you can select a PostScript file using "File", "Print...". In the subsequent menus you can select printer driver, resolution (if the printer supports multiple resolutions), and – in the case of DSC compatible files – the page range you want to print. When Ghostscript has finished processing the file, you can select the printer interface for forwarding the data in a dialog box.

Printing on Windows 95 and NT.   For the newer systems of the Windows family you can use the methods described above for MS-DOS and Windows 3.x. Additionally, you can select a printer queue using its UNC name:

```
gswin32 -q -dNOPAUSE -sDEVICE=ljet4 file.ps
    -sOutputFile="\\spool\<printer name>" -c quit
```

This spools the printer data to the given printer queue. Using the *-sOutputFile="\\spool"* option instructs Ghostscript to present a dialog box in which you can select the desired printer queue or interface.

Printing on Unix.   In Unix it's possible to integrate Ghostscript in the printing process seamlessly. However, some experience with Unix systems administration is required. The variety of available Unix derivatives doesn't really simplify the task of describing the integration of a PostScript emulation for printers. The following notes are not supposed to be a complete description, but should help you get started.

Assuming other system components (especially spooler and backend) are already set up correctly and are able to transfer binary data to the printer unmodified, you can manually use Ghostscript for printing:

```
gs -q -dNOPAUSE -sDEVICE=ljet4 -sOutputFile=\|lp file.ps
    -c quit
```

You can find hints on integrating Ghostscript in systems with a printcap database in the file *unix-lpr.doc*. The accompanying shell script *lprsetup.sh* automatically creates some necessary directories and links as well as printcap entries. Use a text editor to adapt the list of device drivers in this script that Ghostscript is supposed to use. Obviously, these drivers must be compiled into the Ghostscript executable. You can also set up additional printcap filters with *lprsetup.sh*. By default, it creates an input filter consisting of a shell script with the actual Ghostscript call.

After executing lprsetup.sh, follow the instructions in *unix-lpr.doc*, i.e., create some links as indicated in the file, integrate the generated *printcap.insert* file into the system printcap, and adjust the new entries to your local setup (serial interface parameters, etc.). The */usr/local/lib/ghostscript/filt* directory contains several links to the unix-lpr.sh file. In this file you have to add the *-I* option if you didn't install Ghostscript in the standard directories.

On System V, Release 4, and related systems you can define print filters for specific file types. The spooler launches these filters for printing on devices which are not supported directly. To define Ghostscript as a filter, change to the directory */etc/lp/fd* and create a file for the printer, say *ljet_ps.fd*:

```
Input types: postscript,ps
Output types: simple
Command: /usr/local/bin/gs -sDEVICE=ljet4 -q -sOutputFile=- -
```

Integrate this filter in the spool system:

```
lpfilter -f ljet_ps -F /etc/lp/fd/ljet_ps.fd
```

To print a PostScript file, simply declare the file type on the command line:

```
lp -T postscript tiger.ps
```

For serial connections, make sure the backend doesn't change the printer data by using the stty options

```
-opost -cs8 -parenb
```

B.4.3 Ghostscript as Viewer for a WWW Browser

World Wide Web browsers and many E-mail programs classify files according to MIME types (*Multipurpose Internet Mail Extension*). Post-Script files use a MIME type of

```
application/postscript
```

MIME types and corresponding viewers are generally configured in a configuration file or menu. The details vary according to the particular program. Let's take a look at the Windows version of the well-known Netscape WWW browser as an example:

- ▶ Launch Netscape Navigator.
- ▶ Choose "Options", "General Preferences..." and the submenu "Helpers".
- ▶ For the MIME type *application/postscript* enter *ai, ps, eps* in the extensions field (if the entry doesn't exist already). Check "Launch the Application" for "Action" and enter the path of GSview, Ghostview oder Mac GS Viewer as appropriate, e.g., *c:\gs\gsview32.exe*.
- ▶ Click "OK" and "Options", "Save Options".

Unix systems generally use the *.mailcap* file for configuring MIME types. Use the following entry for Ghostview (see below for the *-safer* option):

```
application/postscript; ghostview -safer  %s
```

The relation between MIME types and file extensions is controlled by the *.mime.types* file. If the following line doesn't already exist, add it to the *.mime.types* file:

```
application/postscript   ai, ps, eps
```

Like PostScript, you can also configure Ghostscript and GSview as helper application for PDF files. Proceed as above, using the pdf suffix and a MIME type of

```
application/pdf
```

Note that Ghostview doesn't yet directly support PDF.

PostScript files and security. PostScript – being a full-blown programming language – contains operators for modifying and deleting files. This opens a security gap when downloading unknown files. In the worst case, a file pretending to be a harmless PostScript image may delete files from your local hard disk – possibly even with *root* permission! Although there are no known cases of such "trojan horses", you should protect yourself against this kind of attack. Ghostscript's *-dSAFER* option disables critical file operators; the interpreter refuses to open files other than read-only. GSview launches Ghostscript with this option by default, Ghostview for Unix uses the option if launched with the *-safer* option itself.

B.5 Ghostscript Reference Section

B.5.1 Command Line Options

On all platforms, Ghostscript evaluates several command line options used to control the interpreter:

```
-h
-?
--help
```
These options cause Ghostscript to print a brief help message and a list of available (i.e., built-in) device drivers on screen.

```
@<filename>
```
Ghostscript reads the specified file and treats its contents the same as the command line. This makes it easier to use command line options on Windows or to use command lines longer than 128 characters on MS-DOS.

```
-- <file.ps> arg1 ...
-+ <file.ps> arg1 ...
```
Ghostscript treats the file name as usual but stores the remaining arguments in an array named ARGUMENTS in userdict. This way Post-Script programs can access options and command line arguments.

```
-@ <filename> arg1 ...
```
Same as -- and -+, but expands arguments from *argfile*.

```
-c tokens ...
```
Interprets arguments up to the next "-" as PostScript code and executes them. Each argument must be exactly one token.

```
-Dname=token
-dname=token
```
Defines a name in systemdict with the given definition (equivalent to `/name token def`). This option is mainly used for special names (see below).

```
-Dname
-dname
```
Defines *name* in systemdict with a value of *true*.

```
-Sname=string
-sname=string
```
Defines a name in systemdict with the given string definition (equivalent to `/name (string) def`).

```
-q
```
(*quiet*) Suppress normal startup messages.

```
-f<filename>
```
Execute the given file, even if its name begins with a "-" or "@".
-f provides a way to terminate the token list for *-c*.

```
-g<number1>x<number2>
```
Equivalent to -dDEVICEWIDTH=*number1* and -dDEVICEHEIGHT=*number2* (see below).

```
-r<number>
-r<number1>x<number2>
```

Equivalent to -dDEVICEXRESOLUTION=*number1* and -dDEVICEYRESO-LUTION=*number2* (see below). This is intended for devices that support different horizontal and vertical resolutions, especially dot matrix printers.

```
-u<name>
```

Undefines a name, cancelling *-d* or *-s*.

```
-I<directories>
```

Add a list of directories to the search path for initalization and font files. Multiple directories are separated with a semicolon ";" (MS-DOS, Windows, OS/2) or colon ":" (Unix).

```
-P
```

Ghostscript first searches the current directory for library files. This is the default.

```
-P-
```

Ghostscript doesn't search the current directory for library files, but uses the search path only.

```
-
```

Instructs Ghostscript to read standard input from file or pipe (instead of from the keyboard). Ghostscript reads and processes data from standard input and exits. Note that it's not possible to read PDF files from standard input.

Special PostScript names used as switches.   The *use.doc* file contains some more options for debugging Ghostscript. A couple of names with special meanings is being interpreted by the PostScript code in Ghostscript's initialization files. They work in a similar way to command line options:

```
-dDEVICEWIDTH=<number>
-dDEVICEHEIGHT=<number>
```

Sets width and height of the device, respectively (in pixels).

```
-dDEVICEXRESOLUTION=<number>
-dDEVICEYRESOLUTION=<number>
```

Sets the device horizontal resp. vertical device resolution in dpi.

```
-dCOLORSCREEN
```

On devices with at least 150 dpi resolution forces the use of separate halftone screens with different angles for the process colors (this produces the best-quality output).

`-dCOLORSCREEN=0`

Uses separate screens with the same frequency and angle for the process colors.

`-dCOLORSCREEN=false`

Forces the use of a single binary screen. If COLORSCREEN is not specified, the default is to use separate screens with different angles if the device has fewer than 5 bits per color.

`-dDISKFONTS`

Causes character outlines in fonts to be loaded from disk on demand only. This slows down text rendering but increases the number of fonts which may be loaded into RAM. This technique is mainly intended for low-memory systems such as MS-DOS.

`-dDITHERPPI=<lpi>`

forces all devices to be considered high-resolution, and forces use of a halftone screen or screens with lpi lines per inch, disregarding the actual device resolution. Reasonable values for lpi are N/5 to N/20, where N is the resolution in dots per inch.

`-dFirstPage=<n>`

Starts interpreting on the given page of a PDF document.

`-dFIXEDMEDIA`

Causes the media size to be fixed after initialization. Pages are scaled or rotated if necessary.

`-dFIXEDRESOLUTION`

Causes the output resolution to be fixed.

`-dLastPage=<n>`

Stops interpreting after the given page of a PDF document.

`-dLOCALFONTS`

This is a compatibility option for certain obsolete fonts. This option makes Ghostscript load type 1 fonts always to local VM.

`-dNOBIND`

Disables the *bind* operator (useful for debugging).

`-dNOCACHE`

Disables the font cache (useful for debugging).

`-dNOCIE`

substitutes DeviceGray and DeviceRGB for CIEBasedA and CIEBased-ABC color spaces respectively (useful on very slow systems where color accuracy is less important).

`-dNODISPLAY`

Suppresses normal initialization of the output device. This is useful for debugging and also for PostScript converters that don't produce any screen or printer output (e.g., *ps2ai*).

`-dNOFONTMAP`

Suppresses loading of the Fontmap file.

`-dNOGC`

Disables the level 2 *garbage collector* (useful for debugging).

`-dNOPAUSE`

Disables the prompt and pause at the end of each page. This is useful for driving Ghostscript from another program.

`-dNOPLATFONTS`

Disables platform fonts for X Windows or Microsoft Windows (see Section B.2.4).

`-dNOPROMPT`

Disables the prompt (but not the pause) at the end of each page. This prevents text and graphics output from being mixed on PC displays.

`-dORIENT1`

Exchanges the meaning of the values 0 and 1 for indicating page orientation with *setpageparams*. This is needed for the PostScript code of certain applications.

`-dSAFER`

Disables the PostScript operators for writing or deleting disk files. This is intended for using Ghostscript as viewer for a Web browser in a secure mode.

`-dSHORTERRORS`

Brackets several error messages with %%[and]%% (as Adobe Interpreters do).

`-dWRITESYSTEMDICT`

Systemdict remains writable. This is necessary for some utility programs that must bypass normal PostScript access protection, such as *font2c* and *pcharstr*.

`-sDEVICE=<device>`

Select the initial output device driver.

`-sFONTMAP=<filename1>:<filename2>...`

Defines one or more file names for the font file mapping table. Several file names are separated by a semicolon ";" under Unix and a colon ":" under Windows.

`-sFONPATH=<dirname1>:<dirname2>...`

Defines one or more directory names to be searched for font definitions. Several file names are separated by a semicolon ";" under Unix
and a colon ":" under Windows.

`-sOutputFile=<filename>`

Selects an output file name or pipe. If the file name contains the characters "%d", Ghostscript replaces the "%d" with the actual page number and creates one file for each page, e.g., *page%d.prn* yields
page1.prn, page2.prn and so on.

On Windows 95 and Windows NT you can use UNC path names:
`-sOutputFile="\\spool\printername"` sends the output to the named
printer queue. If the printer name is missing, Ghostscript prompts
for the name of the (local) printer.

On Unix, you can also redirect the output to another program via
pipe: `-sOutputFile=\|lp`. The special name "-" for the output file in-
structs Ghostscript to send the data to its standard output.

`-sPAPERSIZE=<papersize>`

Selects a page size, e.g., *a4*. The file *gs_statd.ps* contains a list of
supported page size names.

`-sPSFile=<file.ps>`

Defines the output file name for PDF to PostScript conversion.

`-sSUBSTFONT=<fontname>`

Selects the named font as substitute for all missing fonts. This
disables Ghostscript's normal font substitution mechanism.

B.5.2 Environment Variables

`GS_DEVICE=<device>`
Defines the initial output device driver.

`GS_FONTPATH=<path>`
Specifies a list of directories that should be scanned for fonts at startup (see Section B.2.4).

`GS_LIB=<path>`
Search path for initialization and font files.

`GS_OPTIONS=<options>`
Defines a list of command line arguments to be processed before the
ones specified on the command line. All command line options are
also allowed in this environment variable.

`TEMP=<directory>`
Directory name for temporary files.

```
DOS4G=quiet
```
Suppresses the usual startup message of the DOS extender for the
386 MS-DOS version.

B.5.3 X Window System Resources

Ghostscript evaluates several X resources under the program name
ghostscript and the class name *Ghostscript*. You can use X resources to
define user preferences or to activate bug workarounds for several X
servers. In the *use.doc* file you can find more information on resources. The table below lists all resources together with their default
values.

Name	Class	Default value
background	Background	white
foreground	Foreground	black
borderColor	BorderColor	black
borderWidth	BorderWidth	1
geometry	Geometry	NULL
xResolution	Resolution	(calculated from
yResolution	Resolution	screen size)
useExternalFonts	UseExternalFonts	true
useScalableFonts	UseScalableFonts	true
logExternalFonts	LogExternalFonts	false
externalFontTolerance	ExternalFontTolerance	10.0
palette	Palette	Color
maxGrayRamp	MaxGrayRamp	128
maxRGBRamp	MaxRGBRamp	5
maxDynamicColors	MaxDynamicColors	256
useBackingPixmap	UseBackingPixmap	true
useXPutImage	UseXPutImage	true
useXSetTile	UseXSetTile	true
regularFonts	RegularFonts	(see use.doc)
symbolFonts	SymbolFonts	(see use.doc)
dingbatFonts	DingbatFonts	(see use.doc)

As an example, the resources below select a resolution of 72 dpi (independent of actual screen size and resolution) and disable platform
fonts:

```
Ghostscript*useExternalFonts:   false
Ghostscript*xResolution: 72
Ghostscript*yResolution: 72
```

If you want Ghostscript to use the same resource settings every time, it's best to put the resources into a file and load it with the *xrdb* program.

B.5.4 Configuration Error Messages

Ghostscript issues the usual PostScript error messages (see Chapter 2). Additionally, there are some messages relating to Ghostscript installation or configuration errors instead of PostScript errors.

`/undefinedfilename in (Fontmap)`
Ghostscript can't find the *Fontmap* file, and the GS_FONTPATH environment variable isn't set. Install a Fontmap file or set GS_FONTPATH to point to an appropriate font directory.

`Can't find (or open) initialization file gs_init.ps.`
Ghostscript can't find its main initialization file. Use the *-I* option or the GS_LIB enviroment variable to point Ghostscript to the directory containing the gs_*.ps files.

`Can't find (or can't open) font file xxx`
The Fontmap file contains a font file entry for a nonexistent file or a file that Ghostscript can't open. Under Unix, check the file permissions.

`Substituting font Courier for xxx`
Ghostscript can't find a requested font and substitutes for it with another font. Processing continues.

`Unable to load default font xxx! Giving up.`
Ghostscript can't find the default font file and hence isn't able to do text output at all. Therefore processing stops. Check the font configuration.

`Can't find library 'libXt.so.6'`
Unix versions of Ghostscript generally are linked dynamically. For this reason, several libraries must be accessible at runtime. Use the *ldd* command to find out which libraries are needed, locate these on your hard disk, and set the LD_LIBRARY_PATH environment variable appropriately. Another solution is to link Ghostscript statically.

`Unknown device: xxx`
Ghostscript has been launched with an unknown device driver name. If you want to use drivers which are not available in the standard configuration, you have to recompile and link Ghostscript with the necessary drivers.

```
gs: Interpreter revision (401) does not match gs_init.ps
revision (353).
```
Ghostscript found an initialization file that doesn't match the program version. Make sure the GS_LIB environment variable or the *-I*
command line option don't point to an obsolete Ghostscript version
on your hard disk.

B.6 More Ghostscript Applications

Many file format conversions and other special applications are possible with the help of Ghostscript drivers and auxiliary programs.
Some of these applications are not PostScript interpreter tasks at first
sight. The descriptions in the following sections provide a summary
of the most important of these applications. Usually you can find
more detailed information in the appropriate documentation or
source files (*.txt, *.ps, *.c).

B.6.1 Graphics File Formats

Displaying and printing graphics file formats. The utility programs
viewgif.ps, viewjpeg.ps, viewpbm.ps, and viewpcx.ps – written in
PostScript – display or print raster graphic files in the GIF, JPEG, PBM,
or PCX file formats without converting them to PostScript. Launch
Ghostscript with the appropriate utility and load a graphics file using
one of the procedures viewGIF, viewJPEG, viewpbm, or viewpcx, e.g.,

```
gs viewjpeg.ps
GS>(file.jpg) viewJPEG
```

Converting PostScript to raster graphics formats. Several file format
drivers enable Ghostscript to convert PostScript files to TIFF, PBM,
PCX, BMP, etc., given the appropriate driver has been compiled into
the Ghostscript executable. The Ghostscript call contains the name
of the driver and (optionally) the resolution. For example, to create a
600 dpi bitmapped TIFF version of a file, use the following command:

```
gs -sDEVICE=tiffpack -r600 -sOutputFile=page%d.tif file.ps
  -c quit
```

Ghostscripts replaces the "%d" variable in the filename with the actual page number (*page1.tif, page2.tif* etc.). By default, the TIFF drivers
use a resolution of 204 x 196 dpi (standard fax resolution).

Enhanced rendering with anti-aliasing. A technique called anti-
aliasing tries to improve text or graphics rendering by making use of
gray levels for smoothing. Anti-aliasing is implemented in a couple

of Ghostscript drivers: Windows and OS/2 display drivers and the Portable Graymap Format (PGM) und Portable Pixmap Format (PPM) file format driver. To make use of anti-aliasing, the bit depth must be at least 8 bits. The following command line can be used to convert a PostScript file to PGM with anti-aliasing:

```
gs -sDEVICE=pgm -dTextAlphaBits=4 -sOutputFile=file.ppm
    file.ps -c quit
```

Possible alpha values are 1 (=no anti-aliasing), 2, and 4. Anti-aliasing for graphics can (independent of text anti-aliasing) similarly be achieved using the -dGraphicsAlphaBits=4 option.

Converting PostScript to PostScript raster graphics.   This conversion makes it possible to print PostScript Level 2 files on devices with PostScript Level 1 interpreters. Ghostscript's *psmono* driver produces (not DSC-compliant) PostScript files containing a raster version of the file as a PostScript Level 1 bitmap. Similar to the TIFF conversion you can select the resolution:

```
gs -sDEVICE=psmono -r600 -sOutputFile=file1.ps file2.ps
```

By default, the *psmono* driver uses a resolution of 300 dpi.

Additional features for EPS files.   The shell script/batch file *ps2epsi* or *ps2epsi.bat* creates ASCII previews for EPSI files. Usage notes can be found in *ps2epsi.doc*. On Windows and OS/2 many additional EPS functions are possible with GSview, including determining a correct bounding box and creating or deleting preview bitmaps. More details can be found in Section 3.5.2.

Converting to the Adobe Illustrator format.   As of version 4.01, a special Ghostscript driver for creating Adobe Illustrator format is not yet available. Instead, Ghostscript uses the sophisticated PostScript program *ps2ai.ps*. Although this conversion is bound to some restrictions, in many cases it yields graphics files which may be opened and edited with any Illustrator-compatible program. On Unix, redirect Ghostscript's output to a file. On Windows, OS/2 and the Macintosh it's easier to have Ghostscript create the file directly. To achieve this, change the variable */jout* at the beginning of *ps2ai.ps* to a value of true. Assign the name of the AI file you want to create to the */joutput* variable. Now launch Ghostscript with the converter and the PostScript file to be converted to AI format:

```
gs -dNODISPLAY ps2ai.ps file.ps
```

For EPS files that are missing the showpage operator at the end, you have to type this operator at the Ghostscript prompt before quitting in order to completely render the page. For the conversion to be successful, it is necessary for Ghostscript to have access to all fonts used in the PostScript file. Note that the conversion isn't perfect: there may be problems concerning color ramps and grouped objects in the converted AI files.

B.6.2 PDF Files

Displaying and printing PDF files. You can list PDF files on Ghostscript's command line just like you can PostScript files because Ghostscript recognizes PDF files automatically. In order to be able to process PDF files, Ghostscript must be configured with the PDF interpreter. By default, this is true on all 32-bit systems except the Macintosh. Ghostscript interprets the printable contents of PDF files only, and ignores hypertext elements (such as links, annotations, and bookmarks) and thumbnails. Although there is no font substitution with Multiple Master fonts, Ghostscript replaces a missing font with a similar one and adjusts the metrics of the substituted font to those of the missing font.

Contrary to PostScript files, it's possible to access random pages of PDF files. Therefore you can select a page range for PDF files when launching Ghostscript:

```
gs -dFirstPage=<n> -dLastPage=<m> file.pdf
```

This works for displaying and printing PDF files and for converting them to PostScript (see below).

Converting PDF files to PostScript. Ghostscript is able to convert PDF files back to PostScript Level 2. In fact, if the PDF file doesn't contain compressed raster graphics or color spaces, the generated PostScript files use Level 1 only. The following command line creates the corresponding PostScript file for a PDF file:

```
gs -dNODISPLAY -sPSFile=file.ps file.pdf
```

A little shell script/batch file contained in the Ghostscript distribution makes this even easier:

```
pdf2ps file.pdf file.ps
```

The following additional options are available for PDF to PostScript conversion:

```
-dPSBinaryOK
```
Allows the generated PostScript files to contain binary data.

```
-dPSLevel1
```
Generates PostScript Level 1 output.

```
-dPSNoProcSet
```
Does not include the PostScript prolog (procset) in the output. Note that the prolog is necessary when sending the generated file to a Post-Script printer.

Converting PostScript to PDF (distilling).   As of version 4.0, Ghost-script is also able to "distill" PostScript files to PDF. Ghostscript must be compiled and linked with the *pdfwrite* device which is the case for Unix and Windows by default. The following command line can be used to distill PostScript files to PDF:

```
gs -q -dNOPAUSE -sDEVICE=pdfwrite -sOutputFile=file.pdf
    file.ps -c quit
```

Again, a shell script/batch file simplifies the process:

```
ps2pdf file.ps file.pdf
```

There are no further options available for PS to PDF conversion. Ghostscript recognizes the *pdfmark* and *setdistillerparams* operators. However, the distiller parameters are ignored with the exception of ASCII85 encoding. Text in any other font than the 13 Acrobat base fonts is converted to bitmaps. Also, there are problems with fonts that use non-standard encodings. Both limitations will be lifted in the future.

PDF files and GSview/Ghostview.   Note that because of the idiosyn-crasies of the PDF format Ghostscript isn't able to read PDF files from its standard input. Due to this fact, displaying PDF files with Ghost-view has its limitations. You can use the following command line for Ghostview on Unix to browse PDF files one page after the other. It's not possible to jump to arbitrary page numbers:

```
ghostview -arguments file.pdf quit.ps
```

GSview for Windows and OS/2 has already been adapted to pro-cessing PDF files. GSview handles PDF files just as PostScript files. Jumping to an arbitrary page in the file is also possible.

Extracting text from PDF files.   Using the *ps2ascii.ps* utility you can extract text from PDF files (see below for details).

B.6.3 Printing and Extracting Text

Printing text files.   The *gslp.ps* utility program implements a line-printer emulation, i.e., printing simple text files with PostScript com-mands. This includes some formating such as headers and footers, page numbers and tabs. Ghostscript optionally creates PostScript code or renders the text on screen or printer. Details on using the emulator and possible options may be found in the *gslp.ps* file. Example for printing a text file on a laserjet printer:

```
gs -q -sDEVICE=laserjet -r300 -dNOPAUSE -- gslp.ps file.txt
```

You may use several options following the file name *gslp.ps*. The *-p* option creates a PostScript file instead of rendering the text on screen or printer:

```
gs -q -dNOPAUSE -- gslp.ps -p file.ps file.txt
```

Extracting text from PostScript and PDF files. To some extent, *ps2ascii.ps* works as a counterpart of the lineprinter emulation as it extracts the textual contents from a PostScript file. Depending on the *-dSIMPLE* option, the utility creates simple or complex output. Simple output consists of text only, whereas complex output additionally contains information about font type and string positions. The positions are given in tenth of a point. More details may be found at the beginning of *ps2ascii.ps*, some usage samples in the batch file *ps2ascii.bat*. A typical command line:

```
gs -dNODISPLAY -dNOBIND -dWRITESYSTEMDICT -dSIMPLE ps2ascii.ps
    file.ps -c quit >file.txt
```

Note that there is good reason to call the utility ps*2ascii*: If the PostScript file contains any special characters (German umlauts, for example), they don't make their way into the output file but get substituted with two-character sequences of ASCII symbols.

B.6.4 Font Tools

Creating AFM files. The *printafm.ps* utility creates an AFM file for any given PostScript font. The metrics files created only contain character width information; kerning data are missing because they cannot be reconstructed from the font. To use the utility, enter the PostScript font name at the end of *printafm.ps*. The program print the AFM file to its standard output which you have to redirect to a file. If the font isn't configured for Ghostscript (via the Fontmap file or the GS_FONTPATH environment variable), enter the font file name on the Ghostscript command line (unfortunately, the redirection doesn't work on Windows or on the Mac):

```
gs -dNODISPLAY -q fontfile -- printafm.ps fontname
    >fontname.afm
```

Printing font tables. The *prfont.ps* utility prints character tables for any given PostScript font. It first prints all characters contained in the encoding vector of the font, then uncoded characters. If the font isn't configured in Ghostscript, enter the font file name on the Ghostscript command line. Then type the font name and the procedure name at the Ghostscript prompt:

```
gs fontfile prfont.ps
GS>/FontName DoFont
```

Character Sets

C

The tables in this appendix are meant to shed light on the rather dubious topic of character sets. They contain complete character sets along with the number (encoding vector position) of each character. Using row and column indexes you can easily find out the respective hexadecimal codes.

Apple Macintosh

	0	1	2	3	4	5	6	7	8	9	A	B	C	D	E	F
0	□ 0	□ 1	□ 2	□ 3	□ 4	□ 5	□ 6	□ 7	□ 8	□ 9	□ 10	□ 11	□ 12	□ 13	□ 14	□ 15
1	□ 16	□ 17	□ 18	□ 19	□ 20	□ 21	□ 22	□ 23	□ 24	□ 25	□ 26	□ 27	□ 28	□ 29	□ 30	□ 31
2	32	! 33	" 34	# 35	$ 36	% 37	& 38	' 39	(40	) 41	* 42	+ 43	, 44	– 45	. 46	/ 47
3	0 48	1 49	2 50	3 51	4 52	5 53	6 54	7 55	8 56	9 57	: 58	; 59	< 60	= 61	> 62	? 63
4	@ 64	A 65	B 66	C 67	D 68	E 69	F 70	G 71	H 72	I 73	J 74	K 75	L 76	M 77	N 78	O 79
5	P 80	Q 81	R 82	S 83	T 84	U 85	V 86	W 87	X 88	Y 89	Z 90	[91	\ 92	] 93	^ 94	_ 95
6	` 96	a 97	b 98	c 99	d 100	e 101	f 102	g 103	h 104	i 105	j 106	k 107	l 108	m 109	n 110	o 111
7	p 112	q 113	r 114	s 115	t 116	u 117	v 118	w 119	x 120	y 121	z 122	{ 123	| 124	} 125	~ 126	□ 127
8	Ä 128	Å 129	Ç 130	É 131	Ñ 132	Ö 133	Ü 134	á 135	à 136	â 137	ä 138	ã 139	å 140	ç 141	é 142	è 143
9	ê 144	ë 145	í 146	ì 147	î 148	ï 149	ñ 150	ó 151	ò 152	ô 153	ö 154	õ 155	ú 156	ù 157	û 158	ü 159
A	† 160	° 161	¢ 162	£ 163	§ 164	• 165	¶ 166	ß 167	® 168	© 169	™ 170	´ 171	¨ 172	≠ 173	Æ 174	Ø 175
B	∞ 176	± 177	≤ 178	≥ 179	¥ 180	µ 181	∂ 182	Σ 183	Π 184	π 185	∫ 186	ª 187	º 188	Ω 189	æ 190	ø 191
C	¿ 192	¡ 193	¬ 194	√ 195	ƒ 196	≈ 197	Δ 198	« 199	» 200	… 201	202	À 203	Ã 204	Õ 205	Œ 206	œ 207
D	– 208	— 209	" 212	" 211	' 212	' 213	÷ 214	◊ 215	ÿ 216	Ÿ 217	/ 218	¤ 219	‹ 220	› 221	fi 222	fl 223
E	‡ 224	· 225	‚ 226	„ 227	‰ 228	Â 229	Ê 230	Á 231	Ë 232	È 233	Í 234	Î 235	Ï 236	Ì 237	Ó 238	Ô 239
F	240	Ò 241	Ú 242	Û 243	Ù 244	ı 245	^ 246	~ 247	¯ 248	˘ 249	· 250	° 251	ˏ 252	˝ 253	ˏ 254	ˇ 255

Windows

	0	1	2	3	4	5	6	7	8	9	A	B	C	D	E	F
0	⬚	⬚	⬚	⬚	⬚	⬚	⬚	⬚	⬚	⬚	⬚	⬚	⬚	⬚	⬚	⬚
	0	1	2	3	4	5	6	7	8	9	10	11	12	13	14	15
1	⬚	⬚	⬚	⬚	⬚	⬚	⬚	⬚	⬚	⬚	⬚	⬚	⬚	⬚	⬚	⬚
	16	17	18	19	20	21	22	23	24	25	26	27	28	29	30	31
2		!	"	#	$	%	&	'	(	)	*	+	,	-	.	/
	32	33	34	35	36	37	38	39	40	41	42	43	44	45	46	47
3	0	1	2	3	4	5	6	7	8	9	:	;	<	=	>	?
	48	49	50	51	52	53	54	55	56	57	58	59	60	61	62	63
4	@	A	B	C	D	E	F	G	H	I	J	K	L	M	N	O
	64	65	66	67	68	69	70	71	72	73	74	75	76	77	78	79
5	P	Q	R	S	T	U	V	W	X	Y	Z	[	\	]	^	_
	80	81	82	83	84	85	86	87	88	89	90	91	92	93	94	95
6	`	a	b	c	d	e	f	g	h	i	j	k	l	m	n	o
	96	97	98	99	100	101	102	103	104	105	106	107	108	109	110	111
7	p	q	r	s	t	u	v	w	x	y	z	{			}	~	
	112	113	114	115	116	117	118	119	120	121	122	123	124	125	126	127
8		□	,	ƒ	„	…	†	‡	ˆ	‰	Š	‹	Œ			
	128	129	130	131	132	133	134	135	136	137	138	139	140	141	142	143
9	□	'	'	"	"	•	–	—	~	™	š	›	œ			Ÿ
	144	145	146	147	148	149	150	151	152	153	154	155	156	157	158	159
A		¡	¢	£	¤	¥	¦	§	¨	©	ª	«	¬	-	®	¯
	160	161	162	163	164	165	166	167	168	169	170	171	172	173	174	175
B	°	±	²	³	´	µ	¶	·	¸	¹	º	»	¼	½	¾	¿
	176	177	178	179	180	181	182	183	184	185	186	187	188	189	190	191
C	À	Á	Â	Ã	Ä	Å	Æ	Ç	È	É	Ê	Ë	Ì	Í	Î	Ï
	192	193	194	195	196	197	198	199	200	201	202	203	204	205	206	207
D	Ð	Ñ	Ò	Ó	Ô	Õ	Ö	×	Ø	Ù	Ú	Û	Ü	Ý	Þ	ß
	208	209	210	211	212	213	214	215	216	217	218	219	220	221	222	223
E	à	á	â	ã	ä	å	æ	ç	è	é	ê	ë	ì	í	î	ï
	224	225	226	227	228	229	230	231	232	233	234	235	236	237	238	239
F	ð	ñ	ò	ó	ô	õ	ö	÷	ø	ù	ú	û	ü	ý	þ	ÿ
	240	241	242	243	244	245	246	247	248	249	250	251	252	253	254	255

ISO 8859/1 (Latin 1)

	0	1	2	3	4	5	6	7	8	9	A	B	C	D	E	F
0	□ 0	□ 1	□ 2	□ 3	□ 4	□ 5	□ 6	□ 7	□ 8	□ 9	□ 10	□ 11	□ 12	□ 13	□ 14	□ 15
1	□ 16	□ 17	□ 18	□ 19	□ 20	□ 21	□ 22	□ 23	□ 24	□ 25	□ 26	□ 27	□ 28	□ 29	□ 30	□ 31
2	32	! 33	" 34	# 35	$ 36	% 37	& 38	' 39	(40	) 41	* 42	+ 43	, 44	- 45	. 46	/ 47
3	0 48	1 49	2 50	3 51	4 52	5 53	6 54	7 55	8 56	9 57	: 58	; 59	< 60	= 61	> 62	? 63
4	@ 64	A 65	B 66	C 67	D 68	E 69	F 70	G 71	H 72	I 73	J 74	K 75	L 76	M 77	N 78	O 79
5	P 80	Q 81	R 82	S 83	T 84	U 85	V 86	W 87	X 88	Y 89	Z 90	[91	\ 92	] 93	^ 94	_ 95
6	' 96	a 97	b 98	c 99	d 100	e 101	f 102	g 103	h 104	i 105	j 106	k 107	l 108	m 109	n 110	o 111
7	p 112	q 113	r 114	s 115	t 116	u 117	v 118	w 119	x 120	y 121	z 122	{ 123	| 124	} 125	~ 126	□ 127
8	□ 128	□ 129	□ 130	□ 131	□ 132	□ 133	□ 134	□ 135	□ 136	□ 137	□ 138	□ 139	□ 140	□ 141	□ 142	□ 143
9	□ 144	□ 145	□ 146	□ 147	□ 148	□ 149	□ 150	□ 151	□ 152	□ 153	□ 154	□ 155	□ 156	□ 157	□ 158	□ 159
A	160	¡ 161	¢ 162	£ 163	¤ 164	¥ 165	¦ 166	§ 167	¨ 168	© 169	ª 170	« 171	¬ 172	173	® 174	¯ 175
B	° 176	± 177	² 178	³ 179	´ 180	µ 181	¶ 182	· 183	¸ 184	¹ 185	º 186	» 187	¼ 188	½ 189	¾ 190	¿ 191
C	À 192	Á 193	Â 194	Ã 195	Ä 196	Å 197	Æ 198	Ç 199	È 200	É 201	Ê 202	Ë 203	Ì 204	Í 205	Î 206	Ï 207
D	Ð 208	Ñ 209	Ò 210	Ó 211	Ô 212	Õ 213	Ö 214	× 215	Ø 216	Ù 217	Ú 218	Û 219	Ü 220	Ý 221	Þ 222	ß 223
E	à 224	á 225	â 226	ã 227	ä 228	å 229	æ 230	ç 231	è 232	é 233	ê 234	ë 235	ì 236	í 237	î 238	ï 239
F	ð 240	ñ 241	ò 242	ó 243	ô 244	õ 245	ö 246	÷ 247	ø 248	ù 249	ú 250	û 251	ü 252	ý 253	þ 254	ÿ 255

ISO 8859/2 (Latin 2)

	0	1	2	3	4	5	6	7	8	9	A	B	C	D	E	F
0																
	0	1	2	3	4	5	6	7	8	9	10	11	12	13	14	15
1																
	16	17	18	19	20	21	22	23	24	25	26	27	28	29	30	31
2		!	"	#	$	%	&	'	(	)	*	+	,	-	.	/
	32	33	34	35	36	37	38	39	40	41	42	43	44	45	46	47
3	0	1	2	3	4	5	6	7	8	9	:	;	<	=	>	?
	48	49	50	51	52	53	54	55	56	57	58	59	60	61	62	63
4	@	A	B	C	D	E	F	G	H	I	J	K	L	M	N	O
	64	65	66	67	68	69	70	71	72	73	74	75	76	77	78	79
5	P	Q	R	S	T	U	V	W	X	Y	Z	[	\	]	^	_
	80	81	82	83	84	85	86	87	88	89	90	91	92	93	94	95
6	`	a	b	c	d	e	f	g	h	i	j	k	l	m	n	o
	96	97	98	99	100	101	102	103	104	105	106	107	108	109	110	111
7	p	q	r	s	t	u	v	w	x	y	z	{	|	}	~	
	112	113	114	115	116	117	118	119	120	121	122	123	124	125	126	127
8																
	128	129	130	131	132	133	134	135	136	137	138	139	140	141	142	143
9																
	144	145	146	147	148	149	150	151	152	153	154	155	156	157	158	159
A		Ą	˘	Ł	¤	Ľ	Ś	§	¨	Š	Ş	Ť	Ź		Ž	Ż
	160	161	162	163	164	165	166	167	168	169	170	171	172	173	174	175
B	°	ą	˛	ł	´	ľ	ś	ˇ	¸	š	ş	ť	ź	˝	ž	ż
	176	177	178	179	180	181	182	183	184	185	186	187	188	189	190	191
C	Ŕ	Á	Â	Ă	Ä	Ĺ	Ć	Ç	Č	É	Ę	Ë	Ě	Í	Î	Ď
	192	193	194	195	196	197	198	199	200	201	202	203	204	205	206	207
D	Đ	Ń	Ň	Ó	Ô	Ő	Ö	×	Ř	Ů	Ú	Ű	Ü	Ý	Ţ	ß
	208	209	212	211	212	213	214	215	216	217	218	219	220	221	222	223
E	ŕ	á	â	ă	ä	ĺ	ć	ç	č	é	ę	ë	ě	í	î	ď
	224	225	226	227	228	229	230	231	232	233	234	235	236	237	238	239
F	đ	ń	ň	ó	ô	ő	ö	÷	ř	ů	ú	ű	ü	ý	ţ	˙
	240	241	242	243	244	245	246	247	248	249	250	251	252	253	254	255

NEXTSTEP

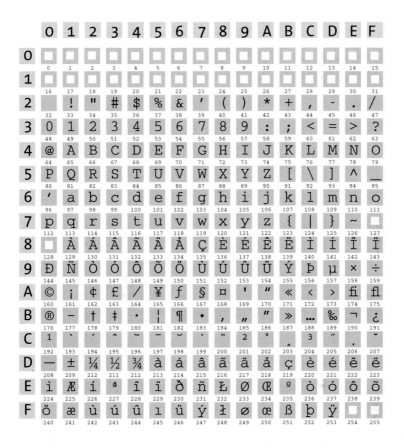

MS-DOS Codepage 437

	0	1	2	3	4	5	6	7	8	9	A	B	C	D	E	F
0		☺	☻	♥	♦	♣	♠	•	◘	○	◙	♂	♀	♪	♫	☼
	0	1	2	3	4	5	6	7	8	9	10	11	12	13	14	15
1	►	◄	↕	‼	¶	§	▬	↨	↑	↓	→	←	∟	↔	▲	▼
	16	17	18	19	20	21	22	23	24	25	26	27	28	29	30	31
2		!	"	#	$	%	&	'	(	)	*	+	,	−	.	/
	32	33	34	35	36	37	38	39	40	41	42	43	44	45	46	47
3	0	1	2	3	4	5	6	7	8	9	:	;	<	=	>	?
	48	49	50	51	52	53	54	55	56	57	58	59	60	61	62	63
4	@	A	B	C	D	E	F	G	H	I	J	K	L	M	N	O
	64	65	66	67	68	69	70	71	72	73	74	75	76	77	78	79
5	P	Q	R	S	T	U	V	W	X	Y	Z	[	\	]	^	_
	80	81	82	83	84	85	86	87	88	89	90	91	92	93	94	95
6	`	a	b	c	d	e	f	g	h	i	j	k	l	m	n	o
	96	97	98	99	100	101	102	103	104	105	106	107	108	109	110	111
7	p	q	r	s	t	u	v	w	x	y	z	{	|	}	~	
	112	113	114	115	116	117	118	119	120	121	122	123	124	125	126	127
8	Ç	ü	é	â	ä	à	å	ç	ê	ë	è	ï	î	ì	Ä	Å
	128	129	130	131	132	133	134	135	136	137	138	139	140	141	142	143
9	É	æ	Æ	ô	ö	ò	û	ù	ÿ	Ö	Ü	¢	£	¥	₧	ƒ
	144	145	146	147	148	149	150	151	152	153	154	155	156	157	158	159
A	á	í	ó	ú	ñ	Ñ	ª	º	¿	⌐	¬	½	¼	¡	«	»
	160	161	162	163	164	165	166	167	168	169	170	171	172	173	174	175
B	░	▒	▓	│	┤	╡	╢	╖	╕	╣	║	╗	╝	╜	╛	┐
	176	177	178	179	180	181	182	183	184	185	186	187	188	189	190	191
C	└	┴	┬	├	─	┼	╞	╟	╚	╔	╩	╦	╠	═	╬	╧
	192	193	194	195	196	197	198	199	200	201	202	203	204	205	206	207
D	╨	╤	╥	╙	╘	╒	╓	╫	╪	┘	┌	█	▄	▌	▐	▀
	208	209	210	211	212	213	214	215	216	217	218	219	220	221	222	223
E	α	ß	Γ	π	Σ	σ	µ	τ	Φ	Θ	Ω	δ	∞	∅	ε	∩
	224	225	226	227	228	229	230	231	232	233	234	235	236	237	238	239
F	≡	±	≥	≤	⌠	⌡	÷	≈	°	∙	·	√	ⁿ	²	■	
	240	241	242	243	244	245	246	247	248	249	250	251	252	253	254	255

MS-DOS Codepage 850

	0	1	2	3	4	5	6	7	8	9	A	B	C	D	E	F
0		☺	☻	♥	♦	♣	♠	•	◘	○	◙	♂	♀	♪	♫	☼
	0	1	2	3	4	5	6	7	8	9	10	11	12	13	14	15
1	►	◄	↕	‼	¶	§	▬	↨	↑	↓	→	←	∟	↔	▲	▼
	16	17	18	19	20	21	22	23	24	25	26	27	28	29	30	31
2		!	"	#	$	%	&	'	(	)	*	+	,	─	.	/
	32	33	34	35	36	37	38	39	40	41	42	43	44	45	46	47
3	0	1	2	3	4	5	6	7	8	9	:	;	<	=	>	?
	48	49	50	51	52	53	54	55	56	57	58	59	60	61	62	63
4	@	A	B	C	D	E	F	G	H	I	J	K	L	M	N	O
	64	65	66	67	68	69	70	71	72	73	74	75	76	77	78	79
5	P	Q	R	S	T	U	V	W	X	Y	Z	[	\	]	^	_
	80	81	82	83	84	85	86	87	88	89	90	91	92	93	94	95
6	`	a	b	c	d	e	f	g	h	i	j	k	l	m	n	o
	96	97	98	99	100	101	102	103	104	105	106	107	108	109	110	111
7	p	q	r	s	t	u	v	w	x	y	z	{			}	~	
	112	113	114	115	116	117	118	119	120	121	122	123	124	125	126	127
8	Ç	ü	é	â	ä	à	å	ç	ê	ë	è	ï	î	ì	Ä	Å
	128	129	130	131	132	133	134	135	136	137	138	139	140	141	142	143
9	É	æ	Æ	ô	ö	ò	û	ù	ÿ	Ö	Ü	ø	£	Ø	×	ƒ
	144	145	146	147	148	149	150	151	152	153	154	155	156	157	158	159
A	á	í	ó	ú	ñ	Ñ	ª	º	¿	®	¬	½	¼	¡	«	»
	160	161	162	163	164	165	166	167	168	169	170	171	172	173	174	175
B	░	▒	▓	│	┤	Á	Â	À	©	╣	║	╗	╝	¢	¥	┐
	176	177	178	179	180	181	182	183	184	185	186	187	188	189	190	191
C	└	┴	┬	├	─	┼	ã	Ã	╚	╔	╩	╦	╠	═	╬	¤
	192	193	194	195	196	197	198	199	200	201	202	203	204	205	206	207
D	ð	Ð	Ê	Ë	È	ı	Í	Î	Ï	┘	┌	█	▄	¦	Ì	▀
	208	209	212	211	212	213	214	215	216	217	218	219	220	221	222	223
E	Ó	ß	Ô	Ò	õ	Õ	µ	þ	Þ	Ú	Û	Ù	ý	Ý	¯	´
	224	225	226	227	228	229	230	231	232	233	234	235	236	237	238	239
F		±	‗	¾	¶	§	÷	¸	°	¨	·	¹	³	²	■	
	240	241	242	243	244	245	246	247	248	249	250	251	252	253	254	255

Adobe Standard Encoding

	0	1	2	3	4	5	6	7	8	9	A	B	C	D	E	F
0																
1																
2		!	"	#	$	%	&	'	(	)	*	+	,	-	.	/
3	0	1	2	3	4	5	6	7	8	9	:	;	<	=	>	?
4	@	A	B	C	D	E	F	G	H	I	J	K	L	M	N	O
5	P	Q	R	S	T	U	V	W	X	Y	Z	[	\	]	^	_
6	'	a	b	c	d	e	f	g	h	i	j	k	l	m	n	o
7	p	q	r	s	t	u	v	w	x	y	z	{	|	}	~	
8																
9																
A		¡	¢	£	⁄	¥	ƒ	§	¤	'	"	«	‹	›	fi	fl
B		–	†	‡	·		¶	•	‚	„	"	»	…	‰		¿
C		`	´	^	~	¯	˘	˙	¨		°	¸		˝	˛	ˇ
D	—															
E		Æ		ª					Ł	Ø	Œ	º				
F		æ				ı			ł	ø	œ	ß				

PDFDocEncoding

	0	1	2	3	4	5	6	7	8	9	A	B	C	D	E	F
0																
	0	1	2	3	4	5	6	7	8	9	10	11	12	13	14	15
1									˘	ˇ	ˆ	˙	˝	˛	˚	˜
	16	17	18	19	20	21	22	23	24	25	26	27	28	29	30	31
2		!	"	#	$	%	&	'	(	)	*	+	,	–	.	/
	32	33	34	35	36	37	38	39	40	41	42	43	44	45	46	47
3	0	1	2	3	4	5	6	7	8	9	:	;	<	=	>	?
	48	49	50	51	52	53	54	55	56	57	58	59	60	61	62	63
4	@	A	B	C	D	E	F	G	H	I	J	K	L	M	N	O
	64	65	66	67	68	69	70	71	72	73	74	75	76	77	78	79
5	P	Q	R	S	T	U	V	W	X	Y	Z	[	\	]	^	_
	80	81	82	83	84	85	86	87	88	89	90	91	92	93	94	95
6	`	a	b	c	d	e	f	g	h	i	j	k	l	m	n	o
	96	97	98	99	100	101	102	103	104	105	106	107	108	109	110	111
7	p	q	r	s	t	u	v	w	x	y	z	{	|	}	~	
	112	113	114	115	116	117	118	119	120	121	122	123	124	125	126	127
8	•	†	‡	…	—	–	ƒ	⁄	‹	›	−	‰	„	"	"	'
	128	129	130	131	132	133	134	135	136	137	138	139	140	141	142	143
9	'	‚	™	ﬁ	ﬂ	Ł	Œ	Š	Ÿ	Ž	ı	ł	œ	š	ž	
	144	145	146	147	148	149	150	151	152	153	154	155	156	157	158	159
A		¡	¢	£	¤	¥	¦	§	¨	©	ª	«	¬		®	¯
	160	161	162	163	164	165	166	167	168	169	170	171	172	173	174	175
B	°	±	²	³	´	µ	¶	·	¸	¹	º	»	¼	½	¾	¿
	176	177	178	179	180	181	182	183	184	185	186	187	188	189	190	191
C	À	Á	Â	Ã	Ä	Å	Æ	Ç	È	É	Ê	Ë	Ì	Í	Î	Ï
	192	193	194	195	196	197	198	199	200	201	202	203	204	205	206	207
D	Ð	Ñ	Ò	Ó	Ô	Õ	Ö	×	Ø	Ù	Ú	Û	Ü	Ý	Þ	ß
	208	209	212	211	212	213	214	215	216	217	218	219	220	221	222	223
E	à	á	â	ã	ä	å	æ	ç	è	é	ê	ë	ì	í	î	ï
	224	225	226	227	228	229	230	231	232	233	234	235	236	237	238	239
F	ð	ñ	ò	ó	ô	õ	ö	÷	ø	ù	ú	û	ü	ý	þ	ÿ
	240	241	242	243	244	245	246	247	248	249	250	251	252	253	254	255

Bibliography

The bibliography gives a commented list of books which expand on this book's topics or contain additional technical details. If you have Internet access, you can obtain many technical notes on Adobe's FTP or WWW server *(ftp.adobe. com and www.adobe.com)*.

PostScript Programming

Adobe Systems Incorporated, *PostScript Language Reference Manual*, Second Edition, Addison-Wesley 1990, ISBN 0-201-18127-4.

Every PostScript programmer needs this book, called the "red book" because of the color of its cover. It completely defines the PostScript language (Level 1 and 2, as well as Display PostScript), and contains several appendixes with the DSC and EPS specifications, and more.

Adobe Systems Incorporated, *PostScript Language Tutorial and Cookbook*, Addison-Wesley 1985, ISBN 0-201-10179-3.

For a long time, the "blue book" was the most important introduction to PostScript programming. But it is outdated because it has never been expanded to cover Level 2.

Henry McGilton, Mary Campione, *PostScript by Example*, Addison-Wesley 1992, ISBN 0-201-63228-4.

This is a comprehensive introduction to PostScript Level 1 and Level 2 programming which is also fun to read. Unlike the red book, it contains hundreds of code samples and instructions. This book in some respect is the successor of the blue book which only covers Level 1.

Adobe Systems Incorporated, *PostScript Language Program Design*, Addison-Wesley 1985, ISBN 0-201-10179-3.

The "green book" conveys a deeper understanding of the programming aspects of PostScript. Although available for quite a long time, it still gives many useful tips for PostScript driver developers. It only covers Level 1.

Glenn C. Reid, *Thinking in PostScript*, Addison-Wesley 1990, ISBN 0-201-52372-8.

Glenn Reid's other PostScript book (he also authored the green book) conveys an understanding of PostScript programming which isn't limited to graphics but covers all programming aspects of Post-Script. This is a useful guide for implementing efficient PostScript programs and drivers.

PostScript Printer Description File Format Specification, Version 4.2, Adobe Developer Support 1993. (Document *5003_42.PPDSpec.pdf* on Adobe's server.)
A description of the PPD file format including many remarks and examples.

Encapsulated PostScript (EPS)

Adobe Illustrator File Format Specification, Version 3.0, Draft, Adobe Developer Support 1992. (Document *5007v3.AI_Spec_3.0_DRAFT.pdf* on Adobe's server.)
This document describes the basics of Adobe Illustrator's file format. The draft is several years old but still the only source of information on the AI format.

Desktop Color Separation Specification 2.0, Quark Inc. 1993, Denver.
Description of DCS 2.0 comments.

Open Prepress Interface Specification 1.3, Aldus Corporation, Seattle 1993. (Document *OPI_13.pdf* on Adobe's server.)
Description of OPI 1.3 comments.

Open Prepress Interface – Version 2.0, Adobe Systems Incorporated. (Document *OPI_2.pdf* on Adobe's server.)
Description of OPI 2.0 comments and applications.

Fonts

Adobe Systems Incorporated, *Adobe Type 1 Font Format,* Addison-Wesley 1990, ISBN 0-201-57044-0 (also available in PDF format on Adobe's server; file *t1format.pdf*).
The "black book" published the Type 1 format's details for the first time. It gives a technical introduction to the outline descriptions and encryption techniques employed in Adobe's primary font format.

Type 1 Font Format Supplement, Adobe Technical Specification #5015. (Document *5015.Type1_Supp.pdf* on Adobe's server.)
This document describes Type 1 format extensions which are not covered in the first edition of the black book, e.g., new forms of hinting and Multiple Master extensions.

Thomas Merz, *TerminalBuch PostScript – Fonts und Programmiertechnik*, Oldenbourg Verlag 1991, ISBN 3-486-21674-0.

Unfortunately, the *TerminalBuch PostScript* is available in German only. It is aimed at PostScript aficionados. It completely describes the Type 1 and Type 3 font formats. The accompanying disk contains utilities (which are completely written in PostScript) to convert both of these formats to the other. Also, the book gives hints on extracting printer-resident fonts.

The Type 42 Font Format Specification, Adobe Technical Note # 5012. (Document *5012.Type42_Spec.pdf* on Adobe's server.)

This is the description of Type 42 fonts, i.e. TrueType fonts which can be directly used in newer PostScript interpreters without prior conversion.

Adobe Font Metrics File Specification, Version 4.0, Adobe Developer Support 1992. (Document *5004.AFM_Spec.pdf* on Adobe's server.)

A description of the AFM format, including the extensions for Multiple Master fonts (AMFM).

Gray Levels and Color

David Blatner and Steve Roth, *Real World Scanning and Halftones*, Peachpit Press 1993, Inc. Berkeley CA, ISBN 1-56609-093-8.

A non-technical introduction to screening, halftoning and scanning. It also gives an overview on relevant PostScript topics. Highly recommended!

Peter Fink, *PostScript Screening – Adobe Accurate Screens*, Adobe Press 1992, ISBN 0-672-48544-3.

Contrary to its title, this book does not only cover AccurateScreens but also gives an excellent overview on halftoning techniques, the associated problems, and PostScript options. Peter Fink discusses all relevant components of the professional production workflow such as film, imagesetter, and printing.

Display PostScript

Adobe Systems Incorporated, *Programming the Display PostScript System with X*, Addison-Wesley 1993, ISBN 0-201-62203-3.

Introduction to programming with Display PostScript in the X Window System including *Client Library, pswrap*, and the *Display PostScript Toolkit*.

Adobe Systems Incorporated, *Programming the Display PostScript System with NeXTstep*, Addison-Wesley 1991, ISBN 0-201-58135-3.

This book gives an introduction to programming NEXTSTEP and Display PostScript. It also contains useful information on EPS and Level 2.

Adobe Acrobat and PDF

Patrick Ames, *Beyond Paper. The Official Guide to Adobe Acrobat*, Adobe Press 1993, ISBN 0-56830-050-6.

A non-technical introduction to Adobe Acrobat and its applications. Due to many practical examples and the pleasing design it's easy reading and doesn't require any prior Acrobat knowledge.

Adobe Systems Incorporated, *Portable Document Format Reference Manual*, Addison-Wesley 1993, ISBN 0-201-62628-4.

The PDF Reference Manual contains the PDF 1.0 specification and hints on optimizing PDF files.

Updates to the Portable Document Format Reference Manual, Adobe Technical Note #5156. (Document *5156.pdf11.pdf* on Adobe's server.)

This update describes the PDF 1.1 extensions which form the basis of Acrobat 2.0.

Document *pdfspec.pdf* on Adobe's server is a PDF version of the reference manual which already contains the PDF 1.1 extensions.

Adobe Developer Support, *PDFmark Reference Manual*, Adobe Technical Note #5150. (Document *5150.Pdfmark_Ref.ps* on Adobe's server. This document is also available with the Distiller software.)

This document describes the *pdfmark* operator which can be used to incorporate hypertext and other extensions in PostScript files which are processed by Acrobat Distiller.

Adobe Developer Support, *Acrobat Distiller Parameters*, Adobe Technical Note #5151. (Document *5151.Distiller_Params.ps* on Adobe's server. This document is also available with the Distiller software.)

This document describes the *currentdistillerparams* and *setdistillerparams* operators which can be used to change Acrobat Distiller's behaviour with PostScript commands.

Graphics and Text File Formats

James D. Murray/William vanRyper, *Encyclopedia of Graphics File Formats*, Second Edition, O'Reilly & Associates 1994, ISBN 1-56592-161-5.

This tome gives a good introduction to programming with file formats and contains technical details for a host of graphics file formats. It is supplemented by a CD-ROM with specifications, sample files and source code.

PostScript Information on the Internet

If you have Internet access you can retrieve diverse information on PostScript and PDF in the "network of networks". The following list gives a selection of relevant sources of information:

News Groups.
- ► *comp.lang.postscript* – General PostScript discussion: programming, drivers, application problems, new Adobe products.
- ► *comp.fonts* – Discussions on fonts and typography.
- ► *comp.text.pdf* – Discussions on PDF and Acrobat software.

World Wide Web.
- ► *http://www.adobe.com* – Adobe's Web server always contains the latest product announcements, specifications, free software, demo versions, etc. A must for all PostScript and PDF enthusiasts!
- ► *http://www.emrg.com* – The Web server of the consulting firm Emerge which specializes on Acrobat products and consulting. The server offers free PDF software, demo versions of commercial plug-ins, much additional information, and links to other servers.
- ► *http://jasper.ora.com/compfont/ifa/ifa3.html* – The Internet Font Archive, compiled and maintained by Norman Walsh, has many links to other Internet Servers with fonts and information on fonts.

Index

servers *407*
Weblink plug-in *272*

X

X Window System (X11) *13, 108*
    and Display PostScript *235*
    change encoding vector *155*
    installing fonts *135*
    resources for Ghostscript *382*
    Type 1 rasterizer *152*
XLFD (X Logical Font Description) *137*
XON/XOFF protocol *32*
xpdf *342*
xv *314*

About the Author

Thomas Merz works as a software developer, translator of technical books, and freelance author in Munich (Germany). He is a system consultant and offers PostScript and Acrobat workshops for users as well as for developers. Thomas self-published the German edition of this book.

The first time he came into contact with PostScript was as a math and computer science student in 1985. Ever since, he stuck to the topic: he developed drivers and converters for a small Unix software company. His interest in fonts and typography arose through private relations ("typography is the mathematics among arts"). As a computer book translator – especially in the fields of computer graphics and Internet – who also does the layout and production work for the books, he has the chance not only to program in PostScript but also to experience the user's point of view.

In 1991 Thomas published his first book on PostScript (a highly detailed treatise on Type 1 fonts). Since then he has been a regular contributor for major German computer magazines and has specialized in DTP, PostScript, and Acrobat.

In 1994, Thomas spent several months in San Francisco. He not only did a book translation in the most beautiful city in the world but also enjoyed exploring the Californian landscape on his racing bike.

Colophon

Book design and illustrations.   The complete book design and all illustrations were done by Alessio Leonardi (Agorà Information Design, Berlin). He created the illustrations with pencil and paper, scanned and digitized the sketches, and finished them in FreeHand, Illustrator, and Photoshop. Screen shots were produced on Mac, Windows, and Unix systems and prepared with Adobe Photoshop. The image inside the front cover was produced with the Alpha device described at the beginning of Chapter 6.

Archetipetti.   The little characters that romp about on the cover and in many illustrations are called Archetipetti *(arke-tee-petti)* and were also created by Alessio Leonardi. The Archetipetti's elite has already assembled to form several PostScript fonts which also contain corresponding symbols (e.g., FF Letterine Archetipetti One). Some of these fonts are commercially available.

Fonts.   The basic text font is TheAntiqua which is used in this book for the first time. This font – like any other fonts in the book (some examples aside) – is part of the Thesis font family designed by the Dutch typographer Luc(as) de Groot in Berlin. Thesis is said to be the largest font family ever digitized: the basic variations TheSans, TheSerif, and TheMix consist of 48 fonts each, carefully matched to each other. Additionally, there is the body text font TheAntiqua, and a monospaced variation which we used for listings and examples. After some experimentation with a Multiple Master version of ThesisMono we decided to use a single fixed font instead. The image on the inside front cover is made of ThesisMono-ExtraBold.

Software.   FrameMaker 5.1 for Macintosh was used to write and layout this book.

Springer-Verlag
and the Environment